PLANNING FOR WAR AT SEA

PLANNING FOR WAR AT SEA

400 YEARS OF GREAT POWER COMPETITION

EDITED BY EVAN WILSON AND PAUL KENNEDY

NAVAL INSTITUTE PRESS
Annapolis, MD

Naval Institute Press
291 Wood Road
Annapolis, MD 21402

Library of Congress Cataloging-in-Publication Data

Names: Kennedy, Paul M., 1945- editor. | Wilson, Evan, 1984- editor.
Title: Planning for war at sea : 400 years of great power competition /
  edited by Paul Kennedy and Evan Wilson.
Other titles: 400 years of great power competition
Description: Annapolis, MD : Naval Institute Press, [2025] | Includes
  bibliographical references and index.
Identifiers: LCCN 2024028582 (print) | LCCN 2024028583 (ebook) | ISBN
  9781612517254 (hardcover) | ISBN 9781612517261 (ebook)
Subjects: LCSH: Naval history, Modern. | Naval strategy—History. | Sea
  control—History.
Classification: LCC D215 .P63 2025 (print) | LCC D215 (ebook) | DDC
  359.009—dc23/eng/20241218
LC record available at https://lccn.loc.gov/2024028582
LC ebook record available at https://lccn.loc.gov/2024028583

♾ Print editions meet the requirements of ANSI/NISO z39.48-1992
(Permanence of Paper).
Printed in the United States of America.

33 32 31 30 29 28 27 26 25   9 8 7 6 5 4 3 2 1
First printing

*The views and opinions expressed by employees of the U.S. Naval War College in
this book are not necessarily those of the U.S. Navy, the Department of Defense, or
the U.S. government.*

CONTENTS

INTRODUCTION

THE BEST-LAID PLANS

Paul Kennedy

The following fifteen scholarly essays were all presented, in shorter form, during a three-day conference in New Haven organized by Yale University's International Security Studies (ISS) and the Hattendorf Historical Center of the U.S. Naval War College in late April 2022. Since the quality and originality of so many of the presentations was extremely high, and all conformed in their ways to the "best-laid plans" idea, the editors were inspired to approach the Naval Institute Press with a view to producing the present collection. The essays are arranged, as they were at the conference, in chronological order and can be perused throughout by the reader in that way, but all are self-standing pieces that, we hope, may be useful additions to the existing naval scholarship of various periods.

The original proposed title of the volume used some poetic license to borrow from the poet Robert Burns' line about "the best-laid schemes [plans] . . . go oft awry." That phrase seemed apt enough when we consider the subject of our symposium.[1] In the long sweep of naval history, many admiralties and their planners have entered into war only to find that things were going awry: their strategic assumptions were flawed, there was "something wrong" with their ships (Admiral Beattie's lament at Jutland), logistics were inadequate, intelligence was badly wrong, and political leaders were either too rash or too timid. Not *all* prewar naval preparations and plans went

1

astray, of course, and it is at least as useful to reflect on those that were successful as it is to analyze the cases of where navies went badly wrong. There are cases here (the Royal Navy in 1914 and the U.S. Navy in 1941) where a leading naval power took heavy losses at the war's beginning but enjoyed so many advantages that strategic recovery was possible; or of where neither side's navy had prepared for the conflict (the First Anglo-Dutch War); or of where a nation's best-laid plans were reasonably well established but swept away by larger circumstances (the French navy in 1940). We have also included, near the end of this collection, some probing essays that consider how well or poorly today's three leading navies—the Russian, the Chinese, and the American—have configured themselves during the Cold War era and may be doing so in preparation for the challenges of future conflict.

Finally, we are aware that a vast literature exists about military incompetence and disasters in *land* warfare, of the best-laid plans of armies going badly awry, of poorly prepared militaries and dreadful generalship.[2] However, our remit will deliberately limit itself to navies and to wars at sea; that realm itself is a great one and covers many centuries of maritime conflict, and of preparing for such conflict. From the mutual confusions of the Anglo-Dutch navies of the seventeenth century to the missteps of the Soviet fleet in the 1970s, planning for the next conflict, as this book shows, was a difficult and error-filled process. There are lessons here, should contemporary naval planners wish to draw them. No navy should presume that, in its plans for the future, it has gotten things right.

The medley of case studies presented in the following fifteen essays is about as rich and varied, and with as many surprises, as any editor might hope for. That each of the protagonists in the First Anglo-Dutch War was almost equally unprepared for the fighting that broke out after 1652 is a remarkable fact, but that explains why it took so long, as Professor Hattendorf describes, for each side to produce a serious fighting navy (chapter 1). Even more remarkable and eye-rubbing was the failure of the vastly superior Royal Navy to inflict punishing blows on its archrival France until the epic Revolutionary Wars were well underway, by which time of course the French military gains on land were more than enough to match Admiral Nelson's striking victories on the sea (chapter 2). And if established maritime nations found it hard to demonstrate "the influence of sea power" in these nearby theaters of war, is it surprising that when the fledgling U.S. Navy undertook actions in the distant waters and complicated politics of the Barbary Coast, the results were indecisive and transient (chapter 3)?

Given the sheer difficulties of communication between admiralties and their overseas squadrons in the age of sail, plus the physical difficulties of the command and control of large numbers of relatively slow three-deckers both before and during battle, it is remarkable that not more incidents occurred during this era when naval planning went badly awry, even though the history reader remembers the long eighteenth century (1689–1815) at sea as being the years of such decisive events and battles as the seizure of Gibraltar, the great incursion at Quiberon Bay, and the battles of the Saintes, Cape St. Vincent, the Nile, and Trafalgar. But it is also worth recalling that very few changes occurred in the design and size of warship types, in the power of their armaments, and in the speed and communications of fleets at sea; premodern fleets had at least a stability in the very weapons-platforms on which they fought. Overall, if the British Admiralty had secured funds from its Parliament to establish efficient battle fleets and lots of swift frigates ready for the next big war with France and Spain, then that, combined with the island country's favorable geographical position and greater fiscal strength, usually ensured decisive victory at sea. The only big exception (1776–83) came when the country's armed forces had been badly run down and Britain itself was diplomatically isolated, something that was scarcely the Royal Navy's fault.

Do very long periods of absence of major wars increase the likelihood of military and naval planning going badly awry when the next great conflicts occur? It is easy to see many reasons this should be so: the naval leadership would now be inexperienced in conducting war, the types of ships and other weapons may have changed greatly in the meantime, a communications revolution could have occurred for which the later navies were not fully prepared, and the battles may be fought in different oceans from earlier, familiar ones. Perhaps, it may be countered, a long period of relative peace should give navies the time to absorb newer technologies and circumstances, train their captains and crews for different sorts of fighting, and revise their systems of command and control. To naval historians, the best test case of all this came at the end of the Pax Britannia (1815–1914) and the vast changes that it brought to industry and technology, the international system of states, and the internal ordering and capacities of the advanced nations.[3] All these background changes, one might assume, would have tested even the most flexible and thoughtful of navies to be ready for another major conflict at sea, like the one that occurred after World War I broke out in the late summer of 1914.

All the same, the geostrategic circumstances for attaining a straightforward naval mastery in this war could hardly have been more favorable for the world's "number one navy"—they were far better, by comparison, than they were during both the Napoleonic Wars and World War II.[4] What was more, Britain's naval directors had begun laying their best plans for a possible future war with imperial Germany since as early as 1903, when the first steps were taken to move some of their fleets back into the North Sea and create new naval bases there. Powerful ironclad warships, propelled by coal- and even oil-based systems, had taken the place of those three-decker sailing ships of Nelson's day. Jellicoe's Grand Fleet practiced again and again for a great shoot-out in the center of the North Sea. New cruiser and destroyer squadrons were readied for dispatch to scout the approach of any German squadrons. Almost immediately after the outbreak of the war in Europe, then, "the King's ships were at sea," and because of alliances, the fleets of France and imperial Russia were as well.[5] The Allied naval predominance was thus overwhelming. Could there, then, be any cause at all for serious setbacks in Britain's naval plans? And if setbacks did occur, what could explain them?

Yet setbacks there were, of a greater and lesser sort, both at the war's beginning and in many later months, tactically, operationally, and strategically, in the North Sea, in the Mediterranean, and farther afield. It would take too much space to analyze them in any detail here, but what rapidly became clear was that the British Admiralty had singularly failed to comprehend the threat posed to their larger warships by the coming of the newer, smaller weapons of war—the torpedo, the naval mine, the submarine.[6] On September 5, 1914, virtually the first day of the war at sea, the light cruiser HMS *Pathfinder* was sunk by a U-boat operating off the Scottish coast. On September 22, the most egregious losses of all occurred when the small German submarine *U-9* managed to sink the three old heavy cruisers (*Aboukir, Cressy, Hogue*) on patrol off the Dutch coastline, with severe manpower losses. Less than a month later the enterprising *U-9* was back in action, sinking the cruiser HMS *Hawke* off Aberdeen. On October 29, the brand-new battleship HMS *Audacious* was sunk by a mine off the coasts of Northern Ireland with heavy loss of life, a catastrophe that was hushed up until the end of the war. A few days later came the news of the crushing of a British heavy cruiser squadron off Coronel, Chile, by Admiral Von Spee's much more powerful raiding group. The Royal Navy was also unready when the time came for large amphibious landings, as the unsuccessful Dardanelles Operation of 1915–16 showed. Its persistent inability to contain the far greater U-boat plundering of the North Atlantic trade routes until forced to adopt convoying merchantmen is also well known.

Explaining these repeated Admiralty failures to understand in advance the newer nature of warfare has been the source of an enormous literature since the first formal Commissions of Enquiry—a literature that was vastly increased in volume following the Royal Navy's controversial losses during that critical Battle of Jutland in May–June 1916.[7] Clearly, a whole number of causes was at work here, but two larger conclusions stand out: first, the existing large surface navies (like Britain's) had not been prepared to meet the newer transformative weapons of asymmetric warfare of the time; and, second, even if those British squadrons had been better led, more sensibly deployed, and far better designed, might sea power itself have far less capacity to influence the strategic outcome of this particular great continental land war than its advocates assumed?[8]

This tally of the many setbacks to the Royal Navy's plans and expectations during the first part of the war forms a backdrop to Kevin McCranie's essay on Sir Julian Corbett (chapter 4) and John Maurer's on Winston Churchill (chapter 5), and to the story of how both those individuals grappled with the coming of World War I at sea. Here were, on the one hand, the most brilliant maritime historian and sea power theorist of his age, and, on the other, the most precociously brilliant political leader of the Liberal Cabinet—the First Lord of the Admiralty to boot. Yet the particular geographic and military-political circumstances of the 1914 war frustrated and puzzled both of them. Churchill's frustration is the easier to understand, yet also the easier to critique, since his notion of seizing the fortress-island of Borkum and using that as a base to pursue victory over Germany was a complete folly: every one of his admirals and other strategic advisers told him so at the time, as did a second generation of admirals when he proposed another Baltic operation (Operation Catherine) some twenty-five years later! Corbett's difficulty was a more nuanced one, as was the man himself. He was perfectly right in calling attention to the cardinal importance of controlling the sea routes between Britain and the outside world, as opposed to mere shoot-outs between rival battlefleets, if naval mastery was not to be lost, and he had to pay a certain price for that view when the Admiralty Board sniffily distanced itself from its own official historian at the time with its commentary on Corbett's *Naval Operations*.[9] But Corbett, like his volatile patron Jackie Fisher, also still seems to have yearned for the navy to have carried out more active operations against Germany even as he saw, and frequently bemoaned, the way the Army General Staff had persuaded the government to go for massive and costly land operations instead. At no point, or so it seems, did this great naval historian of *England in the Seven Years' War* (1907) come to appreciate that the altered technological and geostrategic conditions of 1914 may have made a victory over the Kaiser's Germany so much more difficult than victory over Bourbon France had been back in the eighteenth century. This was not a question of best-laid plans going awry, or of there being a North Sea naval operation of any sort that could have brought Germany down. The only way that the huge Central Powers bloc was going to crumble would be through a combination of the continued grinding Allied economic blockade, plus an enormous American-Anglo-French land offensive in 1918. And all the attempts to secure victory "on the cheap" (at Salonika, or the Dardanelles, or even in northern Italy) were going to be indecisive or disastrous. Borkum was a cheap distraction, and penetrating the Baltic a chimera.

It was well for the Royal Navy that its fleet size was so enormous, and the overall strategic location of the British Empire so favorable, and its fiscal resources so large, that any serious defeat at sea—that is, anything like the loss of command of the North Atlantic back in 1778—was now inconceivable. The loss of so many ships and men at Coronel was a slap in the face, but it was swiftly erased by the sinking of Von Spee's own squadron at the Battle of the Falklands. Jutland may have been a defeat strictly in terms of battleship numbers, but it did not threaten Britain's overall command in the North Sea. And while the Dardanelles operation may have been a fiasco, Allied control of the Mediterranean was unshaken by it. Only the U-boat campaign against the convoys posed a real threat, but even that had been contained by the beginning of 1918. With Fisher and Churchill effectively suppressed in their wish for more dramatic operations against German and Baltic shores, there were no best-laid plans to go awry, because the Royal Navy had failed to create and espouse a theory of victory that would allow it to influence the course of the war.[10] What remained for the Royal Navy was to contain the submarine menace against the vital Atlantic flow of shipping, bottle up the High Seas Fleet at home, and wait until the German military machine in the West crumbled and armistice terms were requested.

And when the German navy surrendered so completely into Scapa Flow in June 1919, and then scuttled itself, it was not difficult to forget about those many naval setbacks of the first two years of the conflict.

But it would be a mere twenty more years before major war again came to Europe, and then (in 1941) to the wider world, challenging the navies of this later age to see how well or poorly their own best-laid plans for maritime warfare would fare. Was there any reason, therefore, not to think that this new phase of naval struggle might produce its own array of cases where Admiralties and their planners had failed to foresee the future? This was not an age of lasting peace and prosperity, as Woodrow Wilson and other world leaders had striven for at Versailles, but instead an age of much confusion, rivalry, and disruption, leaving the planners in all the major navies—the Americans (chapter 6), the French (chapter 7), the Japanese (chapter 8), and the British (chapter 9)—in considerable uncertainty. Battleship-centered fleets still held sway, and their relative numbers and size dominated the great international treaties of Washington and London, yet this was also the revisionist naval age of the coming of the carriers, of land-based airpower, and of the steady growth in the submarine threat to all surface vessels. Moreover, this was still a mul-tipolar great power world, which meant that most navies had to plan for future war in a variety of geopolitical settings. In the U.S. Navy's case this was captured, symbolically, by all those color-codings—War Plan Orange, War Plan Black, and so on! In most cases, the admiral-ties worked hand in hand with their foreign offices so that the fleet dispositions would reflect the nation's diplomatic assumptions, but that did not help things much when the foreign policy scene exhib-ited such frequent political volatility, and in so many different parts of the world, and so swiftly (Manchuria, Abyssinia, the Rhineland, Spain, China, Czechoslovakia, Poland, and the rest).

Perhaps the British Admiralty's planners did it best, even though the large empire was sprawled across the globe and the Royal Navy's fleet dispositions were juggled from one theater to another. Maybe that was simply because the sprawling British Empire was what

Max Beloff once called "a tour de force," and that in turn meant that its naval planning always had to call for flexibility in relocating its squadrons from one ocean setting to the next—a relocation tempo that the coming of war against no less than three Axis navies greatly intensified.[11] Yet even the second-rank naval powers such as Italy and France had to jostle frequently with the possibility of war under varied future circumstances, and with different naval foes, friends, and neutrals, and had to plan their warships' numbers and types (e.g., battle cruisers, fleet destroyers, submarines) accordingly.

By comparison, the U.S. Navy had it somewhat easier. It had, after all, two massive benefits: the American homeland was located a long way from any potential foes, and its own fleets would most probably not be the first to get involved in any future global wars. Still, American naval planners faced the perennial fleet-disposition problem of whether to base the battlefleet in either the Pacific or Atlantic or to divide it according to some other strategic assessment. In the wide Pacific, they argued over whether to place those squadrons a very long way away, in the Philippines or even Singapore; or in the midway base at Pearl Harbor; or safely back home at San Diego. There were also serious differences between the predominant battleship admirals, and the growing carrier lobby in the navy. And this, moreover, was a service that made no serious preparation for the defense of its merchant shipping along its lengthy coastlines, let alone across wider stretches of water. Here, even in the American case, were some best-laid plans waiting to go awry. And if Japan seemed to have things much simpler, strategically speaking, in that it only had to consider planning to fight in one (admittedly enormous) stretch of sea, its own operational assessments were also bedeviled by uncertainties about the direction and timing of the future fleet conflict: Peter Mauch's case study of Admiral Nagano's agonizing changes of thought, until the decision for the Pearl Harbor attack was finalized, captures that planning uncertainty very well.

A great war, the historian Correlli Barnett famously suggested, was the "audit" of a nation's capacity to have gotten things right in a world of constant struggle between the powers.[12] War was also, then, the audit of naval planners and of their plans. And the six years of World War II proved to be an unusually searching test of a navy's capacity to endure, not just because of the severity of the fighting (as compared to 1914–18), but also because things changed so fast. With the entrances and exits of so many players, the different navies found themselves being tested again and again—in their warships' fighting effectiveness, in their fleet arrangements, in their capacity for offensive versus defensive warfare. The French navy's prewar construction and squadron dispositions were basically correct, yet that counted for nought when France itself was swept under by the Nazi blitzkrieg of May–June 1940. Mussolini's large Italian battlefleet (a story not covered here), which entered the war at that same time that France left it, found itself a "prisoner in the Mediterranean" against a larger Royal Navy, as some of its own gloomier admirals had forecast all along.[13] Hitler's Kriegsmarine had a somewhat more impressive record when war came: while its larger surface warships were too few in number to offer more than some brief and fateful (*Graf Spee*, *Bismarck*, and *Scharnhorst*) raids into the Atlantic, its U-boat arm ravaged the Allied convoy routes to a frightening and quite unforeseen degree until finally contained by the summer of 1943.[14] All of this tested Britain's prewar command of the oceans, and in one massive region, the waters of East Asia, it lost control for a critical three years (1942–44) to a stronger Japanese navy—until the latter itself was crushed by America's massive transpacific comeback.

Yet even when that very-well-endowed maritime nation found itself fighting in the ocean in which it had long planned to fight, its main warship types were not necessarily configured for the tough struggle against its Japanese foe. America's great Pacific Battlefleet, the centerpiece of all its prewar planning, was badly weakened and pushed into the background by the Pearl Harbor attack; its carriers were too few in number and disparately used even after Midway, its submarines had the worst torpedoes of any World War II navy, and its destroyer and cruiser squadrons had to learn night-fighting the hard way (chapter 10). Over time, all these warship groups fought with greater and greater effectiveness as the war went on, as did, in an even lengthier and bloodier campaign, the American, Canadian, and British convoy escort forces in the Atlantic War. But it was a long, hard, and costly struggle, and it is a sobering reminder that even the largest navies (such as in this case the American and the British) would encounter many setbacks and unforeseen circumstances when the war for which they had long been planning would eventually break out.

In all our previous cases of prewar naval planning proving either to be basically correct, or of best-laid plans going badly awry, this book's authors could apply the ultimate litmus test of history, that of the subsequent conflict itself. But chapters 11 to 15 constitute a special category here, because they all deal with naval policies and planning during the "long Cold War peace" and into our present times. They detail serious preparations for a war that never took place, and in so doing they offer a caution about deeply frozen mindsets, and the danger of assuming that the world order is going to remain the same. In a curious but interesting way, the U.S. Navy's passionate commitment to the "Maritime Strategy" of the 1970s and 1980s—a strategy that was planned to confront and then crush any North Atlantic operations by the Red Navy—shows many of the characteristics of the famous German Schlieffen Plan of the pre-1914 age: both presumed that war would break out in a specific geopolitical arena and could be won by using specific forces and in specific ways. When Germany's great military strike to the West in the late summer of 1914 foundered on logistical weaknesses and poor leadership, its army found itself unable to adjust. Similarly, when the American Navy found that the raison d'être for its Maritime Strategy had become purposeless at the collapse of the USSR and the shriveling of the Soviet fleets, the service was not very well prepared in terms of the right ships, training, bases, and supply to face newer military challenges in other parts of the world (chapters 11 and 12). Ironically, though, since Russian naval policy and doctrine had mirrored that of its NATO opponent, the twin disruptive blows of the fall of the Berlin Wall and the USSR's own surprising implosion made its own earlier maritime plans in the High Atlantic arena look even more unrealistic, and more inappropriate. What the chastened Russian planners had left was a much-reduced navy with much-reduced finances and a severely reduced field of action (chapter 13). Both sides of the Cold War had, as it turned out, been planning for a battle scenario that would never arise. Once again, though, the vastly endowed American armed services could turn to meet the new world order, or disorders, much more easily than the diminished Russian militaries and navies could.

Far away from all that, a much smaller Chinese navy (the PLAN) had been building itself up and making its own plans for a future naval conflict, which could of course be a war against a whole variety of regional powers (Taiwan, South Korea, Japan, Vietnam) as well as against a giant Pacific power, the United States. In the early stages, the PLAN made the best of what it had at sea, which was not much, and that in turn explains how heavily the Chinese defensive forces relied on having hordes of sea-skimming missiles arrayed on fast attack boats, plus literally thousands of rocket sites along the nation's shorelines. If the U.S. Navy's operational strategy in a future conflict called for forward fleet operations (along the lines, say, suggested in Admiral Stavridis' future-war scenario of 2034), then this Chinese investment in a vast defensive rocket force seems plausible enough. But if the American carrier groups are kept a long way away from the Chinese mainland, and their Aegis antimissile defense systems prove robust enough, and Chinese submarine attacks are also detected and thwarted, then the PLAN's operational assumptions might prove to be no good. The final point to be made here concerns the respective capacity of each side's electronic-warfare systems both to blind the other side as well as to destroy or send astray all incoming missiles. All this will affect China's best-laid naval plans in any case, but one wonders what further changes in planning might emerge as its surface fleet gets more and more powerful, its range becomes far wider, and it becomes ever more of a "blue-water navy," with all the potential and dangers that can flow from it (chapter 14). The reader finishes Erickson's essay with a feeling, more than any of the others have provoked, of the imponderables of modern naval warfare, as well as of the global scene itself.

This collection of essays ends with a return to the subject of the American Navy's evolution and planning in recent decades, from someone who was a close observer and occasional participant (chapter 15). The circumstances here are a long way away from those of the Anglo-Dutch and Anglo-French conflicts in the age of sail, yet in each era there were some unchanging factors involving the disposition of navies, the internal arrangement of fleets, and the overall challenges facing decision-makers. There seems to be general agreement among today's naval commentators that while the Russian navy under Putin offers a hostile and growing force, it really is too small and underfunded to be regarded as a major maritime player—even its submarine forces couldn't compare to America's own. On the other hand, the monies that have been poured into China's fleet growth over the past two decades have turned that country into a serious naval power, and one that is still growing very fast, both qualitatively and quantitatively.[15]

At the end of the day, then, one wonders whether today's U.S. planners will have gotten it right, and while that cannot be answered because the future is unknown, one can ask the same classic questions of this navy that were asked of the navies and admiralties in the past: Have you got the geographic outlines of the future conflict right, and have you disposed of your fleets accordingly? Have you got a secure command and control system built into your navy in the event that shooting breaks out? Are your ships at sea sufficiently equipped to defend themselves? Have you got sufficient reserves of strength if early losses are heavy, and are you equipped, psychologically, to take heavy losses? Is your service trained, so far as this is possible, to expect the unexpected?

And the more the answer to such questions turns out to have been yes, then, obviously, the less likely it would be that the best-laid plans will go badly awry.

NOTES

1. When the Scottish poet Robert Burns first (1785) composed his famous lines "The best laid schemes o' Mice an' Men / Gang aft agley," it was of course his address to a little fieldmouse whose carefully built nest for the cold winter season ahead had been accidentally ripped apart by the farmer's plow: see Burns, "To a Mouse," Poetry Foundation, https://www.poetryfoundation.org/poems/43816/to-a-mouse-56d222ab36e33. The circumstances were utterly different, yet Burns' words remain appropriate to many times and situations.

2. Other than the myriad analyses of military failure surrounding the involved militaries themselves, more historical and specific volumes might include Sir Michael Howard, *The Franco-Prussian War: The German Invasion of France, 1870–1871* (New York: Macmillan, 1961); Jack Snyder, *The Ideology of the Offensive: Military Decision Making and the Disasters of 1914* (Ithaca, NY: Cornell University Press, 2013); David Stahel, *Operation Barbarossa and Germany's Defeat in the East*, Cambridge Military Histories (Cambridge: Cambridge University Press, 2009); and Brian VanDeMark, *Road to Disaster: A New History of America's Descent into Vietnam* (New York: HarperCollins, 2018).

3. For the British "test case" of responses to those nineteenth-century changes, see Paul M. Kennedy, *The Rise and Fall of British Naval Mastery* (London: Allen Lane, 1976), 149–238.

4. Paul M. Kennedy, "The Royal Navy in Three Hegemonic Wars," in N. A. M. Rodger, J. Ross Dancy, Benjamin Darnell, and Evan Wilson, eds., *Strategy and the Sea: Essays in Honour of John B. Hattendorf* (Woodbridge, U.K.: Boydell & Brewer, 2016), 109–39.

5. James Goldrick, *The King's Ships Were at Sea: The War in the North Sea, August 1914–February 1915* (Annapolis: Naval Institute Press, 1984).

6. Of the more notable works, see Arthur Marder, *From the Dreadnought to Scapa Flow*, Vol. 2, *To the Eve of Jutland, 1914–1916* (Oxford: Oxford University Press, 1965); John Keegan, *The Price of Admiralty* (New York: Viking, 1988); Andrew Gordon, *The Rules of the*

Game: Jutland and British Naval Command (Annapolis: Naval Institute Press, 1996); Nicholas A. Lambert, *Planning Armageddon: British Economic Warfare and the First World War* (Cambridge, MA: Harvard University Press, 2012); and Kennedy, *Rise and Fall of British Naval Mastery*, chap. 9.

7. For more on the details of the controversy, see John Brooks, *The Battle of Jutland* (Cambridge: Cambridge University Press, 2016); and Arthur J. Marder, *From the Dreadnought to Scapa Flow*, Vol. 3, *Jutland and After, May to December 1916*, 2nd ed. (Oxford: Oxford University Press, 1978).

8. This is illustrated in Kennedy, *Rise and Fall of British Naval Mastery*, chaps. 7 and 9.

9. Along with chapter 4 in this collection, the details of this conflict and others are covered in Andrew Lambert's recent biography *The British Way of War: Julian Corbett and the Battle for a National Strategy* (New Haven, CT: Yale University Press, 2021).

10. David Morgan-Owen, *The Fear of Invasion: Strategy, Politics, and British War Planning, 1880–1914* (Oxford: Oxford University Press, 2017).

11. Max Beloff, *Imperial Sunset: Britain's Liberal Empire, 1897–1921* (New York: Knopf, 1970), 179–80. For the Royal Navy's operations in the many theaters of war after 1939, simply note the chapter headings in volume 1 of the official history: S. W. Roskill, *The War at Sea, 1939–1945*, 3 vols. (London: HMSO, 1954–61).

12. Correlli Barnett, *The Audit of War: The Illusion and Reality of Britain as a Great Nation* (London: Macmillan, 1986).

13. Some of the most prominent analyses of the Italian naval planning and performance during the war can be found in Robert Mallett, *The Italian Navy and Fascist Expansionism, 1935–1940* (New York: Routledge, 2013); MacGregor Knox, *Mussolini Unleashed, 1939–1941: Politics and Strategy in Fascist Italy's Last War* (Cambridge: Cambridge University Press, 1986); and both volumes of Brian R. Sullivan, *A Thirst for Glory: Mussolini, the Italian Military and the Fascist Regime, 1922–1936* (New York: Columbia University Press, 1984).

14. For more on the Battle of the Atlantic see Paul Kennedy, *Victory at Sea: Naval Power and the Transformation of the Global Order in World War II* (New Haven, CT: Yale University Press, 2022), chaps. 5, 7, and 9; and David Syrett, *The Defeat of the German U-Boats: The Battle of the Atlantic* (Columbia: University of South Carolina Press, 1994), chap. 3. As a detailed overview of German naval operations and armaments, the following volume is superb: Jak Mallmann Showell, *Hitler's Navy: A Reference Guide to the Kriegsmarine, 1935–1945* (Barnsley, U.K.: Seaforth, 2009).

15. Two recent articles demonstrate the dynamic aims of Chinese naval strategy: James Fanell, "Asia Rising: China's Global Naval Strategy and Expanding Force Structure," *Naval War College Review* 72, no. 1 (2019): 11–57; and Lindsey Madero, "The Maritime Silk Road: Concerns for U.S. National Security," *Journal of Advanced Military Studies* 13, no. 2 (October 2022): 99–118.

CHAPTER 1

THE FIRST ANGLO-DUTCH WAR, 1652–54

HOW AN UNEXPECTED ENEMY WITH INNOVATIVE TACTICS STARTED AN ARMS RACE WITH LONG-TERM STRATEGIC CONSEQUENCES

John B. Hattendorf

Before 1652, there had been little thought that the Dutch Republic and England would go to war. The two countries' leaders had not thought in advance about fighting one another in a naval war, nor had their navies. Instead, they had to learn from experience as the war progressed. The First Anglo-Dutch War saw both belligerents adapt quickly to the experience of combat. Their innovations in strategy, administration, logistics, and tactics set the stage for a new era of warfare during the next century and a half of naval warfare.

War arrived suddenly, providing few opportunities for either side to imagine what war with the other might mean. While they were commercial rivals, to be sure, England had supported the Dutch Protestants against Catholic Spain from the 1580s onward. In early 1651, English diplomats at The Hague proposed a union between the new English Commonwealth and the Dutch Republic. There had been a comfortable accommodation and "division of labor" between the two maritime trading powers for several decades, although this division did not create exclusive domains. The Dutch dominated the northern trades, while English trade flourished with Spain, Portugal, and Italy.[1]

As the commercial rivalry grew, both sides remained confident that their established approach to naval warfare was sufficient to subdue the other if the need arose. By the mid-seventeenth century, the English and Dutch navies had developed differently to meet national requirements. As the Dutch Republic entered the apogee of its primacy in world trade, the three kingdoms of the British Isles were wracked by civil war for a decade, from 1642 to 1651, between the Royalists ("Cavaliers") supporting King Charles I and the Parliamentarians ("Roundheads") over issues of religion and government. Then, in January 1649, the Rump Parliament and the leaders of its New Model Army executed King Charles I, leading to further warfare between the two sides. In taking power, Parliament took control of nearly the entire English navy, along with its established complex infrastructure.[2]

Parliamentary forces had to engage various enemies in widely separated areas to consolidate their power. They faced Royalist forces in Ireland, who threatened to eliminate the last Protestant outposts, and a small breakaway Royalist naval force under the king's nephew, Prince Rupert of the Rhine. In addition, the Scots were moving to install Charles II as their king, while Catholic France and Spain threatened the new Protestant government in England. There was also a threat from Royalist privateers. To face foreign and domestic enemies—and even imagined threats—the insecure Commonwealth leaders turned to develop their navy. Initially, it played a pivotal role in supporting their forces ashore. The warships relieved ports held under Royalist siege. Eventually, the Commonwealth navy took up the broader naval role of providing maritime and national security. After 1649, Commonwealth naval forces dealt with a Royalist resurgence at sea and reduced Royalist enclaves as far away as Virginia and Barbados.

The executive body of the Commonwealth, the Council of State, set out to reform the navy and remove anyone disloyal to their cause. Dominated by army officers who placed no trust in naval officers, the fleet command was vested in the newly established position of General at Sea. Three loyal army colonels were appointed to exercise jointly the powers of the office they held in commission. Only one captain who had served under Charles I, Sir George Ayscue, volunteered for the parliamentary naval service.

Having obtained a group of heavy warships at the outset of the civil war, the Commonwealth navy initially had fourteen ships with over fifty guns. The Parliamentary Commission for the Admiralty ordered six new frigates in 1649 and ten more in 1650. Their innovative design foreshadowed British two-decked warships for the next century and a half. Between 1649 and 1650, the Commonwealth expanded its naval force from forty-nine ships to seventy-two and maintained squadrons in the Downs, the Irish Sea, and off Portugal. In addition, the government refined and improved its naval finances, administration at home, and logistics abroad to support overall operations. With these developments, the English Civil War included the foundation of a long-term and slowly developing "Military Revolution at Sea." In February 1652, the navy ordered six new frigates, of which two they subsequently enlarged to third-rate, 50-gun warships. By 1652, the New Model English navy had established the beginnings of a centralized, state-controlled navy. Its officers and men were on paths toward becoming career naval professionals and had experience in combat operations that had played a significant role in defeating Royalist forces. Development in the dockyards, establishing systematic warship design, and growth in infrastructure, finance, and administration all provided elements for future naval development. However, those lines of development were neither straightforward nor consistently successful for England.[3]

In 1652, the Dutch Republic was an established great power and had developed a complex governmental organization. It was a capitalist entrepreneurial state focused on the restructured trade and profits available after 1648.[4] Dutch warships, supplemented as necessary by merchantmen hired and armed for temporary naval service, were primarily intended for convoy- and fishery-protection duties in European waters. The ships of the chartered East and West India Companies had to defend themselves in distant seas.[5] As a result of their dependence on hired merchant ships, in 1650, the Dutch navy numbered on paper only sixty-two vessels with a total displacement of 29,000 tons. These totals were about half the number and 64 percent of the displacement at the height of its strength in 1642. In fact, in February 1652, only thirty-eight sizable Dutch ships were ready for service, including only one warship of more than 50 guns, *Brederode*. Nevertheless, the Dutch navy hired many more vessels, creating a fleet of various types and sizes reflecting the requirements of the shoals and shallow waters of the Dutch coast for small or medium-sized vessels.[6]

Although the Dutch were aware of English naval development, they did not expect to fight England. Nevertheless, there were several underlying tensions and issues between the two nations. A significant issue arose after Parliament passed the Navigation Act in August 1651 to protect English shipping and stop Dutch competition in carrying English colonial goods to England. In addition, the act stopped the Dutch from undercutting English shipping to the Mediterranean by transshipping Mediterranean goods from entrepôts in the Dutch Republic. While the act's provisions hampered Dutch ambitions, they were not in themselves reasons for war.

The English angered the Dutch by stopping Dutch ships on the high seas. Beginning in 1649, England and France fought an informal maritime war following French seizures of English shipping in the Levant. As neutrals in that conflict, the Dutch carried French goods with the idea that a neutral-flagged ship was exempt from capture, even if carrying contraband French goods. The English held the opposite view that they could seize enemy goods, even in a neutral vessel. In 1651, the English took 140 Dutch ships in the Channel, Atlantic, Irish Sea, and the Caribbean. Showing no response to Dutch diplomatic protests, the English escalated their practice, seizing 30 ships in January 1652.[7]

The Dutch began to think seriously about mobilizing the navy to protect merchant shipping. For this purpose, the States-General voted on March 3, 1652, to increase the Dutch navy by 150 ships beyond those in current service. However, the Dutch announcement was no deterrent to London's new and insecure government but rather a challenge. Soon after that, Dutch Admiral Maerten Tromp had orders to engage and, if possible, capture foreign warships attempting to search Dutch ships.[8]

The Dutch policy was an underlying cause of the war, but the spark that lit the flame differed. It arose from the age-old claim of English monarchs to have sovereignty over the Narrow Seas and their demand that foreign warships acknowledge it with a salute. On May 29, 1652, Tromp escorted a large convoy of merchantmen through the Channel. Though he intended to sail along the southern coast of the Channel to avoid encountering the English, foul weather forced him to seek protection under the English headlands. Off Dover with forty-two ships, Tromp sighted the English squadron under General at Sea Robert Blake with thirteen ships, which was precisely the situation Tromp wanted to avoid. Historians incessantly debate who fired first, but it seems Blake fired warning shots for Tromp to salute English sovereignty just as Major Nehemiah Bourne and his squadron approached Tromp on his quarter. Tromp replied with a broadside. While Tromp attempted to disengage, Blake pressed the attack. In the skirmish that followed, Blake inflicted enough damage on the larger Dutch force that the Commonwealth government thought it could now successfully force the Dutch to accept their views. At the same time, the Dutch felt confident that they could prevail. Diplomatic negotiations continued for a few more weeks, but the maritime war had begun.[9]

In geostrategic terms, England held the advantage over the Dutch Republic with its position astride the main routes for Dutch maritime commerce. The British Isles dominated the northern route to Dutch ports, around Scotland, the North Sea, and the Channel. In addition, the sea-lanes from the Baltic were also within reach across the North Sea.

Neither side envisioned a land component in this maritime conflict, and there were no readily accessible colonies for either side to attack. Instead, they both saw that the object of the war was to stop each other's vital maritime commerce on which their economies depended. To achieve this, they both had several strategic options:

- Attacking and capturing enemy trade
- Protecting their own maritime commerce
- Blockading enemy trade
- Attacking enemy warships that protected enemy trade

As the aggressor in the war, the English first chose to attack and capture Dutch trade.[10] At the outset, the Dutch were confident that their long-standing prior successes in defending trade with heavily armed, hired convoy escorts would serve them well again. Typically, Dutch warships had two simultaneous missions to execute. Their primary role was to sail as escorts for convoys to defend trade. If enemy vessels attacked, the Dutch warships had to protect the merchant ships in convoy and fight the enemy.

Early in 1652, the Dutch sent a squadron to the Baltic to protect their trade and suppress neutral trade through the sound. Then, in the summer, the States-General issued a proclamation that forbade all ships from carrying munitions or naval stores to England, either directly or indirectly, and encouraged all the Dutch Republic's friends and allies to follow suit. In response to these Dutch sanctions, Denmark-Norway joined in the effort and inflicted a severe blow on the English supply of naval stores. Although not an active participant in the war, King Frederik III prevented a twenty-ship English convoy from leaving the Baltic. The Council of State sent a squadron of eighteen warships to bring the ships back, but Denmark-Norway refused to release the vessels until the war's end.[11]

Dutch authorities attributed their defeats not to any English superiority but to their admirals' weaknesses as commanders and to the failures of their captains in carrying out their orders. The Dutch admiralties brought legal proceedings against the captains and changed admirals. Meanwhile, the English Council of State ignored their admiral's advice and assumed that the Dutch would not put to sea. Instead of strengthening the fleet at home, as the admirals recommended, they detached ships to the Mediterranean and the West Indies for the protection of trade but made no urgent effort to ready ships to reinforce the home fleet.[12]

In early November, well past the usual season for combat, the States-General ordered Tromp to sail, escorting a convoy to France's west coast. Still facing much discontent among the seamen due to disparities in pay and other difficulties in manning the fleet, Tromp got his convoy to sea on December 1 with an escort of eighty-eight warships in four squadrons. Commanding his reduced squadron of forty-two English ships at the Downs, Blake observed the Dutch passing through the Straits of Dover. Although the English fleet was half the size of the Dutch, Blake engaged Tromp's fleet off Dungeness late in the afternoon of December 10. In the few hours of winter daylight remaining, Tromp defeated Blake's smaller force and continued down the Channel. The disparity in size between the two fleets was undoubtedly a factor in Blake's defeat due to the delay on the English side and the failure to provide timely reinforcements on receiving the intelligence of Tromp's movement. In addition, several English ships had stayed out of the action because unpaid seamen refused to fight.[13]

The first year of the purely maritime war had proved frustrating to both sides. Each had won and lost several battles at the tactical level, but no action had provided a decisive advantage. By the end of 1652, the Dutch victory over the English at Dungeness led both sides to reconsider their approaches. Each side reached different conclusions from their experiences. For the Dutch, the principal issue was the need to change the character of the Dutch fleet. Previously, the Dutch had successfully protected their trade with a small core of warships and a wide range of additional hired and armed merchant vessels of various types and sizes. As early as October 1652, however, Dutch officials reflected on the new difficulties they experienced as they engaged the English navy. They found their enemy increasingly made up of heavily gunned, larger, purpose-built warships manned by a more extensive cadre of professional naval officers and volunteer naval seamen complementing the pressed men.[14] Tromp recommended the construction of large warships equal in size to the English, with a minimum of 40 to 60 guns on two decks. In February 1653 the States-General, in the context of generally strengthening and preparing the fleet for the following year, authorized 2 million guilders to construct thirty new warships. Despite Tromp's recommendation, only one ship was larger than 55 guns, with many smaller warships to meet the traditional concern for the Republic's shallow coastal waters. In December of the same year, the States-General ordered thirty more vessels. However, these new ships could only be ready after some time. Still, the Dutch Navy's perseverance in reacting to English superiority in ships with a shipbuilding program of its own marked a significant change. The Dutch fleet of 154 warships that got to sea in 1653 included 66 admiralty-owned ships, with 46 admiralty-hired ships and another 42 broker- or "directie-" hired ships.[15]

Meanwhile, the English navy had ordered twenty new 50-gun warships in September 1652. The dockyard at Portsmouth, which bore the brunt of repair work, struggled to get supplies.[16] While Parliament made no significant changes to the broad features of English naval organization and administration, it focused on discipline and leadership. Several commanding officers did not bring their ships into battle. As a result, the Council of State ordered an examination of several officers' conduct, resulting in court-martials and dismissals. In November, Parliament acted to find better senior leadership. It ordered Richard Deane to return to service as a General at Sea. At the same time, they appointed Lieutenant-General George Monck as a General at Sea, replacing Popham, who had died in August. England's rising and influential leader, Oliver Cromwell, trusted both men. Monck was the first professional military man to become a General at Sea. During his career in the army, Monck had been an effective military leader, disciplinarian, and artillery expert. Additionally, Parliament replaced the Admiralty Committee of the Council of State with six Admiralty Commissioners, making the Generals at Sea ex officio members.[17]

In the fleet, the situation among seamen differed from that among the officers. Many ships had put to sea undermanned, as seamen found privateers more attractive, given the prospect of prize money. To remedy this, Parliament raised the compensation for seamen, provided bonuses for those who served more than six months at sea, and established a new system for calculating prize money. In addition, Parliament made new provisions for the sick and wounded in the navy. However, the most enduring change was Parliament's establishment of the Articles of War on January 4, 1653. The articles authorized punishments for many of the disciplinary issues that arose at Dungeness while at the same time establishing more clearly the standards expected from officers in combat. In addition, the articles provided the organizational basis on which fleet commanders at sea could further build in refining and implementing battle tactics.[18]

Blake sailed out of the Thames on February 20, 1653, with fifty warships, and more joined him from Plymouth and Portsmouth. His mission was to intercept Tromp and his seventy-five-ship escort on its return passage up the Channel. The opposing fleets were about the same size when the Dutch and English sighted each other off Portland on February 28. During the three-day-long engagement that followed as the fleets moved eastward, Blake engaged with his entire fleet, but Tromp could not bring his whole force to bear while simultaneously protecting the convoy. At the same time, Tromp's ships were running low on gunpowder and provisions. At the end of the action, Tromp retreated home with most of his fleet and convoy, having lost an estimated eleven warships, thirty merchant ships, and some two thousand men, with another fifteen hundred taken prisoner. The English suffered an estimated six hundred men killed and several ships seriously damaged.[19]

The battle created a three-month pause in combat operations. During that time, both sides repaired their battle damage, refreshed their men, recruited additional seamen, and reflected on their battle experiences as the strain of war became deeper. The Battle of Portland closed the Channel to Dutch commercial use and left the North Sea route as the only one available for their commerce. At the same time, the Danish blockade of naval stores from the Baltic seriously hindered the English fleet's return to sea.[20]

On the English side, the Generals at Sea—Monck, Deane, and Blake—reflected on their combat experience. They all had participated in the naval action at Portland, and it was Monck's first experience of a naval battle. Most likely, Monck was the catalyst in seeing the need for a better organization for fighting at sea. An artillery expert, Monck had long experience with military formations and organizations and had already played a leading role in forming the New Model Army. Additionally, he was the second most important military leader in England after Cromwell. English warship design since the Tudor period had been trending toward larger, heavier ships with increasing emphasis on concentrating guns along the sides, but naval tactics had not substantially changed. Although the Dutch preferred smaller vessels, the English approach to naval battle had not been substantially different than the Dutch. Battles tended to end up as melee actions with boarding and hand-to-hand fighting. Although the English typically fired their guns at the enemy's hulls to sink enemy ships, the Dutch fired at the enemy's sails and rigging to disable their maneuvering ability. In tactics, the Dutch preference was to gain the windward position. They divided their fleet into three to five squadrons to maintain order and avoid running afoul of one another while acting as s eparate groups. They swiftly sailed downwind for individual ships to use superior force and overwhelm a selected enemy ship, then board it. Each ship's captain in a squadron took the initiative and did not wait for a flag or squadron commander's direction.

During the Battle of Portland, the Dutch tactics failed. Although they held the windward position, they found they could not get close enough to the English ships to board them in the face of concentrated English gunfire. Nevertheless, for the English ships to achieve the effect they did, they had to have had an open field of fire, suggesting that they were in a line-ahead formation. Seeing the effectiveness of this tactic, the Generals at Sea issued revised Fighting Instructions on April 8, 1653. Previously, the instructions had specified that ships engage "according to the order presented." The new instruction directed that "they are to endeavour to keep in a line with the chief" to "take the best advantage they can to engage with the enemy." Furthermore, if the flagship was in distress, the new instruction was for captains to form a line between the flagship and the enemy to defend the flagship.

Additionally, when the fleet had the windward position, every ship should bear up into the flagship's wake on signal and take station either ahead or astern of the flagship. These instructions marked a revolution in naval tactical thinking, yet this initial statement of the new system marked only the first intention to carry out a complex and challenging task. Numerous unexpected problems arose in solving the practical difficulties involved during the next century and a half. While the new approach concentrated gunfire, it created significant problems for the command and control of large fleets.[21]

The Battle of Portland did not create a similar change in thinking in the Dutch navy. Tromp and his colleagues were reluctant to establish rigid tactical rules that limited their choices. On May 13, 1653, Tromp concluded, "It is impossible to make provision in written orders for all unexpected incidents and eventualities that may occur at sea, whether it be inoffensive or defensive action with an enemy, or in storm, for or other occasion; such would take volumes, which would bewilder the ships' officers."[22]

By April, the English put one hundred warships and a flotilla of fireships at sea. For the season, the Council of State initially wanted to concentrate only a portion of the fleet in home waters and to send a twenty-ship squadron to the Mediterranean. However, by early 1653, English merchants trading in the Mediterranean found their ships uninsurable, making trade untenable. Despite the pressures to send English warships to the Mediterranean, the Generals at Sea advised that the fleet concentrate at home. At this point in the war, the Generals' strategy was to concentrate the main fleet in anticipation of meeting the main fleet of Dutch warships that they expected would be escorting a large convoy. At the same time, single English warships, small squadrons, and privateers would attack and capture Dutch merchant ships sailing independently or in small convoys.[23]

Meanwhile, in late April, Cromwell dismissed the Rump Parliament. Along with it, the Council of State went into abeyance. For the time being, the Army Council took temporary control of governmental affairs for a few weeks until an army-dominated Council of State took control. With the Generals at Sea in charge of the navy, the upheaval at the upper level of government removed some personal tensions. Still, it did not immediately affect English naval policy or strategy.[24]

In light of their recent experience, the Dutch admirals significantly changed their strategy for trade protection. The committee of the States-General on maritime affairs, meeting with Tromp and other leading naval officers, reportedly decided that "our merchant ships should do the best to lie still and not stir outward nor homeward while the English are strong at sea."[25] This logical naval solution failed to account for the Dutch Republic's vital need to continue the maritime trade on which its economy was primarily based. Soon economic pressure forced the trade to resume with naval escort.

After several missed opportunities on both sides, English scouting ships reported the location of Tromp and his headstrong rival Vice Admiral Witte de With.[26] Monck, Deane, and Penn sailed immediately. The two equally sized opposing fleets met off the Gabbard Shoal on the Suffolk coast, where a two-day battle took place on June 12–13, 1653. Unfettered by a convoy, the entire Dutch fleet attacked the English ships intending to use their traditional boarding tactics. But the English, in line of battle formation, quickly repulsed them, dealing them heavy losses. However, the first Dutch broadside killed General at Sea Richard Deane on the English side, leaving Monck as the senior English commander. The next day, Tromp began an orderly retreat toward the Dutch coast. As he did so, he attempted another direct attack from windward, but a sudden lull in the wind left his ships at the mercy of English guns. At this point, the Dutch ships felt their shortage of gunpowder and could not respond as effectively as they might otherwise to the volume of English gunfire. Blake arrived with his squadron to reinforce the English as the combatants drew nearer to the Dutch coast. When the day ended, many Dutch ships were safely behind the sands, where the larger, deeper-draft English ships did not dare to go. Separating into two groups, some Dutch found shelter at the Texel, while Tromp took most Dutch ships to the Wielings in the Western Scheldt. Despite Tromp's tactical skills and the strenuous Dutch efforts, Monck and Blake prevailed due to the greater discipline in gunfire with heavier guns, larger ships, maintaining a line of battle, and the Dutch lack of gunpowder. The English losses involved no ships, but they did lose some four hundred men. The Dutch lost twenty ships—eleven captured as prizes—along with eight hundred casualties and a thousand men captured as prisoners of war.[27]

As the Dutch fleet sought refuge in port, the less-damaged English fleet took the opportunity of their forward position to build on their victory and blockade the Dutch coast. Blake had already demonstrated that he could successfully maintain a blockade when he held Prince Rupert's Royalist squadron and Portuguese trade in the Tagus from March to October 1650.[28] Now, closer to home and with shorter lines for logistical support, Blake and Monck had a much larger blockading force. Focusing on the anchorages at the Texel and Vlie, the blockade paralyzed Dutch shipping and the economy for more than a month. The English maintained the blockade with supplies from small ships and by rotating ships. In late July, a Dutch informant reported, "Since my last hath happened little worth your notice in the matter of trade for indeed the English fleet lie so all along our coast that we can get no ships out nor very few in, only such as outsail the English who now begin to be foul, having been so long at sea."[29]

The economic pressure on the Dutch Republic forced Tromp to hurry the repairs to his fleet. Yet Tromp delayed, faced with a shortage of seamen, gunpowder, and provisions while meting out discipline for those who had misbehaved at the Gabbard. Tromp also had to remast and repair his ships and clean their hulls. The English navy also faced constraints on their blockade. In early July, the English had to leave their blockading station to land many sick seamen, but the Dutch were not yet able to take advantage of the opportunity.

Unopposed, the English ships returned to the Dutch coast, where small vessels supplied them.

Finally, on August 4, Tromp got most of his fleet to sea from the Wielings. To meet the English with any chance of success, he needed to join Witte de With's squadron at the Texel, which Monck was blockading. Tromp sailed north within range of the English, then turned south, drawing Monck away from the Texel and allowing de With to sail as both sides made extensive use of smaller vessels to report tactical intelligence about each other. The two opposing fleets converged in battle on July 8 off Scheveningen. Monck had 130 ships, and Tromp had 100 ships, but de With soon joined with 25 more, making a fleet nearly equal in size. Tromp died during the fierce engagement as Monck drove the Dutch back into port. Despite the victory, Monck's fleet was severely damaged and spent much of August repairing in Southwold Bay (Solebay). They depended on the small dockyard at Harwich, which was unprepared for the massive task due mainly to the shortage of masts and timber. The delays from supply shortages forced the raising of the blockade and allowed the Dutch convoys to sail.[30]

As stormy winter weather approached, both nations concluded it was unwise to risk the largest ships at sea. They reasoned that maintaining the main fleet at sea in winter created unnecessary costs by exhausting their men, consuming stores, and damaging ships in heavy weather. After raising the blockade, the English concentrated a small squadron off Ushant to intercept Dutch shipping entering the Channel, employed another small squadron in the Channel, and created four cruising stations for individual ships in the North Sea, from the Wielings to the Dogger Bank. The Dutch began to escort their delayed convoys again with the coast open. Both sides looked to the winter months to prepare for next year's campaign. By spring, the two sides still suffered from a shortage of seamen, provisions, stores, skilled artisans, and money. The Dutch were in the weaker position, but the new, larger, more heavily gunned Dutch warships were coming down the ways in the spring as English warships began to assemble in the Channel.[31]

Before the opposing fleets could engage, the political leaders of the two exhausted nations ended the war with an uneasy peace in April 1654. Within a few months, however, the States-General decided that the sixty new larger warships it constructed were now to be the property of the States-General and not disposable by the local admiralties, thereby taking a further step in creating a large standing naval force.

While neither side had thought in advance about how they would best fight one another beyond continuing their already established habits and lines of development, the experience of the first year of the war underscored the need for better strategic thinking and operational and tactical changes. Although the war had begun over belligerent rights and neutral trade in international law, the war resolved neither issue. Instead, it marked the beginning of a new era of naval warfare that would last 150 years. Navies expanded their bureaucracies further as they centralized control and developed into professionally manned, state-maintained permanent navies with large purpose-built warships designed to use heavy naval artillery in line-ahead tactics rather than boarding. At this point, organizing battles with ships in a line formation was only an imperfectly realized objective for large fleet battles. At the same time, the navy retained a range of other functions using smaller types of ships. From this point, the Dutch navy's emphasis on convoy escort as the primary purpose of the fleet waned. While convoy operations continued to have a role, fleet battles cleared the way for the safe passage of merchant shipping. Using naval force for economic blockade became more common as a means of war, paralleling the navy's use for trade protection and destroying enemy commerce by both naval vessels and privateers.

NOTES

1. Timothy Venning, *Cromwellian Foreign Policy* (Basingstoke, U.K.: Palgrave Macmillan, 1996), 153–54; Jonathan Israel, *The Dutch Republic: Its Rise, Greatness, and Fall, 1477–1806* (Oxford: Oxford University Press, 1995), 713; Mario Fusaro, *Political Economies of Empire in the Early Modern Mediterranean: The Decline of Venice and*

the *Rise of England, 1450–1600* (Cambridge: Cambridge University Press, 2015), 83–85, 254–60.

2. N. A. M. Rodger, *The Safeguard of the Sea: A Naval History of Britain, 1660–1649* (London: HarperCollins, 1997), 421–23, and *The Command of the Ocean: A Naval History of Britain, 1649–1815* (London: Allen Lane, 2014), 34–35.

3. Rif Winfield, *British Warships in the Age of Sail, 1603–1714: Design, Construction, Careers and Fates* (Barnsley, U.K.: Seaforth, 2009), 41–42, 46; Rodger, *Command of the Ocean,* 1–3; James Scott Wheeler, *The Making of a World Power: War and the Military Revolution in Seventeenth-Century England* (Phoenix Mill, U.K.: Sutton, 1999), 43–46; Richard J. Blakemore and Elaine Murphy, *The British Civil Wars at Sea, 1638–1653* (Woodbridge, U.K.: Boydell, 2018), 71–78.

4. Jan Glete, *War and the Modern State in Early Modern Europe: Spain, the Dutch Republic, and Sweden as Fiscal-Military States, 1500–1660* (London: Routledge, 2002), 171–73.

5. J. R. Bruijn, "The Raison d'Être and the Actual Employment of the Dutch Navy in Early Modern Times," in N. A. M. Rodger, J. Ross Dancy, Benjamin Darnell, and Evan Wilson, eds., *Strategy and the Sea: Essays in Honour of John B. Hattendorf* (Woodbridge, U.K.: Boydell, 2016), 77–78; Glete, *War and the Modern State,* 171–73; Jaap R. Bruijn, *The Dutch Navy of the Seventeenth and Eighteenth Centuries,* Research in Maritime History, no. 45 (St. John's, Newfoundland: International Maritime Economic History Association, 2011), 4–9.

6. Bruijn, "Raison d'Être," 76–87; Jan Glete, *Navies and Nations: Warships, Navies, and Statemaking in Europe and America, 1500–1860,* 2 vols., Stockholm Studies in History, vol. 48 (Stockholm: Almqvist & Wiksell, 1993), 1:156; James Bender, *Dutch Warships in the Age of Sail, 1600–1714: Design, Construction, Careers and Fates* (Barnsley, U.K.: Seaforth, 2014), 30; Herbert H. Rowan, *Johan de Witt, Grand Pensionary of Holland, 1625–1672* (Princeton, NJ: Princeton University Press, 1978), 67; Bernard Ca, *Cromwell's Navy: The Fleet and the English Revolution, 1648–1660* (Oxford: Oxford University Press, 1989), 42–72.

7. Israel, *Dutch Republic,* 714–15.

8. S. R. Gardiner and C. T. Atkinson, eds., *Letters and Papers of the First Dutch War, 1652–1654*, 6 vols. (London: Navy Records Society, 1899–1930), 1:48–169.

9. Gardiner and Atkinson, 1:170–298; Michael Baumber, *General-at-Sea Robert Blake and the Seventeenth-Century Revolution in Naval Warfare* (London: John Murray, 1989), 121–28; Rodger, *Command of the Ocean*, 13; *The Answer of Parliament of the Commonwealth of England to Three Papers Delivered to the Council of State by the Lords Ambassadors Extraordinary of the States-General of the United Provinces* (London: John Field, 1652).

10. Rodger, *Command of the Ocean*, 12–13. The most detailed, document-based, narrative accounts of naval operations are found in the introductions to the various parts of Gardiner and Atkinson, *First Dutch War*; Johan E. Elias, *Schetsen uit de Geschiedenis van ons Zeewesen, 1568–1654*, 6 vols. (Gravenhage: Martinus Nijhoff, 1916–30); and Carl Ballhausen, *Der erste Englisch-Holländische Seekrieg, 1652–1654 sowie der Schewedisch-Holländische Seekrieg, 1658–1659* (The Hague: Martinus Nijhoff, 1923; repr., Springer-Science+Business Media BV).

11. Gardiner and Atkinson, *First Dutch War*, 3:1–2, 12–13; Niels M. Probst, *Christian 4.s Flåde* (Copenhagen: Marinehistoriske Skrifter, 1996), 274–75.

12. Gardiner and Atkinson, *First Dutch War*, 3:220; Herbert W. Richmond, *The Navy as an Instrument of Policy, 1558–1727* (Cambridge: Cambridge University Press, 1953), 120; T. A. Spalding, *The Life and Times of Richard Badiley, Vice Admiral of the Fleet* (Westminster: Constable & Co., 1899), 81–212.

13. Gardiner and Atkinson, *First Dutch War*, 3:1–266; J. R. Powell, ed., *The Letters of Robert Blake together with Supplementary Documents*, Publications of the Navy Records Society, vol. 67 (London: Navy Records Society, 1937), 179–80.

14. Bernard Ca, "Naval Seamen, 1650–1700," in Cheryl Fury, ed., *The Social History of English Seamen, 1650–1815* (Woodbridge, U.K.: Boydell, 2017), 33–35.

15. Bruijn, *Dutch Navy*, 62; Johan E. Elias, *De vlootbouw in Nederland in die eerste helft der 17e eeuw, 1596–1655* (Amsterdam: Noord-Hollandsche

Uitgeversmaatschappij, 1933), 124–61; Pepijn Brandon, *War, Capital, and the Dutch State (1588–1795)* (Leiden: Brill, 2015), 86–89.

16. Robert G. Albion, *Forests and Sea Power: The Timber Problems of the Royal Navy, 1652–1852* (Cambridge, MA: Harvard University Press, 1926; repr., Hamden, CT: Archon Books, 1965), 204–9.

17. Michael Oenheim, *A History of the Administration of the Royal Navy, 1509–1660* (London: Bodley Head, 1896; repr., Aldershot: Temple Smith, 1988), 346–47; Rodger, *Command of the Ocean*.

18. Winfield, *British Warships*, 47; Gardiner and Atkinson, *First Dutch War*, 3:267–452. The Articles of War are on 293–301.

19. Gardiner and Atkinson, *First Dutch War*, 4:1–197; Richmond, *Navy as an Instrument of Policy*, 115.

20. Albion, *Forests and Sea Power*, 108–9.

21. Gardiner and Atkinson, *First Dutch War*, 4:198–396; Julian S. Corbett, *Fighting Instructions, 1530–1816*, Publications of the Navy Records Society, vol. 29 (London: Navy Records Society, 1905), 81–104; Brian Tunstall, *Naval Warfare in the Age of Sail: The Evolution of Fighting Tactics, 1650–1815* (London: Conway Press; Annapolis: Naval Institute Press, 1990), 16–21; N. A. M. Rodger, "The Development of Broadside Gunnery, 1450–1650," *Mariners Mirror* 82, no. 3 (1996): 301–24, reprinted in Jan Glete, ed., *Naval History, 1500–1800* (Aldershot: Ashgate, 2005), 239–62; M. A. J. Palmer, "The 'Military Revolution' Afloat: The Era of the Anglo-Dutch Wars and the Transition to Modern Warfare at Sea," *War in History* 4, no. 2 (April 1997): 123–29, reprinted in Glete, *Naval History, 1500–1800*, 285–309; Bruijn, *Dutch Navy*, 60.

22. Quoted in R. E. J. Weber, "The Introduction of the Single-Line Ahead as a Battle Formation by the Dutch 1665–1666," *Mariner's Mirror* 73, no. 1 (1987): 5–19, reprinted in Glete, *Naval History, 1500–1800*, 313–27; quotations at 8, 316.

23. A. B. Leonard, *London Marine Insurance 1438–1824: Risk, Trade, and the Early Modern State* (Woodbridge, U.K.: Boydell, 2022), 117; Richmond, *Navy as an Instrument of Policy*, 115.

24. Hans-Christoph Junge, *Flottenpolitik und Revolution: Die Enstehung der englischen Seemacht während der Herrschaft Cromwells*, Veröffentlichenden des Deutschen Historischen Instituts London, Band 6 (Stuttgart: Klett-Cotta, 1980), 216–20.

25. Gardiner and Atkinson, *First Dutch War*, 4:251–52; Richmond, *Navy as an Instrument of Policy*, 116.
26. On the career of Witte Cornelisz de With (1599–1658), see J. C. M. Warnsinck, *Drie 17ᵉ Eeuwse Admiraals*, 3rd ed. (Rotterdam: Donker, 1977), 49–98.
27. Gardiner and Atkinson, *First Dutch War*, 5:1–146; Richmond, *Navy as an Instrument of Policy*, 117–18.
28. Rodger, *Command of the Ocean*, 4.
29. Gardiner and Atkinson, *First Dutch War*, 5:263–64.
30. Gardiner and Atkinson, 5:146–429; Richmond, *Navy as an Instrument of Policy*, 120–24; Albion, *Forests and Sea Power*, 209–11.
31. Gardiner and Atkinson, *First Dutch War*, 6:1–260; Richmond, *Navy as an Instrument of Policy*, 120–24.

CHAPTER TWO

WHAT TO EXPECT WHEN YOU'RE EXPECTING THE FRENCH REVOLUTION

Evan Wilson

Perhaps no two navies in world history have had as much time to think about the other, and as much experience fighting the other, as the British and French navies in the eighteenth century. From 1744 to 1815, they were at war with each other for nearly six years out of every ten, a span that one historian has called the "Seventy Years' War."[1] It is an apt term, reflecting the many years of open conflict but also the way each side used peacetime. It was usually assumed that peace would not last, which meant that it was imperative to prepare for the next conflict. At various points, both sides suffered major defeats, and both sides faced serious questions about their ability to recover from them. After losing the Seven Years' War, the French scrambled to fix what had gone wrong, bringing army officers into the navy and launching exploratory missions to gain knowledge and experience.[2] In 1783, the British found themselves in a similar situation, fretting that their isolation in Europe and the loss of the thirteen colonies had caused their geopolitical situation to be irretrievably damaged. Yet some high-profile naval defeats in the last

years of the war in the Caribbean meant that the French were unsat-
isfied with the peace as well. The result was a major naval arms race
in the 1780s, in which the French and Spanish competed with the
British to put themselves in the best possible position when the war
resumed, as everyone knew it would.

The British were remarkably successful in the arms race. Fears
about the consequences of losing the colonies proved overblown, as
trade with the United States quickly returned to its pre-Revolution-
ary levels. The economy boomed in the 1780s, growing at 6 percent
per year. On several measures, this decade saw inflection points in
British growth: tonnage leaving British ports, total exports and imports, and trade with the East Indies, West Indies, and central Europe
all grew substantially.[3] The government taxed this growth, increasing its revenues to such an extent that the new twenty-four-year-old
prime minister, William Pitt the Younger, was able to create a sinking
fund to manage the national debt. He also invested substantially in
naval infrastructure and completed the shipbuilding that had been
started during the war. His investments were sustainable, thanks to
the underlying economic growth, and the British navy entered the
1790s in a much stronger position than many of its officers thought
possible amid the humiliations of the American Revolutionary War.[4]

The French were remarkably unsuccessful in the naval arms race.
That is not to say that they failed to build ships. On the contrary, the
French and Spanish navies combined in 1789 were larger than the
British. The French could put 324,000 tons of warships to sea and
the Spanish 253,000, while the British navy boasted just 473,000 tons.
In theory, here was the opportunity that the Bourbon powers had
let slip through their grasp in 1779, when they had also been able to
deploy more ships of the line than the British. Of course, the opportunity in 1789 never materialized because the vast naval shipbuilding
program of the 1780s made a significant contribution to the financial
crisis of 1788. That crisis caused Louis XVI to call the Estates General,
thereby precipitating the French Revolution. Louis lost his head,
and the navy lost its leadership. All French naval officers were of

noble birth, and many fled into exile. The civil war and chaos of the Revolutionary years left the fleet in no state to meet the British when the European war began in 1792 and 1793.[5]

The Revolution makes it difficult to answer the kinds of questions that this book is asking about the French navy. There was simply too much turnover in too short a time to allow us to unpack how French naval leadership thought in advance about its long-term enemy across the Channel. This chapter, therefore, focuses on the British in the early 1790s. It asks why a navy that had thought about its enemy in advance for decades and invested in its own strength so carefully to fight that enemy should have so badly mismanaged the first years of the war.

Britain joined the war in February 1793 for three reasons. (France technically declared war on Britain, but Britain was clearly prepared to enter the conflict.) The reason often given in surveys of the period is the execution of Louis XVI in January combined with the perceived threat from revolutionary ideology meant that status-quo states around Europe all determined to rid the continent of the French republicans. While that was certainly part of Pitt's rationale for bringing Britain in the war, it was not the primary reason. More important for Pitt was a deeply traditional reason why Britain would join a European war: Britain could not allow a major power to control the Low Countries. Thus, the French invasion of the Austrian Netherlands in September 1792, following victory over Prussian forces at Valmy, was what set Britain on the path to war.[6] It was difficult to invade Britain from the French coast of the English Channel because the prevailing winds blow from the west and there are few good ports along the French side of the coast. It is much easier, however, to launch an invasion from the Netherlands. French Revolutionary armies massed there were possibly an existential threat that could not be ignored.[7]

The third reason Britain went to war was also deeply traditional: to refight the last war. Pitt's investments in the 1780s, combined with the obvious chaos in France, seemed to offer the perfect opportunity for Britain to reverse the losses of the American Revolutionary War. Such a motivation was commonplace in the Seventy Years' War: it explained, in part, the outbreak of the Seven Years' War in 1756 as well as the French decision to support the American rebels in 1778. Our first clue as to why Britain mismanaged the first few years of the French Revolutionary wars can be found here, in these three motivations. The two most important—control of the Low Countries and revanchism—had underpinned British strategy since 1688. Pitt and his ministers approached the conflict as if it were merely another chapter in the ongoing Anglo-French rivalry, which it was, but it was also more than that, as we will see.

Britain's war aims were intimately connected to its reasons for joining the war. Ministers determined to respond to the threat in the Low Countries by tackling French sea power first, but without making the mistakes of the American Revolutionary War. After all, an army in the Netherlands was destined to remain in the Netherlands if it had no fleet to carry it to Britain. While the British navy went about tackling French sea power, Britain could send a small army to the Low Countries to help the larger armies of the German states. Here was the first mistake of the American Revolutionary War that ministers vowed not to repeat. In that war, Britain had not been able to rely on a continental ally; this time, perhaps, would be different.[8]

Pitt had also addressed another mistake from the American Revolution, which was making sure the fleet was mobilized for war. Britain had waited too long to prepare the fleet for a European conflict in 1778; this time, not only had Pitt's investment paid off, but he had mobilized the fleet three times in the peace, against the Prussians in 1787, the Spanish in 1790, and the Russians in 1791. While only the first two had been successful diplomatically, these rehearsals had helped keep the fleet equipped for operations.[9]

Another mistake of the American Revolutionary War had been where the naval war had been fought. While there had been battles in European waters—off Ushant in 1778, in the Channel in 1779, and off Gibraltar in 1781, for example—substantial portions of the war had been fought in North America and the West Indies. While that reflected the cause of the war—a rebellion in North America—it did not play to Britain's strengths. Communications difficulties fundamental to the age of sail meant that once a fleet or squadron left home waters, it was very difficult to get new information to them in a timely manner. Fleets on the other side of the ocean might be six weeks behind the news and end up wandering around aimlessly looking for an enemy that had long since moved elsewhere.[10] Now, in 1793, with the cause of war in France and the Low Countries rather than in the colonies, there was no sensible reason to risk losing control of home waters by dispersing fleets across the ocean.

The three men responsible for directing the war effort were Pitt, Lord Grenville the Foreign Secretary, and Henry Dundas the Home Secretary. They recognized that the focus of this war would be in Europe and organized British forces to prioritize the European theater first. They decided to return British naval strategy to what it had been in the Seven Years' War, when Pitt's father had been prime minister: concentrate British forces in European waters with the goal of keeping the French also in European waters. If that could be done with less than all of Britain's available forces, the remainder would then be free to operate in the empire to capture French colonies. Doing so would, they assumed, bring France to the negotiating table, as it had done in all previous eighteenth-century wars. British deployments in 1793 emphasized protecting the western approaches to the English Channel and watching the French fleet at Toulon. Those two fleets—the Channel Fleet and the Mediterranean Fleet—accounted for a large percentage of the available forces, but not all. There were about half a dozen ships of the line, and possibly as many as thirteen thousand troops, available to be launched at some suitable target. This is what naval theorist Sir Julian Corbett later called the disposal force. The question facing Dundas was where to send it.[11]

Dundas' answer was, again, deeply traditional: the West Indies. It was widely assumed that France's economy depended on overseas trade, in particular from the West Indies. That region generated about two-fifths of France's foreign trade and two-thirds of its deep-sea shipping. Furthermore, the islands in the region were easy to isolate with naval power, weakly defended, and fabulously wealthy. Capturing French islands would strengthen Britain's position at the negotiating table when this war, like all previous wars, inevitably caused financial crises in the major combatants and petered out. The West Indies were therefore a suitable target.[12]

That, then, was the strategic situation for the British in February 1793: Britain had a stronger navy than its traditional enemy, and that navy was unhampered by revolution. Britain had a competent, experienced leadership team—Pitt had been in office for ten years—while France had just guillotined its king. Britain had a coherent strategy that relied on recent history to help it avoid obvious pitfalls. In short, there was every reason to expect that Britain would be able to destroy what remained of French sea power quickly, take control of valuable colonies, and cruise to an easy victory. Having thought about their enemy in advance for a decade, the British were poised to exploit their enemy's weaknesses and capitalize on their own strengths.

But none of that happened. Britain's strategy was wrongly conceived and poorly executed. Five years later, Britain had still not destroyed French sea power. Eight years later, when the war finally ended, Britain had to concede most of her gains to secure a peace, and that peace lasted less than two years before war resumed on a scale previously unknown. The first two years of that new war were characterized by a serious invasion threat, and once again France and her allies had more ships of the line than the British. What went wrong?

Pitt, Grenville, and Dundas failed to understand the ways their enemy had changed during the Revolution. They were no longer fighting Louis XVI's France—literally, as he was dead—and, even more, they were no longer fighting a France whose foreign policy was shaped by dynastic concerns. British leadership was slow to recognize that the Revolution changed both why France was fighting and how France would fight, and that those changes should have major implications for British strategy.

Pitt, Grenville, and Dundas were certainly not alone in their failure, but it is important to note that there were prominent commentators who did not make the same mistake. In August 1792, Lord Auckland, a Member of Parliament and British ambassador at The Hague, wrote to his brother that the French troops on the continent were wholly committed to revolutionary ideologies: "The French troops, however despicable they may be in point of discipline and command, are earnest in the support of the wicked and calamitous cause in which they are engaged." Auckland connected French motivations to British strategy. He said fighting France now required setting aside the "courtesies of the age" and aiming for a total disarmament of the population. He even suggested military executions would be necessary to subdue France.[13] This war would be different. The next month, the French Revolutionary army's shocking victory over the better-equipped royalist and Prussian army at Valmy provided tangible evidence of the power of this new ideology.[14] In January 1793, Pitt read a report on the finances of France, which argued that this was a new kind of war, requiring new strategies. France, the anonymous author told Pitt, was simultaneously broke and in possession of entirely new capabilities: "France has not certain means of making even a first armament and yet may possibly bring into action resources of an extent and efficacy unknown in the history of any age or country."[15]

Given Pitt's preconceived and traditional notions about British goals in the war, it is understandable that he might dismiss comments like Auckland's as overreactions or downplay the possibility that France had unlocked new sources of power. Yet we should be less forgiving about his failure to consider the next logical question: What were France's war aims in 1792 and 1793? If Britain had gone to war with Louis XVI's France in 1787, as had nearly happened, then Pitt might have been able to answer that question easily. France's war aims would have been the same as they had been since 1744: the expansion of the French Empire at the expense of the British, combined with aggrandizement or dynastic expansion on the continent. But Revolutionary France's war aims were both simpler and more difficult to understand: the survival of the French Republic, which was declared two days after the victory at Valmy. Its enemies were both foreign and domestic, and its aspirations were as much ideological as geopolitical. What Pitt, Grenville, and Dundas were doing in 1793, then, was doubly dangerous. Not only were they fighting to recoup losses in the last war; they were also literally fighting the last war. Meanwhile, France was fighting a different kind of war, for different reasons.[16]

Pitt, Grenville, and Dundas failed to understand the strategic consequences of these political changes. Despite the proclamation of the Republic and the execution of the king, they saw France as the old enemy to be dealt with in the usual ways.[17] They committed a common blunder in failing to update their assumptions based on new information. To be fair to them, from the perspective of naval strategy (the cornerstone of all British strategy), there did not appear to be much difference between war against Bourbon France and war against Revolutionary France. The same sound premise should apply to both: prevent the launching of an invasion of Britain and contain French naval forces in Europe. What would be different, though, was the target of the disposal force. War against Bourbon France, it could be assumed, would involve the capture and subsequent exchange of colonies. War against Revolutionary France, however, might not operate under the same assumptions. In a war against this new kind of enemy, how could British sea power best influence events on land?

What to do with the disposal force occupied the Cabinet throughout 1793. Dundas took the lead in preparing the expedition to the West Indies. He had plenty of time to prepare. The war began in February, but the optimal time for launching the expedition was September. That ensured that the expedition would arrive in November, after the hurricanes, and with about six months to campaign before the worst of the sickly season in May or June 1794. Dundas could think carefully about who he wanted to lead the expedition, how large it should be, what its target should be, and what kinds of supplies it would need. That was all to the good. The downside of all this time to prepare was that events quickly overtook Dundas' planning.[18]

In 1793, Dundas held at least four full-time jobs. He was Home Secretary, responsible for suppressing revolutionary unrest in Britain. He was president of the Board of Control, in charge of the East India Company and its operations. He was a Member of Parliament who led a vast patronage network in Scotland, meaning that he carried with him far more than just his own vote. And, finally, he was Treasurer of the Navy. While holding all these jobs simultaneously reflected his abilities and his influence, it also, unsurprisingly, caused him to lose track of some of his responsibilities. He waited until August to order the regiments to be prepared for the expedition, and at the same time, he belatedly realized that he had neglected to tell the Ordnance Board to prepare the expedition's guns. The Duke of Richmond, Master General of the Ordnance, was furious about the poor communication. He managed to get what information he could from his friend Lieutenant General Sir Charles Grey, who had only recently been appointed to command it. Dundas proved to be entirely unhelpful, though, and he and Richmond were at such odds that Pitt had to intervene.[19]

While the two men bickered, events were rapidly overtaking British plans. Since the French had committed so much of their army to the Low Countries, some observers thought the West Indies expedition should be redirected there. Not only would success in that theater eliminate any invasion threat; it would also attack the source of the Revolutionary government's power directly and bolster Britain's standing among possible continental allies.[20]

Meanwhile, a month after the war began, a major rebellion against the French Revolutionary government broke out in the Vendée region. Here was an interesting opportunity for the British because this was a region accessible by sea. There were always likely to be challenges to supply the rebels and coordinate with them, but through the spring, summer, and fall of 1793, it was reasonable to argue that committing British resources here would do major harm to Revolutionary France.[21]

Edmund Burke was among those who made that argument. The Caribbean, he said, was too deadly for invading armies, and any attempt to attack French forces in the Low Countries would be too reliant on allied armies. In any case, Burke argued that the enemy in this war was not France but, rather, Jacobinism—that is, revolutionary ideology. "We are at war with a *principle*," he wrote in August 1793, "and with an example, which there is no shutting out with fortresses, or excluding by territorial limits. No lines or demarcation can bound the Jacobin empire. It must be extirpated in the place of its origin."[22]

As Burke was writing those words, another opportunity presented itself when counter-Revolutionaries in Toulon, site of France's largest naval base in the Mediterranean, took control of the city and offered the French Mediterranean fleet to the blockading British squadron. Admiral Hood, the commander in chief of the Mediterranean, boldly chose to accept their offer and take possession of the city in the name of Louis XVII. Perhaps here a disposal force could be used to take out half of France's naval power in one swoop while simultaneously undermining the authority of the Convention in Paris. As with the Vendée, the rebellion in Toulon could be supported by sea. While neither rebellion seemed likely to bring about a comprehensive counterrevolution, both provided tangible, achievable missions for a disposal force that would contribute to the larger fight against revolutionary ideology, not just France's military power.[23]

Thus, as the West Indies expedition gathered strength in September and October (once the administrative mistakes had been corrected), there were at least three alternative destinations proposed for it: the Low Countries, the Vendée, and Toulon. The Cabinet met at Grenville's office on November 16, 1793, to consider their options. Already, perceptive readers will note, they were running behind schedule. The ideal departure date for the West Indies was two months earlier and, given that the original concept for the expedition had been proposed nine months earlier, there really were no excuses for the delay. Dundas' dithering had fatal consequences, as we will see.[24]

At the November meeting, the Cabinet compared the possible benefits of the expedition to the West Indies with each of the three theaters. First, they correctly dismissed concerns that the French would be able to mount an invasion from the Low Countries, so it was safe to send the disposal force somewhere. A James Gillray political cartoon published that month vividly summed up the consensus view, which was that French attempts to cross the Channel in "bum boats" could be easily repelled. In the cartoon, John Bull, depicted as King George III and embodied as a map of England and Wales, defecates on the invasion forces. "The French Invasion, or John Bull Bombarding the Bum-Boats" is perhaps a more subtle commentary on the wisdom of relying on defecation to protect British shores, but nevertheless, the threat of a French invasion in late 1793 does not seem to have been unduly alarming to Pitt and his ministers.[25]

Second, they compared the West Indies with supporting the Vendée rebels and concluded that it would be worth sending some troops to the Vendée at the expense of the West Indies, even if the chances of real success were low. How to coordinate with the rebels was likely to be an important question, as was what the consequences of a successful rebellion might be. How would Britain's allies respond to the Vendéans if they marched on Paris? Nevertheless, there was clearly some recognition among British leaders that attacking the French Revolution needed to take precedence over expanding the British Empire.[26]

Third, ministers compared the West Indies expedition with Toulon, and Pitt concluded that Toulon might have a better chance of success even than the West Indies. Admiral Hood, the commander in chief in the Mediterranean, had been screaming for more resources for the last two months, both because he recognized the value of the opportunity and because he saw the risk of losing it if he was insufficiently supported.[27]

The result of the Cabinet meeting was, predictably, that the disposal force was divided into three. The original strike force for the

West Indies was 13,000 men; now it was to be just 7,000. The other 6,000 were divided between the Vendée and Toulon.[28] All three expeditions failed.

The worst fiasco was the Vendée. Had the Cabinet not waited until so late in the year, it is not difficult to imagine a different outcome. Following some early victories over Revolutionary forces ("blues") in spring 1793, a loosely bound force of about 20,000 Catholic counter-Revolutionaries ("whites") posed a serious threat to the Convention in Paris. For a brief window in June, the latest draft of Revolutionary manpower had yet to appear, and the Girondin faction's defeat left the Convention distracted and rudderless. The only blue force of any size in the area was a fleet that cruised ineffectually south of Brittany. Here was a ripe target for the Royal Navy, and here was a major opportunity for the whites. Instead, the British squabbled over the gathering of the disposal force and watched the opportunity slip away. Rather than marching on Paris, the whites attacked Nantes, partly in the hopes of providing a port through which they could receive British assistance. But the assault failed on June 29, and soon blue forces began arriving in the region in significant numbers. By the time of the Cabinet meeting in November, there was not much of a rebellion left in the Vendée to support. The mass slaughter of civilians had begun, eventually resulting in 225,000–250,000 deaths.[29]

At Toulon, the outcome was mixed. In August and September, refugees flooded into the city to escape executions by the advancing forces of the Convention. Hood struggled to secure supplies to feed them all while simultaneously negotiating with his allies. The Spanish actually had more military forces in the city than the British, but Hood refused to cede control of the situation. Support arrived in the form of soldiers from Naples and Piedmont, but only the latter had any military experience. But Hood's difficulties with the coalition were nothing compared to his difficulties with his own government. After being promised reinforcements, Hood was shocked to receive an order to detach part of his naval and military forces to Gibraltar so that they could join the West Indies expedition. Hood reluctantly obeyed, but the detachment arrived in Gibraltar to discover that the Cabinet had belatedly realized its mistake and ordered them back to Toulon. By the time they returned, it was too late. Revolutionary forces including a young Napoleon Bonaparte had overrun the city. Hood and the besieged counter-Revolutionary forces managed to destroy nine ships of the line and burn some stores, but thirteen ships of the line and five frigates escaped. It was an enormous missed opportunity.[30]

In the West Indies, as at Toulon, there were some initial successes: the expedition quickly took Guadeloupe, Martinique, and St. Lucia in March and April 1794. The naval and military forces worked well together, in part because of the friendship between the commanders, Vice Admiral Sir John Jervis and Lieutenant General Sir Charles Grey. But then British forces in Europe failed to prevent French reinforcements from sailing, and Grey and Jervis did not take adequate precautions to defend their gains. They also alienated the French planters by extracting as much prize money from their capture as possible. The French landed at Guadeloupe, declared the abolition of slavery, and reversed British gains. The British expedition's attempts to defend the islands during the summer of 1794 were severely hampered by widespread malaria and yellow fever among the soldiers and sailors. More than eight hundred died in May 1794 alone. This was an entirely predictable development, and one that could have been mitigated if the expedition had left on schedule in 1793.[31]

The result was that Britain entered 1794 on the offensive and ended the year retreating on all fronts. The one bright spot that year was the naval victory at the Glorious First of June, when the British took seven French ships of the line, killed or wounded 4,200 French sailors, and took another 3,300 prisoners. But the grain convoy that the French fleet had been sent out to escort got through, so even that tactical win was a strategic failure.[32] Despite their strong position in 1793, the British squandered their opportunities. Why? And what might be of interest in that analysis to practitioners today?

We should be fairly forgiving of British politicians in 1793. Most people most of the time are not living through epochal events that fundamentally shift how human societies are organized. The French Revolution is one of those rare moments in history when international politics changed irrevocably, when the present really was more contingent, dangerous, and riven with significance than the past. It must have been extraordinarily difficult to process those changes in real time, and it is always difficult to judge when and how to update assumptions based on new information.

Nevertheless, enough prominent British observers did just that, and they voiced those observations to leaders in a position to act. There were plenty of signs in 1793 that the Cabinet needed to reconsider its assumptions about France's war aims. For example, the execution of Louis XVI marked a major point of departure in European politics. It sent a clear signal that this was not an enemy likely to compromise at the negotiating table, or likely to have much interest in exchanging colonies. The events of the Terror and the crackdown on the Vendée in 1793 should only have reinforced that conclusion.

It is important to concede that attacking the West Indies was still a reasonable policy choice, even while the Terror raged. If you assume, as Pitt, Grenville, and Dundas did, that the West Indies were vital to France's economy, then cutting France off from those colonies clearly had some strategic value. But in that case, as Michael Duffy argued decades ago, they needed to stick to their original decision and adhere to that most basic strategic principle: concentration of force. The West Indies expedition should have taken precedence over all else, gotten the equipment and men it needed, and sailed on time. Weakening it for low-probability opportunities in France was pointless.[33]

The more prudent course of action would have been to reconsider the point of the West Indies expedition altogether given the developments in France in 1793. Perhaps Dundas and Pitt could have entered the war with a little less hubris. Given that their enemy was clearly "in a state of internal and general frenzy," as Auckland put it, they could have ordered the navy to adopt a blockade-and-see approach.[34] By constricting French sea power to European waters, or even to port, while preparing the disposal force, they could have maintained more flexibility in the face of uncertainty. To adopt this course of action, though, would have required a reconsideration of their own war aims, and they were not able to do that in 1793. Their continued focus on acquiring territory for future negotiations, and their failure to convince the Prussians and Austrians to join a tightly bound anti-French alliance, prevented them from providing support for French men and women who hoped to push back against the Revolutionary changes.[35] The result was that the strategy the British adopted, of half measures in all, was never likely to succeed. They assumed that chaos in France meant weakness in France and, as a result, threw away many of the advantages they had spent the last decade building up.

This episode shows that while peacetime investments provide a platform for success, they are not themselves sufficient. They need to be paired with a good understanding of the enemy's war aims, of how that understanding should shape one's own war aims, and of how one's war aims should shape the deployment of force. Only on that foundation can a coherent strategy be built. The question Pitt, Dundas, and Grenville should have asked themselves was "How might the enemy's new ideological underpinnings cause them to behave, and does that suggest that our best approach is to stick to our prewar strategy, or adjust based on new information?" Both approaches might have worked, but the middle path did not.

NOTES

1. Anthony Page, *Britain and the Seventy Years War, 1744–1815: Enlightenment, Revolution, and Empire* (London: Palgrave Macmillan, 2014).
2. Evan Wilson, *A Social History of British Naval Officers, 1775–1815* (Woodbridge, U.K.: Boydell, 2017), 174–79.
3. Paul Kennedy, *The Rise and Fall of British Naval Mastery* (London: Allen Lane, 1976), 116–22.
4. Roger Knight, *Britain against Napoleon: The Organization of Victory, 1793–1815* (London: Allen Lane, 2013), 21–56.

5. Jan Glete, *Navies and Nations: Warships, Navies and State Building in Europe and America, 1500–1860*, 2 vols. (Stockholm: Almqvist & Wiksell, 1993), 291–92; N. A. M. Rodger, *The Command of the Ocean: A Naval History of Britain, 1649–1815* (New York: W. W. Norton, 2004), 362–63; Jonathan R. Dull, *The Age of the Ship of the Line: The British and French Navies, 1650–1815* (Lincoln: University of Nebraska Press, 2009), 127–36; Wilson, *Social History*, 178–81.

6. Rodger, *Command of the Ocean*, 426.

7. N. A. M. Rodger, "Weather, Geography and Naval Power in the Age of Sail," *Journal of Strategic Studies* 22, nos. 2–3 (1999): 178–200.

8. Daniel A. Baugh disagrees that the lack of a continental ally severely hampered Britain. See his chapter, "Why Did Britain Lose Command of the Sea during the War for America?," in Jeremy Black and Philip Woodfine, eds., *The British Navy and the Use of Naval Power in the Eighteenth Century* (Leicester: Leicester University Press, 1988), 149–70.

9. There is a scholarly disagreement about the significance of Britain's slow naval mobilization before 1778, with some scholars emphasizing how weak the British were relative to the French, and others arguing that it was not until Spanish entry into the war in 1779 that Britain was at a significant disadvantage. Nevertheless, no scholar argues that naval mobilization before 1778 was done with the appropriate sense of urgency. Rodger, *Command of the Ocean*, 334–42, 364–65.

10. This point is made most stridently by Rodger, *Command of the Ocean*, 341–42.

11. Michael Duffy, *Soldiers, Sugar, and Seapower: The British Expeditions to the West Indies and the War against Revolutionary France* (Oxford: Clarendon, 1987), 3–7.

12. Duffy, 7–25.

13. William, Lord Auckland, to his brother Morton Eden, August 10, 31, 1792, as quoted in Jeremy Black, *European Warfare, 1660–1815* (New Haven, CT: Yale University Press, 1994), 170.

14. David A. Bell, *The First Total War: Napoleon's Europe and the Birth of Warfare as We Know It* (New York: Houghton Mifflin Harcourt, 2007), 131–38.

15. "Report on the Finances of France," January 1793, in Pitt's papers, as quoted in Nathaniel Jarrett, *The Lion at Dawn: Forging British Strategy in the Age of the French Revolution, 1783–1797* (Norman: University of Oklahoma Press, 2022), 100.

16. Bell, *First Total War*, 120–51; Joshua Meeks, *France, Britain, and the Struggle for the Revolutionary Western Mediterranean* (London: Palgrave Macmillan, 2017), 80.

17. Jarrett, *Lion at Dawn*, argues that they had a new strategy dating from 1783, which was predicated on the quest for "collective security." But Jarrett also argues that the French Revolution changed little about how they pursued that strategy.

18. Duffy, *Soldiers, Sugar, and Seapower*, 41.

19. Duffy, 41–48.

20. Rodger, *Command of the Ocean*, 426; Jarrett, *Lion at Dawn*, 100–120.

21. Admiral Sir Herbert Richmond, *Statesmen and Seapower* (Westport, CT: Greenwood, 1974), 176–77, appendix 4.

22. Edmund Burke to the Comte de Mercy, August 1793, as quoted in Richmond, *Statesmen and Seapower*, appendix 4.

23. Meeks, *France, Britain*, 91–94.

24. Duffy, *Soldiers, Sugar, and Seapower*, 50–58.

25. James Gillray, "The French Invasion, or John Bull Bombarding the Bum-Boats," November 5, 1793, https://www.james-gillray.org/pop/bum-boats.html.

26. Duffy, *Soldiers, Sugar, and Seapower*, 52–54.

27. Rodger, *Command of the Ocean*, 427.

28. Duffy, *Soldiers, Sugar, and Seapower*, 54–55.

29. Dull, *Age of the Ship of the Line*, 130–32; Bell, *First Total War*, 156–70.

30. Meeks, *France, Britain*, 105–10; Rodger, *Command of the Ocean*, 427.

31. Duffy, *Soldiers, Sugar, and Seapower*, 59–138.

32. Rodger, *Command of the Ocean*, 429–30.

33. Duffy, *Soldiers, Sugar, and Seapower*, 56–57.

34. William, Lord Auckland, to his brother Morton Eden, August 10, 31, 1792, as quoted in Black, *European Warfare*, 170.

35. On the Prussians and Austrians, see Jarrett, *Lion at Dawn*, 92–120.

CHAPTER THREE

"A MAD ACTION"

THE ALMOST-WAR BETWEEN THE UNITED STATES AND MOROCCO, 1801-3

Abigail Mullen

W hen the U.S. Navy arrived in Gibraltar in July 1801, the squadron's commodore, Richard Dale, did not know how many enemies he would be facing. Though the Quasi-War with France was functionally over, the Convention of Mortefontaine had not yet been ratified. The British were not technically at war with the United States, but British privateers had taken numerous American ships since American independence. Within the Mediterranean, the threats were no less grievous: the Americans had been given orders that accounted for the possibility that the United States might be at war with none of the Barbary states—or with all of them.

The First Barbary War (1801–5) was officially between the United States and Tripoli, but over the course of the war, the United States almost went to war (or did for a short time go to war) with each of the other Barbary states. Though the initial orders given to Commodore Dale reflect this possibility, most of the time the United States dealt with these potential enemies just as they had dealt with Tripoli—using haphazard ad hoc strategies that combined the ideas of both the navy and the American consuls in each country. They could rely little on direction from back in the United States, because the crises arose and sometimes passed before word could even reach the United States, much less an instruction be returned to the Mediterranean. However, some of the conflicts ran long enough that the government could make changes or issue orders. In particular, the United States' dispute with Morocco lasted several years. This conflict with Morocco, which will be the focus of this piece, demonstrated not just how important it was to keep a friend from becoming an enemy, but also the immense amount of resources and time necessary to maintain that peace.

The United States had been at peace with all of the states— Morocco, Algiers, Tunis, and Tripoli—since 1797, by which time the United States had a peace treaty with each state individually. As a part of each of these peace treaties, the United States paid a significant sum of money and naval stores to the state, essentially subsidizing the practice that made the treaty necessary: corsairs from the state sailed the Mediterranean, taking ships as prizes and sailors as slaves unless they had a peace treaty. In 1795, the United States spent one-sixth of the federal budget on the treaty with Algiers.[1] However, the payments to Tunis and Tripoli were considerably smaller. The bashaw of Tripoli and the bey of Tunis wanted to be treated more like Algiers, whom the U.S. government believed was militarily and strategically superior to Tripoli and Tunis (and thus worthy of a higher payment). The U.S. consuls in Tunis and Tripoli had their hands full trying to convince the rulers to maintain the treaties they had, rather than breaking them and renegotiating with higher tribute payments. Adding fuel to the fire, the United States was already in arrears on the payments they had already agreed to for each Barbary state. Consul James Leander Cathcart warned multiple times throughout the year 1800 that relations with Tripoli were at a breaking point.

Peace in the Mediterranean was vital to American commerce. The fear of Barbary corsairs had greatly reduced the number of American ships in the area, who faced significant insurance rate increases in addition to the threat of capture. Most European nations had accepted the Barbary demands as a tax on doing business in the

Mediterranean, but the Americans bridled at the practice. Until the end of the Quasi-War, though, there was little the U.S. government could do other than pay the tribute. But one thing was certain: even if the U.S. Navy was able to send over a small force to encourage the Barbary rulers to temper their demands, it would be impossible for them to fight more than one antagonist at a time. The navy was just not big enough, and the Mediterranean not friendly enough to American interests, to fight a multifront war. Therefore, the American squadron went to the Mediterranean in order to keep the Barbary states from declaring war.

However, by the time Dale arrived at Gibraltar in early July 1801, Tripoli had declared war. Dale learned of the declaration at the same time he found in Gibraltar Harbor a 16-gun Tripolitan brig and the flashy Tripolitan flagship, the *Meshouda*.[2] Despite the obvious signs that these two ships were belligerents, it was not politic (or legal) to take them as prizes within the harbor of British Gibraltar. Dale could only leave a ship behind as a one-ship blockade of the port, keeping the *Meshouda* in as best he could. The rest of the squadron was bound for Tripoli, where they planned to execute a blockade in conjunction with the Swedish navy, with whom Tripoli was also at war.

Though the *Meshouda* was Tripolitan, issues related to the ship sparked conflicts with several other nations that spanned almost the entire First Barbary War, testing the Americans' ability to fight one war without starting another. Commodore Dale viewed the presence of the *Meshouda* in Gibraltar as a sign that "our Barbary affairs look very gloomy."[3] This sentiment was exactly the opposite of the optimism his orders exuded, in which interim Secretary of the Navy Samuel Smith posited that it was likely that a simple show of force would keep any of the Barbary states from declaring war in the first place. Though the captain of the *Meshouda*, Murad Reis (a Scotsman who before converting to Islam had been known as Peter Lisle), told Dale that Tripoli was not at war with the United States, Dale knew better than to believe that. He thought "the ship may sail fast enough to catch our Merchant Ships, and would do much damage to our trade, if he gits in the Western Ocean, which I think he intends." So Dale decided to leave Samuel Barron and the USS *Philadelphia* in Gibraltar "to watch his motion, and take him, if possible."[4]

When William Eaton, the U.S. consul in Tunis, learned of the *Meshouda*'s presence in Gibraltar, he wrote to the naval officers that the capture of the crews of the two ships "would be an event so fatal to the Bashaw of Tripoli that it would at once put an end to the war." He argued that because the officers of the two ships came from high-ranking families in the court of Tripoli, their capture would cause those families to turn against bashaw Yusuf Karamanli and "give us the intire command of terms."[5] Eaton tended to overestimate how much individual events would affect the course of the war, but in this case, it was certainly true that the fate of the crews of these two ships became a matter of intense international interest.

The two ships could not be taken while they lay at anchor at Gibraltar, but the Americans could make their stay in Gibraltar as unpleasant as possible. In that regard, the Americans got some help. The dominant naval force in the port in 1801 was the squadron of Rear Admiral Sir James Saumarez, who had fought two battles against the French and Spanish in Algeciras in July and had retired to Gibraltar to regroup.[6] The relationship between Britain and the United States was unclear—the two navies had a complicated and often adversarial relationship. But in this case, they worked together and even assisted each other. Consul John Gavino asked Admiral Saumarez to detain the *Meshouda* for at least twenty-four hours after the departure of any American vessels. He was especially concerned that otherwise the Tripolitan ship would leave alongside the several American ships fitting out for departure from Gibraltar and would be able to take them as prizes as soon as they left.[7] Saumarez agreed to do so.

The Americans also got some help from the British civilian authorities in Gibraltar. The governor of Gibraltar refused to sell provisions to Murad Reis, so the Tripolitans could stay in the port for a limited amount of time before their food and water would run out. By August 8, this lack of provisions was making both the officers and the crews of the two Tripolitan ships restless, and Murad began to show signs of departing to chase the American vessels. If this happened, Gavino told Samuel Barron, he would almost certainly head straight for Tangier or Tetuan for resupply, so the *Philadelphia* would do well to cruise between those two ports.[8] The two ports the *Meshouda* might go to for resupply were both in Morocco. If the ship could not receive what it needed to enable predation on American shipping from the British, Murad would try to turn back to a more familiar ally, another Barbary state. The question for the Americans would be whether they could convince Emperor Mulay Sulayman not to help.

As early as the American Revolution, Morocco had demonstrated an interest in friendly relations with the United States; in fact, the emperor was frustrated by the Americans' reciprocal lack of interest in Morocco. So he ordered the capture of a ship, the *Betsey*, in 1784, in order to get the Americans' attention. And he did get it. Within the year, American negotiators were forging a new treaty with Morocco that granted most-favored-nation status to the United States and a host of other reciprocal benefits to both nations. That treaty, the first of its kind, was ultimately ratified in 1786.[9]

That treaty had been established under Mulay Muhammad bin Abdullah. However, in 1792, Muhammad died; eventually his son Sulayman took the throne. After a few years, the new emperor began to angle for new treaties not just with the United States but with all the so-called Christian nations his country had treaties with. Emperor Mulay Sulayman seemed to wish to break the treaty established in 1786 and negotiate a new one that included annual (or at least frequent) presents to the emperor. The U.S. consul in Tangier, James Simpson, believed that Moroccan assistance to Tripoli was about more than just assisting another Barbary state against a Christian nation. If Tripoli could repel the American threat and force a renegotiation of their own treaty, then Morocco would be primed to be the next in line to renegotiate theirs.[10] So it was vital that the United States not provide the fodder to create their own next enemy.

Morocco was not the only Barbary state interested in help-ing the Tripolitans free themselves from the unofficial American blockade, even as the crews and officers of the two ships began to leave their posts in frustration. On September 2, William Eaton, U.S. consul at Tunis, wrote to Samuel Barron that a ship had just stopped for resupply at Tunis that was headed from Tripoli to Gibraltar to rescue the sailors stranded by the American blockade.[11] So Tunis was also tacitly assisting Tripoli. But the ship was too late—there were almost no sailors left in Gibraltar to be rescued. Instead, the crews that had fled to Tetuan made their way to Oran, a city in Algiers. Once they arrived there, the dey of Algiers could get involved. He asked Richard O'Brien, American consul in Algiers, for passports for all of the crew, whom he intended to send to Tripoli on a ship. O'Brien denied the request, of course, but he knew his decision could have disastrous consequences: "The dey insists I must acquise and I am determined not, even that war should be the result."[12]

By September, even Murad Reis gave up the *Meshouda*—for the moment.[13] However, as Dale was leaving the Mediterranean in February 1802, Mulay Sulayman demanded that the Americans allow the *Meshouda* to leave Gibraltar. In addition, he demanded that the Americans authorize passports for two ships loaded with wheat to travel to Tripoli, where bad harvests had created a famine.[14] Dale demurred, saying that he could not authorize such passports without consulting the president of the United States. James Simpson told the emperor's representative that Dale's imminent departure did not leave him time to consult Admiral Cederström, the Swedish admiral with whom Dale's squadron had been collaborating on the blockade of Tripoli, before departing for the United States. Without Cederström's assent, Dale could not approve any passports. This was obviously a play for time; Simpson wrote, "I hope either Peace with Tripoly, or some other circumstance may happen, to do away the necessity of any farther negotiations on that Topic."[15] Simpson's hope was not to be fulfilled.

According to Simpson, Sulayman's impulse to send wheat to Tripoli could have two possible motives: a "well known charitable disposition" toward all indigent Muslims, or (more likely) a desire to help Tripoli fight against the United States.[16] Despite Dale's evasion, he and Simpson recognized that Morocco was an important part of the community that could make or break the United States' fight against Tripoli. Dale asked Simpson to visit the emperor and try to turn him against the idea of aiding Tripoli, since the emperor's aid could be powerful indeed. Simpson chose to rely instead on the Swedish consul, who was already paying a visit to the emperor and no doubt was doing the same thing.

Complicating matters, Simpson reported in June 1802 that a Moroccan frigate was outfitting at Rabat—a ship of 26 guns, which, though not ready for sea just yet, would likely receive guns the British had brought as presents to the emperor. If the Moroccans were able to put a naval force to sea, then their ability to distract the United States—and force a new treaty—increased significantly. The only solution, Simpson argued, was to keep an American frigate off Morocco until matters could be settled, because "nothing will tend more to keep this Government in awe, than the Ships of War of the United States being frequently seen on its Coasts."[17]

Dale saw the danger clearly—he wrote to the Secretary of the Navy on March 9 that if Morocco declared war against the United States, the emperor "has it in his power, to do us more injury than all the other powers put together."[18] But Dale was leaving, and the new commodore, Richard Valentine Morris, would not arrive for several months. In the meantime, it was up to James Simpson to keep Morocco from becoming an enemy. The emperor had demanded the passports for wheat ships and the *Meshouda* at the behest of an ambassador sent from Tripoli. If the ambassador had requested the wheat passports only, it might have been simple charity by the emperor, but the release of the *Meshouda* could only indicate direct assistance in Tripoli's war effort.[19]

Simpson was not completely alone in his efforts to placate the Moroccan emperor. Peter Wyk, the Swedish consul, had also been asked for passports to evade the Swedish and American blockade. He too had declined to grant them. Wyk's relationship with the emperor seemed much shakier than Simpson's, but Simpson knew that as the emperor treated Sweden, he might soon treat the United States. So when Peter Wyk was invited to leave Tangier on June 10, 1802, because the emperor disdained Wyk's attempts to keep the peace, Simpson must have known that his own position was very weak.[20]

Simpson had reason to be concerned: on June 17, he received word from the emperor that if he did not grant the passports, the emperor would force him to leave the country (an action that amounted to a tacit declaration of war). Faced with the evidence that the emperor had also ordered multiple ships prepared for sea, Simpson tried to convince Commodore Richard Valentine Morris that it was just as much in keeping with national priorities to authorize the passports as it was to deny them—he argued that the danger to American ship-ping, in addition to the inevitable insurance hikes once Moroccan corsairs were out, made the presence of one Tripolitan corsair and a few wheat ships a "far less national injury."[21]

Morris could not be swayed. Thus, on June 24, the emperor declared war on the United States, forcing Simpson to leave Tangier.[22] Simpson now had to reestablish the peace without being able to speak directly to the emperor. Within a few days the emperor did change his mind and give Simpson a six-month extension—but it was too late. Simpson had already decamped to Gibraltar, and he was reluc-tant to return to Tangier without direct orders from the United States or a public peace declaration from the emperor.[23]

The American frigate *Adams* arrived in Gibraltar on the same day that Simpson did. Morris and Simpson had hoped it would bring instructions for how to deal with Morocco, but the orders from Secretary of State James Madison were outdated and of little use. The one valuable thing they did communicate was that the federal government planned to send one hundred gun carriages to Morocco as a gift. With this news, Simpson decided it was safe enough to go back to Tangier to try to negotiate with the emperor.[24]

Simpson arrived back in Tangier on July 26, 1802. On August 3, he met with Abdashaman Hashash, the governor of Tangier, who eventually agreed to withdraw the emperor's authorization for his ships to attack American vessels. Simpson believed that Hashash was the force behind the new hawkishness of the emperor, so if Hashash withdrew authorization, Simpson did not think the emperor would object. When he reported this meeting to the secretary of state, Simpson repeatedly emphasized that the negotiations went much better than they might have, in no little part because of the presence of two American naval vessels off Tangier.[25]

On August 6, 1802, Simpson received a letter outlining the emperor's position. It spoke of restoring the former conditions under which Simpson had operated—which, according to the letter, meant Simpson could return to business as usual, delivering presents to the emperor once a year or every other year. The war "has been occasioned by your own tardiness and neglect in this particular, but Our Master (whom God preserve) now forgives all that." No mention was made in the letter of either the wheat ships or the *Meshouda*.[26] Simpson had actually issued a passport for an unarmed wheat ship to travel from Rabat to Tunis in the course of his negotiations with Hashash, but this new line of dispute surprised him. In his report to the secretary of state, Simpson expressed incredulity that the emperor (or maybe his minister) would so boldly misrepresent the treaty and the customary practices of the consul, neither of which included any kind of annual present. Nonetheless, the emperor was willing to accept the (one-time) present of one hundred gun carriages that President Jefferson had offered, and both Simpson and Sulayman decided to act as though everything had gone back to normal.[27]

Everything had not gone back to normal. Morris had concerns about whether the emperor was truly going to remain peaceful, writing, "How long he may be friendly, is, in my mind, extremely doubtful"; therefore, he left the *Adams* off Tangier just in case.[28] Simpson issued passports for the frigate *Mirboka* and another ship, presuming that the orders to attack Americans had been rescinded. He refused, however, a passport for the *Meshouda* to go to Tripoli. He feared that the emperor was going to claim the *Meshouda* as his own, in which case Simpson would have no choice—he would have to issue a passport or risk going back to war with Morocco. And that is exactly what happened. On September 17, 1802, the emperor issued orders for the *Meshouda* claiming that it "carries our Victorious Flag and goes on the fulfillment of Our Orders and intentions."[29]

Simpson and Morris saw this changing of the flag as a semantic trick, but the practice of non-Moroccan ships flying Moroccan flags had started several years earlier, in the 1790s, when British and Spanish commercial ships both flew Moroccan colors with the sanction of the emperor. In fact, in 1797 hundreds of European ships used this ruse in order to sail as neutrals in the Mediterranean, even without having enough Moroccan sailors or officers to officially meet the parameters for sailing with Moroccan colors.[30] The emperor had only started allowing this practice because he felt pressured to do so by the powerful British influence at Gibraltar, so he must have felt some sense of poetic justice at turning this European practice on its head for a ship in the port of Gibraltar.

On September 27, Simpson issued a passport for the *Meshouda*.[31] According to Midshipman William Henry Allen, this decision was the only thing that kept Morocco from going to war with the United States.[32] Richard Valentine Morris moved on from Morocco to go placate the other Barbary states, who also had the potential to become enemies. The presence of the *Adams* had sufficiently spooked the *Meshouda*'s captain that, passport or not, he chose to lay the ship up in Gibraltar over the winter.[33] But as spring arrived in 1803, it became clear that the *Meshouda* business was anything but settled; the captain began to refit the ship for sea, and it was clear that this time he planned to leave. On April 8, the *Meshouda* left Gibraltar.[34]

On May 12, 1803, the frigate *John Adams*, sent to the Mediterranean expressly because of Simpson's dispatches arguing for the severity of the threat from Morocco, captured the *Meshouda* as it tried to run the blockade of Tripoli.[35] When Captain John Rodgers inspected its cargo, he found guns, cutlasses, hemp, and other contraband items that expressly violated Simpson's passport. It turned out that the *Meshouda* had stopped in Algiers after leaving Gibraltar, though whether its captain had acted on his own or with the emperor's sanction was not yet known.[36] As soon as Simpson learned of the capture, he asked Hashash to explain this "mad action" by Omar Reis, who had taken over as the *Meshouda*'s captain. Hashash disclaimed all knowledge or sanction of Omar's actions, going so far as to request that Omar be sent back to Tangier in order to "lose his head."

Simpson was not sure that this capture was lawful—he believed that the *Meshouda* should simply have been turned away from Tripoli, not captured—but even if it were lawful, he still thought it more politic for the Americans to simply give the ship over to the emperor, giving him "a proof of their Freindship [*sic*] in pardoning the Crime imputed to the Commander of the Meshouda."[37]

Despite his congeniality to the Moroccan officials, Simpson knew the stakes of this dispute: "War with this Country is of all others most to be avoided," he wrote to William Bainbridge. Morocco's position on the southern side of the Straits of Gibraltar meant that they needed very little firepower or ship strength in order to wreak havoc on American shipping; already insurance companies had raised their rates simply because of the threat of war with Morocco, and many commercial vessels waited in Cadiz and other ports close to the straits for convoy for fear of trying the straits unprotected.[38]

Nevertheless, Simpson did not believe that the emperor was blameless. He noted that two more ships were outfitting at Larach and Sallé, and "we have seen the Emperour since the commencement of the War with Tripoly, do what he could to favour them." For Simpson, it was clear that the emperor and the bashaw were colluding, forming a much more powerful enemy than just Tripoli on its own.

The only way to prevent this alliance from mattering was to keep the Moroccan ships from launching at all, so Simpson requested that more ships be left near Morocco.[39]

The problem for Simpson was that there had never been a settled plan for dealing with the *Meshouda*. Alexander Murray, captain of the *Constellation*, had argued in November 1802 that the whole notion of blockading the *Meshouda* in port had been counterproductive—better to have let it go immediately when it was found in Gibraltar in 1801, and then captured it immediately.[40] After the *John Adams* did capture it, James Leander Cathcart, erstwhile consul in Tripoli, argued that the ship had already caused an unaffordable breach with Morocco and had compromised victory against Tripoli because the force had had to be divided.[41] Certainly the prize had limited the squadron's flexibility, as one ship or another in the squadron often had to take it in tow, and once they almost lost it in a whirlpool off the Calabrian coast.[42]

Simpson's concern about the power of collusion between Tripoli and Morocco did not match up with the concerns of the government back in the United States. Though the Secretary of the Navy did issue orders to Edward Preble, the incoming commodore, to be prepared for war with any of the four Barbary states, the secretary of state also reminded Tobias Lear, the incoming consul general to Algiers, that Algiers was "of most importance to the United States"— a position that the United States held mostly because Algiers had been the Barbary state that most aggressively targeted American shipping in the 1780s and 1790s and was perceived to be the state with the most sway over the others.[43] But then again, this dispute between the United States and Morocco would almost definitely have to be settled with little recourse to the government back home—the negotiations would have to take place on the emperor's timeline, not on the U.S. government's.

While the questions over the *Meshouda*'s orders and intentions remained, Simpson reluctantly granted passports to another Moroccan ship, the *Maimona*, a 30-gun ship fitting out at Sallé. The

Maimona and the *Mirboka*, another armed vessel for whom he had issued a passport some time earlier, both carried a sealed letter that was not meant to be opened until the two ships were clear of the Moroccan coast. "This measure shows a stroke against some Nation is determined upon," Simpson wrote, begging Commodore Morris yet again to send more ships to the coast of Morocco in case the nation was the United States.[44]

On August 26, 1803, Captain William Bainbridge found the Moroccan ship *Mirboka* sailing in concert with an American brig, the *Celia*. The Moroccans claimed that the *Celia* was not a prize, but when Bainbridge sent his first lieutenant on board to look for prisoners, he found the crew of the *Celia*. "I made no hesitation in Capturing her after such proceedings on their part and Violation of the faith of Passports which ought to be Sacred," Bainbridge reported to Simpson. In fact, the captain of the *Mirboka*, Ibrahim Lubarez, admitted that he had orders from Hashash, the governor of Tangier, to cruise looking for Americans. Bainbridge had been sailing to the blockade of Tripoli, but now, *Mirboka* and *Celia* in tow, he headed back for Gibraltar to get some answers.[45]

Simpson wrote to the emperor explaining the capture of both the *Meshouda* and *Mirboka* and reminding the emperor that if he wanted peace with the United States, he could not allow ships to cruise for Americans. If the *Meshouda*'s captain had acted without the authorization of the emperor, then Simpson would advocate for the ship's release as a sign of good faith; if not, "the naval force of the United States at this time in these Sea is such as to afford ample protection to its Commerce and for every other purpose it can be required."[46] Despite his bravado, Simpson acknowledged the weakness of his position in a letter to Bainbridge: when he had tried to talk to Hashash about the authorizations, Hashash had detained him overnight. This action, along with a multitude of other signals, proclaimed to Simpson that Hashash was the instigator of these orders, not the emperor himself. So Simpson also wrote directly to the emperor hoping to show him how badly Hashash had mismanaged the emperor's wishes.[47]

The emperor seemed willing to listen. Mulay Sulayman demanded that Ibrahim Lubarez, master of the *Mirboka*, appear before him with all his papers; Sulayman also suggested that Bainbridge should come to tell his side of the story. He reiterated that he was on good terms with Simpson and even sent out a circular to all consuls in Morocco reaffirming Simpson's personal safety no matter the outcome of the conversation about the *Mirboka* and *Meshouda*.[48]

Simpson's suspicions about the purpose of the aggressive orders from Hashash turned out to be accurate; in both the emperor's letter and in a subsequent one from the Moroccan secretary of state, it became clear that the *Mirboka* was meant to capture an American vessel that the Moroccans could hold until the *Meshouda* was returned to the emperor.[49] This strategy harkened back to the *Betsey*'s capture in 1784. The emperor had been different then, but the goal was the same: to get the Americans' attention. In this instance, though, the tables had turned, since instead of taking an American ship, the *Mirboka* had been taken by one.

Up to this point, Simpson had worked with Richard Dale, and then Richard Valentine Morris; the new commodore, Edward Preble, changed both how the United States viewed Morocco and how they dealt with the conflicts. When he arrived in the Mediterranean in September 1803, Preble took a much harder line toward Morocco; he viewed these conflicts as a sideshow of the main event, fighting against Tripoli. He was savvy enough to realize that he had to deal with the problems in Morocco before moving on to Tripoli, but he did not plan to drag out the negotiations for weeks or months as his predecessors had. He asserted that the *Meshouda* was Commodore Morris's province, but the rest he would deal with. From the beginning, he made his position about the *Mirboka* clear: "You may acquaint the Emperor from me," he wrote Simpson, "that it is my intention in future to sink every such vessel as a Pirate, as he denies having given orders to justify their Conduct."[50]

Preble had encountered the other ship with orders to sink Americans as he arrived in the Mediterranean, but he did not know it.

He had stopped the *Maimona* near Lisbon, but when Tobias Lear, incoming consul general to Algiers, inspected its papers, he found nothing amiss. Despite Preble's misgivings, he let the ship go, only to learn from Simpson a few days later that the *Maimona* was one of the ships hunting Americans.[51] Perhaps guessing at Preble's wrath, Simpson tried to persuade him that the path of peace lay through conciliation rather than "a continuation of hostilities."[52] It's not clear whether Preble got Simpson's message before he issued orders to William Bainbridge on September 16 to detain all Moroccan vessels and send them to Gibraltar.[53]

Preble had a whole new strategy: intimidation. Not only did he issue orders for capture of all Moroccans; he also took advantage of the transfer of squadrons as he arrived. Richard Valentine Morris was leaving the Mediterranean in disgrace, but Captain John Rodgers had hoisted his own broad pennant signaling that he now commanded Morris's squadron; thus, two different squadrons, made up of two sets of ships, converged on Gibraltar in the biggest combined force of the war thus far. Rodgers brought with him the evidence of Moroccan perfidy—the *Meshouda* and the *Mirboka*—and Preble brought the will to do something about it.[54]

Nevertheless, it was weeks before Preble could get an audience with the emperor, who was journeying overland to Tangier. In the meantime, Preble, Simpson, and Rodgers debated which ship (if any) to return to Morocco, and Simpson repeatedly reminded Preble that avoiding a conflict with Morocco made fighting Tripoli much easier. Eventually, the three of them agreed to give both the *Meshouda* and the *Mirboka* back, in exchange for a reaffirmation of the 1786 treaty made with Mulay Sulayman's father, as well as the release of the *Hannah*, an American brig that had been detained at Mogadore.[55] In the meantime, the prisoners from the *Mirboka* were spread throughout the squadron, where they made friends with the American officers— Midshipman Henry Wadsworth (so he said) even received an invitation from Ibrahim Lubarez to go with him to Sallé once the peace was restored, where Lubarez would give him four wives.[56]

By the time the emperor's arrival was imminent, Preble and Simpson had worked out all the ceremonies necessary to impress the emperor with the Americans' interest in peace, as well as with the might of their forces. Though Preble agreed to all the ceremonies, he could not quite restrain his wrath, writing to Simpson, "As you think it will gratify his Imperial Majesty, I shall salute him and dress ship, and if he is not disposed to be pacific *I will salute him again*."[57]

In the end, no aggressive salute was necessary. Before the emperor received the Americans, he sent the squadron a present of ten bullocks, twenty sheep, and four dozen fowls, and on October 8 he issued a statement reasserting peace between the two countries. That same day, Preble informed Simpson that he would return the *Mirboka* and Rodgers would return the *Meshouda*; he hoped that the secretary of state would understand that the larger purpose of peace with Morocco trumped the strict interpretation of the legality of their capture.[58] On October 10, the commodore, Lear, and Simpson, along with an entourage of officers, went ashore to talk to the emperor, and both sides agreed verbally to the reestablishment of peace. The *Mirboka* was returned that same day.[59]

By October 14, 1803, the *Constitution*'s log noted, "There is now no American ship in Tangier Except the Constitution"; Preble had wasted no time in sending the full might of his squadron to Tripoli, where he intended they should stay.[60] On October 17, the *Meshouda* sailed from Gibraltar to Sallé, where it would be "hauld up and never go to sea again."[61] However, Preble decided he would leave a ship off Gibraltar just in case, so he issued orders for the *Argus* to stay on the Gibraltar station over the winter.[62]

On October 31, 1803, the secretary of state wrote to James Simpson instructing him to return the *Meshouda*. He also informed him that the gun carriages promised to the emperor years before would finally be arriving on the next ship.[63] By the time Simpson received this letter, peace had already been settled for months, and Preble's attention had turned to Tripoli. That same day, the USS *Philadelphia* ran aground in Tripoli's harbor and was captured by the Tripolitans.

Since Morocco was at peace, Preble and the subsequent commodore, Samuel Barron, were able to focus more fully on winning the war with Tripoli and freeing the more than three hundred prisoners of the *Philadelphia*.

In thinking about their enemies in this war, the Americans had to consider both present and future enemies. The American navy arrived in the Mediterranean with orders that accounted for both of these situations, but the commodores and consuls, rather than the secretary of state or the Secretary of the Navy, had to decide how to balance the present with the future. Conflicts with Morocco, and to a lesser degree similar conflicts with both Algiers and Tunis, made it impossible for this war to be all about Tripoli—instead, the Americans had to divide their forces and their attention. For the United States, the contest with Morocco meant a frustrating delay in fighting Tripoli. For Morocco, it ultimately meant little except that the United States was once again paying close attention to Morocco. For Tripoli, the contest would have mattered a great deal if Morocco had carried their threats into real war. None of the Americans could ever prove definitely that the *Meshouda* affair had been meant to support Tripoli's war effort, but they all suspected it. Instead, all the Bashaw of Tripoli got out of the contest was a delay in fighting the Americans, which may or may not have served him well, and with peace fully restored between Morocco and the United States, he could not expect much more overt assistance. Instead, the Bashaw of Tripoli would have to turn toward Tunis and Algiers if he needed help.

NOTES

1. Frank Lambert, *The Barbary Wars: American Independence in the Atlantic World* (New York: Hill and Wang, 2005), 87.
2. James Leander Cathcart to Thomas Appleton, June 2, 1801, James L. Cathcart Papers, Library of Congress.
3. Richard Dale to the Secretary of the Navy, July 2, 1801, U.S. Office of Naval Records and Library, *Naval Documents Related to the United States Wars with the Barbary Powers*, 6 vols. (Washington,

DC: Government Printing Office, 1939), 1:497 (hereafter cited as *WBP*).

4. Dale to Secretary of the Navy, July 2, 1801, *WBP* 1:497–98.

5. William Eaton to Samuel Barron or William Bainbridge, September 2, 1801, *WBP* 1:566–57.

6. N. A. M. Rodger, *The Command of the Ocean: A Naval History of Britain, 1649–1815*, 1st American ed. (New York: W. W. Norton, 2005), 471–72.

7. John Gavino to Secretary of State, July 18, 1801, *WBP* 1:519.

8. Gavino to Secretary of State, August 8, 1801, *WBP* 1:543–44.

9. Lambert, *Barbary Wars*, 53.

10. Simpson to Secretary of State, May 13, 1802, Despatches from U.S. Consuls in Tangier, Morocco, 1797–1906; Despatches from U.S. Consular Officers, 1789–1906; Record Group 59, General Records of the Department of State, National Archives and Records Administration, Washington, DC (hereafter cited as "Tangier dispatches").

11. Eaton to Barron or Bainbridge, September 2, 1801, *WBP* 1:566–67.

12. O'Brien to Secretary of State, September 26, 1801, *WBP* 1:581.

13. Gavino to Secretary of State, September 14, 1801, *WBP* 1:574–75.

14. Secretary of the Navy to Morris, April 13, 1802, *WBP* 2:114.

15. James Simpson to Secretary of State, March 19, 1802, Tangier dispatches.

16. Simpson to Secretary of State, May 13, 1802, Tangier dispatches.

17. Simpson to Secretary of State, June 5, 1802, Tangier dispatches.

18. Dale to Secretary of the Navy, March 9, 1802, *WBP* 2:81.

19. Simpson to Secretary of State, February 20, 1802, Tangier dispatches.

20. Simpson to Secretary of State, June 5–10, 1802, Tangier dispatches.

21. Simpson to RVM, June 17, 1802, *WBP* 2:181–82.

22. Simpson to Secretary of State, June 25, 1802, Tangier dispatches.

23. Simpson to Secretary of State, July 3, 1801, *WBP* 2:183.

24. Simpson to Secretary of State, July 27, 1802, *WBP* 2:211.

25. Simpson to Secretary of State, August 3, 1802, *WBP* 2:221–22.

26. Mulay Sulayman to Simpson, August 6, 1802, *WBP* 2:226–27.

27. Simpson to Secretary of State, August 12, 1802, *WBP* 2:231.

28. Morris to Secretary of the Navy, August 17, 1802, *WBP* 2:237.

29. Simpson to Secretary of State, September 3, 1802, *WBP* 2:264–65; Orders for the *Meshouda*, *WBP* 2:275.

30. James A. O. C. Brown, *Crossing the Strait: Morocco, Gibraltar and Great Britain in the 18th and 19th Centuries*, Studies in the History and Society of the Maghrib (Leiden: Brill, 2012), 69. This practice backfired on the Moroccans, whose passports then became almost meaningless, since both Britain and Spain knew that a Moroccan passport was no guarantee that a ship was, in fact, Moroccan. Thus, more Moroccans were hurt by this ruse than were helped. Mulay Sulayman ended the practice of issuing Moroccan passports by 1800.

31. Passport for the *Meshouda*, September 27, 1802, *WBP* 2:283.

32. William Henry Allen to General William Allen, November 23, 1802, *WBP* 2:320.

33. Simpson to Secretary of State, December 24, 1802, *WBP* 2:337–38.

34. Wadsworth journal, May 19, 1803, *WBP* 2:409.

35. *John Adams* journal, May 12, 1803, *WBP* 2:402. This is not the same ship as the *Adams* that Morris was waiting for earlier.

36. Morris to Simpson, May 19, 1803, *WBP* 2:408–9; Simpson to Secretary of State, July 9, 1803, *WBP* 2:470.

37. Simpson to Morris, June 20, 1803, *WBP* 2:456–57.

38. Simpson to Bainbridge, September 3, 1803, *WBP* 3:9–10; William Court & Co. to John Gavino, September 5, 1803, *WBP* 3:20.

39. Simpson to Secretary of State, July 9, 1803, *WBP* 2:470.

40. Murray to Secretary of the Navy, November 30, 1802, *WBP* 2:328.

41. Cathcart to Morris, August 15, 1803, *WBP* 2:512–13.

42. Wadsworth journal, July 18, 1803, *WBP* 2:490.

43. Secretary of the Navy to Preble, July 13, 1803, *WBP* 2:476; Secretary of State to Lear, July 14, 1803, *WBP* 2:482.

44. Simpson to Morris, July 26, 1803, *WBP* 2:498.

45. Bainbridge to Simpson, August 29, 1803, *WBP* 2:518; Bainbridge to Secretary of the Navy, August 29, 1803, *WBP* 2:522.

46. Simpson to Mulay Sulayman, September 2, 1803, *WBP* 3:7.

47. Simpson to Bainbridge, September 3, 1803, *WBP* 3:9–10.

48. Emperor of Morocco to Simpson, September 9, 1803, *WBP* 3:25; Emperor of Morocco to consuls, September 9, 1803, *WBP* 3:26–27.

49. Simpson to Bainbridge, September 3, 1803, *WBP* 3:9–10; Emperor of Morocco to consuls, September 9, 1803, *WBP* 3:26–27; Selawy to Simpson, September 12, 1803, *WBP* 3:29.
50. Preble to Simpson, September 13, 1803, *WBP* 3:31.
51. Lear to Preble, September 7, 1803, *WBP* 3:23.
52. Simpson to Preble, September 14, 1803, *WBP* 3:43–44.
53. Preble to Bainbridge, September 16, 1803, *WBP* 3:48.
54. Preble to Simpson, September 17, 1803, *WBP* 3:51–52.
55. Preble to Simpson, September 25, 1803, *WBP* 3:76.
56. Wadsworth to Nancy Doane, September 24, 1803, *WBP* 3:75.
57. Preble to Simpson, October 4, 1803, *WBP* 3:102.
58. Preble to Simpson, October 8, 1803, *WBP* 3:119.
59. Lear to Secretary of State, October 17, 1803, *WBP* 3:148–50.
60. Log of *Constitution*, October 13, 1803, *WBP* 3:134.
61. Log of *Constitution*, October 17, 1803, *WBP* 3:145.
62. Preble journal, October 16, 1803, *WBP* 3:142.
63. Secretary of State to Simpson, October 31, 1803, *WBP* 3:168.

CHAPTER FOUR

THEORY MEETS THE REALITY OF WAR

JULIAN S. CORBETT, HIS THEORIES, AND THE FIRST WORLD WAR

Kevin D. McCranie

J ulian S. Corbett provides a powerful case study that illustrates both the promises and the pitfalls of attempting to apply strategic theory to real-world events. During the first decade of the twentieth century, Corbett forged close links with the British navy's senior leadership and its officer education program. This work allowed him to evolve from a naval historian to a strategic thinker. In 1911, a mere three years before the outbreak of World War I, Corbett published his seminal volume, *Some Principles of Maritime Strategy*. His first biographer has claimed that it "revealed him as a theoretical thinker on war of the first rank," and his most recent biographer, Andrew Lambert, has added, "The book has become the basis of all serious sea power theory" and "remains the single most important text in the canon."[1]

Corbett's career accelerated with the outbreak of World War I as he was drawn into advisory positions as a subject matter expert working for the Royal Navy and the Committee of Imperial Defence. He also agreed to write Britain's official naval history of the war.[2]

Before his death in 1922, he had completed the first three volumes of *The History of the Great War Based on Official Documents: Naval Operations*, taking the war through the Battle of Jutland in 1916.

Thus, Corbett had the opportunity to write about naval history and strategy in a period of great technological change and developing great-power competition before World War I; he then lived through the war, including the uncertainty that shrouded its course and outcome; and finally, Corbett had an opportunity to write the first major naval history of the war. Unlike Alfred T. Mahan, who died in the early months of the conflict, Corbett lived till almost four years after hostilities with Germany had ceased. Until his death in 1922, he remained deeply involved with the Royal Navy. Studying the relationship among his prewar theories, how war interacted with those theories, and his end of war assessments allows today's readers a greater appreciation of the value of theory, its potential pitfalls, and the difficulty in translating theory into practice.

THE IMPORTANCE OF HISTORY FOR INDUCTIVE REASONING

In 1889 Corbett published his first historical work. A biography of George Monk (or Monck), 1st Duke of Albemarle, it was aimed at a popular audience.[3] More than anything else, it whetted Corbett's appetite for historical writing. Throughout the 1890s, Corbett matured as a historian. He read deeply and consulted archives. In 1901 John Knox Laughton, a leading British naval historian, praised the "painstaking and costly research . . . which places Mr. Corbett high on the list of modern historians."[4] In the first decade of the twentieth century, Corbett's work became ever more sophisticated. His volumes on the Seven Years' War and the Trafalgar Campaign, published in 1907 and 1910, respectively, have particularly stood the test of time for their accuracy, use of sources, and sound analysis.[5] Corbett took the study of history seriously. In the period before World War I, he set a high bar for his own historical writings and demanded that others treat historical evidence with the same respect. He even went so far as to critique passages from one of Mahan's books as "too glaring for the dignity of history."[6]

For Corbett, history provided the foundation for strategic theory. Writing just months before World War I, he claimed that people were no longer using "history to prove they were right; now they go to it to find out where they are wrong. . . . They go to history to search for principles, not to prove those which they believe they have already found."[7] Elsewhere, he explained that history worked to "fertilise the mind with examples—wh[ich] may disappear—like manure but leave the soil rich."[8] If the historical evidence was distorted, this necessary foundation for strategic theory became unstable, jeopardizing analysis, weakening the education of British naval officers, and ultimately putting the Royal Navy and his country at risk.

If anything, World War I solidified Corbett's position on the importance of history in the education of Royal Navy officers. Only a few months into the war, Corbett lamented to a colleague, "I have seen a great deal, the mistakes that have been made are due mainly to unfamiliarity with the eternal truths which are enshrined in the history of the old wars."[9] Corbett implicitly understood the value of history, and throughout the war, he saw this as a recurring deficiency among British naval officers. Complaining about the study of history in 1915, he stated, "What a pity it is that our big men don't study it more."[10] When senior officers attempted to apply history, Corbett maintained they often went about it in an ineffective manner. Rather than amass a wide-ranging trove of historical examples to serve as evidence, Corbett described how one officer formed his theory and then used history to prove it.[11]

In writings after World War I, Corbett remained very skeptical of this type of deductive reasoning; instead, he argued strongly for an inductive method that involved the study of numerous historical examples. Only after amassing an array of evidence could a leader use those examples to aid in analysis. Corbett cautioned against deductive approaches and even went so far as to state, "What is best is not to try the deductive method at all. Without training and discipline it is sure to lead astray. . . . Far better to stick to the inductive method. Collect and study the ascertained facts of war history, patiently build up your doctrine on the solid foundations they afford."[12] Those employing the deductive approach generally sought to prove preconceived arguments rather than allow evidence to guide conclusions. Corbett put an exclamation point on this in his official history of World War I, where he contrasted "the child of pure theory" with the "sound doctrine founded on the practical experience of past naval warfare."[13]

GRAND STRATEGIC FOUNDATIONS

A decade before the outbreak of World War I, Corbett outlined the interrelationship among diplomatic, naval, and land strategies:

> No one of the three great national forces can rightly direct its efforts except hand in hand with the other two. Without knowledge of the probable limits and direction which diplomacy can set for a war, and without a clear conception of the political end in view, soldiers and sailors are alike without map or chart wherewith to trace their strategy; nor in like manner can diplomacy be rightly directed without a full grasp of the range and energy of the fighting pressure that can be brought to back it.[14]

Several years later, he more fully emphasized the importance of the political leader for directing Britain's instruments of national power. In addition to diplomacy, the army, and the navy, he added the state's "commercial and financial position."[15] Corbett had a difficult time labeling this an "all instruments of power" approach. He called it alternatively "major strategy," "higher strategy," and what today would be the more familiar term: "grand strategy."[16]

Throughout World War I, Corbett remained a powerful advocate for a grand strategic approach. A navy did not function independently; rather, it was one of several instruments of national power. In the first volume of his official naval history, he explained, "The aim has been to give in narrative form and free from technicalities an intelligible view not only of the operations themselves but of their mutual connection and meaning, the policy which dictated them, their relation to military and diplomatic action, and the difficulties and cross-currents which in some cases delayed their success and robbed them of the expected results."[17]

World War I starkly showcased the importance of a grand strategic approach. It underscored the need for naval and military officers to focus on their areas of expertise while political leaders directed the entire war effort through a comprehensive approach. Following the war, he specifically criticized the Germans for grand strategic failings: "Such differences must necessarily be acute where, as in Germany, soldiers and sailors had come to be regarded as the supreme experts in the conduct of war. They of course could be no more than experts in military and naval operations. Of the other two main factors in war—foreign affairs and economics—they had no special technical knowledge. In these matters the statesmen were the experts."[18] Especially in this area, Corbett's views from before the outbreak of hostilities were if anything solidified in his official history: political leaders guided the war effort to utilize all instruments of national power approach.

The foundations of Corbett's thinking from before World War I survived the war almost unscathed. History continued to inform strategic theory and provided leaders with examples to enhance decision-making. At the grand strategic level, the role of the senior politicians and the interplay of the instruments of national power had if anything become more essential as war touched ever more areas of a country's existence.

THE LETHALITY AND CUSTOMS OF MARITIME WARFARE

Before World War I, Corbett stood in line with many of his contemporaries in arguing that technological advances would have a greater impact on tactics than on strategy. Even so, Corbett admitted, "I venture to submit that torpedoes, wireless telegraphy, and submarines have produced changes of strategical conditions—not fundamental, perhaps, but very important."[19] He supported this statement in the following passage in his official history: "The never ceasing change in the power, range and character of naval material . . . left no stable factors on which a solid scheme could be built up."[20] Technological change is something Corbett in general understood; however, he had a more difficult time grappling with how changes in technology impacted the lethality and morality of war in the maritime environment.

Just days into the war, the Germans began mining international waters. Corbett recounted, almost incredulously, that this was "regardless of neutrals and of all the time-honoured customs of the sea." Corbett saw the use of mines in shipping lanes as a dastardly act that he had trouble fathoming either in real time or as he wrote about it following the war. Even after hostilities concluded, Corbett could not help but contrast what he viewed as the high moral standards of the British with the abominable actions of the Germans.[21] Describing attacks on commerce from early 1915, Corbett still wanted to give the Germans the benefit of the doubt: "In Home waters, as we have seen, there had recently been some inexcusable cases of destruction of merchant ships without warning, and with no attempt to save life, and one shameless attack on a hospital ship, but their offences had been sporadic—explainable possibly by the perverted zeal of individual officers who had lost their heads."[22] In fact, Corbett's official history is in many respects the chronicle of the "increasing disregard with which Germany was treating the accepted limitations of naval warfare." He concluded that the Germans "could not be met within the old canons of war."[23]

Corbett tried to find some precedent from British maritime history. This was very much in line with his views as a historian and the need to follow an inductive approach. Corbett had to look back to the early Tudor period, where the British "had established a reputation that they would always sink rather than surrender. In later times the tradition had not always been maintained, but in the present war there was in this respect, as in so many others, a reversion to the old indomitable spirit—not only, it must be said, in our own Service, but in that of the enemy as well."[24] No quarter was asked and none given. The failure to respect international law, custom of the sea, or even ethics and mores is one area where Corbett's prewar writings failed to capture the coming war. Even after the war, he found it hard to reconcile his studies from the age of sail with the contemporary environment.

Though some might claim that this difficulty to reconcile his theories with actual events reflected his prewar theories on limited war, when Corbett wrote about war limited by its political object, he was emphatic: a "limited object has no relation to the armed force employed, but only to the object for which it is employed. However limited the object, you may, and usually must, employ your whole force."[25] The Russo-Japanese War (1904–5) informed much of his limited war theory: "In this case it was obvious that in Japan the end in view would call forth practically unlimited effort."[26] His concept of limited war dealt with the object and the method of waging war, rather than the means employed. Moreover, his theories of limited war focused on terrestrial objectives. For a maritime state to be successful in limited war, command of the sea was a necessity. In its truest sense, this entailed the elimination of the opposing fleet, yet it is in that domain where Corbett's writings indicated that he had the most difficulty in grappling with World War I's brutality.

Corbett's prewar worldview was of the wealthy English upper middle class, enmeshed in the international maritime economy and the moral foundations of the late Victorian and Edwardian eras. His writings did not grapple with the coming brutality of World War I. This was frankly beyond his comprehension. Even as the first days of the conflict drifted into months, and then years of war, Corbett had difficulty accepting the war's ferocity and the flagrant violation of international custom. He still had not entirely come to grips with the war's brutality when writing the official history.

THE MINOR COUNTERATTACK

The contrast between the age of sail and the contemporary environment was particularly evident in what Corbett labeled the "minor counterattack." He used the term to describe how an inferior fleet could dispute command of the sea through operations aimed at slowly reducing the superiority of the larger fleet. In *Some Principles of Maritime Strategy*, Corbett admitted that technological developments, including torpedoes, had potentially increased the effectiveness of the minor counterattack. Using the Russo-Japanese War, he attempted to draw conclusions, but these were based on a small number of examples and undermined by the rapid pace of technological change.[27]

The official history allowed him to acknowledge that technological advances had a greater impact on minor counterattacks than he estimated before the war: "By the enormously increased power of minor attack Germany could at least hope to reduce our margin of superiority so low as eventually to warrant her taking the offensive." Compared with the possibilities of France using minor counterattacks in the age of sail, Germany "had, therefore, even greater justification and greater promise than that which the French had been wont to adopt in analogous circumstances."[28] When the German submarine *U-9* sank the British armored cruisers *Cressy*, *Aboukir*, and *Hogue* on September 22, 1914, and soon afterward the cruiser *Hawke* on October 15, Corbett explained, "It was clear that the enemy was pushing vigorously his policy of minor attack, and his recent successes confirmed its correctness and its possibilities."[29]

Corbett's prewar writings addressing flotilla craft like submarines did not fully account for their effectiveness in the coming war. The technological infancy of these platforms contributed to his prewar deductions, but Corbett acknowledged their potential in *Some Principles*: "From a strategical point of view we can say no more than that we have to count with a new factor, which gives a new possibility to minor counterattack."[30] When it came to assessing unknowns, he had difficulty speculating. This was likely the result of his background as a historian and his reliance on the inductive method. Corbett preferred to build his arguments off examples from the past. With evolving technologies, Corbett identified possible change but refused to press his conclusions further.

After World War I, Corbett's argument had evolved to account for the increased effectiveness of new technologies. Describing the Germans, he questioned, "Indeed, the wonder is, in view of the results obtained, that a nation credited with so full a measure of the military spirit should so soon have turned its promising method of offence against a commercial objective instead of persevering against the naval one."[31] Corbett was willing to engage with new technologies, assess their effectiveness, and modify his strategic outlook. However, his mindset remained trapped in the customs and ethics of the prewar world. The use of minor counterattacks against warships made perfect sense to him, but the German decision to use submarines and torpedoes against merchant ships was something he found difficult to fathom.

COMMAND OF THE SEA AND COMMERCE DEFENSE

In the opening month of World War I, everything went as Corbett had predicted in the war on commerce. Patrolling British warships had followed Corbett's prewar dictums by focusing on the choke points and terminal points in the sea lines of communication. Because the density of merchant commerce was greatest in those locations, naval patrols effectively minimized the impact of commerce raiding. Outside the terminal and choke points, merchant ships could transit regions with little to fear from commerce raiders because the sheer size of the ocean provided the best ratio between protection to cost.[32] As Corbett explained in the official history, "In this way the vast extent of the Seven Seas was occupied in the traditional manner, not by patrolling the trade routes, but by guarding in such force as our resources permitted the main focal areas where they converged, and where the enemy's commerce destroyers were most likely to be attracted and had the only chance of making a serious impression upon the huge volume of our trade."[33] By such a method, Britain established general, global command of the sea during the first month of the war.[34]

Almost immediately, however, British naval leadership needed to transition from operations to secure command of the sea to operations designed to use command for strategic effects. Corbett described this as "exercising" command of the sea. Such operations were tedious. In his official history, Corbett described them as having that "dead and uneventful character with which our ancestors were so familiar and which public opinion at first found hard to reconcile with its expectations."[35] This differed little from his real-time assessment as 1914 drew to a close: "The sides are too unequal. As far as we can see there will be no question of a struggle for command of the sea—it will only be a question of exercising command. So strongly do I feel this that I do not look forward to writing the history with any pleasure."[36]

Wartime interaction resulted in Corbett changing his views. When writing after the war, he admitted by November 1914:

> Command could no longer be measured by the old standards. If command of the sea meant the power to move fleets, troops and trade freely where we would, then our command was not undisputed, and indeed it seemed to be growing gradually more precarious, as the mining activities of the enemy extended to our western coasts and their submarines with increasing power and range spread further and further afield.

Command of the sea in British home waters appeared increasingly in doubt. Incredulously he asserted, "We found ourselves, in fact, faced with a new struggle of which we had no experience."[37] Describing the loss of the *Lusitania* in 1915, Corbett explained, "For it made suddenly patent how imperfect was the control of the sea which we had already won, and how exacting must be the struggle to perfect it."[38] Exercising command of the sea might be tedious and dull, but as the war progressed, Corbett became increasingly aware of its absolute significance to the outcome of the war.

A critical difference exists between studying past wars and living through a conflict. A historical conflict can be studied dispassionately: the outcome is known. The uncertainty and the emotion of the contemporary environment makes it more difficult in the moment to grasp what is occurring, even for someone like Corbett who possessed an expansive knowledge of naval warfare. Prior to the war in 1911, he had explained, "By no conceivable means is it possible to give trade absolute protection. We cannot make an omelette without breaking eggs. We cannot make war without losing ships."[39] It seems that such conclusions were good and well until merchant ship losses occurred on his watch. Living through a war and all its uncertainties proved far different from studying a conflict that had ended.

How the Germans waged commerce warfare forced Corbett to reconsider his views on command of the sea. Following World War I, Corbett described exercising command as "donkey work," which "besides being dull is of exceptional difficulty." The war demonstrated that it "can't be done so cleanly as of old. The losses & failures must necessarily be more numerous." Sinkings became constant, while Corbett lamented that the "successes we hardly hear of."[40]

It is regrettable that Corbett did not live to write the fourth and fifth volumes of the official naval history. Those volumes would have addressed the war after Jutland, including the Germans' unrestricted submarine warfare campaign. It is, however, important to consider one statement in *Some Principles of Maritime Strategy* written before the war: "Modern developments and changes in shipping and naval material have indeed so profoundly modified the whole conditions of commerce protection, that there is no part of strategy where historical deduction is more difficult or more liable to error."[41] Corbett had an inkling that war would alter his theories relating to the protection of merchant shipping, but he did not live long enough to provide his conclusions based on wartime experience.

THE QUEST FOR BATTLE AND ITS STRATEGIC EFFECTS

The emotions of living day by day through the war also caused Corbett to grapple with the clash between theory and reality regarding the potential of a fleet-on-fleet battle. Naval battle between massed fleets captivated both naval commentators and the general public. Corbett made this point in the opening pages of the first volume of the official history. Describing the battle fleet, he explained, "Of recent years, by a strange misreading of history, an idea had grown up that its primary function is to seek out and destroy the enemy's main fleet."[42] This entirely tracks with his prewar statements. In *Some Principles of Maritime Strategy*, Corbett provided the following explanation, dripping in sarcasm: "The only way of securing such a command [of the sea] by naval means is to obtain a decision by battle against the enemy's fleet. Sooner or later it must be done, and the sooner the better. That was the old British creed. It is still our creed, and needs no labouring." Corbett's sharp pen added, "No one will dispute it, no one will care even to discuss it, and we pass with confidence to the conclusion that the first business of our fleet is to seek out the enemy's fleet and destroy it. . . . To examine its claim to be the logical conclusion of our theory of war will even be held dangerous."[43] After the war, Corbett described this position as "literary rather than historical."[44]

To frame this argument, Corbett looked deeply at the historical evidence to determine how naval battle fit into strategic theory. History indicated that battle needed to be worked for by setting the necessary conditions. In *Some Principles of Maritime Strategy*, Corbett explained: "If circumstances are advantageous to us, we are not always able to effect a decision; and if they are disadvantageous, we are not always obliged to fight." In fact, he would go so far as to argue that the greatest problem in naval warfare "was not how to defeat the enemy, but how to bring him to action."[45]

For a stronger navy, like the one Britain possessed in World War I, Corbett in his prewar writings came up with a simple, and perhaps elegant, solution. If the stronger naval power could "seize a position which controls communications vital to his plan of the campaign," the weaker naval power would be placed on the horns of a dilemma: the weaker naval power would need either to fight to break down the stronger power's position or to allow the stronger naval power to maintain its dominant position.[46]

These prewar views translated clearly into Britain's naval position in the North Sea during World War I. By massing the Grand Fleet between Rosyth and Scapa Flow, British leaders had positioned their fleet to cover the northern exit to the North Sea and intercept any German naval forces that moved against British interests. Following the war, Corbett explained,

> By massing an overwhelming concentration at the vital point the Admiralty had made sure of the command of the Narrow Seas upon which their whole system was built up. They had also made sure of a crushing decision on "the day," but incidentally they had made it inevitable that "the day" would be indefinitely postponed. All experience shows that in conditions such as our home concentration had set up an enemy will never risk a battle except for some vital end which cannot be obtained in any other way.[47]

The congruence between Corbett's pre- and postwar thoughts on naval battle demonstrate the value of studying history in a prewar period. History allowed Corbett to accurately amass evidence that provided broad outlines of the strategic challenges that British and German naval leaders faced with their battle fleets in the North Sea during World War I.

Considering Corbett's comments in the midst of the war, however, provides caution. Even for someone as well informed as Corbett, the endless stalemate in the North Sea proved exhausting. He lamented in 1917 that it seemed impossible "to do anything to get the Navy out of the rut it seems to have got into." He blamed Admiral John Jellicoe, then First Sea Lord: "He is too timid—thinks too much of what might happen to the ships if something hit them. His head is full of pictures—he shirks from risking anything & always seems to want to have a lot up his sleeve—the result is of course that the fleet is never used at its full might." Corbett went on to explain, "His almost childish awe of the Germans has sometimes staggered me. How I lament that there is a chapter of our Naval history that will never be written." He contrasted Jellicoe's timid approach with that of Jackie Fisher, who served as First Sea Lord during the opening year of the war. As Corbett explained, Fisher's "schemes rather take one's breath away, but he had thought them out, was carefully preparing the material. There might have been an awful smash, but what a glorious smash it would have been."[48] That last sentence seems so unlike Corbett's pre- and postwar writings. The careful strategist had for a moment disappeared into wishful thinking for an earnestly sought alternative naval outcome based on Fisher's imaginative plans. Yet by April 1917, when he penned those words, the war was approaching the end of its third year. Maintaining the stalemate at sea had begun to wear on even one of Britain's principal naval strategic thinkers and highlights the stress of living through a war compared with the greater detachment that is possible when thinking of future conflicts or when writing about a war after it is over.

THE MARITIME (OR BRITISH) WAY OF WAR

Corbett's theories recognized that a singular way of war that provided a cookie-cutter approach to strategy that could be applied to every state did not exist.[49] Geographic location, instruments of power, and historical experience are among the multiplicity of factors that inform each country's specific way of war. Corbett's theory posited that Britain's preferred way of war was maritime, in contrast to what he labeled a continental (or Napoleonic) method. *Some Principles of Maritime Strategy* only solidified this preference. Including "maritime" in the book's title was telling, since he defined it as the "part the fleet must play in relation to the actions of the land forces."[50] This neatly supported his grand-strategic, multiple-instruments-of-power approach.

Even after the conclusion of World War I, Corbett remained wedded to the maritime way of war as the most effective means for Britain to obtain strategic effects. He explained, "The problem raised in acute form the fundamental differences between the traditional British method of conducting a great war and the Napoleonic method which with all continental nations had become the strictly orthodox creed." The maritime model involves confronting the opponent "at the weakest point which could give substantial results, and to assume the defensive where he was strongest." This contrasted with the continental method.

It involved attacking "where the enemy's military concentration was highest and where a decisive victory would end the war by destroying his armed forces." Though the continental method had the potential to attain a decisive result more quickly, it required greater means on land than Britain possessed. As Corbett explained, "We never had military force enough to enjoy that preponderance."[51]

Corbett believed that the maritime method gave Britain significant advantages that British leaders failed to exploit in World War I. Even after researching and writing the official history, Corbett still believed that Britain had missed opportunities during the war to "wrest the initiative from the land Powers in our traditional manner, by giving the Continental war a new direction that was best suited to the position and resources of Maritime Powers[,] . . . [by] combining naval and military force against the point where the system of the Central Powers was weakest, while standing securely on the defensive in the main theatre, where its strength was greatest."[52]

In the official history, he named a series of successful examples from the eighteenth and nineteenth centuries. He noted how the British had given the Seven Years' War new direction through their successful expedition to Havana in 1762, how Wellington's campaign on the Iberian Peninsula had allowed Britain to obtain outsized strategic effects in the Napoleonic Wars, and how Britain had obtained similar effects in Crimea. "In all three examples the result was due to the concentration of naval and military force where the enemy was weakest."[53] It is telling that before World War I, Corbett had identified these same campaigns in *Some Principles of Maritime Strategy*.[54] His pre- and postwar writings have a high degree of congruence in both the historical examples and the value of a maritime approach for Britain.

During World War I, Corbett saw the Dardanelles campaign, including operations on the Gallipoli Peninsula, as Britain's opportunity for a maritime approach, though he opposed how it was executed.[55] After the war, Corbett again extolled this operation's intended strategic effects. He believed that Turkey could have been knocked out of the war; this could have for all intents encircled the Central

Powers; and this would have allowed for a concentric attack on Germany and its remaining allies. But about the Dardanelles, Corbett lamented, "It was this venture so rightly aimed—but aimed without the energy of true faith."[56] The failure of the operation meant a "bankruptcy of leadership . . . ignoring the fleet and its oft-proved capacity for substantially increasing the power of the army." As Corbett wrote after the war, "It was impossible not to protest."[57]

What Corbett stated during the war is, if anything, more telling and emotional. As he watched events play out in real time, he remained firmly convinced that British leaders were misguided, costing blood and treasure, while sacrificing Britain's greatest strategic advantages. As he explained in mid-1917,

> Personally I don't believe we shall make any headway until we concentrate on Austria & Turkey . . . & stop playing the German Game in France. To my mind the German attempt at Verdun proved the impossibility of what we are ostensibly trying to do & everything since has gone to condone it.

Here he noted the major 1916 German offensive at Verdun as the example from which Entente leaders should have learned, but as Corbett ranted, "The utter stupidity of soldiers at their own job seems to me to make the sailors look quite brilliant."[58]

Perhaps most damning of all, he wrote in a personal letter to Fisher in mid-1918, "It is a lamentable tale for me to tell. . . . It is the most bigoted 'soldier's' war we have ever fought, and this at the end of all our experience." Pent-up frustration led him to recount how "I wept when our whole Expeditionary Force was going to France, and felt what it would mean, and how Pitt would turn in his grave."[59] Here he referred to Britain's statesman during the Seven Years' War whom Corbett considered the greatest war leader his country ever had. He extolled Pitt's maritime expeditionary approach: "Their power was Pitt's great discovery—the method of employing them his strategical legacy—and it is in the skilful [sic] and instructed use of them that lies the greatest power of a maritime state to this day."[60]

Having failed to see a British leader with Pitt's imagination emerge, Corbett in his letter to Fisher decried, "Oh, these blessed Germanized [British] soldiers with their 'decisive theatre.' Couldn't they see that in Pitt's great war, the best one ever fought, the decisive theatre was Havana—not France."[61]

Before World War I, Corbett had become involved with educating naval officers. This forced him to grapple with strategic theory and introduced him to naval leaders who made use of his analytical skill. They made even greater use of these abilities during World War I, but the fact remains inescapable: Corbett was never a decision-maker. He served as an analyst and strategic thinker who based his arguments on deep historical scholarship. Real-world decisions were made by others. The limits of his influence can be seen in the fact that British leaders followed an alternative script to the one Corbett posited in discussions with leaders and elaborated on in *Some Principles of Maritime Strategy*.

From Corbett's position writing the official history, it was easy to critique leaders for decisions after the fact, but he was not merely content to explain where Britain had gone wrong. Corbett devoted considerable attention to an alternative course of action in his prewar writings. That Britain did not follow his recommendation during the war led to emotional pleas as Corbett saw decision-makers diverge ever more completely from his prewar approach. Right or wrong, Corbett stayed his course, providing a potential alternative to the grinding attritional struggle that occurred in France.

CONCLUSION

Corbett's prewar strategic writings emphasized historical examples to develop inductive arguments based on a maritime approach to Britain's grand strategy. After the war, his involvement with the writing of *The History of the Great War Based on Official Documents* allowed Corbett an opportunity to reflect. He found little need to reassess his reliance on history or his grand-strategic frameworks based on a maritime approach. The closer Corbett's writings got to the actual combat, the less his prewar and postwar writings aligned. This is particularly apparent in areas such as the brutality of the war and the German use of submarines to attack merchant shipping. To his death, he remained steeped in Victorian and Edwardian values even though the war had shattered the edifice on which they existed.

Most poignant were Corbett's statements during the war. It should be noted that the majority of his pre- and postwar writings come from publications, while those written during the war are mainly found in letters to friends and colleagues, which were never intended for a wide audience. Even so, his statements during the war indicate how difficult it is even for a strategic thinker well versed in theory and history to maintain reasoned arguments. He even admitted as such in a speech he gave in 1917: "Never, perhaps, has it been more difficult to see beyond the tumult of passing events."[62] His views on battle are particularly instructive in this regard. Moreover, the loss of merchant shipping weighed heavily on Corbett. His prewar writings indicated that losses would occur, but living through the experience and witnessing the employment of new technologies created uncertainty and caused Corbett to forgo his historical approach. Such a critique might require the abeyance of human nature, but even during the war, Corbett recognized its importance: "Never has it been of more vital consequence to keep sure hold of well-tried guiding lines."[63]

Overall, Corbett's prewar arguments posited a maritime approach to war. British leaders during World War I did not follow that approach, and this weighed heavily on him. In 1917, Corbett explained to a friend, "Your belief that the Service might have learnt a little more from my books is a comfort to me. I seem to have written so entirely in vain & seldom see any effect except where someone has mistaken or misapplied the teachings & consequently gone wrong."[64] Corbett saw miscalculations and mistakes at every turn. In real time, decision-makers face difficult choices. While Corbett was close to Britain's decision-makers, he remained an adviser, a historian, and a theorist. He demonstrates the limits of influence a theorist must grapple with when positing thoughts about future war, living through wartime uncertainty, and finally trying to make sense of it afterward.

NOTES

1. D. M. Schurman, *Education of a Navy: The Development of British Naval Strategic Thought, 1867–1914* (repr., Malabar, FL: Krieger, 1984), 174; Andrew Lambert, *21st Century Corbett: Maritime Strategy and Naval Policy for the Modern Era* (Annapolis: Naval Institute Press, 2017), 3–4. For a more complete assessment of Corbett's significance and his theories, see Kevin D. McCranie, *Mahan, Corbett, and the Foundations of Naval Strategic Thought* (Annapolis: Naval Institute Press, 2021).

2. Andrew Lambert, *The British Way of War: Julian Corbett and the Battle for a National Strategy* (New Haven, CT: Yale University Press, 2021), 307.

3. Julian S. Corbett, *Monk* (London: Macmillan, 1889).

4. [John Knox Laughton], "Mr. Corbett's Drake and His Successors (Review of *Drake and the Tudor Navy*, *The Successors of Drake*, and *Papers Relating to the Navy during the Spanish War*)," *Edinburgh Review* 397 (July 1901): 2.

5. *England and the Seven Years' War: A Study in Combined Strategy*, 2 vols. (London: Longmans, Green, 1907) and *The Campaign of Trafalgar* (London: Longmans, Green, 1910).

6. Corbett, review of *Types of Naval Officers Drawn from the History of the British Navy* by Alfred Thayer Mahan, *American Historical Review* 7 (April 1902): 558.

7. Julian S. Corbett, "Staff Histories," in Julian S. Corbett and H. J. Edwards, eds., *Naval and Military Essays: Being Papers Read at the Naval and Military Section of the International Congress of Historical Studies* (Cambridge: Cambridge University Press, 1914), 24.

8. Lecture on Naval History, n.d., Corbett, box 1, Liddell Hart Centre for Military Archives, King's College, London.

9. Corbett to Calendar, December 2, 1914, Michael Arthur Lewis Papers, LES/4/1, National Maritime Museum, Greenwich (hereafter NMM).

10. Corbett to Richmond, December 18, 1915, Herbert Richmond Papers, RIC 9, part 1, NMM.

11. Corbett to Richmond, January 28, 1916, RIC 9, part 1, NMM.

12. Corbett, "Methods and Discussion," *Naval Review* (1920): 322, 324.

13. Corbett, *History of the Great War Based on Official Documents: Naval Operations* (London: Longmans, Green, 1921), 2:4.

14. Corbett, "United Service," *Naval Review* (1923 [originally written in 1904]): 204.

15. Corbett, Strategical Terms and Definitions used in Lectures on Naval Strategy [hereafter Green Pamphlet], Corbett Papers, CBT, 6/15, p. 1, NMM.

16. In *England and the Seven Years' War*, he mixed the terms (see 1:2, 77, 273). In the first edition of the Green Pamphlet, he mixed grand and major strategy as well (see CBT, 6/15, NMM). The 1909 edition of the Green Pamphlet only used major strategy (see CBT, 6/16, NMM). Corbett continued to use major strategy in *Some Principles of Maritime Strategy* (London: Longmans, Green, 1911; repr., Annapolis: Naval Institute Press, 1988).

17. Corbett, *History of the Great War*, 1:vii.

18. Corbett, *History of the Great War*, 3:45.

19. Corbett, "The Strategical Value of Speed in Battle-Ships," *Journal of the Royal United Service Institution* 51 (1907): 831.

20. Corbett, *History of the Great War*, 1:3.

21. Corbett, *History of the Great War*, 1:41.

22. Corbett, *History of the Great War*, 2:260.

23. Corbett, *History of the Great War*, 1:257.

24. Corbett, *History of the Great War*, 1:368.

25. Corbett, "Methods and Discussion," 324.

26. Corbett, *Maritime Operations in the Russo-Japanese War, 1904–1905* (repr. with intro. by John B. Hattendorf and Donald Schurman, Annapolis: Naval Institute Press, 2015), 2:398.

27. Corbett, *Some Principles*, 227–32.

28. Corbett, *History of the Great War*, 1:163.

29. Corbett, *History of the Great War*, 1:216.

30. Corbett, *Some Principles*, 231.

31. Corbett, *History of the Great War*, 1:216–17.

32. Corbett, *Some Principles*, 261.

33. Corbett, *History of the Great War*, 1:15.

34. Corbett, *History of the Great War*, 2:1.

35. Corbett, *History of the Great War*, 1:161.

36. Corbett to Calendar, December 2, 1914, LES/4/1, NMM.

37. Corbett, *History of the Great War*, 2:1–2.

38. Corbett, *History of the Great War*, 2:383.

39. Corbett, *Some Principles*, 279.

40. Corbett, Lecture, Sea Commonwealth [1919], Corbett, box 2, Liddell Hart Centre for Military Archives, King's College, London.

41. Corbett, *Some Principles*, 266.

42. Corbett, *History of the Great War*, 1:2.

43. Corbett, *Some Principles*, 167.

44. Corbett, *History of the Great War*, 1:2.

45. Corbett, *Some Principles*, 164.

46. Green Pamphlet, CBT, 6/15, p. 11, NMM. The same wording is in the 1909 edition of the Green Pamphlet, CBT, 6/16, p. 11, NMM. A similar argument can be found in *England and the Seven Years' War*, 1:309.

47. Corbett, *History of the Great War*, 1:161–62.

48. Corbett to Richmond, April 24, 1917, RIC 9, part 1, NMM.

49. Lambert, *British Way of War*, 12.

50. Corbett, *Some Principles*, 15.

51. Corbett, *History of the Great War*, 3:41.

52. Corbett, *History of the Great War*, 2:290.

53. Corbett, *History of the Great War*, 2:291.

54. Corbett, *Some Principles*, 56–57.

55. Corbett to Richmond, January 28, 1916, RIC 9, part 1, NMM.

56. Corbett, *History of the Great War*, 3:40.

57. Corbett, *History of the Great War*, 3:219.

58. Corbett to Richmond, July 26, 1917, RIC 9, part 1, NMM.

59. Corbett to Fisher, June 12, 1918, in *Fear God and Dread Nought: The Correspondence of Admiral of the Fleet Lord Fisher of Kilverstone*, ed. Arthur J. Marder (London: Jonathan Cape, 1952–59), 3:538–39.

60. Corbett, *England and the Seven Years' War*, 1:100.

61. Corbett to Fisher, June 12, 1918, in *Fear God*, 3:538–39.

62. Corbett, "The Sea Commonwealth," in A. P. Newton, ed., *The Sea Commonwealth and Other Papers* (London: J. M. Dent, 1923), 1.

63. Corbett, "Sea Commonwealth," 1.

64. Corbett to Richmond, December 23, 1917, RIC 9, part 1, NMM.

CHAPTER FIVE

CONTESTING THE GERMAN ISLAND CHAIN

WINSTON CHURCHILL AND THE SEARCH FOR A NAVAL OFFENSIVE DURING THE FIRST WORLD WAR

John H. Maurer

Winston Churchill wanted Great Britain's Royal Navy to undertake an offensive maritime strategy against imperial Germany during World War I. The strategy that Churchill advocated called for the navy to attack into German home waters to seize an island for use as a forward base. The island chain of Borkum, Heligoland, and Sylt were examined as potential bases for forward operations along the Germany's North Sea coastline. Of the three islands, Borkum was selected by Churchill as the best suited for use as a base to support forward-deployed naval forces. Once in control of Borkum, British naval forces would carry out an aggressive campaign of minelaying and submarine operations in Germany's home waters. Churchill expected that this offensive would force the German battle fleet to come out from its bases to fight against the British invaders and thus allow Britain to achieve one of its principal war aims: destroying Germany's battle fleet. He also envisioned the seizure of Borkum as providing a springboard for potential follow-up efforts to draw Denmark and the Netherlands into the war, to surge British naval forces into the Baltic Sea, and even to conduct ground and air campaigns to strike into the German homeland.

Churchill presented these proposals for an aggressive maritime strategy as a strategic alternative to the British army's plans for launching ground offensives on the Western Front in France and Belgium. In pressing his views on Prime Minister H. H. Asquith, he used graphic language to ask, "Are there not other alternatives than sending our armies to chew barbed wire in Flanders? Further, cannot the power of the Navy be brought more directly to bear upon the enemy?"[1] Instead of fighting costly battles of attrition on the stalemated western front, he called for campaigns against Germany from the sea that he believed would be a better way to bring British power to bear in winning the war. Churchill developed his ideas for an offensive maritime strategy throughout the war, culminating in a lengthy proposal printed for the Cabinet in July 1917.

In advocating offensive operations in the war at sea, Churchill saw the navy as reviving a traditional maritime strategy that had enabled Britain to triumph over rival great powers in past wars. As First Lord of the Admiralty, he had a painting hanging in his office of the hard-fought Battle of Camperdown, in which a British fleet smashed the Dutch navy off the coast of the Netherlands in 1797. Going on the offensive at sea against Germany, the Royal Navy would be crowned with new triumphs to add to those gained over the Danish, Dutch, French, and Spanish navies in earlier wars. Before the war, he opposed a "purely passive defensive" naval strategy and advocated instead plans to impose a close blockade of the German coastline.[2] Churchill was not alone in viewing offensive operations to seize command of the seas as part of a traditional British way of war. The British public, their leading political figures, and a few prominent naval leaders also expected that the navy would seek to destroy the Kaiser's fleet, enabling a triumphant Britannia once again to rule the waves.

Churchill's calls for offensive operations against the German coastal island chain, however, ran into stiff opposition from a larger group of naval leaders. Whatever the strategic merits of a traditional maritime strategy, the navy's leading commander at sea and naval planners on the Admiralty staff deemed Churchill's plans both impractical and much too dangerous. Admiral Sir John Jellicoe, commander of Britain's Grand Fleet in the North Sea and later First Sea Lord, refused to execute Churchill's plans for the offensive. In Jellicoe's view, the lethality of modern naval warfare made inoperable the strategic verities passed down from wars fought a century before. Technology trumped tradition.

Although Churchill's maritime strategy was not put to the test of combat, an examination of it can contribute to understanding what realistic strategic options were open to Britain's leaders during the Great War. Were offensive operations by the Royal Navy practicable against the panoply of defenses and naval forces concentrated in German home waters? Did modern weaponry make obsolete prewar strategic dogmas for fighting at sea? How did naval commanders assess risk, and how did these assessments influence their operations? Could Britain have won a victory at sea comparable to Camperdown in the machine age, this time fought out by steel-clad dreadnoughts amid swarms of destroyers, in waters infested with submarines and mines? These questions underscore the operational problems that limited the strategic courses of action open to Britain's leaders for conducting the war at sea.

The naval arms competition between Germany and Britain was a defining feature of the international strategic environment before World War I. Germany's naval buildup posed what Churchill called an "ever-present danger" to Britain's security. In the years just before the war, Churchill, then in his late thirties, served as First Lord of the Admiralty, the civilian government minister most responsible for overseeing Britain's naval defenses. To keep Britain ahead of the German navy, he called for an "ample margin" of superiority in warships because "the consequences of defeat at sea are so much greater to us than they would be to Germany."[3] Staying ahead of Germany in the prewar competition in large surface ships conferred on Britain an important strategic advantage in going into the war.

At the war's outbreak, the two most powerful battle fleets in the world steamed to their war stations, ready for action. Contrary to the prewar expectations of many analysts and commentators, however, the British and German fleets did not rush to grapple with each other in mortal combat. Unlike the generals who threw their armies into horrific battles in search of a quick victory, the cult of the offensive did not motivate the admirals. Neither side showed themselves as eager to settle the struggle for naval mastery by taking the offensive to bring on a major fleet action. Instead, the battle fleets of both countries adopted a defensive stance. Naval commanders on both sides of the North Sea feared putting their big surface ships at risk in combat. The risk-averse strategic posture adopted by British and German naval leaders did not mean they wanted to avoid a clash of battle fleets: both navies were built up and trained for the day when the opposing battle lines would trade blows and a new chapter in the history of sea power's influence on history would be written. Those holding high command at sea, wanted to fight a fleet action only if it could be fought under strategic and operational conditions of their own choosing. They engaged in strategic script writing, assigning to their adversary a role that would end in their defeat. Naval leaders refused to cooperate by playing the part assigned to them in their adversary's script. Apart from the Battle of Jutland, the two battle fleets kept their distance, in the safety of their protected bases, and only ventured forth when a glimmer of hope appeared to indicate that their enemy would play the fool and fight at a disadvantage.

The defense suited Germany's naval leaders, who hoped to defeat Britain at sea by following what today we call a strategic offset of an antiaccess, area-denial strategy. Germany's leaders expected that Britain's admirals in the early twentieth century would emulate their illustrious forebears and attempt to establish a close blockade of the German navy's main bases. A British fleet attacking into the defensive bastion formed by the island chain of Borkum, Heligoland, and Sylt would get entrapped in a lethal killing zone made up of mines, small surface craft, submarines equipped with torpedoes, and accurate land-based artillery. Armed with these weapons, German forces could inflict heavy losses on British surface ships before the clash of battle fleets occurred. The attacking British fleet, weakened by losses, crippled, and reduced in its fighting efficiency by damage, would then be finished off by German battleships in a major surface engagement.[4]

Much to the chagrin of the German navy's leadership, Britain's naval leaders refused to follow this strategic script. Jellicoe was not in the mold of Britain's great naval hero Admiral Lord Nelson. Indeed, Jellicoe was quite the reverse of Nelson when it came to calculating risk in naval operations. While Nelson strove to fight battles of annihilation, the spirit of safety first possessed Jellicoe. The commander of Britain's main fleet saw preserving his own ships from danger as the pinnacle of strategic wisdom. He had no intention of playing the role written for him by the German naval staff, even if it meant breaking with what was widely regarded as a strategic tradition that had served Britain well in the glory days of the Napoleonic Wars. Jellicoe determined that the risks of an offensive in the North Sea far outweighed the rewards. He refused to carry out an offensive that he feared would jeopardize Britain's overall naval superiority. "The danger is very real and the disaster may occur in a few minutes without warning," he warned. "It only requires the fleet to be inadvertently taken over one minefield for a reversal to take place in the relative strength of the British and German fleets. The existence of the Empire is at once in the most immediate and grave danger."[5] To Jellicoe, a North Sea offensive appeared an act of strategic folly. The Grand Fleet was too valuable to be wasted like the Light Brigade, thrown into an unnecessary charge against the enemy's guns and torpedoes.

Jellicoe had good reason to be risk averse. The opening stages of World War I underscored the danger to surface ships. The battleship *Audacious*, representing the latest generation of British capital ships, hit a mine and sank off the north coast of Ireland. In the naval assault on the Dardanelles, the attacking Allied fleet suffered heavy losses to mines. Six British and French battleships were sunk or heavily damaged by mines and Ottoman gun batteries when the Allied fleet tried to force its way past the defenses guarding the Dardanelles. Stealthy German submarines could also wreak havoc with surface ships. This danger was brought home by the loss of three British armored cruisers—the *Aboukir*, *Cressy*, and *Hogue*—torpedoed on the same day by the German submarine *U-9* off the coast of the Netherlands. The British naval leader Lord Fisher of Kilverstone lamented that "with the holocaust of the three cruisers" Britain had lost "more officers and men than in all Lord Nelson's battles put together."[6] A German submarine sank the battleship *Formidable* in the North Sea. One officer serving with the Grand Fleet, Commander Dudley Pound, viewed these losses as a "warning to us—we had almost begun to consider the German submarines as no good and our awakening which had to come sooner or later and it might have been accompanied by the loss of some of the Battle Fleet."[7] The lesson was clear: there was nothing heroic or strategically advantageous about pitting large surface ships against an antiaccess, area-denial strategy built on mines, torpedoes, coastal defense artillery, and submarines. The age of Nelson was past; modern weapons technology had tamed the heroic virtues of aggressive command leadership.

Furthermore, no strategic imperative compelled Britain to attack into the German island chain. Britain's strategy of what nowadays is called offshore control imposed a naval stranglehold on Germany's seaborne trade with the outside world. The Royal Navy could carry out this task by setting up a distant blockade that did not risk capital ships. British armed merchant cruisers—operating outside an arc stretching from the English Channel, Britain, the Orkney, Shetland, and the Faroe Islands to the coast of Norway—could monitor and control trade to the European continent. This advantageous geographic position meant that the British battle fleet could avoid the hazard of attacking into the strong German defenses in home waters, or even risk fighting a major battle in the North Sea, while still hurting Germany's economy and war effort. The combination of Britain's geographic position, superiority in large surface ships, and defensive strategy prevented Germany's battle fleet from breaking the British stranglehold on the German economy.[8] On the maritime chessboard, the most valuable pieces, the queens of the British and German na-vies—the squadrons of modern battleships—kept away from each other, staying on the defensive. This stalemate in the North Sea con-stituted a British strategic victory.

At the war's beginning, Churchill favored conserving the Grand Fleet's strength because Germany's defensive strategy made it difficult to force a fleet-on-fleet engagement. "The enemy in my judgment pur-sues a wise policy in declining battle," Churchill wrote Jellicoe. "By remaining in harbor he secures for Germany the command of the Baltic with all that that implies both in threatening the Russian flank and protecting the German Coast and in drawing supplies from Sweden and Norway." Churchill considered Germany's defensive strategy "the best use to which in present circumstances they can turn their Fleet."[9]

Staying on the defensive, however, did not sit well with Chur-chill. He wanted to see the navy seize the strategic initiative in the war at sea by making a transition from defense to offense. Soon after the war's onset, in a major speech before an audience of 15,000 listeners in Liverpool, Churchill called for an offensive to destroy the German fleet if it did not venture out for battle in the North Sea. "Although we hope the navy will have a chance of settling the question of the German Fleet," he declared, "yet if they do not come out and fight in time of war they will be dug out like rats in a hole." Churchill's fiery rhetoric received loud cheers from the crowd. Alas, the timing of his speech could hardly have been worse for him. The very next day the cruisers *Aboukir*, *Cressy*, and *Hogue* were torpedoed and sunk, in waters not far from where the Battle of Camperdown had been fought. The king reproached Churchill for using language that "was hardly dignified for a Cabinet Minister." Churchill's "threat was unfortunate," the king emphasized, because "the rats came out of their own accord and to our cost."[10] Despite the Palace's displeasure at the speech, the crowd's reaction indicated that the British public expected the navy to attack and destroy the German fleet.

Nor was Churchill alone in wanting to go over to the offensive. Admirals Fisher and Sir Arthur Wilson at the Admiralty also proposed offensive operations against German coastal defenses.[11] Churchill prodded Jellicoe to take the offensive. "In balancing the risks of an offensive," he wrote to Jellicoe, "one must not overlook the perils & losses of our present policy." While the Admiralty had access to the German navy's radio signals from having broken its naval codes, this "amazing advantage" was not a guarantee of strategic success. "Even with the priceless information," Churchill maintained, "the dangers of surrendering the initiative to the enemy are great & obvious." Furthermore, this advantage might not last if the Germans realized that their codes had been compromised by British intelligence. "At any moment the information may cease, & then we should have to have a patrolling battle & battle cruiser squadron at sea frequently—with all the added dangers that implies." Another danger that Churchill saw emerging was the increase in Germany's submarine construction and aggressiveness: "New submarines are being built for Germany & must be finishing in a few months. Those they have increase in daring & skill each week."[12] To Churchill, the increasing German submarine threat was a spur for offensive action.

Churchill sought to persuade the reluctant Jellicoe by arguing, "Everything convinces me that we must take Borkum as soon as full & careful preparations can be made." After studying the problem, he concluded that Borkum was the best suited of the German islands to establish an advanced base from which British flotillas of submarines and smaller surface vessels could operate in Germany's home waters. With the possession of Borkum, "we must make it the most dreaded lair of submarines in the world, and also the centre of an active mining policy." The British navy would have seized the strategic initiative in the North Sea. "It seems to me necessary to dominate the area with flotillas to make the Germans face at his very doors the dangers he has invites us to come across the seas to seek," Churchill maintained. "Once established there we should confront him with all the ugliest propositions."[13] An attack on Borkum would likely spur the German high command to risk their battleships in a large battle. Jellicoe would then have an opportunity to win a crushing victory—a Camperdown or Trafalgar—over the German fleet. If the German fleet remained in port, then the seizure of Borkum would enable an aggressive mining of Germany's home waters. The German fleet would effectively be sealed in, unable to emerge from its bases. Churchill wrote to Jellicoe, "I beg you most earnestly to brood over these things with a view to the assertion of our naval strength in its highest and most aggressive form."[14]

Churchill believed that the taking of Borkum and the fighting at sea would provide a springboard for follow-up offensives against Germany. Once Borkum had been captured, he thought, Britain could establish an advanced "aeroplane base of 60 machines" to support more offensive operations. He also maintained that "in the North strategy & politics move together, & it [should] be possible by a proper use of our fleets & armies in that combination [which] sea-power renders possible, to bring both Holland and Denmark into the fighting line."[15] Destroying or penning in the German battle fleet, along with gaining Denmark as an ally, would give the added strategic advantage of permitting an offensive into the Baltic Sea. British naval forces could then tighten the blockade noose around the German economy by cutting the flow of imports to Germany from the neutral Scandinavian countries. In addition, a successful drive into the Baltic would enable Britain to cooperate with Russia in undertaking offensives against Germany.

The arguments presented by Churchill persuaded neither Jellicoe nor his principal naval staff planners. Herbert Richmond, then serving as a planner, poured scorn on Churchill's arguments for an offensive to seize the island of Borkum. "It is *quite mad*," Richmond confided to his diary. "The reasons for capturing it are NIL [sic], the possibilities about the same. I have never read such an idiotic, amateur piece of work as this outline in my life." Richmond prepared an assessment of the difficulties that British forces would face in storming the island. Weather conditions, navigational difficulties, mines, gun batteries, and problems that gunfire from warships would face in hitting targets presented severe challenges, and all would need to be overcome for the island to be captured. His conclusion was blunt: "The condemnation of the whole scheme as outlined lies in the fact that it violates the simple and well-established law that you cannot make an oversea expedition of troops until you have command of the sea over which the troops have to pass."[16]

The senior naval officers serving with the Grand Fleet also warned Churchill that offensive operations to attack the fortified German islands were ill conceived and dangerous. Jellicoe had the support of his fleet commanders in opposing offensive actions in German home waters deemed high risk: "The opinions of these officers were unanimous," he later wrote.[17] Churchill could not convince Jellicoe to go on the offensive. Jellicoe remained committed to a strategy of only seeking battle if the German main fleet made the first move by coming out of its defensive bastion into the North Sea.

The failures at the Dardanelles brought about the downfall of Churchill and Fisher at the Admiralty. With their departure, the impetus for offensive action in the North Sea went away. The new First Lord, Sir Arthur Balfour, while trying to revive plans for the offensive, could not get Jellicoe to budge. When Balfour raised the question of the Grand Fleet undertaking a "naval offensive against Germany in the Baltic or elsewhere," Jellicoe persisted in rejecting a more aggressive stance. He maintained that no "naval offensive appears to me practicable unless and until our objective, the High Sea Fleet, gives us the opportunity . . . and until the High Sea Fleet emerges from its defences I regret to say that I do not see that any offensive against it is possible."[18]

When the German battle fleet did emerge, Jellicoe had his chance to deliver a crushing blow at the ensuing Battle of Jutland. This fleeting opportunity, however, was lost: the German battle fleet escaped the British trap and annihilation. Although the German fleet inflicted heavier losses on their British opposite, the battle confirmed the stalemate in the North Sea. Admiral Reinhard von Scheer, commander of the German fleet at Jutland, reported to the Kaiser, "There can be no doubt that even the most successful result from a high sea battle will not compel England to make peace."[19] Germany's battle fleet could not win the war at sea—a startling admission from its commander. Instead of the battleship serving as the decisive weapon, the German navy's leadership turned to the submarine to deliver the knockout blow by going on the offensive to disrupt Britain's control of the world's shipping lanes. If Germany's naval leaders were deterred from using their battle fleet in an aggressive strategy, they were not at all inhibited in their willingness to use submarines to take the fight to Britain on the high seas. German submarines could get around the British lead in capital ships and advantage of geographic position by undertaking a deep strike against the network of oceanic trade. The submarine force—not the vaunted battleships—constituted Germany's real high seas fleet.

To be effective in disrupting Britain's maritime trading network, German submarine skippers had to receive authority to fire without warning on merchant ships, neutral as well as Allied. Practically all shipping had to be treated as hostile. Operating under these permissive rules of engagement (known as unrestricted warfare), German submarines proceeded to inflict a stunning blow against world trade, just as Germany's naval leaders predicted. In January 1917, before the submarine campaign began, German submarines sank 145 British, Allied, and neutral ships, totaling 291,459 tons of merchant shipping. In April, German submarines sank 354 ships, totaling 834,549 tons of shipping.[20] If permitted to continue, losses of this magnitude would bring about a German victory. Churchill called the fight against the German submarine offensive "a life and death struggle" to command the maritime commons.[21]

German success in sinking merchant tonnage owed much, however, to the British Admiralty's mismanagement of trade defense. The Admiralty could not have been a more cooperative adversary, acting according to the script written for it by German naval planners. Now ensconced at the Admiralty was Jellicoe, whose lackluster performance as commander of the Grand Fleet had not prevented him from being promoted to First Sea Lord. This choice would prove unfortunate. Jellicoe's failure to move quickly to adopt convoys magnified shipping losses.[22] Jellicoe was losing the war at sea to the German submarines—not in an afternoon, but in a protracted attrition battle involving merchant shipping losses. While unwilling to risk battleships, keeping them heavily defended by destroyers against attack by submarines, Jellicoe proved content to send merchant shipping into dangerous waters. Yet Britain's war effort depended on the protection of shipping. Britain could no more afford to lose the Battle of the Atlantic than it could to suffer defeat in the North Sea.

Germany's submarine offensive marked a turning point by bringing the United States into the war. For Churchill, the American decision to enter the war shifted the balance of power decisively against Germany. "I rejoice at the advent of America into this struggle," he told the House of Commons. He believed that but "for the entry of the United States into the war at this juncture it is perfectly clear that we should have been in measurable distance of a highly unsatisfactory peace." He was confident American power "restores at a stroke the fortunes of the struggle and offers the finest prospects that have yet been open to us of assured and indubitable victory."[23] Churchill outlined his strategic assessment and prescriptions in a speech before a secret session of the House of Commons. What was critical was to bring the resources of the United States into the struggle across the Atlantic. Thus, crucial to winning the war was the necessity of reducing the shipping losses that threatened to cripple the Allied war effort. The ability to bring American power to bear on the battlefield of Europe required mastering the German submarine menace. In addition, he argued that Britain and France should conserve their manpower by not undertaking major offensive operations on the western front. Britain and France should await the arrival of a large American army before undertaking major offensives. In the meantime, the Allied armies should pursue a strategy of active defense. The time could be used to better arm the Allied armies and retrain them in new tactics that held promise of breaking the trench deadlock, restoring mobility to the battlefield, and defeating the German army.[24]

Churchill's comprehensive strategic review impressed his listeners and especially found favor with Britain's prime minister, David Lloyd George, who was looking for political allies to buttress his wartime coalition government. Churchill was out of office, having resigned from the government with the cloud of the Dardanelles debacle hanging over his head. After serving a tour of duty as a battalion commander on the western front, Churchill was eager to play an active role in government by holding a high-level executive office. Lloyd George obliged, appointing him to the important government post as minister of munitions.[25] At the Ministry of Munitions, Churchill presided over the production of weapons and supplies for the British army and Royal Air Force.

Before taking up the new assignment, Churchill worked up a strategic appraisal of the merits and means for undertaking a major offensive in the North Sea. This appraisal brought together many of his earlier views advocating an assault into German home waters and added some new and novel ideas. He began his memo by sketching out the "traditional war policy of the Admiralty" that guided British naval operations in earlier great wars against France. Churchill insisted, "The experience of 200 years had led all naval strategists to agree on this fundamental principle, 'Our first line of defence is the enemy's ports.'" While the main theater of war had shifted from the Channel to the North Sea, the strategic imperative of taking the offensive into enemy home waters still applied. He also maintained that the decision at the war's outset to follow a strategy of a distant blockade of Germany "implied no repudiation on the part of the Admiralty of their fundamental principle of aggressive naval strategy, but only a temporary abandonment of it in the face of unsolved practical difficulties; and it was intended, both before and after the declaration of war, that every effort should be made to overcome those difficulties." In his memo, Churchill wanted to show how these difficulties could be overcome.[26]

Churchill argued that Britain possessed an overwhelming superiority of force, enough to take the offensive in the North Sea. He called for the establishment of two battle fleets, each greater in battleship strength than the German navy. One fleet would act as an inshore force to cover and support the invasion force that would seize Borkum and establish a forward base of operations. This "Inshore Aggressive Fleet" would consist of older but still well-armed battleships, which would be modified to get extra protection against underwater damage from torpedoes and mines. Cruisers, flotillas of destroyers, submarines, mine warfare vessels, and seaplane ships would support the battleships. The inshore naval force, he maintained, was superior in strength to the German navy in its home waters. He calculated that the firepower of the massed German battle fleet was but 70 percent of the battleships making up the inshore British battle line. Capturing Borkum from the German garrison defending the island, he estimated, would also require a landing force of two divisions of ground troops supported by tanks. To get the assaulting infantry and tank forces ashore, he proposed the construction of what would later be called landing craft.[27]

The campaign to take Borkum, Churchill predicted, would result in "hard fighting at every step." He did not minimize the losses that the British navy would suffer in taking the fight into enemy home waters. He conceded that the German navy was a formidable fighting force. Indeed, he reckoned that British losses suffered by the inshore fleet might well equal those suffered by the German navy. This attrition, however, worked in Britain's favor given the superior force that would be concentrated for the offensive. Churchill maintained, "We can pursue a policy of ship for ship losses. . . . With overwhelming superiority, mutually destructive fighting is the surest road."[28]

While the German navy would be ground down by the British inshore forces, Britain's main battle fleet—what Churchill called the "the blue water fleet," consisting of the latest and most powerful battleships—would stay in reserve. The preservation of this force meant that Britain would retain overall naval superiority, despite the losses he anticipated that the inshore fleet would suffer. While the fighting took place in German home waters, "our Blue Water Fleet, sufficient in itself to assure the supremacy of the ocean and the broad seas, would remain safe and intact like the gold reserve in the Bank of England, as the ultimate guarantee." In addition, American naval forces arriving in European waters could take part in an offensive. The combined naval might of Britain and the United States, in Churchill's calculations, ensured an overwhelming superiority of force.[29]

What losses would Britain have suffered in the "mutually destructive fighting" to seize Borkum? Churchill did not give an estimate, although he did acknowledge that the contest would be hard-fought. Naval actions fought during the war offer some indication of the losses that might have been incurred during offensive operations in the North Sea. At the Battle of Jutland, British losses amounted to fourteen ships sunk and over 6,000 dead in a day's fighting. In trying to storm past Ottoman defenses at the Dardanelles, the attacking British and French squadrons suffered the loss of three old battleships, along with 700 dead. The sinking of the *Aboukir*, *Cressey*, and *Hogue* resulted in the loss of over 1,400 lives. Capturing Borkum would have involved several days of intense combat for the warships at sea and for the ground forces storming ashore. Breaching the German island defenses, then, might have entailed taking losses like those Britain suffered on the first day of the Battle of the Somme, when almost 20,000 soldiers lost their lives. Taking Borkum, too, was just the beginning of what would have been a protracted effort to grind down the German navy. The attrition of ships and men would have continued in following actions. In his memorandum, Churchill said he thought the attacking British naval forces would give as good as they got in a battle of attrition with the German navy. What if, however, British losses, in relation to the German navy, amounted two-to-one or greater, like the loss ratio that the Grand Fleet suffered at the Battle of Jutland? Given the magnitude of losses the navy might have suffered, it is little wonder that Britain's naval leaders opposed Churchill's plan.

If navy and army planners concluded that capturing Borkum was not feasible, then Churchill proposed a novel idea of building an artificial island anchorage on the Horns Reef in the North Sea. Building this island anchorage would require sinking large concrete structures onto the reef's seabed. He imagined "a torpedo and weather-proof harbour, like an atoll, would be created in the open sea, with regular pens for the destroyers and submarines, and alighting platforms for aeroplanes." This improvised man-made island would serve as a forward base to support offensive naval operations. Like China's construction projects in the South China Sea today, this man-made island would help Britain to command the waters around it. Churchill estimated that it would take a year to make the preparations to carry out this construction project. This innovative idea, then, afforded no immediate relief to the pressing problem of reducing merchant shipping losses to German submarines.[30]

In addition to making the case for how to execute an aggressive strategy, Churchill provided a strategic rationale for going over to the offensive. The main driver for undertaking an offensive naval strategy was the need to curtail the heavy shipping losses being inflicted by Germany's submarines. He emphasized, "The submarine attack upon commerce ruptures the basis upon which the policy of 'distant blockade' and still more the policy of 'distant blockade and nothing else' stand." In the North Sea, Churchill estimated, Germany's navy was "neutralising and containing Allied forces at least four times the strength of his own fleet, while ravaging all our sea communications with his submarines." Meanwhile, he pointed out that German submarines were imposing heavy costs on Britain, "such as eating less bread, ploughing up the land, cutting down the forests, dispersing thousands of guns on merchant ships, building more merchant ships for the submarines to sink, consuming hundreds of destroyers and thousands of small craft in escort and submarine hunting." Churchill condemned the Admiralty's defensive naval strategy as "the negation of war." He contended that "a naval offensive will force the enemy to concentrate his submarines—or a large portion of them—upon his own defence . . . and collateral relief to our own trade routes." The mining of Germany's home waters would also hinder the ability of German submarines to get to the open seas. The contest against German submarines would shift to Germany's home waters instead of the sea approaches to the British Isles. A naval offensive would cause sinkings of merchant shipping to drop even as the British navy took higher losses in combat. This strategic trade-off, Churchill contended, worked to Britain's favor.[31]

Churchill was confident that the Royal Navy would prevail in the fighting that would take place in German home waters. Once Britain dominated the German navy, he wanted to see follow-up operations to take place. Britain could move, "*if we thought fit*, to invite both Holland and Denmark to join the coalition against Germany, and to support either or both of them by adequate armies either in Holland or Denmark, or conceivably we could ourselves invade Schleswig." What would induce Denmark and the Netherlands to join the Allied coalition, Churchill did not elaborate. But even if this northern front did not come together, the threat of invasion, Churchill believed, would still force Germany to withdraw forces from other fronts. By inducing Germany to move forces to strengthen its northern defenses, "this fact in itself might exercise an all-important influence on the great battles on the Western front, and consequently upon the fate of the war."[32]

The success of these operations required that Britain "maintain aerial supremacy." Churchill was an air enthusiast, so much so that he attempted to learn how to fly. In his quest to qualify as a pilot, however, he came close to losing his life on several occasions. His wife Clementine, concerned about her husband's safety, insisted that he stop taking flying lessons; most reluctantly, he took her advice and gave up on the quest. Churchill put great store in the value of "an aerial offensive on the greatest scale" against the German homeland. "We should establish on the captured or improvised island aerial stations and bombing bases of a very powerful character," he wrote, "and from these, in easy striking distance of the most important military and naval places in Germany, we should levy a continued bombing attack. Essen, Wilhelmshaven, Cuxhaven, Kiel, the whole line of the Canal, all the dockyards, all the anchorages would be brought under continuous bombing by night and day from quite short distances." Aircraft would also provide intelligence: "Every movement of the enemy would be known."[33] As minister of munitions, he wanted to ensure the production of "very large quantities of explosives [that] will be required for strategic bombing, and all our resources will be involved."[34] Churchill received support for his plans to build up Britain's airpower from Lord Fisher. The old admiral disapproved of the Admiralty's handling of the war at sea. Eager to get on Churchill's good side and find employment at the Ministry of Munitions, Fisher declared, *"The Air will win the war now."*[35]

In arguing for an offensive strategy, Churchill admitted that if naval officers were not wholeheartedly committed to making the effort, then it should not be attempted. His experience with reluctant naval leaders at the Dardanelles had provided him with a painful lesson in leadership in war. If naval leaders could not bring themselves to undertake the offensive, then Churchill called for a reorientation in the allocation of resources going into the British war effort. He saw the Ministry of Munition and the Admiralty as in direct competition for resources in labor, steel, and financing. He estimated the Admiralty possessed "surplus *matériel*, stores, and expert personnel [that] should be released for other purposes." A change in priorities would result in more resources going to the army and air force.[36] "I am impressed with the unsatisfactory character of the arrangements in regard to Admiralty priority which obtain at the present time," he complained. "It is not right that one department should claim and secure priority for all its work, however unimportant some classes of that work may be, over the most important work of all other departments."[37] He called for a review of "the Admiralty use of steel for other purposes than merchant shipbuilding."[38] He believed the Admiralty made exaggerated demands for resources. He feared that if the government did not take steps to curb the Admiralty's appetite, "we may fail to have the strength available for the general offensive war, and may consequently be compelled impotently to witness the defeat of our

Allies one by one."[39] Churchill saw his ministry as manufacturing the weapons required to support war-winning offensives against Germany and thought it should get more resources at the Admiralty's expense.

Churchill's return to high executive office within the government and his proposal for offensive operations were most unwelcome news at the Admiralty. Nothing had changed Jellicoe's mind in judging offensive schemes to be "extraordinarily wild theories . . . which are absolutely and absurdly impracticable." He feared that offensives into German home waters would result in "another Dardanelles in the Heligoland Bight." Moreover, dealing with proposals for offensive action forced Jellicoe "to spend . . . valuable time in endeavoring to show amateur strategists the impossibility of their ideas."[40] Jellicoe's boss, First Lord of the Admiralty Sir Eric Geddes, also resented what he considered to be a power play by Churchill in an interdepartmental struggle over the allocation of resources. An infuriated Geddes even threatened resignation to stop what he saw as attempts by the minister of munitions to interfere in the direction of the war at sea. Lloyd George showed considerable skill in adjudicating disputes within his government and keeping his two ministers in line.[41]

To answer Churchill, the Admiralty tasked Captain Dudley Pound, then serving on the naval staff. Pound was an up-and-coming officer, marked for higher leadership roles. He had recently come to the Admiralty from command of the battleship HMS *Colossus*, which had taken part in the Battle of Jutland. Pound's assessment of Churchill's proposal was thoughtful, thorough, and reflected recent combat experience from having served with the Grand Fleet in the North Sea. He acknowledged that the "proposals put forward by Mr. Churchill comprise various operations on the enemy coast with presumably the ultimate object of sealing the enemy's ports to prevent the egress of his submarines." Pound analyzed the problems involved in seizing and holding Borkum and using it as a base of operations to blunt the German submarine offensive. "The taking of Borkum even by its greatest advocates is recognised to be a very difficult task," Pound contended. If the island was stormed, he argued that it would be difficult to hold against a determined German counterattack. Even if British forces held the island against counterattacks, its anchorages would remain within range of German artillery batteries on the mainland. The only way to secure the anchorages from artillery fire would be to establish an enclave on the German mainland. "Whether the occupation of the mainland opposite the Island is feasible only the military can say but undoubtedly large forces would be required," Pound insisted. "It is clear however that only by such occupation could we make use of Borkum as a base." In Pound's judgment, Borkum could not serve the purpose of an advanced base for subsequent operations in German home waters.

Pound also emphasized that Churchill's plan "would necessitate our keeping a large fleet in these unhealthy waters for the whole period taken to reduce Borkum." This concentration of British naval forces in the North Sea to support offensive operations would draw away warships from the defense of trade. The concentration of escort vessels would mean "that our present measures for trade protection would have to be discontinued." Further, he warned of the dire strategic consequences if the offensive failed in blocking Germany's ports: Britain would then "be very much worse off than before." While demonstrating the difficulties and risks that an offensive entailed, Pound did not minimize the problem of beating back Germany's submarine offensive. He admitted the stark reality before the Admiralty: "Should the present measures against submarines fail we shall be faced with the alternative of dealing with the menace at its root or concluding a peace other than we desire."[42]

Admiral Sir George Hope, the director of the operations division of the naval staff, concurred with Pound's assessment. Hope conceded that the "correct" strategy was the traditional British strategy of a "'close and aggressive blockade' of the enemy's ports . . . with the object of finding a means of fighting and compelling the enemy to fight and of thus establishing a greater control of the sea approaches to his harbours." An offensive strategy, he pointed out, confronted the problem of "the vulnerability to submarine attack of the ships engaged, and another is the great risk of mines." He seconded Pound's view that Britain lacked the necessary naval forces to go on the offensive in the North Sea and still protect oceangoing trade. Hope added that an offensive into German home waters would result in British naval forces suffering from "attrition to such a point as to reduce our superiority to nothing. When this point has been reached, the German submarines would be freed to carry out a more extended campaign against our trade, while our flotillas of small craft would have been so much reduced that we should be in a much worse position to counteract them."[43] In Hope's view, an offensive carried too high a risk of ship losses that would endanger Britain's overall command of the seas.

Pound's assessment, along with Admiral Hope's comments, gave Jellicoe the analysis that he needed to push back against offensive plans. Also working in Jellicoe's favor was that merchant shipping losses came down as the number of ships escorted in convoys increased. Convoys turned the tide in the battle against the German submarine offensive. The reduction in merchant shipping losses made less compelling one of the main arguments for taking the offensive in the North Sea. In addition, Jellicoe convinced American navy leaders that the dangers and difficulties of offensive operations were too great. Jellicoe reported that an offensive maritime strategy "was discussed with the USA & French naval authorities who agreed that the proposals were not a practical matter and who stated that they were not prepared to supply the ships required."[44] The Admiralty thus put to rest Churchill's plans.

Did Churchill's calls for major offensive operations in the North Sea make sound strategic sense? Was an aggressive maritime strategy a realistic and worthwhile endeavor, a return to a traditional British way of war that would avoid the huge losses of the attrition battles of the western front? After the war, when Churchill turned to writing *The World Crisis*, his account of the recently concluded conflict, he sought to analyze Britain's strategic options for fighting Germany. As part of his assessment of strategic alternatives, he considered including a section on his proposals for offensives on Germany's northern flank.

Churchill, however, "had great doubts" about whether to include the chapter. To obtain expert professional opinion on his strategy, he turned to Admiral Sir Roger Keyes, then serving as commander of Britain's Mediterranean Fleet. Keyes was one of the most aggressive naval commanders of the war, and Churchill valued his views about plans for offensive operations at sea. He sent a copy of the draft chapter to Keyes for comment. Churchill wrote, "It explains as nothing else can my view as to the offensive strategy of the Navy. I should like you to consider carefully whether it would be ridiculed by Service opinion. I remain obstinately convinced that the lines of thought are sound."[45] Churchill hoped to convince Keyes that his offensive schemes had merit.

Keyes' response was unequivocal and disappointing: plans for an offensive against the German island chain in the North Sea carried too high a risk of failure and loss. Various plans to seize Borkum, Keyes wrote Churchill, were simply not "*war* under modern conditions." The difficulties of seizing and holding an advanced base were daunting. It was also not clear whether an offensive campaign would bring strategic benefits commensurate with the costs and risks. To convince Churchill to drop the section on the naval offensive, Keyes turned to none other than Dudley Pound to write a response. Pound, who had been promoted to rear admiral, was serving as Keyes' chief-of-staff with the Mediterranean Fleet. Keyes made clear that Pound's analysis reflected the weight of professional naval opinion about the difficulties and dangers of combat in German home waters. Keyes hoped that the critique of Churchill's section on the naval offensive "will induce you to eliminate it!"[46] Eliminate it Churchill did. "So many thanks for your searching criticism of my Borkum plan," Churchill wrote back to Keyes. "It has proved fatal to the enclosing of the chapter in any form, which is probably a good thing."[47]

While Churchill followed Keyes' recommendation and did not include his plan for a naval offensive in *The World Crisis*, he remained convinced of its strategic merit. When Churchill returned as First Lord of the Admiralty at the outbreak of World War II, he pushed again for an offensive maritime strategy to carry a British fleet into the Baltic Sea. In a replay of 1917, it was none other than Dudley Pound, now serving as First Sea Lord, who pushed backed against Churchill's offensive scheme, code-named Plan Catherine. Naval planners once again stood against Churchill's plan, which they found reckless. They understood far better than Churchill the dangers that surface ships would face in carrying out a naval offensive into Germany's home waters.[48]

The back-and-forth arguments between Churchill and British naval leaders over strategy underscore the harsh realities of the struggle for naval mastery during World War I. The Royal Navy would have paid a fearful price in ships and personnel if it had undertaken an offensive to seize an island base in German home waters. The prospect of taking heavy losses and uncertainty about the fighting's outcome deterred the British navy's leadership from offensive action. Jellicoe, as commander of the Grand Fleet and later as First Sea Lord, never wavered in his opposition to attacking into German home waters. In his opposition, Jellicoe was supported by his principal advisers and staff. When an aggressive naval leader like Keyes, too, condemned Churchill's best-laid plan, that surely indicates the weight of opposition from navy professionals. Churchill's strategy thus remained a paper plan, a strategic alternative to what might have been.

NOTES

1. Martin Gilbert, *Winston S. Churchill* (Boston: Houghton Mifflin, 1973), companion vol. 3, part 1, 336–49, 350–56.
2. Arthur J. Marder, *From the Dreadnought to Scapa Flow*, vol. 1 (London: Oxford University Press, 1961), 373–77.
3. Speech by Winston Churchill, March 18, 1912, in Robert Rhodes James, ed., *Winston S. Churchill: His Complete Speeches, 1897–1963* (New York: Chelsea House, 1974), 1928.
4. Paul M. Kennedy, "The Development of German Naval Operations Plans against England, 1896–1914," in Paul M. Kennedy, ed., *The War Plans of the Great Powers* (New York: Routledge, 2014), 171–98.
5. Jellicoe to Balfour, January 25, 1916, Jellicoe Papers, Ad. Ms. 48992, vol. 4, ff. 6–13, British Library.

6. Arthur J. Marder, ed., *Fear God and Dread Nought: The Correspondence of Admiral of the Fleet Lord Fisher of Kilverstone* (London: Jonathan Cape, 1959), 3:112–13.

7. Paul G. Halpern, ed., "Dudley Pound in the Grand Fleet, 1914–15," in *The Naval Miscellany* (Aldershot, U.K.: Ashgate for the Navy Records Society, 2003), 6:413.

8. Michael Epkenhans, "The Imperial Navy, 1914–1915," in Michael Epkenhans, Jörg Hillmann, and Frank Nägler, eds., *Jutland: World War I's Greatest Naval Battle* (Lexington: University of Kentucky Press, 2015), 117–42.

9. Churchill to Jellicoe, October 8, 1914, Jellicoe Papers, Ad. Ms. 48990, ff. 158–64, British Library.

10. Martin Gilbert, *Winston S. Churchill*, vol. 3 (London: Heinemann, 1971), 84–87.

11. Jan Rüger, *Heligoland: Britain, Germany, and the Struggle for the North Sea* (Oxford: Oxford University Press, 2017), 133–44; Richard Dunley, "Operation Q: Churchill and Fisher's Invasion of Germany, 1915?," *Journal of Military History* 86, no. 3 (July 2022): 612–41.

12. Churchill to Jellicoe, January 4, 1915, Jellicoe Papers, Ad. Ms. 48990, ff. 175–77, British Library.

13. Churchill to Jellicoe, January 11, 1915, Jellicoe Papers, Ad. Ms. 48990, ff. 178–82, British Library.

14. Churchill to Jellicoe, March 9, 1915, Jellicoe Papers, Ad. Ms. 48990, ff. 191–93, British Library.

15. Churchill to Jellicoe, March 9, 1915, Jellicoe Papers.

16. Arthur J. Marder, ed., *Portrait of an Admiral: The Life and Papers of Sir Herbert Richmond* (London: Jonathan Cape, 1952), 134–39.

17. Admiral Viscount Jellicoe of Scapa, *The Grand Fleet, 1914–1916: Its Creation, Development and Work* (London: Cassell, 1919), 128–29.

18. Balfour to Jellicoe, January 17, 1916, Jellicoe Papers, Ad. Ms. 48992, vol. 4, ff. 1–3; Jellicoe to Balfour, January 25, 1916, Jellicoe Papers, Ad. Ms. 48992, vol. 4, ff. 6–13, British Library.

19. Admiral [Reinhard] Scheer, *Germany's High Sea Fleet in the World War* (London: Cassell, 1920), 169.

20. Arthur J. Marder, *From the Dreadnought to Scapa Flow*, vol. 4 (London: Oxford University Press, 1969), 102.

21. Winston S. Churchill, in James W. Muller, ed., *Thoughts and Adventures* (Wilmington: ISI Books, 2009), 134.
22. See Marder, *Dreadnought to Scapa Flow*, 4:99–192.
23. CHAR 9/54, ff. 81, 88, Churchill Archives Centre, University of Cambridge (hereafter CAC).
24. Churchill, *World Crisis*, part 1, 254.
25. Churchill, *World Crisis*, part 1, 255.
26. "Naval War Policy, 1917," CHAR 27/1, ff. 42–54, CAC.
27. "Naval War Policy, 1917," CHAR 27/1, ff. 42–54.
28. "Naval War Policy, 1917," CHAR 27/1, ff. 42–54.
29. "Naval War Policy, 1917," CHAR 27/1, ff. 42–54.
30. "Naval War Policy, 1917," CHAR 27/1, ff. 42–54.
31. "Naval War Policy, 1917," CHAR 27/1, ff. 42–54.
32. "Naval War Policy, 1917," CHAR 27/1, ff. 42–54.
33. "Naval War Policy, 1917," CHAR 27/1, ff. 42–54.
34. Churchill note, August 12, 1917, CHAR 8/104, f. 32, CAC.
35. Fisher to Churchill, CHAR 2/92, f. 19, CAC.
36. "Naval War Policy, 1917," CHAR 27/1, ff. 42–54.
37. CHAR 8/104 f. 36, CAC.
38. Churchill to Curzon, July 26, 1917, CHAR 8/104, ff. 291–93, CAC.
39. "Duplication and Waste of Effort," November 6, 1917, CHAR 8/104, ff. 336–37, CAC.
40. A. Temple Patterson, *The Jellicoe Papers* (London: Naval Records Society, 1968), 2:181, 191, 203–4.
41. Martin Gilbert, *Winston S. Churchill* (London: Heinemann, 1977), vol. 4 companion, part 1, 139–40.
42. "CNS Naval War Policy," Jellicoe Papers, Ad. Ms. 48992, vol. 4, ff. 100–106, British Library.
43. Comments by Admiral Hope, July 20, 1917, Jellicoe Papers, Ad. Ms. 48992, vol. 4, ff. 107–18, British Library.
44. Handwritten note, Jellicoe Papers, Ad. Ms. 48992, vol. 4, f. 97, British Library.
45. Churchill to Keyes, October 29, 1926, CHAR 8/203, ff. 210–11, CAC.
46. Keyes to Churchill, November 23, 1926, CHAR 1/188; Keyes to Churchill, December 12, 1926, CHAR 8/174, ff. 1–30, CAC.
47. Churchill to Keyes, December 18, 1926, CHAR 1/188, CAC.
48. Karl Lautenschläger, "Plan 'Catherine': The British Baltic Operation, 1940," *Journal of Baltic Studies* 5, no. 3 (1974): 211–21.

CHAPTER SIX

THE WARS YOU WANT VERSUS THE WARS YOU GET

THE LIMITATIONS OF THE INTERWAR U.S. NAVY AS A HISTORICAL MODEL

Ryan Wadle

I n October 1960, Admiral Chester W. Nimitz, who had spent almost the entirety of the war as the Commander in Chief of the Pacific Fleet, gave a speech at the Naval War College. Reflecting on the time he and other senior leaders spent in Newport—a majority of flag officers at the start of World War II were Naval War College graduates—Nimitz made this bold claim: "The war with Japan had been reenacted in the game room here by so many people in so many different ways that nothing that happened during the war was a surprise—absolutely nothing except the Kamikaze tactics toward the end of the war; we had not visualized those."[1] The statement, given as Nimitz extolled the value of the Naval War College, has been subject to wildly diverging analyses of its accuracy by historians in the decades since. Setting aside this debate for the moment, it raises an important question: How effective was the U.S. Navy at preparing for and anticipating future conflicts, and then, when war came in 1941, how quickly did the service adapt to the realities of combat?

Note here at the outset the distinction between *innovation* and *adaptation*. Following Williamson Murray, this chapter defines innovation as a peacetime process characterized by the ability to capitalize on the "time available to think through problems" to develop new ideas and technologies slowly and deliberately and to incorporate them into the force. Conversely, adaptation is a much more rapid wartime process driven by the "feedback of combat results, which can suggest necessary adaptations."[2] Even while these two processes have distinct differences, they are closely interrelated. The period between World War I and II is one almost tailor-made for military and naval historians to examine these concepts. Bookended by the two most destructive wars in human history—the first of which was seemingly marked by stalemate and pointless bloodshed, while the second, featuring many of the same combatants but equipped with new generations of weapon systems, expanded the scope of the devastation in almost unfathomable ways—the interwar period offers up a tantalizing example of how militaries can change or "transform" themselves in peacetime.[3]

Yet in the first decades after World War II, some of the most prominent literature on the U.S. Navy, including Clark Reynolds' *The Fast Carriers: The Forging of an Air Navy* (1968) and Clayton Blair's *Silent Victory: The US Submarine War against Japan* (1975), focused much more on the wartime adaptation and expansion of the fleet.[4] Not until the 1970s did scholarly attention begin to examine seriously the interwar innovation of the fleet, and the studies that emerged in the 1990s concurrent with the national security community's emphasis on the concept of "Revolutions in Military Affairs"—in at least one case from a study funded by the Office of Net Assessment—allowed this narrative to take hold.[5] If one combines these perspectives, as Trent Hone has done in his outstanding *Learning War: The Evolution of Fighting Doctrine in the U.S. Navy, 1898–1945* (2018), one can see that the U.S. Navy was a healthy and robust learning organization capable of identifying and solving problems using a combination of tactics, doctrine, and technology.[6] The Navy's structure at the time was far from ideal given that the relative independence of the service's powerful bureaus led to somewhat confusing chains of command across the civilian and military leadership, but the various organizations as well as the Navy's culture created an environment conducive to learning.

Because so much of the extant historiography, regardless of whether it focuses more on the interwar or wartime years, retains a certain element of triumphant problem solving, historians should be wary of overconfidence in understanding and then drawing lessons from the Navy of the period. In particular, the Navy's ability to learn during the period was intimately linked to the ability of its uniformed leaders to anticipate the nature of the conflict they believed most likely to occur. Predicting the future is a difficult task to undertake under even the best of circumstances, so the Navy made a series of assumptions about a future conflict that served to simplify the process.[7] These assumptions were reflected in the strategic priorities made by the service's War Plans Division and the resulting force structure that civilian and uniformed leaders advocated for from the early 1920s through the late 1930s. They show a service that overwhelmingly focused on the projection of power across the Pacific against Japan as expressed by War Plan Orange. Every aspect of the Navy oriented around this threat, profoundly influencing its force structure, operational concepts, and doctrine, and even the service's educational system. As a result, the service developed many new capabilities, including aviation, amphibious warfare, and submarines, with varying degrees of success. These capabilities promised to alter radically how the U.S. Navy intended to seize control of the sea and then exploit it by shifting away from a traditional surface fleet into a true "three-plane" Navy that could also contest control in the skies above and in the depths below.[8]

In concentrating on transpacific power projection, the Navy's learning organization elected not to devote much attention to other conflict scenarios. Thus, despite the recent experience in protecting the sea lines of communication between North America and Europe in the Great War, the Navy placed little priority on antisubmarine warfare and the development of escorts. This oversight created a significant problem in 1942 as the Navy struggled to contain both the menace of German submarines along the East Coast and the rampages of the Japanese fleet in the Pacific, and the latter problem could have been significantly worse had the Imperial Japanese Navy (IJN) not suffered from their own forms of myopia that led them to ignore critical concepts, such as unrestricted submarine warfare, that could have turned the tide in the Pacific. Thus, while the U.S. Navy developed a learning system capable of innovating and adapting, there was plenty that the institution overlooked, underestimated, or simply got wrong. Many of the seeds of the Navy's turnaround from a beleaguered service into a force capable of global sea control had been laid by the end of 1942, but these were not readily apparent at the time.

THE U.S. NAVY AND POWER PROJECTION

Historians have paid relatively little attention to the contextual factors that made such a consensus possible and allowed the U.S. Navy to be so single-minded in its strategic outlook between the world wars. Its leaders and planners lacked any meaningful strategic guidance from civilian policymakers for much of this period, allowing them to plan, for better or worse, largely in a policy vacuum free of interference. Furthermore, the United States' geographic isolation and the demise of imperial Germany meant that the Navy did not seriously consider the possibility of a challenger appearing in the Atlantic world, depending on how one interprets the Navy's views on Great Britain. In essence, the Navy behaved as if it existed in a bipolar world when there still existed multiple poles of global power. Bipolarity at sea—the United States and Japan—played to the navy's preference for a power projection model. As the Navy gradually began to identify the means by which it would execute a transpacific campaign, some capabilities received more attention and resources than others, leaving critical gaps when the nation entered the war in 1941.

Reconciling these vastly different visions of how the U.S. Navy viewed itself, the world, and its ability to solve problems is critical to understanding the interwar period. At the risk of oversimplifying the matter, the roots of the Navy's conflicted view of itself and the world can be traced back to Alfred Thayer Mahan. There is a side of Mahan that remains underappreciated today: the sober analyst of geopolitical and naval affairs. He called for a rapprochement between the United States and Britain well before this became an unofficial policy in the early twentieth century. He believed that "cordial recognition of the similarity of character and ideas will give birth to sympathy, which in turn will facilitate a cooperation beneficial to both." Mahan also judged that the U.S. Navy's future was in the Pacific but that it would exert "influence, not supremacy" because, he continued, "the Western Pacific will remain Asiatic, as it should."[9]

Yet there is the other, more famous, side of Mahan: the evangelist of sea power and the international celebrity. He was a creature of the late nineteenth century, but he also had a profound effect on both his contemporaries and future generations of officers.[10] This is the Mahan whose influence could still be felt so acutely decades later that led Secretary of War Henry Stimson to complain about the "the peculiar psychology of the Navy Department, which frequently seemed to retire from the realm of logic into a dim religious world in which Neptune was god, Mahan his prophet, and the U.S. Navy the only true church."[11]

Mahan preached the importance of the United States becoming a sea power, but the country went about it in ways that differed from the British model. As Andrew Lambert suggests, the United States remained a continental power and built a Navy in that strategic visage; even with the takeover of the Philippines and Guam and the assumption of de facto or de jure control of Latin America, it did not possess an overseas empire that required the development of the vast trade networks that marked the British Empire at its peak during Mahan's lifetime. Dismissing Mahan as someone who "did not engage with soul of sea power, only the strategic surface,"

Lambert also describes Mahan's strategic model as using a battlefleet to "advance total-war strategies of annihilation or unconditional surrender."[12] When analyzing the buildup of the U.S. Navy from its late nineteenth-century rebirth through the interwar period, Lambert writes, "The 'New' American navy was 'Roman,' serving the interests of a continental great power."[13] While there is much about Lambert's reading of Mahan that can be scrutinized, the point remains that the U.S. Navy built a fleet that reflected national strategic concerns and emphasized power projection rather than presence or the protection of the sea lines of communication.[14]

After the end of the Great War, the Atlantic world did not offer the opportunities for power projection that had appeared in the Pacific. Britain remained the strongest power in the region, and the U.S. Navy often benchmarked itself against the Royal Navy in war games at the Naval War College in the 1920s. In 1924, for example, the "Battle of Sable Island" served as a test of how naval warfare might be affected by the presence of aircraft carriers among both fleets.[15] The selection of the Royal Navy as an adversary of war games ("Red" in the color scheme of the day) had more to do with the need to test the students against a fleet of similar size and relatively comparable composition than with a significant interest in Britain as a potential adversary. Tellingly, even though some American civilian and naval leaders viewed the Washington Conference agreement as designed to limit British power, planning for war against Britain occurred only intermittently in the years thereafter. The Red-Orange war plan of 1931 pitted the United States against a hypothetical renewal of the Anglo-Japanese alliance. It was noteworthy for being the only war plan prior to the Rainbow plans that involved more than one adversary in more than one ocean, but it was more of a thought exercise than a serious strategic contingency. The Navy showed little interest in either the Red or Red-Orange plans. The U.S. Army, by contrast, used a potential invasion of Canada to justify the creation of a larger standing peacetime force, which meant it had a far greater stake in maintaining Red as an enemy than the Navy did.[16]

The identification of Japan as the nation's likeliest threat by war planners had many credible justifications. The neutralization of Germany after 1919 removed a former foe from the international scene, one that had once occupied much of the Navy's intellectual energy. Instead, the first generation of postwar planners fixed their attention on Japan for several reasons. These included the desire to guarantee the few extant overseas U.S. political commitments, such as the Open Door, which was codified into international law with the signing of the Nine-Power Pact at the Washington Conference, and legal possession over the Philippines and Guam. The ongoing domestic political turmoil over Japanese immigrants to the United States, which occurred amid a much larger backlash against open immigration from both Europe and Asia, had already provoked political crises with Japan and provided a possible justification for a future conflict.[17] There were also more subtle cultural influences over the selection of Japan as a potential enemy. In a September 1919 lecture to the Command and General Staff School, Captain Harry Yarnell, who was then serving as a member of the Navy's War Plans Division, spoke of Japanese immigration as an issue worth fighting over, because "white labor cannot compete with Asiatic labor without descending to a scale of life wholly incompatible with white ideals and traditions."[18]

Most importantly, identifying Japan as an enemy had an institutional bias: Japan posed a strategic problem that meant the Navy would be the primary instrument of a solution. But while there was broad-based agreement in this strategic framing, there was a corresponding lack of consensus on how best to defeat Japan in a coming conflict. Throughout his career Yarnell favored a more Corbettian strategy that sought to economically isolate Japan from potential resources and markets rather than confronting the Japanese in the Home Islands. He sought to incorporate aircraft and submarines more fully into his strategic calculations as these weapons systems matured. As he wrote to the Chief of Naval Operations, Admiral William Leahy, in 1937, "The old dyed in the wool strategists declare that a naval war cannot bring a country to terms; that there must be an invasion of the enemy territory and the defeat of his armies. This may be true of some countries, but not in the Pacific. Some nations can be strangled to death. The invasion theory is a legacy from Clausewitz who was writing from the European standpoint of 100 years ago with self-contained countries and permanent armies." Such a strategy promised to avoid the "horrors of land warfare" of the Great War.[19]

Yarnell, however, was in the minority. The dominant strain of thought instead focused on power projection, almost as an end in itself. The desire to project American power caused the Navy to inflate the importance of Philippines as a national security priority even as the Army, save for General Douglas MacArthur, spent much of the interwar period seeking to downgrade its commitment to protecting the islands from a foreign assault. In fact, disagreements over the power projection mission as expressed in War Plan Orange caused a breakdown of interservice relations for a time in the mid-1930s.[20]

The Navy's commitment to a power projection conflict led it to focus almost its entire physical and intellectual energy on solving the problem. From 1919 to 1939, the Navy's Plans Division, sometimes in concert with its Army counterparts who sat on the Joint Plans Committee, rigorously studied the subject. The plans received nearly constant attention and updates and constituted almost living documents. To test assumptions made in these plans, the Navy turned to war games, which became a significant part of the curriculum at the Naval War College throughout the period. As with studies on other aspects of the U.S. Navy, opinions on the value of the college in preparing the service for an upcoming conflict vary widely. Ronald Spector and especially Michael Vlahos frame the college's wargaming-heavy curriculum, which was first designed by Admiral Williams Sims in 1919 and carried on, with some modifications, by his successors, as a center of rote indoctrination for generations of naval officers seeking to partake in the navy's mission. For Vlahos, battle, as expressed through the chart and board maneuvers performed by students at the college, became a ritual culmination of the naval officer's career. Red and Orange existed not as geopolitical threats but as half-realized foes against which officers commanding their paper fleets could test themselves, but these mental exercises ultimately did little to advance the art of naval warfare.[21]

Meanwhile, other sources, including Hone's *Learning War*, view the Naval War College as a focal point of organizational learning and an essential element in preparing many key senior leaders, including Nimitz and Ernest King, for the complexities of naval warfare. Instead of Vlahos' numbly ritualistic Navy, Hone instead portrays the Navy as a "complex adaptive system" capable of learning, processing, and disseminating information at a responsive pace. This organizational and cultural ability to learn allowed the Navy to think through strategic problems and develop solutions that could be passed down to the tactical level and individual units. As Hone himself acknowledges, the Navy did spend time in the interwar period studying Jutland. But instead of a backward-looking exercise akin to armchair admiralship, Hone says the Navy refought Jutland so it could win a future naval battle against a peer competitor.[22]

In addition to the many dozens of war games played in Newport during the period, the Navy also had its system of Fleet Problems that could examine these ideas in a real-world setting. Arguably, the Fleet Problems offered more value to the Navy because these were not games played among an exclusive number of aspiring senior officers but instead a means to have the entire fleet engage in mock campaigns and engagements. The twenty-one Fleet Problems conducted between 1923 and 1940, combined with an additional three similarly sized exercises played in cooperation with the Army, sought to test only the most important problems identified in plans and war games. Lessons learned were then fed back toward the planners so that the cycle could begin again. For example, war games suggested that maximizing the number of aircraft carriers in the fleet under the terms of the Five-Power Treaty would be the most beneficial option, but the Fleet Problems demonstrated that larger carriers with their superior seakeeping and their ability to launch larger "pulses" of aircraft in a single strike ultimately mattered more. This revelation led the Navy to abandon the smaller and more constrained design of the carrier *Ranger* in favor of the larger *Yorktown* class, and it ultimately pointed the way toward the successful *Essex*-class carriers designed on the eve of World War II.[23]

By reducing the number of possible strategic paths through the joint and service planning processes and then employing the feedback mechanisms to test that strategy and to design the force structure to execute it, the U.S. Navy had theoretically simplified the problems facing any peacetime military organization. The effect of this can best be understood when comparing the U.S. Navy against the Royal Navy in the interwar period. Historians and political scientists have compared the relative performance of the two navies in the arena of naval aviation, and Emily Goldman devised a model that helps to explain the phenomenon in more generalizable and systemic terms. The diversity and intensity of threats, she argues, can help to explain the results of military transformation. The British, already enduring financial constraints brought by the high cost of waging World War I, faced a wide range of strategic threats in the two decades that followed. None of them was clearly compelling enough to allow the Royal Navy, the army, and other parts of the government to coalesce around a strategic design, at least before German rearmament in the 1930s. Conversely, by focusing solely on the strategic problem in the Pacific, the U.S. Navy could seek to build a force especially well suited to the region.[24]

Force structure, itself the purview of the Navy's General Board, likewise derived from the focus on power projection. American aircraft carriers, unlike their British counterparts, emphasized range and a large aircraft complement of specialized aircraft carrying out air superiority, strike, and reconnaissance roles. Battleships, which spent most of the interwar period static in numbers thanks to the construction holiday and tonnage limits agreed on in Washington, received updated protection and superelevated guns that widened the radius of a naval engagement. Unlike the British, who sought to build a fleet of light cruisers to show the flag and protect trade routes, the United States instead built heavy cruisers that could both scout ahead of the battle line yet remain formidable combatants during an engagement. Finally, submarines, which remained a bit of an afterthought in fleet doctrine, received attention as the Navy experimented with different designs before settling on a "fleet boat" standard that could operate independently across the Pacific. In short, the U.S. fleet was built from top to bottom to fulfill the power projection mission.[25]

The ethos of power projection as expressed through War Plan Orange pervaded all aspects of naval life during the interwar period. In one sense, it speaks to the incredible amount of organizational, bureaucratic, and cultural cohesion within the Navy that this broad consensus existed. Obviously, some major disagreements existed within the officer corps, such as the importance of naval aviation in both contemporary and future naval engagements and views relating to arms limitation treaties.[26] Additionally, there also existed a disagreement over how a campaign against Orange would be waged. So-called "thrusters," who believed the fleet and a relief ground force could be dispatched across the Pacific within weeks of the outbreak of hostilities, initially dominated the planning process. Armed with experiences learned during Naval War College war games and the Fleet Problems, "cautionaries" supplanted the "thrusters" and imposed a slower, more realistic advance across the Japanese-held islands of the Central Pacific.[27] These disagreements largely focused on the ways and means by which a Pacific war would be fought—the focus on Japan remained virtually unquestioned.

The pronounced shift toward a cautionary strategy by the 1930s also created a much clearer need for the Marine Corps to develop the capability to seize advanced bases for use by the fleet in a trans-pacific campaign. The Corps had first assumed this responsibility at the turn of the century, but the British experience in the Dardanelles campaign as well as the advent of the Japanese mandates in the Central Pacific had led many in the Corps, including Major Earl Ellis, to begin studying the possibility of amphibious operations against a defended possession. Experience gathered in joint exercises with the Army and Navy fed into a series of landing exercises that the Marines conducted in the late 1930s. These exercises led to the identification of several critical capabilities, including landing craft that could beach themselves as well as tracked landing vehicles that could traverse the reefs and other offshore obstacles present at many of the Central Pacific atolls. The Marine Corps also began to develop their own landing doctrine, which proved so successful that the Army, which had largely abandoned any idea of needing to conduct amphibious operations, adopted the Corps' doctrine on the eve of war with only minimal changes.[28]

THE COSTS OF MYOPIA

Many regard the Navy's approach during the interwar period as an excellent example to study because of its successes, but not enough attention is paid to what the service missed. Most prominently, the Navy paid little attention to protecting sea lines of communication. Even during war games and Fleet Problems, it was assumed that the fleet could protect the ships carrying the relief force and their supplies. Using a combination of escort vessels and aerial patrols, the Navy appeared to have solved this problem. This was, however, at best a tertiary concern among the litany of problems the Navy sought to address in experiments.[29]

As a progressive institution that was reborn during a time of incredible scientific process, the U.S. Navy remained comfortable with developing and deploying new technologies. Indeed, the advances first conceived during World War I to overcome the submarine menace came into use during the interwar period, none of which was more important than sonar. Completed too late to see service in World War I, the Navy placed sonar aboard ships during the interwar period; destroyers from the mid-1930s onward were outfitted with the new technology, although the highly classified nature of the technology made it difficult to assess how much rigorous testing occurred in exercises.[30] The same assumptions that inhibited the development of effective submarine tactics had a corresponding effect on antisubmarine warfare (ASW) whereby the effectiveness of sonar and aerial patrols proved vastly overstated, giving the Navy a false sense of security. More fundamentally, as C. C. Felker notes in his history of the Fleet Problem system, the interwar Navy's fundamental approach to antisubmarine warfare was flawed. The Navy had the tools and the concepts developed in World War I to successfully defeat concerted submarine attacks, yet never truly believed that this could happen again. To quote Felker, "The Mahanization of antisubmarine warfare was reinforced through simulation. And therein lay the problem. Critical fallacies in simulation informed expectations. The fleet problems nurtured a false sense of security."[31] The same fleet problems that had a hugely beneficial effect on the development of naval aviation and other capabilities failed miserably with regard to ASW.

One need only look at the combat records of World War II to see these disparate failures fully manifested. The United States had gradually extended its security responsibilities in the Atlantic throughout 1941, culminating in September, when the torpedo attack on the USS *Reuben James* led President Roosevelt to allow American warships to fire on German submarines. Thus, by the time Germany had declared war on the United States shortly after Pearl Harbor, the Navy had acquired many valuable months of experience of conducting ASW operations in coordination with experienced British and Canadian personnel and against a battle-hardened German foe. These ties would only deepen and become more formalized after the United States joined the Allied cause.

Even so, the scope and scale of the German submarine menace in the first half of 1942 caught the U.S. Navy completely off guard. In fairness, there existed confused command responsibilities at sea between the Atlantic Fleet and the Naval Frontier Commands as well as at the top between the offices of the Chief of Naval Operations, Admiral Harold "Betty" Stark, and the Commander in Chief of the U.S. Fleet, Admiral Ernest J. King. The latter was resolved in March 1942, when King assumed responsibility for both positions, but the former lingered to some degree until the creation of the Tenth Fleet in March 1943 centralized control over ASW in the Atlantic. While these command and control issues contributed to the disaster, King's refusal to apply lessons learned from the British and Canadians about convoys played a significant role. What resulted was a "happy time" of German U-boat captains having almost free rein to attack individual merchants off the coast with little fear of organized reprisal. Well into 1942, small numbers of German submarines disrupted the movement of commerce and especially oil, leading to the halving of fuel stocks on the Eastern Seaboard.[32] In essence, the U.S. Navy misunderstood the problem, focusing too much on trying to find and sink submarines and too little on the much more prosaic task of protecting merchants. Adaptation, in the form of new escorts, better doctrine, escort carriers, and long-range patrol aircraft, later in 1942 eventually reduced the threat, and by one estimation the Battle of the Atlantic was nearly won by the end of the year.[33] Still, whether due to structural or matériel problems or outright malpractice, the U.S. Navy's efforts in the first half of 1942 and Admiral King's performance in particular left something to be desired.[34]

The Japanese strike on Pearl Harbor on December 7, 1941, was but a prelude to a months-long campaign to seize the resource-rich areas of Southeast Asia and establish a defensive perimeter in the Central and South Pacific capable of staving off any counteroffensive staged by the Americans. The poor performance of the U.S. Navy in these early months of the war can easily be explained by the shock of the Japanese attacks, even though invasions on the Philippines and Guam had been anticipated for years and air attacks on Pearl Harbor had factored into multiple interwar exercises, including Grand Joint Exercise 4 in February 1932. At nearly every juncture during these campaigns, the Japanese had the advantages of surprise and experience as well as numerical superiority. Perhaps most importantly, the Japanese also possessed local air superiority that allowed its forces to locate and strike Allied forces at will, leading to the destruction of the British capital ships of Force Z and the combined American British Dutch Australian (ABDA) fleet in the first months of the war.[35]

Ironically, however, the disaster could have been far worse for the United States. Japan, unlike Germany, never attempted to initiate any interdiction campaign against American shipping. The Japanese possessed submarines even larger than their American counterparts, capable of transpacific voyages, and some carried small numbers of aircraft, although they were less maneuverable and far noisier than the smaller American fleet boats. Japanese submarines inflicted some losses between Hawaii and the West Coast in the early weeks of the war, but they did little to interdict the valuable convoys that maintained the vital lifeline between North America and Australia. Had they done so, especially during 1942 when shipping and ASW escorts remained scarce, they would have stood a good chance of stretching American resources to the breaking point while likely limiting the possibility of an Allied counterstrike. One of the *Yorktown's* first assignments in Pacific waters involved providing air cover for a Samoa-bound convoy; American leaders may have been forced to assign the immensely valuable fleet carriers to shepherd other convoys, thus forestalling the counterattacks that eventually drew the IJN back into the Central and South Pacific in spring and summer of 1942. The aircraft-carrying submarines also could have attempted to disable the locks of the Panama Canal, which could have created additional strategic or psychological problems for the Navy and the larger American war effort.[36] In his blunt style, Admiral King said of the missed Japanese opportunity to wage a sustained interdiction campaign with their submarines that "they might have raised hell."[37] Instead, the Japanese remained wedded to doctrine dictating that submarines play a role in fleet engagements, not attacks on merchantmen. They inflicted some critical losses during 1942, including sinking the carriers *Yorktown* and *Wasp* and disabling the *Saratoga* on two separate occasions, leaving her unavailable for much of the first year of the war, but the potential for even greater effects remained unrealized.

Surface actions remained a critical component of naval thought during the interwar era, even exceeding the importance placed on developing naval aviation. Nevertheless, the Navy failed to develop effective night-fighting doctrine prior to the war. In the series of naval battles in the waters around Guadalcanal in late 1942, these problems came at a high cost, especially at the disastrous Battle of Savo Island in August. However, by the time of the Battle of Guadalcanal in mid-November, the U.S. Navy began to leverage its advantages in radar to mitigate Japanese superiority in optics and torpedoes.[38] Furthermore, from the chaos of these early surface battles came a critical adaptation that would pay dividends for the remainder of the war: the Combat Information Center (CIC). Soon after Admiral Nimitz and his staff issued a call to create CICs in November 1942, the commanding officer of the destroyer *Fletcher* conducted an experiment that sought to harness the constant input of information from radar and radio to improve his ability to command his ship in battle. To solve this, he stationed a junior officer (the future naval strategist J. C. Wylie) adjacent to the radar plot to feed him information. This successful test went beyond the parameters initially issued by CINCPAC, but it was reported back to Pacific Fleet headquarters and subsequently disseminated throughout the fleet so that all American warships had a CIC by the following year.[39]

The problems of translating interwar theory to wartime practice were even more acute among the Navy's submarine force. The declaration of unrestricted submarine warfare against Japanese merchant shipping made immediately after Pearl Harbor unleashed the submarine force to sever the sea lines of communication between the Home Islands and Japan's resource-rich conquests in Southeast Asia. The Navy had developed a submarine design—the *Gato*-class fleet submarines—capable of long-range patrols in warm Pacific waters that was well suited to this mission. However, torpedo development and the doctrine to employ the submarines lagged far behind. Sinkings of Japanese merchant vessels throughout 1942 remained embarrassingly small.[40] Replacing conservative captains with more aggressive hunters and creating and implementing the U.S. Navy's version of German wolf-pack tactics eventually paid dividends, but these solutions still eluded the fleet by the end of 1942.

The Navy's failure to develop effective submarine torpedoes severely hampered submarine operations in the first two years of the war. While the Navy had been testing automobile torpedoes since the 1890s, its processes were flawed. Testers, often under pressure to limit expensive tests, applied rigid and unrealistic controls to the inconsistent numbers of tests conducted at the Newport Torpedo Station or by vessels among the fleet. This situation worsened during the interwar period, and submariners entered the war not realizing that their torpedoes utterly failed at sea.[41] The visibility of the failures was humiliating; at the Battle of Midway, a torpedo fired by the submarine *Nautilus* broke apart on impact with the hull of the already damaged Japanese carrier *Kaga*, allowing some of the carrier's crew to use the torpedo wreckage as a makeshift life raft.[42] Thus, even when American submarine captains found themselves in a position to attack enemy vessels, their weapons failed them. Only in 1943 with the introduction of both new torpedo designs and a much more effective contact warhead could submarines finally attack vessels with reasonable confidence in their chances of success.

THE BENEFITS OF MYOPIA

Despite the many frustrations the U.S. Navy endured in 1942, the service had proved far more prescient in its understanding of carrier warfare. The destruction inflicted by the Japanese at Pearl Harbor may have thrust the Navy's carrier force into a somewhat unexpected role of serving as the fleet's primary capital ships until the first of the new battleships arrived in late 1942, but it did not necessarily alter the roles the Navy had expected carriers would play in wartime. As they had shown in the Fleet Problems, the carriers proved to be excellent raiding platforms in the early months of 1942, attacking Japanese bases in the Central and Southwest Pacific and launching the April 1942 Doolittle Raid on the Japanese homeland. These raids, which provided valuable combat experience for American airmen and sailors, constituted part of what Clark Reynolds argues was a "fleet in being" strategy. The early raids compelled the Japanese to divert some of their own carriers away from their planned operations, but the Doolittle Raid led Admiral Yamamoto Isoruku to press for the seizure of Midway atoll in the hopes of drawing out and destroying the remaining strength of the U.S. fleet in battle.[43]

At the battles of Coral Sea and Midway, other American assumptions about carrier warfare also proved true and had a dramatic effect on the conduct of the war. The importance of striking first in carrier warfare had been demonstrated as early the mid-1920s in war games, and it remained a critical factor in combat. The American emphasis on developing an organic reconnaissance and strike capability for its carriers paid big dividends in both battles, especially at Midway, when SBD Dauntless dive bombers sank four Japanese carriers while the IJN, which had prioritized offensive strike for its carrier air groups and relegated scouting duties to floatplanes, struggled to find their American foes as quickly and easily. The Japanese losses suffered at Midway forced Admiral Yamamoto to cancel the operation, but the setbacks suffered in both battles also led to the cancelation of Operation FS, a series of invasions planned for Samoa, Fiji, and New Caledonia in the summer of 1942. Had these invasions occurred, the Japanese could have put themselves in position to interdict the strategically invaluable supply lines to Australia and greatly hamper the Allied war effort in the Pacific.[44]

Another critical lesson from the interwar era also proved true regarding carrier combat: their incredible vulnerability to air and submarine attacks. The advent of radar had helped to provide some advance warning for American combat air patrols to intercept incoming Japanese air strikes at sea and ashore, allowing the less experienced American aviators in inflict losses on the far more experienced Japanese pilots, but the carriers themselves remained vulnerable throughout the first year of the war.[45] Of the Navy's prewar fleet carrier force of six hulls, only *Enterprise* and *Saratoga* remained afloat by the end of 1942; the former had narrowly averted a potentially fatal air attack due to weather, and the latter had spent half the year undergoing repairs from two separate submarine attacks. This was not a unique problem: the IJN fared little better, losing four heavy and two light carriers during the 1942 engagements, indicating that the ships themselves were both high priority targets for the opposing navies and extremely difficult to defend.[46] Some of the elements necessary to defend carriers were present by the end of 1942, but better doctrine and technology that would eventually allow for carrier task forces to adequately defend themselves from conventional air attack were still months away.

By the end of 1942, the U.S. Navy remained locked in a deadly stalemate with the IJN in the South Pacific. The situation appeared somewhat better in Atlantic waters as escort vessels came off the slipways and gradually began to mitigate the threat posed by German U-boats. In addition, despite the harried and improvised nature of the assaults, the Navy had successfully transported and landed American divisions ashore in North Africa. These were tangible signs of progress, but victory was by no means assured by the end of the year.

The U.S. Navy's ability to innovate in advance of war and adapt once it entered combat is perhaps more mixed than historians often admit. The estimate of the strategic situation by its leaders and planners had led them to commit to a strategy of power projection. They transformed the entire Navy Department to prepare for such an eventuality. The Navy benefited from the United States' robust scientific and industrial capacity, which it leveraged through the creation several mechanisms capable of providing feedback on their plans. As a result, the Navy became quite effective at innovating and identifying the capabilities it would need to project power across the Pacific. Many of the weapon systems that would go on to play a significant role in the eventual Allied victory were in service or under development by the time war began. That said, the Navy's ability to correctly anticipate the nature of the next war proved far less prescient, especially once one looks away from the successful experiments to develop the fleet's carrier force. Many of the critical components of victory, including the ability to protect the vulnerable carriers, simply did not exist by the end of 1942. In the area of torpedo development, the Navy had utterly failed to provide its ships with effective weapons, and this debacle ultimately had a profoundly negative effect on the war effort. The Navy's problem-solving process continued to search for solutions, but only some of them had been discovered after a year of war. As the war unfolded, the U.S. Navy was able overcome the problems its limited strategic worldview had created due to its strengths in identifying and solving problems by applying feedback mechanisms first used during interwar war games and exercises to draw lessons from operational commands and combat vessels. However, drawing lessons from a conflict in which the United States also possessed the advantages of geography, time, and prodigious productivity must be done carefully so that one can separate the factors under the Navy's control from its inherited advantages.

NOTES

1. Fleet Admiral Chester Nimitz, Speech to U.S. Naval War College, October 10, 1960, folder 26, box 31, RG 15, Guest Lectures, 1894–1992, Naval Historical Collection, Naval War College, Newport, RI.

2. Williamson Murray, *Military Adaptation in War: With Fear of Change* (New York: Cambridge University Press, 2015), 2. See also Frank Hoffman's *Mars Adapting: Military Change during War* (Annapolis: Naval Institute Press, 2021).

3. Williamson Murray and Allan R. Millett, eds., *Military Innovation in the Interwar Period* (New York: Cambridge University Press, 1996), is but one of several volumes devoted to change among interwar militaries.

4. Clark Reynolds, *The Fast Carriers: The Forging of an Air Navy* (New York: McGraw-Hill, 1968); Clay Blair Jr., *Silent Victory: The U.S. Submarine War against Japan* (Philadelphia: Lippincott, 1975).

5. Charles Melhorn, *Two-Block Fox: The Rise of the Aircraft Carrier, 1911–1929* (Annapolis: Naval Institute Press, 1974); Norman Friedman, Thomas C. Hone, and Mark Mandeles, *American and British Aircraft Carrier Development, 1919–1941* (Annapolis: Naval Institute Press, 1999); Gary Weir, *Building American Submarines, 1914–1940* (Washington, DC: Naval Historical Center), 1991.

6. Trent Hone, *Learning War: The Evolution of Fighting Doctrine in the U.S. Navy, 1898–1945* (Annapolis: Naval Institute Press, 2018).

7. Some scholars have argued that a so-called rational learning model of military innovation is highly dubious given the complexities and intangibility of warfare. See J. C. Sharman, *Empires of the Weak: The Real Story of European Expansion and the Creation of the New World Order* (Princeton, NJ: Princeton University Press, 2019), 18–33.

8. E. G. Lowry, "Three-Plane Navy," *Saturday Evening Post*, June 11, 1921, 16.

9. Alfred Thayer Mahan, *Mahan on Naval Strategy: Selections from the Writings of Rear Admiral Alfred Thayer Mahan* (Annapolis: Naval Institute Press, 2015), 248.

10. Peter Karsten, *The Naval Aristocracy: The Golden Age of Annapolis and the Emergence of Modern American Navalism* (New York: Free Press, 1972).

11. Henry L. Stimson, *On Active Service in Peace and War* (New York: Harper, 1948), 506.

12. Andrew Lambert, *Seapower States: Maritime Culture, Continental Empires, and the Conflict That Made the Modern World* (New Haven, CT: Yale University Press, 2018), 2, 16.

13. Lambert, 301.

14. Sir Julian Corbett, not Mahan, wrote in much more detail about power projection and joint warfare. See Kevin D. McCranie, *Mahan, Corbett, and the Foundations of Naval Strategic Thought* (Annapolis: Naval Institute Press, 2021), 191–206.

15. Thomas Wildenberg, *All the Factors of Victory: Admiral Joseph Mason Reeves and the Origins of Carrier Air Power* (Washington, DC: Potomac Books, 2003), 106–13.

16. Steven T. Ross, *American War Plans, 1890–1939* (London: Frank Cass, 2002), 93–160. See also William R. Braisted, "On the

American Red and Red-Orange Plans, 1919–1939," in Gerald Jordan, ed., *Naval Warfare in the Twentieth Century, 1900–1945* (London: Croom Helm, 1977), 167–85.

17. Interestingly, the passage of the Immigration Act of 1924 may have partially neutralized the issue in American domestic politics but had no appreciable effect on the calculation of Japan as a potential enemy.

18. Captain H. E. Yarnell, "Strategy of the Pacific," lecture delivered before the Army General Staff College, Washington, DC, September 9, 1919, roll 6, entry A1-4, RG 38, National Archives and Records Administration, College Park, MD.

19. Admiral Harry Yarnell to Admiral William Leahy, October 15, 1937, President's Secretarial File, Departmental: Navy Department, October 1936–37, Franklin Delano Roosevelt Library.

20. Ryan Wadle, "Failing to Speak the Same Language: The Roots of 'Jointness' in the United States, 1919–1941," *Journal of Military History* 84, no. 4 (2020): 1119.

21. Ronald Spector, *Professors of War: The Naval War College and the Development of the Naval Profession* (Newport, RI: Naval War College Press, 1977), 144–51; Michael Vlahos, *The Blue Sword: The Naval War College and the American Mission, 1919–1941* (Newport: Naval War College Press, 1980), 131–56.

22. Hone, *Learning War*, 140–43.

23. Albert A. Nofi, *To Train the Fleet for War: The U.S. Navy Fleet Problems, 1923–1940* (Newport, RI: Naval War College Press, 2010), 1–9; Friedman, Hone, and Mandeles, *American and British Aircraft Carrier Development*, 53, 81–82. See also Mark Allen Campbell, "The Influence of Air Power upon the Evolution of Battle Doctrine in the U.S. Navy, 1922–1941" (master's thesis, University of Massachusetts at Boston, 1992).

24. Emily O. Goldman, *Power in Uncertain Times: Creating Strategy in the Fog of Peace* (Palo Alto, CA: Stanford Security Studies, 2011), 78–124. See also Emily O. Goldman, "International Competition and Military Effectiveness: Naval Air Power, 1919–1945," in Risa Brooks and Elizabeth Stanley, eds., *Creating Military Power: The Sources of Military Effectiveness* (Stanford, CA: Stanford University Press, 2007), 158–85; and Kendrick Kuo, "Military Innovation

and Technological Determinism: British and US Ways of Carrier Warfare, 1919–1945," *Journal of Global Security Studies* 6, no. 3 (2021): 1–19.

25. John T. Kuehn, *Agents of Innovation: The General Board and the Design of the Fleet That Defeated the Japanese Navy* (Annapolis: Naval Institute Press, 2009); Norman Friedman, *U.S. Battleships: An Illustrated Design History* (Annapolis: Naval Institute Press, 1985), 189–207; Norman Friedman, "Naval Strategy and Force Structure," in John H. Maurer and Christopher M. Bell, eds., *At the Crossroads between Peace and War: The London Naval Conference of 1930* (Annapolis: Naval Institute Press, 2014), 216–18; Joel Ira Holwitt, *"Execute against Japan": The U.S. Decision to Conduct Unrestricted Submarine Warfare* (College Station: Texas A&M University Press, 2009), 67–75.

26. Admiral William Veazie Pratt, who served as the Chief of Naval Operations from 1930 until 1933, was ostracized by the naval officer corps for his support for naval arms limitations. See Gerald Wheeler, *Admiral William Veazie Pratt, U.S. Navy: A Sailor's Life* (Washington, DC: Government Printing Office, 1974), 185–86, 342, 355.

27. Edward S. Miller, *War Plan Orange: The U.S. Strategy to Defeat Japan, 1897–1945* (Annapolis: Naval Institute Press, 1991), 167–79.

28. Jeter A. Isely and Philip A. Crowl, *The U.S. Marines and Amphibious War: Its Theory and Its Practice in the Pacific* (Princeton, NJ: Princeton University Press, 1951), 3; Allan R. Millett, *Semper Fidelis: The History of the United States Marine Corps*, rev. and expanded ed. (New York: Free Press, 1991), 335–43, 349–50. See also David John Ulbrich, *Preparing for Victory: Thomas Holcomb and the Making of the Modern Marine Corps, 1936–1943* (Annapolis: Naval Institute Press, 2011), 45, 55, 94–97.

29. Nofi, *To Train the Fleet for War*, 290–91.

30. Norman Friedman, *Winning a Future War: Wargaming and Victory in the Pacific War* (Washington, DC: Naval History and Heritage Command, 2017), 173–74.

31. Craig C. Felker, *Testing American Sea Power: U.S. Navy Strategic Exercises, 1923–1940* (College Station: Texas A&M University Press, 2006), 85–87.

32. Michael Gannon, *Operation Drumbeat: The Dramatic True Story of Germany's First U-Boat Attacks along the American Coast in World War II* (New York: Harper and Row, 1990), 390–94; Werner Rahn, "The War at Sea in the Atlantic and in the Arctic Ocean," in Horst Boog, Werner Rahn, Reinhard Stumpf, and Bernd Wegner, eds., *Germany and the Second World War*, Vol. 6, *The Global War* (Oxford: Oxford University Press, 2015), 369–79; Craig L. Symonds, *World War II at Sea: A Global History* (New York: Oxford University Press, 2018), 240–48; Phillips Payson O'Brien, *How the War Was Won: Air-Sea Power and Allied Victory in World War II* (Cambridge: Cambridge University Press, 2015), 234–41.

33. O'Brien, *How the War Was Won*, 256, 262.

34. For a close critique of King during the Battle of the Atlantic, see Thomas B. Buell, *Master of Seapower: A Biography of Admiral Ernest J. King* (Boston: Little, Brown, 1980; Annapolis: Naval Institute Press, 1995), 282–99.

35. Paul S. Dull, *A Battle History of the Imperial Japanese Navy, 1941–1945* (Annapolis: Naval Institute Press, 1978), 35–93.

36. Carl Boyd and Akihiko Yoshida, *The Japanese Submarine Force and World War II* (Annapolis: Naval Institute Press, 1995), xi–xiii, 53–112, 189–90; Glen Williford, *Racing the Sunrise: Reinforcing America's Pacific Outposts, 1941–1942* (Annapolis: Naval Institute Press, 2010), 302. Many early supply ships traveled unescorted, and convoys often traveled with only cruisers as their escorts.

37. Quoted from Buell, *Master of Seapower*, 299.

38. Trent Hone, "Mastering the Masters: The U.S. Navy, 1942–1944," in Vincent P. O'Hara and Trent Hone, eds., *Fighting in the Dark: Naval Combat at Night, 1904–1944* (Annapolis: Naval Institute Press, 2023), 182–90.

39. Hone, *Learning War*, 212–15, 223–25, 228–32. See also Timothy S. Wolters, *Information at Sea: Shipboard Command and Control from Mobile Bay to Okinawa* (Baltimore: Johns Hopkins University Press, 2013), 170–221.

40. Blair, *Silent Victory*, 359–62.

41. Buford Rowland and William B. Boyd, *U.S. Navy Bureau of Ordnance in World War II* (Washington, DC: Government Printing Office, 1953), 90–131. See also Audrey Duke, "The Quest to

Achieve 'One Accurate Shot': U.S. Navy Torpedo Development and Testing, 1896–1917" (certificate thesis, U.S. Naval War College, 2023), https://apps.dtic.mil/sti/trecms/pdf/AD1203110.pdf.

42. Blair, *Silent Victory*, 243–45.
43. Clark G. Reynolds, "The Fleet in Being Strategy of 1942," *Journal of Military History* 58 (January 1994): 103–18; Jonathan Parshall and Anthony Tully, *Shattered Sword: The Untold Story of the Battle of Midway* (Washington, DC: Potomac Books, 2005), 32–33; and Craig L. Symonds, *The Battle of Midway* (Oxford: Oxford University Press, 2011), 97–106.
44. Wildenberg, *All the Factors of Victory*, 120–95; Thomas Wildenberg, *Destined for Glory: Dive Bombing, Midway, and the Evolution of Carrier Airpower* (Annapolis: Naval Institute Press, 1998), xiii–xiv, 183–216; Mark R. Peattie, *Sunburst: The Rise of Japanese Naval Airpower, 1909–1941* (Annapolis: Naval Institute Press, 2001), 47–50; Michael W. Myers, *The Pacific War and Contingent Victory: Why Japanese Defeat Was Not Inevitable* (Lawrence: University Press of Kansas), 36–37.
45. Eric M. Bergerud, *Fire in the Sky: The Air War in the South Pacific* (New York: Basic Books, 2000), 463–65.
46. Dull, *Battle History*, 113–32, 145–71, 197–208, 227–35.

CHAPTER SEVEN

JANUS AND MARS

FRENCH NAVAL AND DEFENSE PLANNING IN THE INTERWAR YEARS, 1922-40

Martin S. Alexander

f there was anything certain about attempting naval planning and defense procurement during the kaleidoscopic and anarchic world of no less than seven competing great powers in the interwar years, it was that uncertainty ruled. Each admiralty, each naval ministry, had to worry about threats to their east and their west, and some to their south. The Royal Navy tried to prepare for war in three theaters, against three separate foes. American attention twisted between its Atlantic and Pacific fronts. Italian admirals looked for war against France but fretted anxiously about fighting the French navy's partner, Britain's Royal Navy. What was more, every claim for more naval construction had to stand against rival claims for extra army divisions, or more bomber squadrons. Even within navies, planning forecasts threw up disputes and disagreements: Would large battleships be the best guarantor of naval mastery in a future war, or carrier divisions, or the ever more dangerous submarine fleets?

Before we pass judgment on those who built and ran the French navy of the interwar years and the war plans they devised for possible future conflict, we should recollect this larger, relative context. After all, ever since the emergence of rival, egoistical nation-states from the 1500s onward, the great powers had strenuously competed against one another and demanded that their armed services be able to do the same. In consequence, this laid a heavy burden on the senior staffs of every army and navy. Crystal ball–gazing was no easier for service chiefs between 1922 and 1939–40 than in earlier or later eras of statecraft. As a previous volume that examined the powers from the early nineteenth century to the high Cold War put it, planning and futureproofing has always occurred in the chilly, gray, and swirling "fog of peace." Naturally, the publicity for that volume further asked, "How do we plan under conditions of uncertainty? Do military planners see themselves as preparing to administer a peace, or preparing to fight a future war?"[1]

France and its naval planners faced specific dilemmas, and this chapter focuses primarily on naval planning in France. But that planning, it needs to be clearly understood, was part of a coherent structure that addressed overall war aims. Perhaps for several powers it was harder than it was for France, the geostrategic binds arising at a time when most powers with substantial militaries still had empires on several continents. And those territories, whether constituting a near-abroad like Morocco-Algeria-Tunisia for France or a far-flung colony like Indochina, offered both the symbols and substance of prestige and power. Nonetheless they had, after 1919, become just as much points of vulnerability.[2] In Paul Kennedy's phrase made notorious, France like all the other powers faced "imperial overstretch."

Complicating these structural challenges was the fast pace of technological change. Because ever-newer and more powerful weapons appeared in these years, it might be unwise to pour too much money into, say, a new type of tank, or plane, or submarine. Five years was now enough for 1934 designs to be obsolete as war began. As recent publications on this phenomenon explain, technical designers and inventors were fast becoming the "wizards of Armageddon."[3] With this "technological turn," so to speak, the powers with comparatively weaker industrial bases faced detriment. Italy was an easy example here and soon became Europe's "man of straw," even if the bombastic Mussolini disregarded counsels that told him Italian military clout was deficient, and plunged his country into overseas ventures for which Italy's armed forces were ill equipped in Ethiopia from 1935 onward and the Spanish Civil War in 1937–38.[4]

Italy was always, in Richard Bosworth's telling phrase, "the least of the Great Powers," whereas France was unquestionably potent.[5] All the same, France also faced serious problems for its defense after 1919. The country was, as Robert Doughty has aptly termed it, "the Pyrrhic victor" among the Allies. It had suffered appalling exsanguination: 16.2 percent (i.e., 1.39 million) of Frenchmen who enlisted in 1914–18 were killed. Another 3 million had been wounded, a third of them so badly maimed they could never work again.[6] A shocking number of French adult men after 1919 were sickeningly disfigured after collisions on the western front battlefields between *chair et acier* (in Michel Goya's chilling words)—hot and jagged steel smashing into human flesh. For France, 1919 was a victory of much more pain than gain. The nation emerged in a kind of shroud of sad grandeur, to face two generations of misery (in the formula of Georges "Tiger" Clemenceau, prime minister 1917–20).[7]

To this demographic and psychological damage must be added the ways geography had bequeathed France a challenging position vis-à-vis its aggressive Italian and German neighbors—and put the metropole or "hexagon" (i.e., mainland continental France), far from its imperial resources and reserves. Thus, France's strategic and operational dilemmas of the interwar decades—and not just for the French navy but all its armed forces—meant it faced very particular difficulties to achieve homeland security.

Security for the "hexagon" was, however, the principal demand made as a whole on the French navy and fleet commanders after 1919, and urgently after 1935: Can you, in these incredibly difficult and worrying circumstances, give your country, a weakened yet still substantial great power, both safety from foreign foes and a chance of victory against them in the event of another world war?

What, then, about the specifics of France's military and naval planning, enemy net assessment, and war preparations? The remainder of this chapter will consider these issues for this troubled and Janus-faced power, from around 1931 till the recast required after France's defeat and armistice in June–July 1940.

France's most familiar defense project between the world wars was the Maginot Line—a fortified zone to block off one hundred miles of eastern frontier and the whole of Alsace and Lorraine. The fortifications had a clear purpose on a grander scale too: to be a force multiplier. The French army, as just noted, had bled white in World War I. Therefore after 1919 it came to rely on restricting the battlefields where combat might reoccur. By delimiting future killing grounds, France could optimize precious manpower.

Even these measures would be insufficient if forces were raised only from metropolitan France—even given additional frontier security by the Maginot Line. After retiring from the French high command in January 1935, General Maxime Weygand wrote in October 1936 in the *Revue des deux mondes* (a periodical much quoted by the chattering class in Paris) that "France with its population of forty million, many of them elderly, cannot pretend to arm so many men as a youthful Germany of sixty million." By lowering the age of conscription for military service, the French army managed after autumn 1936 to increase the recruits incorporated annually from 230,000 to 280,000.[8]

Of special alarm to the French defense elite in the mid-1930s was the long land border with their poorly protected neighbor, Belgium. This risked being a "a fatal avenue," as then Lieutenant Colonel Charles de Gaulle described it, along which German invading armies could advance straight to Paris. Farther southeast, the frontier with Italy was shorter. The French army could anchor its left flank on the Alps, and defense plans there demanded fewer troops and fortifications. Italy, even under its Fascist regime after 1922, was by no means regarded—in contrast to a revanchist Germany—as an inevitable enemy. When France's 1927–28 Army Acts were invoked in March

1935 to lengthen conscription to two years, some retired generals urged bigger measures. "The immediate support of British armored brigades," wrote General Baratier, last chief of staff to Marshal Foch and now military chronicler for the newspaper Le Temps, "and everything Italy will be able to give France seems indispensable." Italy's friendship, or at least benevolent neutrality, was discussed in Rome in June 1935 between Weygand's successor, General Maurice Gamelin, and the Italian chief of general staff, Marshal Pietro Badoglio. An understanding might, it was thought, permit the bulk of French imperial reinforcements to move safely to Europe and concentrate against Germany.[9]

If Italy became an unfriendly neutral or enemy, the threat from the German menace would make French imperial manpower crucial for French defense. "Overseas France" (La France Outre-Mer) had supplied supplementary troops for French operations in World War I. Those contingents had arrived thanks to far-sighted geostrategic thinking over several decades. In the years 1892–1905 Joseph Galliéni, a general who served in Indochina and then as governor of Madagascar, and Louis-Hubert Lyautey, French proconsul in Morocco, urged the harnessing of imperial manpower, plus the minerals and raw materials needed in munitions manufacture. In 1911, a book of startling boldness appeared from General Charles Mangin. It sketched out a strategy to match Germany's intrinsically superior military capability by means of drawing a compensating "Black Force" (La Force Noire) recruited in the colonies. To be utilized were the supposedly "martial races" of French Equatorial and West Africa, plus draft labor from Indochina and the French Antilles. Mangin offered a vision wherein overseas formations would spring forth as from human reservoirs. Not long after, this vision was realized: the French army recruited over 140,000 West Africans into combat assignments on the 1914–18 western front.[10]

After 1919 it was essential that France keep its overseas military assets at the heart of strategic plans. The military manpower pool at home was just too low. In the 1920s the birthrate in metropolitan France dropped, owing to 1.39 million young French men having been recently killed. In a remark aimed as an external deter‑ rent as much as a domestic morale‑booster, Weygand said in Decem‑ ber 1938 that any power challenging the Third Republic must reckon on confronting not just 39 million mainland French but legions from La France Outre‑Mer. The African manpower reservoir, one listener noted, "inspires General Weygand to refer to France and French Africa as one country with a population of 110 million and to urge his countrymen to realize and make use of this fact."[11]

Overseas troops and colonial labor would need maritime trans‑ port to the theaters of operations, as well as to factories and building yards. So here was a core mission for the French navy—one that required well‑regulated and protected convoys of freight ships; secure SLOCS (sea lines of communication); ports equipped with cranes; oil storage tanks and fueling pipes; and rail tracks laid to the docksides. Maritime infrastructure on this scale would then enable soldiers and laborers from France overseas to arrive wherever they were needed— and be secure in transit and speedy in arrival. Therefore France in the 1930s invested steeply in its merchant marine as well as in new French navy warships.

For centuries France had been a major maritime actor. In World War I its fleet had been free to concentrate in the Mediterranean, with just a few dispersed squadrons, thanks to the 1912 Anglo‑French naval accord. The interwar years were more difficult. A serious wob‑ ble in relations with London occurred when the Royal Navy "sailed solo" to conclude its own deal on warship ratios with Nazi Germany in 1935, announced with crass insensitivity on June 18 (120 years to the day since the Battle of Waterloo). But France had embarked four years before, after the 1930 London Naval Conference, on a large‑ scale program to build new and state‑of‑the art fighting ships. Driv‑ ing developments was the minister Georges Leygues, a parliamentary deputy from the Lot‑et‑Garonne. Laying a strong claim to be called "the father of the modern French navy," Leygues served as minister of marine in 1926–30 and 1932–35. One French fleet executive officer in those years—later an admiral—wrote that the 1930s saw French people "really get an interest in their Navy." Leygues and his successors brilliantly grasped "how to manage the inevitable political horse-trading, and work with teams of remarkable officers such as Admiral [Louis] Violette and Admiral [Georges] Durand-Viel, so that they surmounted the financial, administrative and technical difficulties they faced."[12]

As a result the French fleet and its shore establishments enjoyed cross-party backing and the necessary finance for its building programs. Consistency in the choice of naval materials and in the annual budget exercise was the hallmark of successive navy ministers after Leygues, namely François Piétri, César Campinchi, and Alphonse Gasnier-Duparc. With this support the modernization and expansion launched by Leygues gained momentum and advanced apace.

Besides these astute navy ministers, France in the 1930s had a senior naval officer corps of rare talent. Standing out were Vice Admirals Durand-Viel (1875–1959), Chief of Naval Staff (CNS) 1931–36, and his successor Jean-Francois Darlan (1881–1942), CNS January 1937–41, along with Admiral Raoul Castex (1878–1968), France's greatest naval theoretician. Castex wrote the five-volume *Theories stratégiques*, published in 1939. He applied cold logic rather than romantic dreams to strategic ends-means calculations. Above all, Castex insisted unsentimentally that naval commitments must align with naval capabilities and recognize that, if a war came about, distant Indochina would be indefensible.[13]

The officers beneath Durand-Viel and Darlan were tried and trusted professionals, with extensive seagoing command experience that they alternated with stints at the Naval Staff College and in advisory posts with government ministers. Still others in 1939–40 undertook liaison to the Admiralty in London, fashioning a work manlike if not always completely cordial partnership with the Royal Navy (French Atlantic division units, including the battle cruiser *Dunkerque*, patrolled in the 1939–40 winter in formation with warships of the Home Fleet including the battle cruiser HMS *Hood*).[14]

The armed forces of France—as those of every nation's armed forces—needed a "brain" to guide them, and a capable system for strategic assessment. Historians of the interwar era describe how almost all the powers, middling and great alike, were unavoidably Janus-faced as they peered through the fog to discern the contours of future war. None had especially well-developed bureaucratic machinery to produce agreed-on, coherent, and consistent grand strategy. But Britain and France came closest. The former's Committee of Imperial Defence (CID) had existed since 1902. Global thinking about war and resources for war was the remit of the Imperial Defence College, established in 1926. To this apparatus was bolted in 1936 the newly formed Joint Intelligence Committee (JIC). And in France there was from 1906 a CSDN (Superior Council for National Defense), enhanced in 1932 by the establishment of the HCM (High Military Committee) for interservice discussions. The HCM evolved in summer 1936 to become the CPDN (Permanent Committee of National Defense), and the army minister of the day, then Edouard Daladier, was made minister for national defense and war. In January 1938 France's most distinguished active-duty soldier, General Gamelin, became the first chief of French national defense staff.[15]

France and Britain therefore compared favorably with the dysfunctional and disjointed Third Reich military procurement and planning processes. In the Axis capitals military strategizing and resource allocations remained a primeval jungle where "beast ate beast." It may be averred that disconnected or "parallel" wars were waged by imperial Japan's army in China; by its navy in the Pacific and East Indies; and by Germany and Italy in Europe and Africa.[16]

Were matters better in the United States? It is arguable. The War Department under Henry L. Stimson and the Navy Department of Secretary Frank Knox did not major in coordination. Not only did the U.S. Army and U.S. Navy retain separate air corps until 1947; the fragile linkages within the U.S. strategic planning apparatus also gave long life to discrepancies between U.S. Navy and U.S. Army plans—with feeble political-bureaucratic means to reconcile divergent views as between the two services. In comparison, perhaps the setups of France and Britain by 1939 appear quite impressive, even coherent, efficient, and resilient. They were democracies well equipped with bureaucracies of war.

Throughout this period, the French fleet trained for multiple roles. One that is noteworthy but rarely highlighted was its mission assigned from September 7, 1938, to defend the airspace of littoral France. The navy's core function was, however, to help the Royal Navy enforce a blockade on Germany and maintain the SLOCs so that Allied merchant shipping had freedom of movement. The realities of power and the extensive French metropolitan littoral from the North Sea, along the Bay of Biscay and into the Mediterranean, meant France's naval posture never veered far from the priorities of the Admiralty in London. As Paul Reynaud—a political leader of the Democratic Alliance conservatives and a past and future prime minister—put it in the Chamber of Deputies on December 27, 1935, during the height of the Ethiopian crisis, "If we get separated from England, it means war."[17] Schemes of offensive operations were mooted in the summer of 1939, with Anglo-French colonial and naval planning and joint staff work taking place in May, June, and August in meetings at Rabat (Morocco) and Djibouti, as well as in London and Paris. Valuable coordination was also agreed by the respective senior navy, army, and air officers in work done together at Singapore from June 22 to 29, 1939, led by Admiral Sir Percy Noble for the British and conducted in what Admiral Decoux, the senior French officer, termed "an atmosphere of comradely trust."[18] The French fleet of 1939 owed much to many actors, civilian and military, but "first and foremost to parliament which . . . voted with splendid regularity the budgetary allocations that were asked of it."[19] This echoes Admiral Philippon's view that it is no slight on Leygues and Piétri, Darlan, Durand-Viel and Violette to "underline how from 1926 to 1939, parliament accorded pretty much continuous support to their vast [naval] enterprise."[20]

French forces were primarily responsible for the SLOCs to North Africa, which had increased in importance as a result of interwar investments in cargo-handling facilities, docking capacity, oil storage tanks, and railway freight uplift from the quays. The chief beneficiaries were Oran in Algeria, along with Bizerte and Sousse in Tunisia. Improvement of the infrastructure was keenly monitored by the French legislature's defense committees. These projects gained backing from 1937 onward from sympathetic parliamentarians such as Edmond Miellet and Henri Ponsot who tutored themselves on the strategic issues by visiting French North Africa. By 1939–40 a coastal network of rail tracks linked the ports of Algeria to those of Tunisia.

The vulnerability of factories near the frontiers to a surprise attack meant that planners were justifiably concerned with the industrial districts crammed with coal mining and steel production adjoining Belgium and Germany, which was the expected main battlefront in a future European conflict. Nevertheless, the French North African frontiers also got attention. Albeit incomplete by July 1940, from late 1937, this effort started to establish munitions, artillery, aeroengine, and airframe manufacturing, along with more training facilities, in dispersed locations in the French Empire's "strategic hinterland," where it would be far less vulnerable to German or Italian air attack.[21]

France did not come close to the shift of Soviet war industry behind the Urals in 1941–42. But France did display vision and systematic planning born of the same grand strategy. Withstanding an opening enemy onslaught, and then enduring while reserves mobilized, were central themes in French planning. But no one in Paris thought a future war winnable by defense alone. Rolling back and defeating enemies would be the work of later French and Allied offensives after a middle phase of stalemate and "wearing down." For as it was spelled out in June 1937 by General Denis-Auguste Duchêne, "The simplistic system of a Wall of China, no matter how solid and well-defended, must be rejected. An army for the defensive is an army for defeat."[22]

With regard to warships and bases, the French navy had built a substantial submarine force of thirty-nine boats with three more in construction, and plans for another two got the green light in 1940; there were also forty existing coastal submarines, eight under construction, and twelve more authorized. Coastal submarines were well suited to the Mediterranean, where larger submarines were easily detected.

The French Channel division's harbors, crammed with stockpiled shells, fuel, and provisions, lay at Dunkerque, Le Havre, and Cherbourg (the last sheltering three torpedo boats and four coastal submarines). The Atlantic Fleet was disposed between Brest, Lorient, and Dakar (Senegal). Brest was the base of France's sole aircraft carrier *Béarn* (launched 1927), three torpedo-boat destroyers, twelve fleet destroyers, and twelve submarines, along with the 1st Fleet Squadron's two battleships, a further two elderly training battleships, three light cruisers, and six destroyers. A further three torpedo boats were at Lorient. Dakar was the base for four light cruisers, one being detached at Casablanca and another to France's Caribbean territories of Guadeloupe, Martinique, and Guyane.

The Mediterranean Fleet anchored at Toulon, Bizerte, and Mers el-Kebir. Toulon sheltered three destroyers, six torpedo boats, eleven patrol submarines, eight coastal submarines, and eight training submarines. Toulon also accommodated 3rd Fleet Squadron, with its six heavy cruisers and twelve torpedo-boat destroyers. Bizerte, for its part, had been substantially improved in the later 1930s. It was the home port for six patrol and eight coastal submarines, and 4th Squadron's four light cruisers and six destroyers. Mers el-Kebir was the base of 2nd Fleet Squadron, with the three *Bretagne*-class modernized battleships (originally built 1910–12) and nine destroyers. This force distribution allowed mitigation against a surprise attack. The key warships of the French fleet were never amassed like eggs in one basket. Powerful escorts for merchant shipping were likewise assured by means of fleet subunits whose officers were familiar from peacetime exercises with the approaches and tides at each end point of the voyages across the Mediterranean.

In more distant waters, however, the French were stretched thin. Beirut, headquarters for the territories of the French Levant (Syria and Lebanon), had just three patrol submarines; Casablanca, two destroyers and four patrol submarines; Saigon, a heavy cruiser and a light cruiser. Admiral Jean Decoux, dispatched to Indochina in April 1939 to take over as commander in chief, quickly learned what his colleague, Castex, had prophesied: the territory was too distant and too vast, with insufficient armament or factories to make more on the spot. It would have no chance of reinforcement or survival if fighting spread to the Far East and engulfed it.[23]

Meanwhile, if the Marine Nationale faced a fight with Italy, it was confident it could win. French intelligence on Mussolini's fleet was well informed and assisted a radical recalibration of French strategic thinking about Italy that amounted to a very fast turn from treating Rome and its forces as a likely ally to preparing against Italy as probable enemy. So after 1936 the face of the French Janus presented a sterner countenance.

Italian military support for Franco's Nationalist cause in Spain raised the stakes: some ministers in the French center-left Popular Front government of 1936–37 angled to supply weapons to the Spanish Republicans while the French fleet shadowed Italian and German warships in the western Mediterranean and along the Atlantic coast of Iberia. While maintaining wary communications with the Italian navy, French warships joined the patrols agreed under the Nyon Accord—a League of Nations arrangement to prevent seaborne resupply to Spain's belligerents.[24]

Assuring the quarantine helped hone the French navy's battle readiness by revising its tactical procedures, practicing its signal drills, and undertaking greater volumes of live firing at towed targets. The naval archives and parliamentary papers point to a "colonial-naval school" coalescing informally by 1939–40. This loose grouping of like-minded service chiefs and ministers was ready, one might almost say eager, to fight Italy and knock down Mussolini's regime. In Paul Halpern's summation, "Darlan's plans in the event of war with Italy were aggressive."[25]

Perspectives depended to an extent on whether in Paris the French strategic glass was viewed as half-empty or half-full.[26] By 1939 France's naval renaissance was one factor underpinning greater confidence about the Mediterranean and East Africa. The *Dunkerque* (laid down in 1932) and the *Strasbourg* that soon followed were fast and heavily armed, "built allegedly as 'a reply' to the German 10,000 ton armor-clad ships (the three *Deutschland* type pocket-battleships) but also with an eye to the up-and-coming Italy."[27] The editor of the bellwether *Jane's Fighting Ships* wrote in the annual volume's foreword for 1939, "[An] exceptionally heavy programme of new construction has been initiated in France. With two supplementary votes, the total number of ships provided for under the 1938–39 Estimates exceeds 100, a record for recent times." Some improvement in the pace of building warships had been achieved. Nevertheless, continued *Jane's* editor, "it still lags behind that of Germany and Italy."[28] The new battleships were fast nearing completion, along with large quantities of light cruisers, destroyers and submarines, all crewed by 70,000 men with proportionately more career sailors than was the case with the army's manpower.

In Spain, moreover, the Italian army had lost men, material, and morale. It once more failed to secure a speedy and prestige-boosting overseas victory when, in April 1939, it invaded Albania but got bogged down. Substantial Italian ground troops and air squadrons meanwhile remained stuck in East Africa where Ethiopia remained uncharted and unconquered. That was despite the deployment of Mussolini's best general, Pietro Badoglio, and 400,000 troops that got split between garrison work, lines of communication, and counter-insurgency.[29] Whether or not opportunities existed for France and Britain to knock out Mussolini from the Rome-Berlin Axis, French leaders maintained focus on their assumed "big war": the one against next-door Nazi Germany. In this regard, Admiral Castex "recognized the crucially important role that the exercise of naval mastery often has in strategically positioning land forces against even the most redoubtable continental opponent."[30]

It was just as well that the French naval leadership with strong support in Parliament had got the fleet, maritime SLOCS, and well-resourced shore bases in such good shape, because the French air force, by contrast, was utterly unready in 1939. It had been a doctrinal football, kicked between the apostles of strategic bombing and the rival high priests of tactical support to the ground forces. Too many air armament programs had come and gone, amid breathtaking technological advances and near-instant obsolescence for aircraft. The French Parliament had agreed in 1928 to upgrade the war ministry's aeronautical undersecretariat to a full-fledged third service. Laurent Eynac became the first French air minister, a post he held till December 1930, and again from March to June 1940 under Paul Reynaud's premiership. Moreover, by 1933 the separate service had the structures to fashion air strategy, with an air staff and an Ecole de L'Air for officer training, independent of the army. Air rearmament schemes followed suit from Plan II in 1934 to Plan V in 1938–39. Damagingly, however, a "policy of prototypes" meant aircraft were made in tiny batches by too many companies, from non-interoperable designs. Only 650 airworthy modern machines stood on French airfields in May 1940.[31]

Insufficient airpower undermined, partly, the confidence possessed by France's land and naval services toward Italy. Concern about vulnerability to Italian strikes from the sky against Toulon and Marseilles forced the basing of some of the limited air assets in southern France. Even in September 1939 it was judged essential by the chief of air staff, General Joseph Vuillemin, and the air minister, Guy La Chambre, to state plainly to the prime minister, Edouard Daladier, that the air force could not sustain combat operations before another six months of rearmament and aircrew training had taken place—that is, not before April 1940. Better this, however, than the forecast in 1938 that war for Czechoslovakia would see the annihilation of French aviation in two weeks.[32] Ironically, in the eighteen months after that, matters improved, though unavailingly in the end. "I am not saying this of our bombardment aviation where we could not catch up lost time," wrote General Giraud in his after-action report on the 1940 defeat, "but our facilities in Morocco, our French factories and American factories enabled achievement of our fighter air force."[33] Yet did that matter if the Luftwaffe was always much stronger?

Consequently, French strategic action in the "home" theater remained confined inside long-established thinking. Once again, comparison with the British is instructive. The Royal Air Force (RAF) staff had studied Germany's bomber raids on London in 1917–18 and worried about the civilian home front and the damage a German air offensive might cause to Britain's southern and southeastern ports: Felixstowe, Harwich, Tilbury, Dover, Portsmouth, and Southampton. Stanley Baldwin, who served three terms as British prime minister between 1923 and 1937, warned in 1934 that "for our defence we must no longer think of the Channel, the white cliffs of Dover, but of the Rhine; that is where our frontier now lies."[34] France also feared devastating air attack. Almost as Baldwin made his "White Cliffs" speech, France in 1934 established a specialized new national command for the "Air Defence of the Territory." Sound-ranging and directional antennas, plus observer posts to provide early warning of inbound bomber raids, were constructed across northeastern France. All gained direct telephone links to the new national air defense headquarters. On September 15, 1939, Colonel William Fraser, Britain's military attaché in Paris, opined as Poland got defeated, "We have perhaps . . . a month before the air war starts on this side."[35] Judging the German air force much stronger than the French and RAF together, those in Paris and London "responsible for the conduct of the war obsessed about not provoking the enemy," in the words of one chief of the French Air Historical Service. Consequently, strategic actions by French aviation "never had more than a derisory scope."[36]

And the sky above Western Europe was not the only arena of inaction. Allied moves on land were also cautious and limp. French mobilization took three weeks from September 1, 1939, while

Britain's deployable army—a modest expeditionary force of just four motorized infantry divisions—was not on the French-Belgian border till early October. Allied grand strategy was predicated on a long war, something expertly examined in print by Robert Young.[37] Therefore, as Britain's military attaché wrote, "all stories of attacks on the Siegfried Line are 'bunk.'" The French general staff realized that Poland, a nominal ally, had seen through French talk of attacks into the Rhineland. The passivity of the phony war had been foretold years before. For instance, Marshal Smigly-Rydz (Polish commander in chief) returned from visiting the Maginot Line in 1936 convinced that an army that possessed such formidable defenses "would be most unlikely to venture beyond them to help its allies."[38] The Poles were of course proven correct.

Within the imperial-naval arena in 1939–40 the Allied naval authorities were transfixed by the German threat, but the French navy proved ready and well prepared for the war it got. The maritime "left flank," the littoral of the Bay of Biscay and Channel, was secured by the alliance with Britain. Heavy units of the French fleet, including *Dunkerque* and *Strasbourg*, with many cruisers and destroyers, conducted joint patrols with Royal Navy's Home Fleet and Gibraltar-based elements, including HMS *Hood*, to hunt German surface raiders such as the *Admiral Graf Spee*, run to ground in December 1939. French escort groups and covering cruiser squadrons plied up and down the African coast from Dakar and Casablanca to Brest, Nantes, and Bordeaux. Further cargo ships safely crossed the Mediterranean to Toulon and Marseilles from the Algerian and Tunisian ports of Oran, Algiers, Bône, and Bizerte, while yet more troop transports and freighters navigated the Red Sea and along the East African coast. From September 1939 French troopships and "certain high-value transports," in Paul Halpern's term, traveled in convoys with a naval escort. The sister battleships *Bretagne*, *Provence* and *Lorraine*, for example, screened a flow of military convoys between North Africa and France from September 1 to October 5, 1939. These SLOCS formed a strategic umbilical cord; no significant troopship loss was suffered. It was an impressive and overlooked achievement, one that Darlan, his planning staffs, and French crews at sea could be proud of.[39]

Eloquent tribute was also paid to the French navy by General Henri Giraud, commander of Seventh Army in 1939–40 and rival of de Gaulle for the leadership of Free France in 1942–43:

> Only the navy, one can say, was ready for war. Since 1920, methodically, patiently, the French fleet had renovated itself. As much from the standpoint of morale as material, the navy had regained confidence in itself, in its traditions, in its faith. Its ships were often better than foreign vessels in each type. Its crews were disciplined[;] . . . it had wanted to retain its own aviation and it had done. It had wanted to prove wherever it was called upon that it was superior to the German fleet, and that it was competitive with the British fleet. Wherever it was required to collaborate with the French army, the navy demonstrated a comprehension, a broad outlook and a comradeliness to which a land lubber is happy to attest after observing the happy results that were achieved.[40]

All of which is not to say that the French fleet was heavily engaged in the war's opening months. In June 1940 it floated at anchor intact, but "virtually in mothballs."[41]

That was not entirely by choice, from the perspective of French strategists. Mussolini's fence-sitting—Italy remained neutral till June 10, 1940—caused widespread frustration. Darlan's intentions were indeed aggressive. In summer 1939 operational thinking to seize the initiative in the whole Red Sea, Gulf of Suez, and Gulf of Aden region was finalized with the British Middle East service chiefs during meetings at Aden and Djibouti. Complete control of communications via the Red Sea and Suez Canal was the objective. "The best way to attain this goal is to destroy the enemy forces operating in and from Italian East Africa," they concluded.[42] This would have seen real war, not phony, given half a chance. So the uneasy peace with Italy represented a kind of missed opportunity. By January 1940 the French naval staff was crafting ambitious projects, and Admiral Darlan, their chief, "sought to use his growing influence in French strategic councils," in the words of Talbot Imlay, "to galvanize French military planning."[43] French bomber aircraft groups stood on runways no great flying time from Italy's heavy industries in Turin and Milan, and its shipyards at La Spezia and Livorno. For their part, French forces on the Alps and the Tunisia-Libya frontier were raring to go. A *Daily Mail* newspaperman reported from Gamelin, "If the Italians come in against us, we shall need 5 divisions to defeat them; if they are neutral we shall need ten divisions to watch 'em; if they come in with us, we shall need 15 divisions to reinforce 'em."[44]

So, with Italy neutral and operations against the German navy in the North very limited, the Marine Nationale, along with the colonies, survived as major components in the calculus of power right up until the British attack on the French battle squadron at Mers el-Kébir on July 3, 1940. For the British fleet, matters then took a different course. Soon the opportunity would come about through the bold carrier-launched strike against Italy's battleships at Taranto in November 1940. Sadly, that occurred too late for the fine French navy to play the parts it had trained for, because it was the Third Republic—not Fascist Italy—that got knocked out of the conflict.

Ironically the Mediterranean did become what Reynolds Salerno called the "vital crossroads" on the Allied advance to victory in Europe—though it would be 1943–44, not 1940–41, before the Axis was assaulted from the south.[45] Knowing this later outcome, we may feel that things could have been very different. "Had the French Navy rallied to the Allies" after the armistice of June 1940 or even just before the Toulon squadron's scuttling to forestall German capture in November 1942, judged Chalmers Hood, "it would have provided overwhelming maritime superiority in the European theatre, possibly releasing more Anglo-American forces for duty against Japan."[46] Even prior to that, such superiority would surely have annihilated Mussolini's imperial pretensions. Furthermore, though the French fleet was bombarded by its former British ally at Mers el-Kébir, the units that survived remained potent. As Paul W. Doerr noted, reviewing George Melton's book on interwar Anglo-French naval relations, "The *Dunkerque* was damaged, not destroyed, and the *Strasbourg* escaped to Toulon, where it headed a formidable force of cruisers, destroyers, and some seventy-odd submarines. Meanwhile the *Richelieu* and the incomplete *Jean Bart* escaped destruction at Dakar and Casablanca, respectively. Melton concludes that Mers el-Kébir actually worsened Britain's strategic situation. Fortunately, nothing came of the potential threat from the Vichy navy."[47] How to sum up this poignant French case? Although France was a beaten power in Europe and adjusting to Hitler's "New Order," it possessed, ironically, an unbeaten navy. Darlan's fleet had "done its bit."[48] French interwar strategists were correct that their navy and empire's power to strike back would be crucial to winning the next war; but they were right, also, that mainland France itself had to avoid defeat. A splendid set of warships and admirals might, one feels, have contributed far more in World War II, had the French army and air force done "their bit" a lot better in 1940.[49]

Perhaps the shock of that summer masks how the case of interwar France was not really so different from that of most other powers. None had a clairvoyant to show them beyond doubt what their armed forces would have to face, survive, and overcome. All sensed they would be unwise to prepare for a conflict of just one kind or in just one theater. Was there ever a case where the armed forces of any nation, however powerful, could be confident they were planning correctly for future war? One doubts it, even for today's United States. Writing of the U.S. military after the Iraq and Afghanistan interventions of the 2000s, Max Boot has argued that "irregular warfare . . . doesn't mean that the US can ignore the dangers of major warfighting. . . . Innovation must be organizational as much as technological, and it needs to focus on potential threats across the entire spectrum."[50] Welcome to the 1920s and 1930s—for such counsel seems as pertinent as ever in the 2020s and 2030s.

NOTES

1. Description of Talbot C. Imlay and Monica Duffy Toft, *The Fog of Peace and War Planning: Military and Strategic Planning under Uncertainty* (London: Taylor & Francis, 2006), at https://www.routledge.com/The-Fog-of-Peace-and-War-Planning-Military-and-Strategic-Planning-under/Imlay-Toft/p/book/9780415366977 (accessed April 19, 2022).

2. Admiral Jean Decoux, *A la Barre de L'Indochina: Histoire de mon Gouvernement-Général (1940–1945)* (Paris: Plon, 1949), 3–39, 73–83; Christopher M. Andrew and A. S. Kanya-Forstner, *France Overseas: The Great War and the Climax of French Imperial Expansion* (London: Thames & Hudson, 1981).

3. Acknowledging Fred Lawrence Kaplan's seminal book on the Cold War nuclear technocrats, *The Wizards of Armageddon* (New York: Simon & Schuster, 1983).

4. See Robert Mallett, *The Italian Navy and Fascist Expansionism, 1935–1940* (London: Taylor & Francis, 1998); John Gooch, *Mussolini's Generals: The Armed Forces and Fascist Foreign Policy, 1922–1940* (Cambridge: Cambridge University Press, 2007).

5. R. J. B. Bosworth, *Italy, the Least of the Great Powers: Italian Foreign Policy before the First World War* (Cambridge: Cambridge University Press, 1979).

6. Robert A. Doughty, *Pyrrhic Victory: French Strategy and Operations in the Great War* (Cambridge, MA: Belknap Press of Harvard University Press, 2005).

7. Georges Clemenceau, *Grandeurs et misères d'une victoire* (Paris: Plon, 1930).

8. General Weygand, "L'état militaire de la France," *Revue des deux mondes* 35 (October 15, 1936): 721–36 (esp. 730, 736).

9. Baratier to Reynaud, April 3, 1935, Papiers Paul Reynaud 74AP12, Archives Nationales (AN), Pierrefitte, France; cf. Martin Thomas, "At the Heart of Things? French Imperial Defense Planning in the Late 1930s," *French Historical Studies* 21, no. 2 (1998): 325–61.

10. Martin Thomas, *The French Empire between the Wars: Imperialism, Politics and Society* (Manchester: Manchester University Press, 2005), 17–28; Claude Carlier, *Les troupes coloniales dans la Grande Guerre* (Paris: Economica, 1999).

11. Great Britain: The National Archives: Public Record Office (hereafter TNA-PRO), FO371 series: General Correspondence File 22915: C16018/36/17: Col. William Fraser: "Appreciation of the French Strategic Policy after Munich," December 22, 1938, 3.

12. Vice-amiral Hilarion Philippon, *Le métier de la mer* (Paris: France-Empire, 1971), 139–40.

13. R. Castex, *Strategic Theories*, selections translated and edited, with an introduction, by Eugenia C. Kiesling (Annapolis: Naval Institute Press, 1994). Similarly for Britain, see Christopher M. Bell, "'Our Most Exposed Outpost': Hong Kong and British Far Eastern Strategy, 1921–1941," *Journal of Military History* 60, no. 1 (1996): 61–88. Other notable French interwar admirals were Marcel Gensoul (1880–1973) and Emmanuel Ollive (1882–1950), Jean-Pierre Estéva (1880–1951), Jean Decoux (1884–1963), Jean-Marie Abrial (1879–1962), Célestin Bourragué (1886–1955), Jean-Ernest Odend'hal (1884–1957), Paul Auphan (1894–1982), and Pierre Muselier (1882–1965). The last-named became the first French general or flag-rank officer to rally to de Gaulle's France Combattante (Fighting France) after the June 25, 1940, Armistice. The naval leadership has been termed the "Royal Republicans," in the wordplay of one historian, with the ministry located on the fashionable rue Royale in Paris. R. Chalmers Hood III, *Royal Republicans: The French Naval Dynasties between the World Wars* (Baton Rouge: Louisiana State University Press, 1985).

14. Space precludes a systematic tracking of flag-rank careers, but a fine example is Admiral Odend'hal. After seagoing assignments and work in naval intelligence to support the French army at Salonika in World War I, he served on the 1919 peace conference secretariat in Paris. Etienne Taillemite said Odend'hal had "in very difficult functions, shown himself an exceptional staff officer who delivered the very greatest services" during the negotiations. In the rank of commander (*capitaine de frégate*) he accompanied Admiral Le Bon, chief of the French navy, to the naval limitations conference in Washington in 1921–22. Further sea experience for Odend'hal included time in 1924 as Channel and North Sea divisional chief of staff and, in 1925, command of 6th Torpedo Boat Squadron on the Moroccan coast during the Abd-El-Krim insurgency. Odend'hal was selected for the CHEN

(the Centre des Hautes Études Navales, or Center for Higher Naval Studies)—the route to the top for talented officers. Promoted full captain (*capitaine de vaisseau*) on graduation in 1928, Odend'hal took the heavy cruiser *Tourville* on a global "show the flag" cruise before becoming naval chief of staff to the minister of marine in 1931–32, and passing a year as an instructor at the CHEN in 1932–33. Promoted to rear admiral in July 1933, Odend'hal became deputy secretary of the joint services planning body, the CSDN (Superior Council for National Defense). This led to his second stint in 1935 as chief of staff to the minister, by this time Francois Piétri. From 1936 to 1938 Odend'hal commanded 2nd Light Cruiser Squadron on the Atlantic station, flying his flag on the *Emile Bertin*. Commandant of the French naval war college in March 1938, he attained the rank of vice-admiral and became head of the French Naval Mission to the British Admiralty in September 1939. Three months later he was promoted to four-star rank (vice-amiral d'escadre), his career preparing him well, along with fellow French admirals of his generation, for inter-Allied negotiations, higher staff planning, and intelligence assessment as well as seagoing command.

15. Hervé Coutau–Bégarie and Claude Huan, *Darlan* (Paris: Fayard, 1989), 105–212.

16. MacGregor Knox, *Common Destiny: Dictatorship, Foreign Policy and War in Fascist Italy and Nazi Germany* (Cambridge: Cambridge University Press, 2000).

17. Robert J. Young, "French Military Intelligence and the Franco-Italian Alliance, 1933–1939," *Historical Journal* 28, no. 1 (1985): 143–68.

18. Decoux, *A la Barre de L'Indochine*, 17; André Reussner, *Les conversations franco-britanniques d'Etat-Major, 1935–1939* (Vincennes: Service Historique de la Marine, 1969).

19. Thomas Vaisset, "La puissance navale de la France (1919–1942)," *Historiens et Géographes*, no. 459 (August 2022), https://www.aphg.fr/La-puissance-navale-de-la-France-1919-1942.

20. Philippon, *Le métier de la mer*, 140.

21. Thomas, *French Empire between the Wars*, 324–39; France AN (Assemblée Nationale et Sénat): 3ᵉ République, Sixteenth Legislature (1936–42). Dossiers of the committees for the Army, Marine, Aeronautics, Public Works, Labor, Foreign Affairs, Commerce and Industry.

22. Duchêne had commanded Tenth Army, then Sixth Army, in 1916–18; quotation from his *Echo de Paris* review, June 17, 1937, of Paul Reynaud's book *Le probleme militaire français* (Paris: Flammarion, 1937), in France: AN Papiers Reynaud 74AP, box 12 (press cuttings, reports, reviews); cf. Judith M. Hughes, *To the Maginot Line: The Politics of French Military Preparation in the 1920s* (Cambridge, MA: Harvard University Press, 1971).

23. "Fleets in 1939," WW2-Weapons.com, https://www.ww2-weapons.com/fleets-in-1939/ (accessed June 25, 2023); Francis E. McMurtrie, ed., *Jane's Fighting Ships, 1939* (London: Sampson, Low, Marston, 1939; repr., Newton Abbot: David & Charles, 1971), 169–216; Decoux, *A la Barre de L'Indochine*, 3–22, 27–39, 73–89; Philippe Masson, *La marine française et la guerre, 1939–1945* (Paris: Tallandier, 1991), 24–75.

24. Willard C. Frank Jr., "Multinational Naval Cooperation in the Spanish Civil War, 1936," *Naval War College Review* 47, no. 2 (1994): 72–101; Jean-Marie Palayret, *L'Alliance impossible: Diplomatie et outil militaire dans les relations franco-italiennes (1929–1938)* (Vincennes: Service Historique des Armées, 2004).

25. Paul Halpern, "French and Italian Naval Policy in the Mediterranean, 1898–1945," in John B. Hattendorf, ed., *Naval Strategy and Policy in the Mediterranean: Past, Present and Future*, chap. 4 (London: Frank Cass, 2000), 98.

26. See Reynolds M. Salerno, "The French Navy and the Appeasement of Italy, 1937–39," *English Historical Review* 112, no. 145 (1997): 66–104.

27. Siegfried Breyer, *Battleships and Battle Cruisers, 1905–1970* (New York: Doubleday, 1973), 77.

28. McMurtrie, *Jane's Fighting Ships, 1939*, v; cf. John Jordan and Robert Dumas, *French Battleships, 1922–1956* (London: Seaforth, 2009).

29. John Gooch, *Mussolini's War: Fascist Italy from Triumph to Collapse, 1935–1943* (London: Allen Lane, 2020).

30. John Arquilla, review of Castex, *Strategic Theories*, ed. Kiesling, *Naval War College Review* 47, no. 4 (1994): 114–17 (quotation, 116).

31. See Robert J. Young, "The Strategic Dream: French Air Doctrine in the Inter-war Period, 1919–1939," *Journal of Contemporary History* 9, no. 4 (1974): 57–76; Herrick Chapman, *State Capitalism and Working-Class Radicalism in the French Aircraft Industry* (Berkeley: University of California Press, 1990).

32. Patrick Facon, *L'Armée de L'Air dans la tourmente: La bataille de France, 1939–1940* (Paris: Economica, 1997).

33. TNA-PRO: FO 371, file 32082: "Rapport Giraud. Les Causes de la défaite," July 26, 1940, 7.

34. House of Commons Debates, July 30, 1934, vol. 292, cc. 2325–2447, https://api.parliament.uk/historic-hansard/commons/1934/jul/30/armaments (accessed June 25, 2023); cf. Uri Bialer, *The Shadow of the Bomber: The Fear of Air Attack and British Politics, 1932–1939* (London: Royal Historical Society, 1980).

35. General Niessel, General Chabord, and G. de Guilhermy, *D.A.T.: Défense Aérienne du Territoire* (Paris: Editions Cosmopolites, 1934); William Fraser to his wife in England, September 15, 1939 (letters seen at Isington Mill, U.K., September 1983, thanks to General Sir David Fraser).

36. Lucien Robineau, "L'Armée de L'Air dans la Bataille de France," *Les armées françaises pendant la Seconde Guerre Mondiale*, Colloque de L'Institut d'Histoire des Conflits Contemporains, Paris, May 7–10, 1985.

37. Robert J. Young, "La guerre de longue durée: Some Reflections on French Strategy and Diplomacy in the 1930s," in Adrian Preston, ed., *General Staffs and Diplomacy before the Second World War* (London: Croom Helm, 1978), 41–64.

38. TNA-PRO: FO371, file 22915, C16018/36/17, December 22, 1938.

39. Halpern, "French and Italian Naval Policy in the Mediterranean, 1898–1945," 99.

40. TNA-PRO: FO371, file 32082, "Rapport Giraud. Les Causes de la défaite," July 26, 1940; Contre-amiral Raymond de Belot, *La Marine française pendant la campagne, 1939–1940* (Paris: Plon, 1954).

41. R. Chalmers Hood, "Bitter Victory: French Military Effectiveness during the Second World War," in Allan R. Millett and Williamson Murray, eds., *Military Effectiveness*, vol. 3: *The Second World War* (London: Unwin Hyman, 1988), 221–55 (quotation, 223).

42. Vincennes: Service Historique de la Défense, 1N47 (Etat-Major du Général Georges). Ministère des Colonies—Conférence tenue à Aden, 30 mai–3 juin 1939. Appendix A: "Problème Naval."

43. Talbot C. Imlay, "Paul Reynaud and France's Response to Nazi Germany," *French Historical Studies* 26, no. 3 (2003): 497–538 (quotation, 529).

44. *Daily Mail* quote in N. J. Crowson, ed., *Fleet Street, Press Barons and Politics: The Journals of Collin Brooks, 1932–1940* (Cambridge: Royal Historical Society, 1998), 254. As Italy's nonbelligerence continued, prognoses hardened. On May 13, 1940, the U.S. naval attaché in Berlin said his Spanish counterpart doubted "Italy will remain out long, but has little respect for her ability. He attributed a remark to General Gamelin that a neutral Italy would cost France ten divisions for border patrol, a hostile Italy would cost twenty divisions to neutralize them, and an Allied Italy would cost forty divisions to bolster them up." National Archives and Records Administration: Franklin Delano Roosevelt Library, Hyde Park, New York: President's Secretary's File Box 201, U.S. Naval Attaché, Berlin: War Diary, vol. 1 (September 1, 1939–May 26, 1940).

45. Reynolds M. Salerno, *Vital Crossroads: Mediterranean Origins of the Second World War, 1935–1940* (Ithaca, NY: Cornell University Press, 2002); MacGregor Knox, *Hitler's Italian Allies: Royal Armed Forces, Fascist Regime and the War of 1940–43* (Cambridge: Cambridge University Press, 2000), chaps. 1–4.

46. Hood, "Bitter Victory," 242.

47. Paul W. Doerr, reviewing George E. Melton's *From Versailles to Mers el-Kébir: The Promise of Anglo-French Naval Cooperation, 1919–1940* (Annapolis: Naval Institute Press, 2015), in *Michigan War Studies Review*, 2016-089 (August 22, 2016), https://www.miwsr.com/2016/downloads/2016-089.pdf (accessed March 3, 2023).

48. Alexander John Upward, "Ordinary Sailors: The French Navy, Vichy and the Second World War" (PhD diss., West Virginia University, 2016), 146.

49. See the useful assessment of the Vichy and Free French navies in Hugues Canuel, *The Fall and Rise of French Sea Power: France's Quest for an Independent Naval Policy, 1940–1963* (Annapolis: Naval Institute Press, 2021).

50. Max Boot, *War Made New: Technology, Warfare and the Course of History, 1500 to Today* (New York: Gotham, 2006); William H. McNeil, "Conspicuous Proliferation," *New York Review of Books*, December 21, 2006.

CHAPTER EIGHT

ADMIRAL NAGANO OSAMI AND THE JAPANESE NAVY'S DECISION FOR WAR AGAINST THE UNITED STATES

Peter Mauch

A dmiral Nagano Osami remains, by any standard of judgment, one of the Imperial Japanese Navy's most puzzling officers. He could, in a service that prided itself on its understanding of the United States, boast long experience in that country, so that he understood as well as any uniformed naval officer the preponderance of power the United States could bring to bear in the event of war in the Pacific. Even so, Nagano positioned himself, soon after his April 1941 appointment as Navy chief of staff, as a leading proponent of war against the United States. The "time for war," he shouted at his government colleagues in a characteristic statement in early November 1941, was "now!" It would "not come later!"[1]

This essay locates Nagano's bellicosity in an admixture of decades-old strategic doctrine, pre–Pearl Harbor intelligence, and dysfunction in the Japanese policymaking process. Readers will hopefully discern a two-way approach: I trace Nagano's career against the backdrop of naval policy and, at the same time, I use Nagano as a conceptual lens through which to examine Japanese naval policy. There are three key points of focus. First, Nagano's career provides a microcosm of the Japanese navy's decades-long fixation on fleet ratios, particularly a doctrinal belief that victory in war in the Pacific was possible only if the Japanese fleet was at least 70 percent the size of its U.S. antagonist. Second, Nagano's abovementioned appointment atop the Navy General Staff coincided with intelligence indicating attainment of the all-important 70 percent ratio vis-à-vis the U.S. Pacific Fleet; satisfaction therewith was tempered by the grim certitude that U.S. president Franklin D. Roosevelt's massive fleet expansion programs rendered maintenance of this ratio a practical impossibility. This dovetailed neatly with this essay's third point of focus: Nagano felt almost entrapped by Navy Minister Vice Admiral Oikawa Koshirō's inability to speak clearly and unambiguously about the navy's position on the issue of war and peace in the Pacific. Oikawa's reticence contrasted sharply with the Imperial Japanese Army's forceful representation of its views, and it seemed to Nagano to raise the likelihood of Japan drifting aimlessly into war against the United States. That outcome could only be to the detriment of Japan's chances of victory in the Pacific, and Nagano championed instead a proactive embrace of war in the hope of maximizing Japan's chances of victory.

NAGANO, NAVAL ORTHODOXY, AND THE U.S. NAVY

Nagano was born in June 1880 into a formerly high-ranking samurai family of the Tosa domain. The navy had long since rejected hiring and promotion practices that favored sons of former samurai, but Nagano's proud parentage nonetheless meant that ambition came naturally to him. He marked himself, from the outset of his career, as one of the Japanese navy's best and brightest young officers, and he graduated, in December 1900, second in his Naval Academy class. He subsequently specialized as a gunnery officer. This was the most prestigious specialization in the navy and was a sure path for any young man hoping one day to command battleships, squadrons, and even fleets. Nagano completed two stints at the Naval Gunnery School in Yokosuka—the first in 1903 and the second from 1905 to 1906—and his exploits during the intervening Russo-Japanese War of 1904–5 placed him at the cutting edge of his service's junior gunnery officers.[2]

Nagano entered the Naval Staff College in 1909. Here he and his classmates studied maritime strategy and tactics, naval administration, naval history, and general education subjects including foreign languages. They also learned the art of operational planning. Across many classes, there was a preoccupation—shared by all the world's great navies—with major fleet engagements, and the Combined Fleet's annihilation of Russia's Baltic Fleet in the Battle of Tsushima comprised a subject of both intense national pride and most intensive study. This "doctrine" of "major fleet engagement" had a big-guns-and-big-ships corollary: big guns were seen as the decisive factor in any fleet engagement, and big ships provided the best possible means of shortening the battle line and concentrating big-gun fire.[3]

The Meiji emperor had, in the meantime, sanctioned the Imperial National Defense Policy, which designated the United States as the navy's primary hypothetical enemy. This did not necessarily mean that Japan's sailors were hoping for war against the United States; it was a dispassionate designation, based primarily on U.S. capacity. Whatever the case, it was the considered opinion of the service's foremost strategists that war with the United States would most likely follow a three-step process whereby (1) Japanese forces would in the war's opening stages overrun the Western Pacific, including the U.S. colony in the Philippines; (2) the U.S. fleet would subsequently advance through the Central Pacific while the Japanese fleet lay in wait in the waters around the Ogasawara Islands; and (3) a major fleet engagement would ensue, with each side seeking to annihilate the other. Japan's maritime strategists were satisfied that a fleet at least 70 percent the size of the U.S. fleet would maximize Japan's chances of emerging victorious from such a war. On this basis, the navy set its sights on the so-called eight-eight fleet, at the core of which were eight new dreadnought battleships and eight armored cruisers.[4]

Nagano remained peripheral to war planning and decisions concerning the eight-eight fleet, but his time at the Naval Staff College meant he was steeped in all these aspects of naval orthodoxy. After graduation, he spent time at sea and also in the Navy Ministry in Tokyo before leaving, in January 1913, for a two-year stint at Harvard Law School. He returned thereafter to sea and, among other assignments, commanded the cruiser *Hirado*. His time aboard *Hirado* coincided with Navy Minister Admiral Katō Tomosaburō's securing of the funding for the eight-eight fleet, which meant that the Japanese navy would finally accomplish its long-cherished 70 percent fleet ratio vis-à-vis the U.S. Navy.

NAGANO AND THE ERA OF NAVAL ARMS LIMITATION

Nagano served for three years from December 1920 as attaché to the Japanese embassy in Washington. The assignment coincided with the Washington Conference of 1921–22, where the world's great naval powers agreed to a U.S. proposal for a radical reduction in capital ship strength according to the ratio of 5:5:3 for the United States, Britain, and Japan. This experiment in naval arms limitation ended efforts at attaining a fleet strength 70 percent that of the United States, and it torpedoed the eight-eight fleet. It also rent asunder Japan's officer class and gave rise to two diametrically opposed factions within the Japanese navy. The so-called treaty faction welcomed the system of naval arms limitation, on the grounds that war against the United States was unwinnable, whatever fleet ratio Japan was able to attain. The treaty faction also believed that the 5:5:3 ratio limited U.S. shipbuilding capacity even more than it restricted the Japanese navy. Officers in this faction pointed to other agreements reached at the Washington Conference, including particularly an Anglo-American undertaking not to build fortifications in the Western Pacific, which afforded Japan command of East Asia's seas. On the other side of the divide, officers in the so-called fleet faction opposed any international agreements that undercut what they regarded as the irreducible operational requirement of a 70 percent fleet ratio vis-à-vis the United States.[5]

Nagano gravitated toward the fleet faction. It could hardly be otherwise, given his long identification with the major fleet engagement doctrine and its big-guns-and-big-ships corollary, along with the 70 percent ratio and the eight-eight fleet plan. In short, Nagano believed that the agreements reached at the Washington Conference handed the United States an unassailable operational advantage without so much as a shot having been fired in the Pacific. He became convinced of the fundamental correctness of his position after he paid US$300,000 to acquire a confidential study prepared by the Plans Division in the U.S. Navy's Office of the Chief of Naval Operations. The study, titled "The Conduct of an Overseas Naval Campaign," concerned itself with the objective of wresting from Japan command of the sea in the Western Pacific, and it specified that such would be possible in war if only *the Japanese fleet were less than 70 percent the size of the U.S. fleet.*[6] The case, for Nagano, was closed.

Nagano returned to Tokyo in late 1923 and was almost immediately promoted to flag rank. He remained aloof from the factional infighting that beset the navy for the remainder of the 1920s and the early 1930s. In the mid-1920s, he headed the General Staff's Intelligence Division and then took command of the First Overseas Service Fleet, which existed to protect Japanese nationals and property along China's Yangtze River. He was back in the United States, as commander of the training squadron, when the Geneva Naval Conference of 1927 brought Anglo-American-Japanese delegates together to discuss limitations on auxiliary vessels not covered by the Washington Conference. Discussions at Geneva ended in Anglo-American disagreement, and Nagano returned to Tokyo. He was serving as the Naval Academy commandant when the London Naval Conference met in 1930, so he was removed from the bruising battle that took place within the Japanese navy over the Anglo-American–Japanese agreement to limit auxiliary vessels including cruisers, destroyers, and submarines at levels considerably lower than the Japanese navy sought.[7]

Nagano returned to Tokyo in the summer of 1931 and was serving as the navy's vice chief of staff when the Japanese army launched its conquest of Manchuria. Japan's relationship with not only China but the rest of the world fell into a sharp decline; the Japanese navy, while nonplussed by its sister service's actions in Manchuria, paid careful attention to America's declared refusal to recognize any forceful changes to Chinese sovereignty. Next thing Nagano knew, the navy appointed him as its delegate to the sixty-nation Geneva Disarmament Conference of 1932–33. In an address to reserve officers on the eve of his departure, he disparaged "idealistic arms limitation treaties" that did not account for each nation's "security" needs. He labeled the naval arms limitation treaties that Japan had hitherto concluded with the Anglo-American powers "unsatisfactory," and he insisted that Japan had henceforth to insist on a naval strength that would enable "protection" of its rights and interests.[8] The naval ratios that defined Anglo-American-Japanese naval arms limitation nonetheless played no particular role at Geneva, and Nagano kept a low profile as the conference bogged down amid Franco-German mistrust and disagreement.[9]

Nagano returned to Japan and served as commander of the Yokosuka Naval District and subsequently as a member of the prestigious but largely ceremonial Supreme Military Council. In 1935, he was appointed the chief delegate to the Second London Naval Conference. The provisions of the Washington and London treaties were set to expire, and Nagano's role was to renegotiate the entire raft of naval arms limitations agreements. He traveled to London and tabled an approach, defined not by ratios but instead by a common upper limit in naval arms. He proposed, in a word, parity between and among the Anglo-American-Japanese powers. Nagano's individual role in defining this position is unclear;[10] what is clear is Nagano's personal identification with the proposal. He explained to his emperor after returning to Tokyo in early 1936 that he had championed the "best" approach to naval arms limitation, precisely because it left untrammeled within the confines of the common upper limit each nation's sovereign right to determine how to arm itself and cater to its own particular security needs.[11] Nagano's positive assessment notwithstanding, the Anglo-American powers were nonplussed by the proposal. Nagano led the Japanese delegation out of the London Conference and out of the era of naval arms limitation.[12]

NAGANO AND ARMY-NAVY RIVALRY

Nagano returned from London to a delicate political situation. Tokyo was still reeling from the February 26 Incident, which involved young army officers in a bloody rebellion. The coup attempt failed, but three of the navy's senior-most officers—Lord Keeper of the Privy Seal Admiral Saitō Makoto, Grand Chamberlain Admiral Suzuki Kantarō, and Prime Minister Admiral Okada Keisuke—had been targeted by army assassins. The interservice relationship had reached its nadir.

Amid the ensuing political change, Nagano emerged as navy minister. On the day of his appointment, Nagano told Army Minister General Terauchi Hisaichi of his refusal to follow the convention whereby policy toward China was considered almost solely the army's prerogative. He put Terauchi on notice: the army's actions in China were damaging Japan's relationships with other nations, including the United States, and were therefore of direct and central concern to the Japanese navy.[13] Some months later, when he learned that the army had been conducting clandestine negotiations with Nazi Germany with a view to concluding a Japanese-German alliance, Nagano told Terauchi that although the navy felt "goodwill" toward Germany, a "political partnership" was "unjustifiable."[14]

Nagano also looked askance at the army's insistence on preparing for the possibility of war against the Soviet Union. Hostilities on the continent—against China, against the Soviet Union, or a combination thereof—would be, for all intents and purposes, an all-army affair and preparation for such a possibility would almost invariably result in increased budgetary allocations for the army. This could only mean a lean budget for the navy. Nagano could not help but think of such an outcome in terms of fleet ratios: in mid-1936 he calculated that neglecting to build ships would, in the best-case scenario, result by late 1941 in a near-catastrophic 58 percent ratio vis-à-vis the U.S. Navy.[15]

Nagano's ministerial responsibilities included securing a budgetary allocation that would enable the navy to replenish and augment its fleet now that the era of arms limitation had ended. To contest the army and to justify his budget requests, Nagano argued publicly that the Manchurian Incident had fostered hostility and enmity in every direction. A strong navy was necessary, if only to deter other nations like the United States from taking stronger measures against Japan. Nagano also fell back on what had long been considered a distinctly naval prerogative, namely the so-called southward advance. As he explained to the Imperial Diet in May 1936, the navy needed to build ships in order not only to defend the empire and secure its interests but also to lead the way in penetrating the resource-rich colonial regions of Southeast Asia and thereby contribute materially to the "stabilization" of the people's livelihoods.[16] His position was encapsulated by the phrase *hokushu nanshin* (northward defense, southward advance), which entailed a defensive posture for the army in Korea, Manchuria, and northern China and the navy's peaceful but proactive penetration of Southeast Asia.[17] Ever the big-ships-and-big-guns proponent, Nagano prioritized what he regarded as the urgent need to build battleships.[18]

NAGANO AND THE QUESTION OF WAR OR PEACE WITH THE UNITED STATES

Nagano left Tokyo in February 1937 to take command of the Combined Fleet. He remained at sea in early July when fighting with Chinese forces broke out on the outskirts of Tientsin. Nagano's role was minor: not only did the cabinet in Tokyo adopt a policy of nonescalation of the so-called Marco Polo Bridge Incident; the army, of necessity, bore the brunt of the fighting. A big-ships-and-big-guns advocate like Nagano was little interested in the relatively mundane tasks assigned the navy in the early days of the fighting. He entrusted to his subordinates things like protecting troop transports and evacuating Japanese residents from the Yangtze River basin. From August, he showed somewhat more interest in the naval air arm's efforts at attaining control of the skies over Nanking and elsewhere, and also in preparations for the possibility of Anglo-American or Soviet entry into the hostilities against Japan.[19] But before the year was out, he was transferred back to Tokyo.

Nagano returned to the Supreme Military Council. There he remained for almost three and a half years, until April 1941, when he succeeded Prince Fushimi Hiroyasu as chief of staff. In the interim, the war in China dragged on indefinitely, the army got its nose bloodied in a short war fought against the Soviets along the Manchurian border, World War II began in Europe, and Japan's relationships with the Anglo-American powers deteriorated precipitously. In Washington, the administration of President Franklin D. Roosevelt in early 1940 went so far as to abrogate the Japanese-U.S. Commercial Treaty, which meant it could at a moment's notice impose commercial sanctions and trade embargoes against Japan. Then the German army conquered continental Western Europe, and in September 1940 Japan joined Nazi Germany and Fascist Italy in a military alliance. The Japanese-German-Italian Tripartite Pact signaled Japan's newfound intention to advance forcefully into the suddenly defenseless colonial regions of Southeast Asia. The pact also threatened the United States with a two-front war in the Pacific and Atlantic Oceans, in an effort at frightening it away from a policy of support for Britain.[20]

The Tripartite Pact left Nagano aghast. Like most Japanese naval officers, he was convinced of Anglo-American inseparability, and he refused to believe the United States would allow Britain to fall. Testimony to this conviction came in the form of the Lend-Lease Act, which President Roosevelt signed into law in March 1941 and which made it possible for the United States to provide Britain with sorely needed matériel despite Britain's inability to pay for it. Nagano worried that Lend-Lease practically guaranteed U.S. entry into Britain's war against Germany. He also worried that Germany would, in this instance, call on Japan to fulfill its alliance obligations and open hostilities against the United States. On the eve of his appointment as navy chief of staff, he was heard denouncing the alliance as the "root of all evil." He also worried about the impact on the Japanese-U.S. relationship of the army's unending war in China. "Unless we withdraw from the Tripartite Pact and withdraw troops from China," he told Rear Admiral Fukudome Shigeru, "reaching an agreement in the Japanese-U.S. negotiations is impossible."[21]

Almost immediately upon his appointment as navy chief of staff, Nagano received from Captain Yokoyama Ichirō, naval attaché to the Japanese embassy in Washington, a cable recommending pursuit of a proposal for peace in the Pacific known as the Draft Understanding between Japan and the United States. The Draft Understanding was the product of quasi-official negotiations in Washington involving Japan's ambassador and retired admiral Nomura Kichisaburō, a Japanese army colonel, a Japanese banker, and two Roman Catholic priests. Nomura and Yokoyama had, from the outset of those negotiations, kept the naval leadership in Tokyo fully informed of the Draft Understanding's terms and conditions. It required that the United States (1) reopen normal commercial relations with Japan, (2) scale back its defensive preparations in the Southwest Pacific, and (3) cooperate with Japan in its efforts at procuring resources from Southeast Asia. At the same time, the Draft Understanding required that Japan (1) forsake its alliance obligation to enter the war on Germany's side in the event the United States went to war in the Atlantic, (2) foreswear a forceful advance into the defenseless colonial regions of Southeast Asia, and (3) commit to peace terms with China that were agreeable to the United States, which would in turn require that Roosevelt use his good offices to bring Chinese leader Chiang Kai-shek to the negotiating table.[22]

It is fascinating to speculate on what might have been had Nagano been serving as navy minister in April 1941. It is at least conceivable that he would have supported Nomura's diplomatic efforts and steered Japan away from war. But Nagano, as chief of staff, was not responsible for questions of war or peace. So far as the navy was concerned, that responsibility rested solely with Navy Minister Vice Admiral Oikawa Koshirō. He hoped to avoid war with the United States for the very good reason that he regarded a war in the Pacific as unwinnable, but he was willing to confront neither his subordinates nor his ministerial colleagues with the imperative of avoiding a war the navy could not win. He did nothing to support the Draft Understanding and seemed simply to hope that somebody else would somehow see it through to fruition. In this way, Oikawa ceded the initiative to the volatile and doggedly pro-German foreign minister, Matsuoka Yōsuke, who through May 1941 went to almost absurd lengths to reassert Japan's obligations to its alliance partners.[23]

Nagano despaired at Oikawa's ministerial performance. "Whatever you say to Oikawa," Nagano charged, "he is hopeless. He says he does not want war, but he has not taken a single policy that would prevent war." Nagano was also critical of the cabinet of Prime Minister Konoe Fumimaro as a whole. "While the government says it does not want to go to war," he moaned, "it continues along a path leading directly to war, and has not changed direction in the least."[24] Nagano was satisfied, in other words, that Oikawa and the cabinet on which he served had rendered war in the Pacific a virtual inevitability.

So far as Nagano was concerned, the question of war or peace was no longer at issue. This meant his constitutionally defined prerogative—namely, operational viewpoints—must necessarily take priority. Nagano almost instinctively focused his attention on fleet ratios and was satisfied that the fleet had surpassed a 70 percent ratio—it had, in fact, attained a 75 percent ratio vis-à-vis the Americans.[25] That was good news, but Nagano was also overtly conscious of the two-ocean navy being built by the Roosevelt administration.[26] With this, Japanese industry could not keep pace, and the

75 percent ratio could not be maintained. If war was, as Nagano believed, unavoidable, then it really only made operational sense so long as the fleet ratio remained favorable. The conclusion was obvious: war sooner was far better than war later.

NAGANO AND THE SOUTHWARD ADVANCE

Nagano's fast-firming belief in the desirability of a decision for war sooner rather than later coincided neatly with a stunning turn in the war in Europe, where Hitler had determined to forsake the long-anticipated invasion of Britain and instead launch war against the Soviet Union. Code-named Barbarossa, the fast-approaching German invasion of the Soviet Union sparked a powerful, aggressive impulse within (particularly) the Japanese army. The Army Ministry and Army General Staff resembled hives of activity throughout June, as they tried to determine the best possible response. Nagano and his subordinates were acutely aware of what was a wildly swinging debate within the army: on the one hand, there were arguments for a northward advance against the Soviet Union, and on the other hand, there were arguments for an advance into Southeast Asia. By mid-June, the army coalesced around the curiously worded *junbi-jin taisei* (preparatory-formation setup), which allowed for possible action in both the North and the South. If the decision were reached to advance north, a total of twenty-four army divisions would fight. If, however, the decision were reached to advance south, ten army divisions would be involved.[27]

The disparity spooked Nagano and many of his professional colleagues. They saw in the army's "preparatory-formation setup" a predetermined focus on the army's traditional enemy to the north. Naval officers fretted at the money and matériel the army would need in the event it went to war against the Soviets. This would come at the navy's direct expense and would almost necessarily result in a critical slowdown in shipbuilding, even as the Roosevelt administration pursued its abovementioned, immense fleet expansion program. Recalling Nagano's conviction that a Japanese-U.S. war was now a practical inevitability, the nightmarish scenario of war against the Soviets held out the prospect of the United States launching operations in the Pacific at a time of its own choosing. This would presumably be only after the Japanese navy had been thoroughly emaciated by the voracious appetite of its sister service.[28]

To Nagano's horror, the ever-submissive Oikawa remained silent and refused to represent the navy's perspective at cabinet level. Nagano now took the bit between the teeth. Contesting the army over budgetary allocations was old hat for Nagano, who (readers will recall) engaged in precisely such a contest when he served as navy minister. A southward advance was his ace in the hole. But, whereas he had as navy minister argued for peaceful penetration into Southeast Asia, the terrible repercussions of anything but a prompt decision for war in the Pacific meant Nagano now called for a forceful advance. He took the case to the highest counsels of state on June 11. "We must build bases in French Indochina and Thailand in order to launch military operations," he said. "We must resolutely attack anyone who tries to stop us."[29]

A few weeks later, a subordinate approached Nagano. He reminded the admiral that the army still seemed likely to march to war against the Soviets, and asked, "What are you going to do?" The pep talk was all Nagano needed. He stormed into a meeting of the naval leadership and again propounded on the need to launch a forceful southward advance, all the while insisting that Japan must not be deterred by the possibility of war against the United States. Oikawa meekly submitted.[30]

The arguments for a southward advance ultimately carried the day, and the army too agreed to a southward advance. Enthusiasm within its ranks for war against the Soviets had by no means subsided, but the army agreed at least to advance as far as southern Indochina. It was attracted by the likelihood of a largely bloodless advance, and it knew that the Indochinese advance was the necessary first step if any further advances southward were to be taken. An Imperial Conference on July 2 formalized a twofold decision:

(1) to advance into southern Indochina, and (2) to prepare to advance farther south or instead to the north against the Soviets.[31] Most Japanese decision-makers convinced themselves that the United States was unlikely to take drastic measures in response to the Indochinese advance. Nagano thought otherwise. "This means war," he was heard muttering to himself after the decision to advance into Indochina was reached.

NAGANO AND WAR

Japanese forces began advancing into Indochina on July 28. The Roosevelt administration was tipped off by French colonial authorities and preempted the Indochinese advance by freezing all Japanese assets in the United States. The British and Dutch followed suit. Nagano now began speaking of American-British-Chinese-Dutch (ABCD) encirclement. Those nations were, he avowed, placing an "iron chain" around Japan's neck and he insisted that Japan's only hope was to "break through this iron chain" before it was complete.[32]

Nagano's subordinates were in lockstep with their boss. They met on July 26 with Army General Staff officers and propounded on the need for war in the Pacific. The war's opening shots ought, they explained, to be directed against the Dutch East Indies, Malaya, and the Philippines. Then, if the United States engaged in a major fleet engagement, fleet ratios were such that Japan would in all likelihood emerge victorious. Nagano's subordinates also allowed that Japan did not necessarily have the means to force the U.S. Navy into such a major fleet engagement. They admitted that the United States might opt instead for a protracted war of attrition and, tellingly, they refrained from speculating on the prospects of victory in such a war. One day later, Nagano reported to the emperor. He explained that the Tripartite Pact rendered a Japanese-U.S. war a practical inevitability. Nagano added that, in the event of war, Japan's oil stocks would be exhausted within a year or two. This meant, he said, there was no choice but to strike southward immediately and secure access to the Dutch East Indies' oil. An attack on the Dutch East Indies required an attack on the British positions in Malaya and Singapore and the U.S. position in the Philippines. Then, to the emperor's chagrin, Nagano allowed that he had no confidence in the prospects of victory over the United States.[33]

On August 1, the Roosevelt administration slapped a total embargo on the export of oil to Japan. The British and the Dutch followed suit. Japan had no access to oil and could rely only on its reserves. Nagano was now feeling the pressure of not only a favorable fleet ratio that could not possibly be maintained but also a reliance on oil stocks, which must invariably dwindle. He joined with others in the Japanese decision-making process and, by the end of August, he had helped forge a consensus to "complete preparations for war, with the last ten days of October as a tentative deadline, resolved to go to war with the U.S., U.K., and the Netherlands if necessary."[34] An Imperial Conference met on September 6 and agreed that, if Japanese-U.S. negotiations had not been concluded by early October, the government would immediately resolve to start war.[35]

The hapless Oikawa placed all his hope in a summit meeting between Konoe and Roosevelt. A Japanese government proposal, the summit meeting was the subject of intense Japanese-U.S. negotiation. Importantly from Oikawa's perspective, the summit meeting proposal absolved him of the need to speak up and to confront his colleagues with difficult policy choices. By early October, Nagano had lost all patience. There was, he said, "no longer time for discussion." He added, "We want quick action."[36] There was considerable ambiguity in Nagano's remarks. Was he arguing for an end to "discussion" between the Japanese and U.S. governments, and for "quick action" in opening hostilities in the Pacific? Or was he instead calling for an end to "discussion" among Japanese policymakers, and for "quick action" concerning the approaching deadline and the need for a definite decision for either war or peace? Was it a combination thereof? Only one thing is certain: Oikawa's abject performance as navy minister left Nagano in the almost impossible situation of arguing for a war that he worried might well prove unwinnable. He slept through quite a number of meetings in 1941 and, although his subordinates joked that this must be due to the energies he was expending on his much younger wife, it seems at least as plausible to suggest Nagano was wracked by anxiety, confusion, and even distress.

Contributing to Nagano's difficulties was Combined Fleet commander in chief Admiral Yamamoto Isoroku's Pearl Harbor attack plan. Nagano first sighted the plan in August, and it struck him as altogether too risky. He also worried that the Pearl Harbor attack plan required a long-range cruising capacity that the Combined Fleet did not possess. Recent scholarship holds that this was precisely Yamamoto's point. Yamamoto actually hoped Nagano would ultimately reject the plan. This would then enable Yamamoto and Nagano to confront Oikawa with the impossibility of war, and the need for a drastic change in Japanese policy. If this were indeed Yamamoto's hope, it failed. Perhaps he put up too good a front, for Nagano in early October washed his hands of the Pearl Harbor plan. "If Yamamoto is that confident," he declared, "I'll leave it to him."[37]

A last-minute change in government erased the October deadline for war, but the pressures confronting Nagano remained unchanged. For one thing, the cabinet of Prime Minister General Tōjō Hideki made no policy U-turns that might have steered Japan away from war. Then there were Japan's oil supplies, which were dwindling by the day. And, of course, an unassailable number of keels were being laid in American shipyards. Nagano presented in early November as "clearly determined that we must go to war now."[38] As always, he sweated on fleet ratios. He told an Imperial Conference on November 5, "The ratio of our fleet to that of the United States is 7.5 to 10." With that ratio, he was confident that the Combined Fleet could "destroy their fleet if they want[ed] a decisive battle."[39]

CONCLUSION

This essay has demonstrated that Nagano's role in Japan's decision for war needs to be understood in the context of his long adherence to naval orthodoxy, including a threefold preoccupation with major fleet encounters, with big guns and big ships, and with the perceived need for a fleet ratio of at least 70 percent vis-à-vis the U.S. Navy. It has also demonstrated that naval intelligence in 1941 was itself framed within the context of fleet ratios, so that Nagano was particularly animated by intelligence indicating that (1) the Japanese navy had surpassed a 70 percent fleet ratio vis-à-vis the U.S. Navy, and (2) that this percentage was, in the medium to longer term, utterly unsustainable. Finally, this essay has demonstrated that Nagano posited himself as Tokyo's leading war hawk because he believed that the government's policies practically guaranteed war. The key issue was Oikawa, who was unwilling to confront his colleagues with the need for policies that might steer Japan away from war in the Pacific and who seemed unable to rein in the Imperial army's aggressive impulses. Nagano could do nothing to salvage transpacific peace, but he could do something to guard against a northward advance against the Soviets: he could—and did—champion a southward advance into Southeast Asia. He almost welcomed the prospect of war against the United States, on the grounds that the earlier war began, the better were Japan's prospects of victory. But even then, Nagano recognized how minuscule were Japan's chances of anything but shattering defeat. He presents as almost a tragic figure whose positions in 1941 made a major contribution to the demise of the navy he had served with distinction for decades.

NOTES

1. "66th Liaison Conference, November 1, 1941," in Nobutaka Ike, ed., *Japan's Decision for War: Records of the 1941 Policy Conferences* (Stanford, CA: Stanford University Press, 1967), 202.

2. Hata Ikuhiko, ed., *Nihon rikukaigun sōgō jiten* [Comprehensive encyclopedia of the Japanese army and navy, 1868–1945], 2nd ed. (Tokyo: Tokyo Daigaku Shuppankai, 2005), 237; Nihon Hakugaku Kurabu, eds., *Nichi-Ro sensō no jinbutsu ga yoku wakaru hon: Ano meishō/gushō no igai na "sono ato"* [Understanding the persons of the Russo-Japanese War: The unexpected "after" of the great commanders and strategists] (Tokyo: PHP Kenkyūjo, 2008), 29.

3. For the "doctrine" of "major fleet encounter" quotation, see Bōe-ichō Bōei Kenkyūjo Senshishitsu (BBKS), eds., *Senshi sōsho (100): Daihon'ei kaigunbu daitōa sensō kaisen keii 1* [War history series, vol. 100: Imperial headquarters, navy, circumstances leading to the outbreak of the greater East Asia war, vol. 1], 42. See also BBKS, eds., *Senshi sōsho (31): kaigun gunsenbi (1) shōwa 16nen 11gatsu made* [War history series, vol. 31: Naval armament and war preparation (vol. 1) up to November 1941], 108–9; Sadao Asada, *From Mahan to Pearl Harbor: The Imperial Japanese Navy and the United States* (Annapolis: Naval Institute Press, 2006), 26–44; and David C. Evans and Mark R. Peattie, *Kaigun: Strategy, Tactics, and Technology in the Imperial Japanese Navy, 1887–1941* (Annapolis: Naval Institute Press, 1997), 129–32.

4. The text of the Imperial National Defense Policy appears in Shimanuki Takeji, "Nichiro sensō ikō ni okeru kokubō hōshin, shōyō heiryoku, yōhei kōryō no hensen" [The development of the national defense policy, the naval strength requirement, and the general plan for strategy since the Russo-Japanese War], *Gunji shigaku* 8, no. 4 (March 1973): 2–16. For Japanese naval strategy and the eight-eight fleet, see Evans and Peattie, *Kaigun*, 152–91.

5. Regarding factionalism in the Navy, see Asada, *From Mahan to Pearl Harbor*, 69–125.

6. See Iwamura Kentarō, "Nihon kaigun ni okeru kaikaku no keizokusei no sogai yōin: gendai no gunji soshiki ni ataeru inpurikēshon" [Impediments to the continuity of reforms in the Japanese navy: Implications for contemporary military organizations], *Kaikankō senryaku kenkyū* [Japan Maritime Self Defense Force command and staff college review], vol. 8, no. 2 (January 2019): 32–33. Japanese sailors' focus on the 70 percent issue meant they overlooked other aspects of this study. It called for amphibious warfare and aircraft carriers, long before the U.S. Navy acquired such capabilities. Both featured prominently in the Pacific War. See Carl H. Amme, "Seapower and the Superpowers," U.S. Naval Institute *Proceedings*, October 1968.

7. Regarding the London Conference and the brawling it sparked within the Japanese navy, see Asada, *From Mahan to Pearl Harbor*, 126–57.

8. "Nagano zenken tōji" [Plenipotentiary Nagano's formal response], December 10, 1932, Gunshuku ni kansuru 2,3 kōen, Rikugunshō gunshuku kankei, kokusai renmei/kafu kaigi/gunshuku kankei shorui, Rikugunshō Dainikki, Japan Ministry of Defense Archives, JACAR reference code: C08051917500.

9. Japanese diplomacy at Geneva remains an understudied episode. For an excellent account of the Geneva Conference, see Thomas R. Davies, "France and the World Disarmament Conference of 1932–34," *Diplomacy and Statecraft* 15, no. 4 (2004): 765–78.

10. See, e.g., BBKS, eds., *Senshi sōsho (91): Daihon'ei kaigunbu/rengō kantai (1) kaisen made* [War history series, vol. 91: Imperial headquarters, navy/combined fleet (vol. 1) until war's opening] (Tokyo: Asagumo Shuppansha, 1975), 278–83.

11. "Fukumei jōsōbun" [Text of report to the throne], in Gaimushō, eds., *Nihon gaikō bunsho: 1935nen Rondon kaigun kaigi keika hōkokusho* [Documents on Japanese foreign policy: Proceedings of the London Naval Conference of 1935] (Tokyo: Gaimushō, 1986), 183–91 (quotation, 186).

12. See Asada, *From Mahan to Pearl Harbor*, 203–6; and Stephen E. Pelz, *Race to Pearl Harbor: The Failure of the Second London Naval Conference and the Onset of World War II* (Cambridge, MA: Harvard University Press, 1974), 1–63, 152–64.

13. BBKS, *Senshi sōsho*, 91:291.

14. BBKS, *Senshi sōsho*, 91:337. He later agreed to a Japanese–German Anti-Comintern Pact (concluded on November 25, 1936), but justified this on the grounds that it was not a political partnership that targeted a particular nation but was instead an expression of a shared ideological antipathy for communism and the Communist International.

15. See Nagano's remarks before the House of Representatives' budget committee on May 13, 1936: "Dai-69-kai Teikoku gikai shūgiin yosan iin dai4punkakai (rikugunshō, kaigunshō) dai1gō," May 13, 1946, https://teikokugikai-i.ndl.go.jp/#/detailPDF?minId=006913604X00119360513&page=1&spkNum=0&current=16.

16. "Dai-69-kai Teikoku gikai shūgiin kessan iin dai1punka (ōkurashō, rikugunshō, kaigunshō, nōrinshō oyobi shōkōshō

shokan) kaigiroku (sokki) dai1kai," May 21, 1936, https://
teikokugikai-i.ndl.go.jp/#/detailPDF?minId=006910705X
00119360521&page=10&spkNum=29&current=4.

17. BBKS, *Senshi sōsho*, 91:297. The emphasis was on a peaceful—as
opposed to a forceful—southward advance. See BBKS, *Senshi
sōsho*, 100:121.

18. See, for example, Nagano's remarks to the House of Peers on
May 20, 1936: "Dai-69-kai Teikoku gikai kizokuin yosan iin
dai4punkakai (rikugunshō, kaigunshō) dai1gō," May 20, 1936,
https://teikokugikai-i.ndl.go.jp/minutes/api/emp/v1/detail
PDF/img/006903612X00119360520.

19. BBKS, *Senshi sōsho*, 91:355–58. See also BBKS, eds., *Senshi sōsho
(72): Chūgoku hōmen kaigun sakusen (1) Shōwa 13nen 4gatsu made*
[War history series, vol. 72: Naval operations in the China theater, vol. 1, until April 1938] (Tokyo: Asagumo Shuppansha,
1974), 335–53.

20. See Peter Mauch, *Sailor Diplomat: Nomura Kichisaburō and the
Japanese-American War* (Cambridge, MA: Harvard University
Asia Center, 2011), 114–23.

21. Fukudome Shigeru, *Kaigun no hansei* [Naval reflections] (Tokyo:
Nihon Shuppan Kyōdō, 1951), 64. Regarding Lend-Lease, see
Warren F. Kimball, *The Most Unsordid Act: Lend-Lease, 1939–1941*
(Baltimore: Johns Hopkins University Press, 1969).

22. Regarding Yokoyama's cable, dated April 18, see BBKS, *Senshi
sōsho*, 100:253. Regarding the Draft Understanding, see Peter
Mauch, "A Bolt from the Blue? New Evidence on the Japanese
Navy and the Draft Understanding between Japan and the United
States, April 1941," *Pacific Historical Review* 78, no. 1 (2009): 55–79.

23. Mauch, "A Bolt from the Blue?"

24. Fukudome, *Kaigun no hansei*, 64.

25. See BBKS, *Senshi sōsho (101): Daihon'ei kaigunbu daitōa sensō kaisen
keii 2* [War history series, vol. 100: Imperial headquarters, navy,
circumstances leading to the outbreak of the greater East Asia
war, vol. 2] (Tokyo: Asagumo Shuppansha, 1979), 331–32; and
BBKS, eds., *Senshi sōsho (69): Daihon'ei rikugunbu, daitōa sensō kaisen keii 3* [War history series, vol. 69: Imperial headquarters, army,

circumstances leading to the outbreak of the Greater East Asia war, vol. 3] (Tokyo: Asagumo Shuppansha, 1973), 160.

26. See Samuel Eliot Morison, *The Two-Ocean War: A Short History of the United States Navy in the Second World War* (Boston: Little, Brown, 1963), 20–25, 30.

27. BBKS, eds., *Senshi sōsho (73): Kantōgun (2) kantokuen / shūsenji no taisosen* [War history series, vol. 73: Kwantung Army (vol. 2), Kwantung Army special maneuvers / war against the Soviet Union at the end of the war] (Tokyo: Asagumo Shuppansha, 1974), 8.

28. See Peter Mauch, *Tojo* (Cambridge, MA: Harvard University Press, forthcoming).

29. "29th Liaison Conference, June 11, 1941," in Ike, *Japan's Decision for War*, 47–51 (quotation, 50–51).

30. Mauch, *Sailor Diplomat*, 183.

31. "Imperial Conference, July 2, 1941," in Ike, *Japan's Decision for War*, 77–90.

32. Kobayashi Seizō, *Kaigun taishō Kobayashi Seizō oboegaki* [Memoranda of Admiral Kobayashi Seizō], ed. Itō Takashi and Nomura Minoru (Tokyo: Yamakawa Shuppansha, 1981), 127.

33. BBKS, *Senshi sōsho*, 101:402–4.

34. BBKS, *Senshi sōsho*, 101:454–55. See also BBKS, *Senshi sōsho*, 70:491–95, 499–508.

35. "Imperial Conference, September 6, 1941," in Ike, *Japan's Decision for War*, 133–63.

36. "57th Liaison Conference, October 4, 1941," in Ike, *Japan's Decision for War*, 179–81 (quotation, 180).

37. Todaka Kazushige, "Shinjuwan wa sōteigai! Kaisen o tomerarenakatta 'sekinin' to 'gosan'" [Pearl Harbor was unexpected! "Responsibility" and "miscalculations" that were unable to prevent the opening of war], in Rekishi kaidō henshūbu, eds., *Nichi-Bei kaisen no shin'in to gossan* [The opening of the Japanese-U.S. war: Real causes and misunderstandings] (Tokyo: PHP Kenkyūjo, 2021), chap. 5.

38. "66th Liaison Conference, November 1, 1941," in Ike, *Japan's Decision for War*, 199–207 (quotation, 207).

39. "Imperial Conference, November 5, 1941," in Ike, *Japan's Decision for War*, 208–39 (quotation, 233).

CHAPTER NINE

WHICH ADVERSARY, WHEN?

THE STRATEGIC DILEMMAS OF THE ROYAL NAVY, 1939-45

Geoffrey Till

THE PLANNER'S PROBLEM

In World War II, British naval planners, like those of every other navy in every other period, faced a gap between their resources and their possible commitments. This iron law of naval procurement meant choices and adjustments had to be made between various competing courses of action. The resultant dilemma for the British was particularly bad before and during World War II. Both immediately and for an indeterminate future, they needed to service expanding commitments in Europe, the Mediterranean, and the Indo-Pacific all at the same time, but with insufficient resources. "We are a country," said Lord Curzon, summarizing the problem, "by virtue of our insular position in Europe and of our Imperial position abroad, with maritime approaches on every side, that makes everyone our neighbor, our frontier are the frontiers of every state, or almost every state, in the world." Although we should indeed "ditch the idea that Britain had entered into an inevitable state of decline in the early twentieth century," this still meant its policymakers and planners faced a multitude of resource-constrained choices.[1]

First, there was the issue of deciding which enemy to fight. Since this was a matter of objectives and grand strategy, it was something politicians had to decide rather than the military, and still less the Royal Navy.[2] Its task was to implement, and maybe guide, if it could, the decisions of its political masters. Naval planners had not simply to decide how to allocate ships, people, and capabilities between the competing theaters of war, difficult though that was. It was also a question of determining what *kind* of forces they would need to be, because the geographic and strategic distinctiveness of different theaters would likely demand varying types and mixes of ships and capabilities.

Then, second, there was an important *temporal* aspect to the problem as well. Anticipations (or just plain guesses) about the likely course of events, mean that decision-makers, then as now, had to prepare for future priorities that could be quite different from current ones because of circumstantial changes that were certain to take place but also likely to be unpredictable in nature. Further, this process of preparation for the future would need to be conducted alongside that for current operations. As a result, a navy's "capability deliverers" (to use the modern term) could find themselves servicing two different sets of strategic priorities at the same time. This delicate balancing act between the demands of the present and future is exceedingly difficult for fleet designers to manage as Admiral Doenitz, with his reliance on the currently available U-boat Type VII, discovered when his much-vaunted Type XXI, XXIII, and even the XXVIB arrived too late to have material effect.

Third, as Anthony Eden remarked, "One of the disturbing factors in the situation was that so much was incalculable."[3] Accordingly, there was every possibility that all of those "looking through a glass darkly" would come to different conclusions about all of this, whether from strategic conviction or sectional and service interest. Finally, since strategic change was the only constant, this was a continuous process—a race without a finish-line tape.

All these problems and issues are manifest in the Royal Navy's evolving strategic policy toward Japan as its main antagonist at sea. They are equally clear, operationally, in its worst disaster, the destruction of Force Z in December 1941, and in one of its main accomplishments, the British Pacific Fleet of 1944–45. The decisions made reflected both the long period of strategic reflection and adaptation through the interwar years and then the experience of war in the European theater from 1939 to 1941.

NAVAL POLICY AND JAPAN: CHOOSING THE ENEMY TO FIGHT

During the interwar period, the broad consensus had been that Britain should aim at developing a navy ultimately capable of covering against Japan, while at the same time keeping sufficient force at home to deter any significant European threat. In the 1920s, the navy focused strongly on the Japanese threat where it came up against the redoubtable Chancellor of the Exchequer, Winston Churchill.[4] The more immediate need, though, was to be able to respond quickly and effectively to specific developments that seemed likely to threaten the empire wherever they arose. Accordingly, the Royal Navy found itself involved in an apparently endless series of crises, such as the Russian, Turkish, Chinese, and Spanish Civil Wars. These lesser demands, of course, in the modern jargon, "consumed readiness" and aggravated the navy's capacity to manage its strategic dilemma in an age of austerity.[5]

By the early 1930s, it was clear that a combination of disarmament arrangements, defense cuts, and the linked atrophy of the British defense industrial base were making dealing with both present and future increasingly challenging. The 1935 mobilization for the Abyssinian Crisis revealed the problem all too clearly. Both the British and the Italian navies understood that the Royal Navy would win any such war, but the likely damage it would suffer could make the deterrence of anyone else problematic.[6] For that reason, Admiral Chatfield, the most impressively far-sighted of the First Sea Lords of the time, argued for a foreign policy expressly designed to reduce the number of potential adversaries that the Royal Navy might need to deal with. In a way, this made the state of the navy a driver of national strategy, rather than merely one of its instruments. As an attempt at threat reduction by diplomacy, however, it failed. For a while, the Abyssinian Crisis made it politically impossible to regard Italy as a possible partner; later, however, in 1938–39, planners needed to remember it might be. Most of the time the Germans and the Japanese appeared to be generally unappeasable, but on occasion even they could be seen as at least deferred adversaries.

This shape-shifting strategic ambiguity about who and what to concentrate on made the naval planners' problem very difficult. For this reason, they stuck to their New Standard Fleet (NSF) of 1936, on the basis that with it the Royal Navy could deal with almost anything. Such a fleet would mitigate the dilemmas of choice. The NSF was indeed a "breath-taking" project. It comprised twenty capital ships, fifteen carriers, one hundred cruisers, nearly two hundred destroyers allocated to twenty-two flotillas, eighty-two submarines, and "the usual proportion of smaller vessels." It would have been an effective and balanced force. It was designed to provide a range of options likely to come in handy when dealing with a reasonable range of contingencies. At the same time, it could be (just about) affordable in peacetime. The expectation was that, once war came, the resultant mix of capabilities and forces would need to be adjusted to suit circumstances as they unfolded.

This was problematic, despite or perhaps because of, the accepted need to spread the resultant construction program over seven years. Moreover, given the urgent need to cope with the possibility of horrific air attacks at home and then to bolster the French, respective governments prioritized first "Fortress Britain" and the RAF and then the construction of an army capable of a serious continental commitment. Against the navy's focus on the Far East, there was also the countervailing argument that Japan was unlikely to move against the empire unless and until Britain was embroiled in a demanding war in Europe. By focusing on preserving peace in Europe, in other words, two birds could be killed with one stone This resultant budgetary and industrial constraint meant that the chances of the navy's NSF being built in time, or even at all, were low.

With that, the capacity to handle the German, Italian, and Japanese naval threats simultaneously became extremely problematic and inspired the long campaign to turn either Japan, Germany, or Italy into at least a deferred adversary. As a result of this strategic uncertainty the Royal Navy went to war in 1939 against an enemy that had not been its main focus of concern for most of the interwar period. Worse, the operational requirements of the Euro-Atlantic and Indo-Pacific theaters were significantly different. The latter was likely to demand the capacity to operate across vast distances and in open water; the former suggested limited range operations in coastal and narrow waters well within the reach of land-based airpower. Of course, both could be accommodated to a limited extent, but the last-minute switch in priority from the Indo-Pacific to the Euro-Atlantic required a major conceptual adjustment and also meant that both campaigns proved to be critically underresourced.

THE EXPERIENCE OF WAR, 1939–1941

From the grand-strategic point of view, the war started quite well for the Royal Navy in that only Germany was initially involved, although there remained the prospect of the other two Axis powers joining in at some later date. Nonetheless, some urgent adjustments were required. Recognizing that despite the attention paid to the RAF and the army, the navy needed to get bigger, faster had led to a cut-down but still substantial fleet construction program in the late 1930s. No one knew, of course, how long the war would last, nor how long would the navy accordingly have in which to expand its fleet. From the start, though, it was agreed that battleship construction would actually need to be delayed because its completion would probably take too long. This delay would also facilitate the earlier construction of other types of warships more urgently required, particularly convoy escorts, escort carriers, amphibious warfare ships and merchant ships, the construction of which was in any case less demanding.

Britain's capacity to both build and crew a bigger fleet depended on the strength of its industrial base and its manpower pool. These, and their limitations, were major preoccupations for the government before and during the war and a subject of much dispute among historians ever since. Resource limitations did much to frame naval responses to the operational challenges the Admiralty faced. In particular, the extent to which the comparatively new air dimension of war sucked up manpower and industrial resources while not providing sufficient compensating rewards for the navy was a major constraint. After a period in which the Air Ministry had very serious doubts about the extent to which the British aviation industry could produce aircraft in the number and of the quality a major war would require, Britain did indeed become a very substantial aircraft producer. In part, this relied on early preparations to reconcile the ultimate strategic interest of the state with the immediate commercial interest of the arms manufacturer.[7] But to an extent, the emphasis on the air dimension came at the expense of the country's maritime industrial base, and arguably of the Fleet Air Arm too.

The result was a need to import armor for the new carriers from Czechoslovakia and the equipping of battleships with old 14-inch guns, while its adversaries were producing theirs with 15-inch, 16-inch, and even 18-inch guns. All the same, the Royal Navy ended the war far stronger than it had been at its start, and in a style that casts significant doubt on "declinist" propositions about Britain's industrial-technical limitations and comparative lack of innovation.[8] The real commitments-resources issue instead was an excessive reluctance to risk the civilian economy in peacetime, and the strategic choices that were in the end reluctantly made.

For the Royal Navy in 1939 the worst consequence of this dilemma was the disappointing state of naval aviation and the associated vulnerability of the fleet to land-based airpower. The dire consequences of this were apparent in the Norwegian, Dunkirk, Crete, and Mediterranean campaigns, all of which were fought in close proximity to land. Land-based airpower, particularly in the shape of Fliegerkorps X, proved a much more serious threat than had been anticipated. Hard experience in the first two years of the war had clearly demonstrated that, in the pithy words of Rear Admiral Henry E. Eccles, "it is literal hell to have to fight against air power without it."[9] This is often portrayed as the triumph of aircraft over battleships, of airpower over sea power, and of the failure to take the required responses attributed to the "sclerotic conservatism" of the Royal Navy.[10] Although often endorsed by air enthusiasts of the time, such impressions are simplistic and overdrawn.

Instead, deficiencies in the number and quality of its aircraft were in large measure due to the underinvestment and design compromises that came about in consequence of the Dual Control system by which responsibility for, and the management of, the Fleet Air Arm was unhappily shared between the navy and the RAF. This contributed to the low numbers and poor quality of most British naval aircraft, and in particular of its fighters. For such reasons, British naval aviation had slipped from complete predominance in 1918 to inferiority, relative to the U.S. and Japanese. It is important however not to slip into the trap, remarked on by Andrew Boyle, of unconsciously basing criticism of the Royal Navy's relative air mindedness on a comparison of British naval aviation of 1939 with that of the U.S. and Japanese navies of 1941.

The result of the indifferent performance of British naval fighters was an excessive and unwarranted reliance on defensive antiaircraft (AA) gunfire. Moreover, there were substantial and realistic doubts in pre-radar days about the prospects for the preemptive interception of incoming air attack. The performance of the AA fire that had to be relied on instead, however, was particularly disappointing. This was especially true of the High Angle Control System (HACS), on which much depended. Nonetheless, a radically new emphasis in fleet defense against air attack was already in train. British experiments before the war had already shown that radar could profitably be taken to sea in a way that would much improve the chances of air interception, especially when the lessons of fighter direction learned during the Battle of Britain were applied. This was speedily done. When in 1942 the carrier HMS *Victorious* was loaned to the

American fleet in the Pacific, its fighter direction capabilities were much admired. Making up for past deficiencies by getting the high-quality fighters best able to exploit it, however, took much longer. The strategic bombing offensive and the battle for air superiority over land continued to have a higher national priority.

The vigor with which the navy fought, eventually successfully, to recapture the Fleet Air Arm from the RAF (together with operational control of Coastal Command), however, shows that the Royal Navy was certainly not blind to its potential. Before the war, the Admiralty had pushed for better means of measuring the performance of its AA defenses, and, as already remarked, the development of sea-based radar along with the fighter direction this made possible. It had stressed the need to armor its aircraft carriers, a move that was controversial in that it reduced their aircraft complement but enhanced their survivability against air attack. Through the interwar period, the Admiralty had thoroughly investigated the prospects for carrier attacks on enemy bases and targets ashore, and even toyed with the notion of combined carrier groups especially for a putative high seas battles with the Imperial Japanese Navy. Only with the resources that came later in the war could these sometimes-misty aspirations be translated into operational reality, in the shape most notably of the British Pacific Fleet.[11]

Again, if the operational performance of the HACS was overrated and had speedily to be compensated for, much the same could be said of ASDIC (an early version of sonar). Partly because of this, but also in part because Germany was nominally only allowed to construct a limited submarine fleet under the 1935 Anglo-German Naval Agreement, the U-boat threat to shipping was underestimated. Moreover, there was an understandable failure to anticipate the German army's overrunning France and much of Scandinavia and so winning much better access to the Atlantic. Instead, the navy worried rather more about the surface raider. This threat did indeed need to be taken seriously, especially when conducted in conjunction with submarine attack, but the U-boat proved to be of much greater concern and required major operational and policy adjustments.

Dealing with the U-boat thereafter called for a significant redistribution of fleet energy and resources, away from the high seas battle for sea control, which had dominated planning and construction in the interwar period. Instead, the emphasis had to be on a massive construction and training effort, and the devotion of much scientific effort to the antisubmarine war. Necessarily at the expense of other of its roles, this campaign demanded an antisubmarine navy in a state of permanent revolution. It had constantly to adjust to new tactical-technical challenges, ultimately with great success.[12] This was just as well, since the argument that the Battle of the Atlantic was by far the most strategically important naval campaign of the whole war is strong and justifies the resources devoted to it, even if at the price of preparing for high seas encounters.[13] Once this existential threat was rendered manageable, beginning with American entry and certainly by the spring of 1943, more attention could be paid to other aspects of the war at sea, not least in the Far East.

WAR AND THE FAR EAST COMMITMENT, 1939–41

For the British, in the first two years of the war, there was little question about ultimate priorities. Even the Australians and the Americans accepted that for the British the European situation would have to come first. Strategically this seemed nothing but sensible. Only a war in Europe would threaten Britain itself, the heart of the empire. Moreover, given Japan's continuing preoccupations with the long, messy, and costly war in China; its possible intentions against Russia; an increasingly assertive United States waiting in the wings of the Pacific theater; and Britain's residual prestige as still the world's preeminent global power in the interwar period, it was reasonable for Churchill to conclude that "Japan is unlikely to attack us unless and until she is sure we are going to be defeated (in Europe)."[14] As Churchill himself later admitted, this view was based on an apparently reasonable assumption that Japanese action could be reconciled "with prudence or even sanity."[15] Perceptions of Japan's industrial backwardness relative to Britain and the United States seemed to reinforce the point.[16]

Moreover, there was the temporal aspect noted earlier. Once the European war started, in the words of Australian prime minister Robert Menzies, Britain faced a choice between "taking a risk with an existing war in order to guard against a possible one."[17] Even after the fall of Malaya and Singapore, Churchill, was quite unrepentant about his choice: "If the Malay Peninsula has been starved for the sake of Libya and Russia, no-one is more responsible than I, and I would do exactly the same again."[18]

His rationale at the level of grand strategy was perfectly clear. With the fall of France and before the entry of the United States into World War II, Britain and its empire stood alone against Germany and Italy, with Japan waiting menacingly in the wings. The German invasion of Russia in June 1941 ended this especially dangerous period, and thus it seemed critically important to keep this new ally in the war. In the short term, the woeful Soviet unpreparedness for dealing with Operation Barbarossa demanded urgent British help. Hence the decision to supply Russia in its apparent hour of need with fighters and other aircraft, as well as the tanks that might otherwise have made all the difference in the Malaya campaign.

The Mediterranean theater seemed increasingly important as a crucial staging point for supporting, and being supported by, imperial possessions in the Indo-Pacific, not least for their fighting manpower. The oil of the Persian Gulf was important too and had to be guarded from both the Germans and, more remotely, the Japanese. The same applied to the oil of the Caucasus which was seen as critical to the survival of Russia as a fighting ally. For both these reasons, much was hoped for from General Auchinleck and his Operation Crusader, beginning on November 18, 1941. Hopefully, this would consolidate the security of Britain's hold on North Africa once and for all. Accordingly, the demands of the Libyan campaign had a much higher priority in manpower and military matériel than did a possible Malaya campaign—which might not have even happened at all if Britain was clearly victorious in the Mediterranean.

The consequence of these priorities was clear. Such expectations contributed to the relatively slow progress in developing the naval base at Singapore before the war. During the first two years of the European war, Far Eastern priorities slipped still further. The basic idea had been that the deployment of the "main fleet" to Singapore would sufficiently deter the Japanese from attacking Malaya. But this deterrent posture was gradually weakened through the interwar period and into the early stages of the war in Europe. It was accepted back in 1922 that the local defenders might have to stick it out for six weeks or so before the "main fleet" arrived. By 1939 this "period before relief" had extended to six months, and in the following year, until Italy had been defeated in the Mediterranean, there was doubt that the main fleet would arrive at all. In the meantime, as the chiefs gloomily noted in July 1940, "In the absence of a Fleet our policy should be to rely primarily on airpower. The air forces required to implement that policy, however, cannot be provided for some time to come. Until they can be made available we shall require substantial additional land forces in Malaya, which cannot in present circumstances be found from British or Indian resources."[19] Worse still, the size of the relieving naval force that could be spared from the European theater got progressively smaller with the unanticipated fall of France in 1940, the German intervention in the Mediterranean, and the start of the Arctic convoys in the autumn of 1941.[20] Churchill and the Admiralty hoped things would get better from the spring of 1942, which indeed they eventually did, making it possible to build up a substantial Eastern Fleet to guard the all-important Indian Ocean.[21] But, for now, and despite some professional advice to the contrary, most notably from General Dill, the Chief of the General Staff, Churchill persisted in his broad lack of sympathy for "further dispositions for the defense of Malaya and Singapore, beyond the modest arrangements which are in progress."[22]

The result of this was a running down, rather than a buildup, of naval, army and air resources in the theater. For example, the crack fifteen-strong 4th Submarine Flotilla, arguably the very best in the

Royal Navy, which had practiced wolf-pack tactics against invasion fleets in the Gulf of Thailand, was withdrawn from the theater in 1940 and sent to the Mediterranean.[23] While overall personnel numbers in Malaya and Burma were kept high, this was by dint of mobilizing large numbers of barely trained soldiers, especially from India. There were key manpower shortages in all three services, not least in the various intelligence agencies. For the same reason, the British had no tanks in Malaya, too few first line aircraft, and were short in all manner of military supplies, not least in telephone wire, which later made battlefield communication difficult. When from June 1941 it looked as though the Soviet Union might succumb to the German assault, Britain sent six hundred fighters there rather than to Singapore, where such critical shortages were to make it far easier for the Japanese to control the skies.

In their Far Eastern policy, though, the British had concerns other than the direct and immediate operational defense of Malaya and Singapore. These derived from that other way of dealing with a potentially superior adversary, namely, to rally support from allies and partners. As the situation in the Far East deteriorated, the Australians and the New Zealanders started to put the pressure on for more resources to be devoted to the defense of Singapore in support of Britain's promise of 1922 to see to their security in the Far East. Imperial rather than solely British defense, therefore became a policy driver. But the two merged, as the British always said they would, because both dominions made a crucial contribution to the campaign in Libya on which Churchill pinned so much hope. In the Australian case in particular, this support was thought conditional on Britain satisfying antipodean security needs close to home.

There was an American angle to this as well. One of Churchill's major priorities was to secure the entry of the United States into the war. Roosevelt, for his part, was slowly trying to persuade the American public that they should do so. But politically Roosevelt needed physical proof that the British were a going concern out in the Far East and were not simply a decaying colonial empire desperate for help. While the Dutch were prepared to say they would help in Malaya as much as they could with submarines and aircraft, the Americans initially were not.[24] The physical proof that Roosevelt needed was what he called an "adequate token force" that should contain "some capital ships."[25] From this point of view, Force Z was to be a British sprat to catch an American mackerel, along with some antipodean ones.

Building on this, Churchill revived the idea of sending out a high-profile "Flying Squadron." Strategically, he was inspired partly by his own "glittering phrase,"[26] and more substantively by the effectiveness of German capital ships in distracting and tying down numerically superior allied forces over the past two years. He hoped that the vague menace of these intrinsically powerful units being able to "appear and disappear amongst the islands" would deter the Japanese from early aggression, particularly at a time when they would need to focus on what the U.S. Pacific Fleet was, or might be, doing elsewhere.[27] In his view, the threefold aim was for the force to act as the nucleus of a new Eastern Fleet, to protect vital communications in the Indian Ocean, and to spur the United States to greater effort in Southeast Asia. Such a deterrent strategy depended on Japan's not knowing where Force Z was, and on its having the fueling and supply resources needed for such a roaming brief.[28]

Traditionally, the Admiralty is said to have vehemently opposed this strategy. Instead, they (including the Vice Chief of Naval Staff, Admiral Sir Tom Phillips who, paradoxically, went on to command Force Z) advocated a slower buildup of forces in the Indian Ocean, while making it clear that before such a force was ready it would need to be kept out of harm's way.[29] Unfortunately, this more stately accumulation of strategic force in the wider area would meet neither Churchill's *political* requirement for reassurance of Australia and New Zealand nor act as a promissory note to Roosevelt. Churchill was thinking of a fleet to deter war; the Admiralty were more concerned about fighting it and defending sea communications across the Indian Ocean.[30] More recent analysis, however, suggests that this was a much more harmonious process of continual adjustment than is usually said, and that, if anything, it was Admiral Pound and his colleagues, not Churchill, who ended up urging for the Royal Navy adopting a riskier forward posture for Force Z earlier than arguably proved wise.[31]

There was also an important timing dimension to this series of rolling and cumulative strategic decisions. Although the two-stage Japanese advance into French Indochina in September 1940 and July 1941 had clearly changed and potentially worsened the calculus, it was by no means clear that these moves necessarily portended an attack on British and Dutch holdings to the south rather than one on China to the north. As late as November 19, 1941, the Far East Combined Bureau (FECB), despite high-level intelligence to the contrary, dismissed the Japanese buildup in what is now southern Vietnam as merely a prelude to intended offensive operations in southern China.[32] As far as a possible assault on Malaya or the East Indies was concerned, it was widely but not exclusively believed that the Japanese were unlikely to make any seaborne move until the monsoon was over—in perhaps late February or March 1942. FECB was aware of the fact that the Japanese navy had changed ship and shore base call signs on November 1 and then again, most unusually, on December 1. "It can be assumed," they said the following day, "that this change is made in preparation for an operation"—but they still weren't sure where, and generally did not think it would be against Singapore.[33] Over the next few days, however, they began to suspect an attack might indeed be imminent. Up till then, like everyone else, Churchill and his local commanders overestimated the time available for the assembly of the necessary deterrent or defensive forces.

The result of all this was a compromise between the various positions. Thus, when HMS *Prince of Wales* and *Repulse* made their grand entry into Singapore on December 2, they were seen as the first earnest of a stronger force—the Eastern Fleet—that would be built up later. Indeed, HMS *Exeter* of the Battle of the River Plate fame arrived eight days later, as did the U.S. 57th Destroyer Division, where, as one participant later recalled, "[they] were supposed to act as anti-submarine screen for the *Prince of Wales* and *Repulse*."[34] Not realizing how short time was, Admiral Phillips dispersed Force Z immediately upon arrival. HMS *Prince of Wales* went in for a long-overdue refit of her boilers and distillers that was expected to take a week, the *Repulse* plus two of her destroyer escorts, HMAS *Vampire* and HMS *Electra*, steamed off to Darwin to reassure the Australians. Additionally, Phillips himself flew to Manila to confer with the Americans and arrange for the dispatch of U.S. destroyers to Singapore. He also planned to hold talks with the Dutch to integrate their aircraft and submarines into the overall effort. Asked by his British host in Labuan on the way to Manila on December 4 whether there would be war with Japan, Phillips replied, "I don't think so."[35] In fact, the Japanese had made the final decision to attack the day before Force Z arrived in Singapore. They sank the two capital ships on December 10, killing more than eight hundred sailors.

There is some justification for the argument that the men on the spot in the Malaya theater did not make the best use of what was available.[36] Nonetheless, the overwhelming reason for Britain's catastrophic defeat by the Japanese and the fall of Singapore can be attributed to the all-round resource shortages that resulted from the exercise in radical strategic readjustment that successive governments felt forced to make in the five or so years preceding it.

THE PERIOD OF RECOVERY IN THE FAR EAST, 1942–45

Thereafter, British strategic choices in the Far East, especially after the final, cataclysmic fall of Singapore in February 1942, were above all heavily contingent on what the Japanese and Americans did, but this still required making choices first about the balance in resource allocation to be made between the Pacific and European wars. Naturally, this also depended on the nature of the operations to be conducted in both. Increasingly, this was a process of adjusting back, to some extent at least, to the navy's earlier strategic assumptions.

In the Far East, Churchill was initially reluctant to sanction major operations against Rangoon and Singapore, or even smaller-scale and more dubious operations such as the reconquest of the Andaman Islands. He was long averse to the "laborious reconquest of Burma, swamp by swamp."[37] Instead, he sought Operation Culverine, the seizure of the western tip of Sumatra, as a base from which to prosecute the war against the Japanese in Malaya, with the possibility of linking up with Australian and MacArthur campaigns along the Dutch East Indies to the Philippines, and as a possible means of strategically retaking Singapore from the soft underbelly of Southeast Asia. The British service chiefs and the Americans were able quickly to show that the means for such a bold and demanding operation were simply not available. Sumatra wasn't as soft as all that.

Accordingly, recovering Britain's position in the Far East, this "grave of a dozen schemes," resolved into two competing strategic alternatives, both of which would call for radically different naval responses.[38] The first was to consolidate and build up imperial strength in India and then launch into a major sea-based land campaign to drive the Japanese out of Burma and Malaya. To Churchill, the empire "striking back" in this way had resonance.[39] Such a major operation, however, seemed likely to be painfully attritionalist in nature, long, difficult, and wholly reliant on the Royal Navy providing the conditions under which the necessary manpower and matériel could be brought into the theater and supplied. In the end, under General Slim, this campaign was impressively successful, but the war ended before its final consummation with Operation Zipper, a planned amphibious operation against occupied Malaya to retake Singapore.

The more maritime alternative was initially pushed by General Alanbrooke and his colleagues. This was for a campaign focused on directly joining the Americans in the final assault on Japan in the Pacific. Sweeping across the spaces of that vast ocean, this would be an entirely different style of operation for the Royal Navy, requiring major adjustments in its composition and procedures. In the end, the British found that they had, just about, the resources to do both. The existing Eastern Fleet in effect became the British East Indies Fleet, supporting operations in the Indian Ocean, while another new fleet was sent out from the United Kingdom to become the British Pacific Fleet.[40]

By this time the Royal Navy had "adjusted" to changing circumstances by expanding to a fleet of some 900 major units and with a personnel strength that had grown from 129,000 in 1939 to 863,5000 by mid-1944. Manpower, however, had become a major concern in every way. Such a huge shift of focus to the Pacific, at a time when Britain and its navy were both exhausted and regarding the postwar future with some foreboding, could hardly be more demanding. Nonetheless, as a major exercise in strategic readjustment, the effort was successful, and, for all its manifold difficulties, Britain's objectives in the Far East were largely achieved.

FORMING THE BRITISH PACIFIC FLEET

The British Pacific Fleet (BPF) of 1944–45 was a remarkable and successful exercise in radical adaptation,[41] despite acting merely as Task Force 57 of Admiral Spruance's 5th Fleet and being dwarfed by the sheer scale of American naval forces already in the Pacific. Even at the end of a totally exhausting war, the British produced a new fleet of four armored fleet carriers, two modern battleships, seven light cruisers, and three destroyer flotillas that performed all their tasks successfully in the final campaign against Japan. The experience and the level of operational expertise gained in such operations were excellent strategic preparations for the postwar world.

Refocusing back onto Japan instead of Germany as the main adversary required major adaptation in the Royal Navy's approach to the conduct of operations. But changed circumstances meant this was not to be simply a return to the habits of thought and planning assumptions of the interwar years; this was to be an aggressive campaign, quite different from the limited and defensive operations imagined in the 1930s. Moreover, while the sheer size of the theater of military operations was the same, now there were virtually none of the bases and port facilities that the Royal Navy as an imperial navy had got used to relying on for support and maintenance when operating in distant seas. Sydney was 12,500 miles from Britain and 2,000 from Manus Island, the BPF's main operating base. As Admiral Fraser put it, "The distances involved are similar to those of a fleet based in Alexandria, and with advanced anchorages at Gibraltar and the Azores, attacking the North America coast between Labrador and Nova Scotia."[42] Facilities in Australia were the nearest to hand, but even they were very far away from Japan's home waters, the likely area for the conduct of final operations.

Moreover, styles of operation would be different too. By the time the British Pacific Fleet would be able to arrive in strength, the cataclysmic Battle of Leyte Gulf had more or less finished off the Japanese navy as a serious contender for sea control. Thus, the Japanese did not mount a serious assault on allied merchant shipping as had been expected. As a result, the operational focus of the BPF was on neither sea control nor the defense of sea communications against the residual threat posed by submarines, fast attack craft, mines, and aircraft. Instead, it was on the projection of offensive power ashore.

The Royal Navy *was* experienced in offensive operations, but largely by means of amphibious landings in which operational and tactical surprise was a key factor. But that was not the style of operations in the later stages of the campaign in the Central Pacific, where very heavily defended islands had to be seized methodically, one by one, in predictable operations where surprise could hardly be relied on. Here the emphasis would be on long-lasting attritional bombardment to reduce air and ground defenses as much as possible, before the troops landed. By the time the British arrived, this support had to be delivered under completely novel kamikaze air attack. These conditions required especially high levels of both defensive and offensive firepower and resilience in naval supporting services. The BPF's level of performance in both would have astonished their forebears in the Norway and Crete campaigns.

All this demanded constant replenishment at sea for long periods of time, far from any bases. It meant that to participate fully in such operations, the Royal Navy needed to develop a fleet train, really for the first time on this scale. Admiral King pointedly emphasized the need for this. The extent of the challenge was demonstrated on July 22–24, 1945, when a U.S. task group of fifteen tankers, five support ships, and four freighters supported TF 38 and the British TF 37 (redesignated from TF 57 in May) in their final devastating attacks on Japanese naval bases in the war at sea's biggest display of underway replenishment.[43] Moreover, this requirement occurred at a time when pressure on Britain's manpower and merchant fleet was at its most acute, given the urgency of the need to wind the European war down and the British economy up.

Finally, the British Pacific Fleet would very much be acting as junior partner in a campaign that the U.S. Navy, especially in the person of Admiral King, regarded very much as its own. This plus its reliance on the Americans for practical assistance of every kind meant that the BPF had to accept another way of doing things, to an extent it was decidedly not used to. The BPF's commanders handled this transition to junior partner with skill and grace. It helped that the British still had things to offer even in carrier operations, such as the angled deck and light landing systems that were to prove themselves in postwar operations. The requirement to make this adjustment nevertheless symbolized the gradual transfer of strategic weight from Britain to the United States during the course of World War II. The arrival and performance of the BPF nonetheless helped ensure that Britain could stay at the postwar top table, with some credibility, at least for a while.

Almost as a form of osmosis through close association, the Royal Navy picked up unfamiliar habits of thought and procedure across the whole range of naval operations. This included more modern ways of treating the lower deck, its people, as for instance in the acceptance of centralized messing; insuch gradual ways, the old democratic feudalism that had distinguished relations between officers and ratings up to then was transformed. This fitted the shift in social attitudes back home that resulted in the election in 1945 of a Labour government and the ushering in of the welfare state.

In this, the navy was responding to an even wider set of challenges than those simultaneously posed by the military power of Germany, Italy, and Japan. Events were to show that holding the line against two while the third was dealt with was strategically impossible. Instead, Britain was pinned down in Europe until late 1942 to such an extent that it could not adequately service the Far East. Thereafter with the considerable American, imperial, and other Allied help, resources began matching commitments much better. For all its initial setbacks, the Royal Navy proved sufficiently resilient to absorb the attrition that resulted from its inability to choose which enemy to fight when, and ultimately to emerge exhausted but triumphant. In consequence of the lessons painfully learned and the adjustments made in and after the heat of battle, the victorious postwar Royal Navy was to be very different from the one that had gone to war in 1939. All the same, it could not escape the simple fact that postwar Britain continued to have more commitments than resources and the Navy's traditional capacity to "make do and mend" was to be repeatedly called on in the years to come.

NOTES

1. Quoted and sourced in David French, *Deterrence, Coercion and Appeasement* (Oxford: Oxford University Press, 2022), 137–38.
2. French, 15–65, explorers, who made grand strategy.
3. Quoted and sourced in French, 251.
4. John H. Maurer, "'Winston Has Gone Mad': Churchill, the British Admiralty and the Rise of Japanese Naval Power," *Journal of Strategic Studies* 35, no. 6 (2012): 775–97.
5. G. H. Bennett, *The Royal Navy in the Age of Austerity, 1919–1922: Naval and Foreign Policy under Lloyd George* (London: Bloomsbury Academic, 2016).
6. French, *Deterrence*, 329–57.

7. David Edgerton, *Warfare State: Britain, 1920–1970* (Cambridge: Cambridge University Press, 2006); Mathew Powell, "Capacity for War: Preparing the British Aviation Industry in the 1920s," *RUSI Journal* 163, no. 3 (June–July 2018): 28–34.

8. See, for example, Correlli Barnett, *The Audit of War: The Illusion and Reality of Britain as a Great Nation* (London: Macmillan, 1986).

9. John B. Hattendorf and Pelham Boyer, eds., *To the Java Sea: Selections from the Diary, Reports and Letters of Henry E. Eccles, 1940–1942* (Newport, RI: U.S. Naval War College Press, 2022), 258.

10. The phrase is Corelli Barnett's. See Geoffrey Till, *Airpower and the Royal Navy* (London: Jane's, 1979).

11. Till, *Airpower*, 137–71.

12. Malcolm Murfett, *Naval Warfare 1919–1945: An Operational History of the Volatile War at Sea* (Abingdon, U.K.: Routledge, 2009), 464–65.

13. Evan Mawdsley, *The War for the Seas: A Maritime History of World War II* (New Haven, CT: Yale University Press, 2019), 475–78.

14. Quoted in Andrew Gordon, "The Admiralty and Imperial Overstretch," in Geoffrey Till, ed., *Seapower: Theory and Practice* (London: Frank Cass, 1994), 80.

15. Robert Rhodes James, ed., *Churchill Speaks, 1897–1963: Collected Speeches in Peace and War* (New York: Barnes & Noble, 1980), 784–85. The notion that Japan, with its weak economy, shaky relations with Soviet Russia, deep embroilment in the China War, would also choose to take on the United States and the British Empire simultaneously indeed strained credulity.

16. Mawdsley, *War for the Seas*. This was a point continually made in the local press in Singapore and goes some way to explain its complacency about the prospects for Japanese attack.

17. Sir Robert Menzies, *Afternoon Light: Some Memories of Men and Events* (London: Cassell, 1967), 31.

18. Churchill to Clement Attlee, December 30, 1941, quoted in Christopher J. Baxter, "A Question of Blame? Defending Britain's Position in the South China Sea, the Pacific and South-East Asia, 1919–1941," *Journal of RUSI* 142, no. 4 (1997): 66–75.

19. Report by Chiefs of Staff Committee, July 31, 1940, COS(40)592 and WP(40)302, Cab 66/10, the National Archives, U.K.

(hereafter TNA). This assessment fell into the hands of the Japanese after the SS *Automedon* was captured by the Germans.

20. Mawdsley, *War for the Seas*, 132–34.

21. Andrew Boyd, *The Royal Navy in Eastern Waters: Linchpin of Victory, 1935–1942* (Barnsley, U.K.: Seaforth, 2017) makes a persuasive case that this policy was sensible, clear, and much more harmonious between Churchill and the Admiralty than traditionally thought.

22. Directive of April 28, 1941, WO 106/2620, TNA, quoted in Peter Elphick, *Singapore: The Pregnable Fortress* (London: Coronet Books, 1995), 209.

23. Alastair Mars, *British Submarines at War, 1939–1945* (London: William Kimber, 1971), 21, 24, 47–52. Thirteen Dutch submarines were based in the East Indies, however, and they joined in the British defense effort and fought very bravely. Tennant Report, Ten/22/1, National Maritime Museum, Greenwich.

24. Arthur J. Marder, *Old Friends, New Enemies: The Royal Navy and the Imperial Japanese Navy. Strategic Illusions, 1936–41* (Oxford: Oxford University Press, 1981), 141–52.

25. Commander T. C. Hampton, RN, Report of Meeting (with Admiral Leahy, USN), June 27, 1939, in Michael Simpson, ed., *Anglo-American Naval Relations, 1919–1939* (London: Naval Records Society, 2010), 288–89.

26. A typically acute observation in Menzies, *Afternoon Light*, 66.

27. The validity of Churchill's "Tirpitz option" remains controversial. Arthur Nicholson, *Hostages to Fortune: Winston Churchill and the Loss of the Prince of Wales and Repulse* (Stroud: Sutton, 2005), 36–38; and Christopher Bell, *Churchill and Seapower* (Oxford: Oxford University Press, 2013), 240.

28. For a forceful criticism of Churchill's "fleet-in-being" ideas see Captain Russell Grenfell, *Main Fleet to Singapore* (London: Faber, 1951), 131–36.

29. Bell, *Churchill and Seapower*, 244.

30. Illustrating the point, the Admiralty made it clear that should the Japanese fleet advance on Singapore or indeed Ceylon, their proposed deterrent fleet would probably need to retreat out of harm's way should deterrence fail.

31. Boyd, *Royal Navy in Eastern Waters*.
32. FECB.1948(56) in COIC Daily Summary of Operational Intelligence, Royal Australian Navy (RAN) Sea Power Centre, Canberra.
33. "Most secret sources" (ULTRA) in COIC Daily Summary, December 2, 1941, RAN Sea Power Centre, Canberra.
34. Hattendorf and Boyer, *To the Java Sea*, 183.
35. Peter Elphick, *Far Eastern File: The Intelligence War in the Far East* (London: Hodder & Stoughton, 1997), 324.
36. A detailed account of the failure of the Singapore campaign is beyond the scope of this paper. The critical literature is vast. For some sympathetic treatments of the problems faced by local commanders, see Mathew Wills, *In the Highest Traditions of the Royal Navy* (Stroud, U.K.: Spellmount, 2011); Ronald McCrum, *The Men Who Lost Singapore, 1938–1942* (Singapore: NUS Press, 2017); Geoffrey Till, *Understanding Victory* (Santa Barbara: Praeger, 2014); Peter Dye, *The Man Who Took the Rap* (Annapolis: Naval Institute Press, 2020).
37. Bell, *Churchill and Seapower*, 299–301.
38. H. P. Willmott, *Grave of a Dozen Schemes: British Naval Planning and the War against Japan, 1943–1945* (Annapolis: Naval Institute Press, 1996).
39. Andrew Roberts, *Walking with Destiny* (London: Allen Lane, 2011), 838.
40. Murfett, *Naval Warfare*, 404–5.
41. Jon Robb-Webb, *The British Pacific Fleet: Experience and Legacy, 1944–50* (London: Ashgate, 2013).
42. Mawdsley, *War for the Seas*, 468.
43. Murfett, *Naval Warfare*, 448.

CHAPTER TEN

FROM WATCHTOWER TO ICEBERG

THREE CASES OF DOCTRINAL ADAPTATION IN THE PACIFIC WAR, 1941-45

John T. Kuehn

LOVE DAY (L-DAY), THE PHILIPPINE SEA
April 1, 1945

As far as the eye could see, there were ships. Among them, over twenty aircraft carriers of various sizes, from the big fleet carriers to the "Jeep" escort carriers. On them were embarked over a thousand aircraft, providing safe escort for transports with 183,000 troops. As they began Operation Iceberg (the invasion of Okinawa and the Ryukyus), General Curtis Lemay's B-29s hammered Japanese airfields in Kyushu and southern Honshu, while U.S. Army bombers from the Philippines did the same on Taiwan.[1]

April 12, 1945

Radar operators on the picket destroyer *Stanly* picked up a large target. It was a "Betty" type bomber (G4M2E) from the Japanese airbase in Kanoya, carrying two Ohka piloted bombs to attack Allied forces at Okinawa. This force, a mix of Ohka, kamikaze special attack aircraft, and their non–special attack escorts, attacked the picket destroyer, which was supported for close-in air defense by LCS(L) 32. The Ohka, intended for large targets, was so fast that it failed to explode until after it had passed through the destroyer's thin superstructure. Due to their speed and balsa wood construction, the Ohka were difficult to destroy with munitions that were fused electro-magnetically like the Mark 30 and 40 projectiles. Combat air patrol (CAP), alerted after the first radar detections and rolled in to assist in the defense of the picket ship, shooting down at least six aircraft of various types. After the attack, *Stanly* sailed under her own power to the Kerama anchorage. She was repaired in an advanced base repair dock (ARD) and was back in action in five days.[2]

The operations by American forces at Okinawa did not just happen. There were many paths to the organizations, systems, platforms, men, and doctrine in place for the complex combat just described. These things were not improvised but the result of developments going back prior to the start of the war. Operations on this scale did not result from improvisation. Nowhere was this more the case than in the area of tactical and operational doctrine for submarines, aircraft, and surface ships.

The present analysis follows from the scholarship of Trent Hone on adaptive innovation by the U.S. Navy as an organization during World War II. It looks at U.S. naval doctrine adaptation during World War II in the Pacific from 1942 to 1945, thus the titular reference to Operations Watchtower (Guadalcanal) and Iceberg (Okinawa). There is one taxonomic difference with Hone in this regard, and that is that the U.S. Navy is an institution made up of organizations.[3] Institutions have staying power. One of the reasons for that staying power has to do with their sheer bureaucratic size, history, and culture, as well as how that history and tradition reflect societies' own history and culture. President John F. Kennedy's iconic quotation captures a truth about the Navy, both for America's cultural perception of the Navy and for the Navy's image of itself: "Any man who may be asked in this century what he did to make his life worthwhile, I think can respond with a good deal of pride and satisfaction, 'I served in the United States Navy.'"

It would have been apt to add "in World War II," and especially "in the Pacific." If we look at the timing—preparing for a reelection campaign, mere months before his assassination—I think it difficult to deny the power of this artifact of naval institutional culture as a reflection of American culture. Finally, look where it is posted—on the Navy History and Heritage Command website, easily found via a simple internet search.[4] Institutional culture is a powerful thing, and it does not come from the ether. The Navy Kennedy talked about was the institution that adapted during World War II in the Pacific in ways that urgently need reconsideration, study, and reflection.

The three case studies herein address what some have labeled the "great apes," or primary tribes of U.S. naval officers: the submarine, surface, and aviation communities.[5] The first order of business discusses what these Navy tribes were adapting *from* (their context prior to adaptation) and in response to *whom*.

THE AMERICANS

Wayne Hughes has written, in his book on naval tactics, that "tacticians had to adapt in the midst of the war so extensively that by the end of it no major category of warship except minecraft was employed in the U.S. Navy tactically for the purpose for which it had been built."[6] This assessment has stood the test of time but must be "scrubbed" against something Fleet Admiral Chester Nimitz said in 1965:

> The enemy of our games was always—Japan—and the courses were so thorough that after the start of WWII—nothing that happened in the Pacific was strange or unexpected. Each student was required to plan logistic support for an advance across the Pacific—and we were well prepared for the fantastic logistic efforts required to support the operations of the war—The need for mobile replenishment at sea was foreseen—and practiced by me in 1937.[7]

How to resolve this apparent contradiction? It is a question of humans and machines—Nimitz commented on the overall strategy, while Hughes talked about prewar design decisions about weapons of war and their tactical purposes. In resolving this, we will see the first of Hone's major points about why the U.S. Navy adapted successfully, perhaps more successfully in comparison to the Japanese: its changes illustrate its adaptive capacity. This term comes from the cognitive sciences, and for large groups like organizations and institutions we might label them "adaptive systems." Adaptation is not an all-or-nothing process; rather, it involves rates of change relative to other adaptive systems or organizations, as well as the overall "fit" for the institution. Adaptive capacity comes from the "potential for modifying what worked in the past to meet the challenges in the future."[8]

In other words, adaptive capacity comes from learning, not just as individuals but also as organizations and institutions. The relationship between the influence of the learning and size of the learning collective is also important. Individuals tend to learn faster, institutions slower. Learning has a greater effect in larger groups, but in smaller groups it tends to occur more easily. Prior to World War II, the U.S. Navy's officers spent large amounts of time increasing adaptive capacity in two ways. The first was in wargaming at the Naval War College in Newport, and the second was in annual fleet exercises conducted every year with major units of the fleet.[9] This brings us back to Nimitz's quotation "Nothing that happened in the Pacific was strange or unexpected." Nimitz has clearly overstated the case, but what they had learned was to expect the unexpected and how to adapt to the unexpected within the framework of War Plan Orange. For example, the Navy planned for advance bases. When Australia, in a breathtaking windfall, became a huge "advance base," Navy leaders and planners quickly adapted to its use and ensured that sea lines of communication to it were a strategic priority.[10] Orange as the template innovation has been examined much in the literature, especially regarding the development of U.S. Marine Corps amphibious doctrine in the interwar period. From 1920 to 1941 this doctrine has often served as the "poster child" for successful peacetime innovation.[11] During the first major amphibious landings in New Georgia, Bougainville, and Tarawa in 1943, it delivered success to varying degrees—but it was primarily the success of an interwar idea, little modified until afterward, and then only in the margins. By contrast, the doctrinal developments discussed below encompass major conceptual developments and changes in a more urgent and unforgiving environment.

ORANGE AND COMMONALITY OF DOCTRINE

Both the interwar Japanese and U.S. navies were shaped by the constraints of the Washington Naval Treaty while they thought about a war over vast distances in the Pacific. For the U.S. Navy these ideas coalesced into War Plan Orange, a contingency plan to protect American interests in the Pacific, especially in the Philippines, should war break out with Japan. Planning over the course of the interwar period led to the same vision of the environment of operations and combat in both fleets. Both foresaw a complex naval campaign as the U.S. fleet fought through the Japanese mandated islands of the Pacific against primarily Japanese air and naval forces. The U.S. Navy's plan involved two distinct courses of action. The first, which became known as the "through ticket" or "thrusting" option, focused on defending the Philippine Islands, which both services identified as Japan's likely first target in any war with the United States. By seizing the Philippines, Japan could deny the naval, air, and land forces a secure advance base from which they could wage war against the Japanese Empire in the Western Pacific. The thrusting option held the promise of preventing this. A second course of action, first introduced as a minority course of action after the Washington Naval Treaty in 1922, became known as the "step-by-step" or "cautionary" plan. This plan involved the U.S. Navy advancing slowly across the Pacific, seizing island "advance bases" where they could dock the fleet and build airfields.[12]

The U.S. Marines developed doctrine and trained to seize and defend these islands as locations for advance bases for the fleet. Once in the vicinity of Guam, the U.S. Navy would fight a climatic "decisive battle" and defeat the Japanese navy, after which it would liberate the Philippines and apply a blockade against Japan to force her to terms. Before the outbreak of war in late 1941, U.S. Army Air Force planners focused on Europe, although there was an implicit assumption that they would conduct a strategic bombing campaign to supplement the naval blockade from bases seized (or recaptured) in the Western Pacific.[13]

On the Japanese side, there were senior officers in the imperial navy and army who were deeply offended by the Washington Naval Treaty and the "inferior" position it assigned Japan by the 5:3 naval ratio for its capital ships. Elements of the naval officer corps, later characterized by historian Sadao Asada as the "fleet faction," clearly identified the United States as their primary enemy.[14] During the 1920s the fleet faction trained relentlessly to the motto of the "few overcoming the many."[15] This resulted in lethal accidents at sea during training exercises due to realistic and risky operations, many at night. Japan's strategic plans for a defense of the Pacific, based in part on compromised American war plans, outlined a campaign of attrition against the American Navy advancing from the West Coast of the United States into the Central Pacific. At some point, probably in the Western Pacific, the Japanese intended to offer decisive battle against a whittled-down American fleet in the manner of Admiral Togo's victory over the Russian fleet at the Tsushima Strait in 1906. In sum, the desired decisive battle would not take place until the U.S. fleet, pushing out from California, had been reduced to force levels where the Japanese could prevail in a replay of Togo's victory in the same general area that the U.S. Navy envisioned a fleet action.[16]

Trent Hone has characterized the U.S. Navy's battle fleet doctrine on the eve of war as "decentralized development of plans and doctrine in small units and the movement of a large, consolidated battle fleet across the Pacific as a single main body." He further argues that a "radical change" occurred during the war, especially in carrier doctrine and surface warfare night doctrine.[17] Hughes identified five tactical problem areas for the U.S. Navy on the eve of war. Hone used these in his analysis to varying degrees. Hughes tended to focus on the use of aircraft carriers, but his problems apply to submarines and surface ships as well. Those problems were "Tactical Formation; Dispersal or Massing; Offensive versus Defensive firepower; Daytime versus Nighttime tactics; Dual Objectives (e.g., battle force versus invasion force protection)."[18] Given the time and space constraints here, I will not examine each item on this list but will instead provide context for the discussion and a point of reference. I will first discuss adaptation in undersea warfare by the U.S. submarine fleet, then aircraft carrier doctrine, and finally surface Combat Information Center (CIC) doctrine.

SUBMARINE WARFARE

"'EXECUTE UNRESTRICTED AIR AND SUBMARINE WARFARE AGAINST JAPAN.' . . . This directive hadn't been expected."[19] These words open the official, and initially classified, history of the World War II operations of the Pacific Submarine Force (SUBPAC). One goes to war with the submarine force one has, and in this case the original mission orders, as cogently outlined in that long-ago directive, implied that the tactics and the doctrine required were not developed or expected. Although some thinking had been done inside the General Board of the Navy and the Submarine Officers' Committee (SOC) about using submarines to attack Japanese merchant shipping, the war they got was not the war they expected or planned for in the submarine force.[20]

Returning to Plan Orange, Japanese and American submarine doctrines were almost identical, and with good reason: they were based on the same assumptions of what war in the Pacific would look like. Both envisioned submarines as auxiliaries to the fleet. Long range and endurance for reconnaissance would be at a premium in such a war. Given the constraints of the Washington Treaty until

1937, the Japanese intended to use submarines, as well as airpower (both land- and carrier-based), to provide that reconnaissance. They would build the picture for the commanders of the major battle fleets. Similarly, the U.S. Navy intended the same role for its submarines and aircraft like the PBY Catalina flying boat. U.S. Navy submarine prewar exercises focused on submerged approaches to well-screened enemy formations, which led to tactics and patterns unsuited to attacking unscreened Japanese merchant ships and convoys. Both submarine forces focused on conserving torpedoes for high-value targets like battleships and aircraft carriers, remaining hidden, and not giving their position away so they could continue to (1) collect and develop [the tactical disposition of] the enemy fleet and, if the opportunity arose, (2) sink a capital ship and contribute to the goal of attrition of the enemy fleet.[21]

Pearl Harbor completely undid this approach, at least for the U.S. submarine fleet. Its skippers were thrown into battle with a doctrine that was poorly matched to their training and torpedoes that turned out to be almost useless as weapons of war until 1943. What is often missed was the revolutionary nature of the directive itself. The authors of the SUBPAC report noted, "This all-embracing directive, issued by the Chief of Naval Operations within six hours after the first bomb fell on Pearl Harbor, started the submarines on their campaigns. . . . It was as startling as the Japanese attack, and, in the final analysis of enemy dead, and enemy ships sunk or damaged, a hundredfold more devastating." The United States was adopting the same approach to submarine warfare it had used as one of its pretexts to enter war against Germany in 1917.[22]

How did the U.S. submarine force adapt?[23] All accounts agree that it initially did not adapt that well. Unlike air and surface forces, the doctrine of formation remained focused on individual submarines, and it was only later in the war that submarines engaged routinely in group tactics. Of the tribes, submariners remained the most independent and reliant on their commander's skill and initiative. The chief problem had to do with the cautious doctrine implied by the fleet scouting mission of the prewar era. Their tactics emphasized stealth and not giving their position away. Under these guidelines, the Navy designed what some have called the "accidental commerce raider": large, fast, modern submarines of the *Tambor* and *Gato* classes. The *Tambor* and *Gato* classes additionally had ten torpedo tubes mounted both fore and aft (six bow and four stern) as well as the ability to mount a 5-inch deck gun to replace the small 3-inch gun if required. They were also air-conditioned.[24] Despite their ideal design for unrestricted warfare in tropical waters, American submarines remained relatively ineffective until 1943. As already noted, the U.S. Navy went to war with one of the worst torpedo designs of any of the major naval powers—for submarines, destroyers, and airplanes. Only the personal efforts of Vice Admiral Charles A. Lockwood, commander of SUBPAC, resulted in workarounds and fixes for the submarine variants. Lockwood, supported by Nimitz (who also had time in submarines), demonstrated the flaws in the torpedoes and had fixes put in place, including deactivation of the magnetic exploders and new parameters for the use of contact exploders.[25] The increase in numbers of merchant tonnage sunk in 1943 reflects these fixes, and then the additional sunk tonnages in 1944 reflect an entire year of these excellent submarines with a now-serviceable torpedo at work. The other key element in their effectiveness was the use of signals intelligence (Sigint) cueing. By late 1943 Allied (not just American) submarines were often being cued by SUBPAC to attack targets using Sigint in a way that did not exist earlier in the war but that still protected the sources of the cueing.[26]

Ironically, the dismal torpedo situation worked in the U.S. submarine force's favor by reinforcing complacency in the Japanese navy about commerce protection. But other factors also pertain. It has been noted that fully a third of the submarine force's skippers were relieved in the first year for poor performance that was the result of a combination of bad torpedoes and timid interwar operational doctrine designed for major fleet engagements. These officers were often replaced with a new breed of aggressive young officers such as

Dudley "Mush" Morton of *Wahoo* fame and Dick O'Kane One can suggest that the new breed of incoming skippers, antheir often informal sharing of knowledge ashore in Pearl Harbor and Fremantle, also increased adaptive capacity in the submarine force.[27]

U.S. submarines were refitted with the 5-inch gun mentioned previously in order to allow them to better attack targets on the surface when the torpedoes malfunctioned or after the combat load of "fish" had been expended. This interacted with Japanese actions with favorable results. Japan's merchant marine fleet constituted the great Achilles heel for her maritime empire. The ineffectiveness of the U.S. submarine campaign during the first eighteen months of the war reinforced a false sense of security in the Japanese navy as well as contributed to an ongoing Japanese failure to adequately emphasize antisubmarine warfare (ASW) in its training and doctrine. In fact, there was only one Japanese officer on the Naval General Staff primarily tasked with oversight of ASW prior to the outbreak of war with the United States. Japanese officers and sailors disparaged protection of merchant ships as a lesser and even dishonorable naval mission.[28]

The other factor favoring adaptation had to do with operational leadership. Lockwood, one of the prewar advocates of the *Tambor* class boats, received orders to take over submarine operations out of Fremantle, Australia, in 1942, and his aggressive leadership resulted in Admiral Nimitz bringing him back to Pearl Harbor to command SUBPAC in early 1943 after the untimely death of Admiral Thomas English. Lockwood employed an operational analytical approach in utilizing America's huge intelligence windfalls from code-breaking and was instrumental in fixing the torpedo problem. Yet it all took time, and contingency of course played its role.[29]

Did the Japanese adapt once they realized the scope of the threat? In fact they did, by forming convoys, covered not only by ASW escorts but also by aircraft, since many of these ships moved through littoral waters of archipelagoes with Japanese air bases on them, especially in the Philippines and along what the Chinese today call the "first island chain."[30] As the Japanese adapted, forming escorted convoys, so did the Americans. Once the convoys were formed and effective, Admiral King, cognizant of the effectiveness of German "wolf packs" against convoys, pushed for Lockwood to form his own American "wolf packs." By June 1944, Lockwood had formed a "convoy college" curriculum to train his crews to use group tactics against convoys similar to the German wolf packs (*Roedel* tactics) in the Atlantic. Actual patrol areas were then part of a convoy college plan that envisioned a rotating series of patrols to practice group tactics in combat around Luzon and Formosa, especially since shrinkage of the operations area and new forward submarine bases made additional U.S. submarines available for group tactics. Fascinatingly, another outgrowth of this effort was to establish patrol areas based on expertise and named after college degrees. The newer submarine crews went to "undergraduate" patrol areas, while the more seasoned skippers went to the "graduate" and "doctoral" areas.[31] The formation of these patrol areas also created the problem of fratricide, such as Allied aircraft attacking unidentified submarines, giving birth to a system of water space management doctrine to avoid friendly attacks. For example, the most "exclusive" areas, where attacks on submarines were entirely prohibited, were called Class A areas. This doctrine is still in use in the U.S. submarine service today.[32] Also, note how elements of offensive purpose and massing of firepower were in evidence for the specifics of the military situation, in this case escorted Japanese merchant convoys.

AIRCRAFT CARRIER DOCTRINE: PAC-10

Hughes' list, mentioned above, primarily focused on aircraft carrier development during the war. For the first eighteen months of the war, carrier doctrine used prewar approaches, with one exception: mission.[33] For much of the interwar period the use of carriers was predicated on ensuring fighter cover for the battle fleet, followed by fighter protection for transport and logistics ships needed for advanced base resupply or even seizure (assault shipping). After Pearl Harbor,

Nimitz withheld using his surviving battleships (TF-1) because they were not considered fast enough and used too much fuel to accompany his carriers in executing his raiding strategy, especially with the paucity of oilers at that stage of the war. The carriers were used to provide protection to the Wake Island Relief Force. During the period prior to August 1942 and the air cover for the Guadalcanal (Watchtower I) invasion convoys, they provided cover, especially for convoys building up land bases (Samoa) as they were built up along the major sea lines of communication (SLOC) through the South Pacific.[34] The carriers' primary role, though, consisted in being used for a raiding strategy against Japanese targets, both on shore and at sea. Air defense of battleships was no longer the primary mission. As the raiding strategy was executed, the Navy learned it needed more fighters aboard its carriers, so that by the time of Midway, fighter strength aboard carriers had increased by almost a third, while the number aboard Japanese carriers remained the same. This enabled dual mission use of protection for the carrier as well as escorts for raiding carrier bombers and even use as light fighter-bombers.[35]

One could surmise that Nimitz and his carrier commanders might decide to copy their Japanese counterparts given the success of *Dai Ichi Kido Butai*, the six-carrier striking force that attacked Pearl Harbor. However, after *Saratoga*'s damage and operational loss to a submarine torpedo shortly after Pearl Harbor, there simply were not enough carriers to try the massed carrier approach, especially given the wide-ranging raids and their distances from the areas raided. Also, Midway seemed to teach that massing carriers in large groups could be disastrous. However, by mid-1943 the Two-Ocean Navy Act of 1940 began to deliver fleet and light carriers in sufficient numbers to require standardization of formation, organization, and doctrine for multicarrier groups. Nimitz anticipated this problem and convened a special board in 1943 to standardize carrier doctrine. The board adopted many of the innovations and brevity codes first developed by Admiral William V. Pratt in the late 1920s. It was titled *Current Tactical Orders and Doctrine, U.S. Pacific Fleet* (1943). In June, this doctrine, which became known as PAC-10, was promulgated to the fleet as the fast carrier task force almost doubled in size from the previous year.[36]

The Americans had been experimenting with various carrier configurations but had finally decided on both mass and dispersion: mass because they could, with all the new carriers coming online in 1943; and dispersion as a result of what happened to the Japanese at Midway. The Americans clearly wanted to avoid that scenario and now had the luxury to employ both approaches. For Galvanic—the invasion of the Gilbert Islands—Spruance organized his six large fleet carriers and five light carriers (CVL) into four carrier task groups (CTGs), each built around two or three aircraft carriers. The standard configuration included two fleet (large) carriers. To these CTGs Spruance attached the new fast battleships, which provided antiaircraft cover and protection from enemy battleships. They could also be repurposed for shore bombardment. Battleships followed three doctrinal paths, these two—carrier support operations and amphibious fire support—and one discussed in the last section of this chapter for surface-on-surface engagements. This narrative belies that of the obsolete battleship of World War II. In this manner Nimitz and Spruance achieved tactical mass and operational dispersion. The CTGs were then grouped into a carrier task force (CTF) whose first commander was Rear Admiral C. A. Pownall. Also in direct support of the landings were eight of the new escort carriers (CVE). It was the first comprehensive test of PAC-10 and proved a major success.[37]

An element in carrier use involved what would become standard practice, to first sweep through the target area to suppress enemy air (and warships if found) as much as possible, especially in areas outside the coverage of Allied land-based aircraft. Afterward, Pownall pressed Nimitz to equip the light carriers entirely with fighters for fleet defense, but King insisted on keeping some multimission Avenger (Grumman TBF) bombers on these ships. Another key feature that occurred was the standardization of fighter direction doctrine using radar and plots aboard the carriers, the forerunner of the modern carrier combat direction center (CDC). By the time of Flintlock, the Marshalls operation in early 1944, the standards imposed by PAC-10 had ameliorated the need to "learn anew" procedures should one change CTGs aboard a warship, giving the Fifth Fleet staff great latitude in task organizing as new ships and veterans came and went during operations.[38]

SURFACE CIC DOCTRINE

It is well known how poorly the U.S. Navy performed in combat at night during much of the Guadalcanal campaign in the southern Solomon Islands. During the campaign in the central Solomons, however, the Japanese navy found itself faced with American surface ships that were improving—that gave as good as they got and had begun to skillfully use their radars in night actions.[39] By mid-1943 tests had determined both workarounds and fixes for the contact exploders on the entire inventory of American torpedoes, not just those on submarines. Also, the destroyer community solved many of its problems by setting much shallower depth runs for its torpedoes. Although it took time for the improved methods and equipment to reach the battlefield, U.S. destroyer-launched torpedoes soon began to exact a deadly toll on the Japanese.[40]

But the Japanese learned, too. The first battle of the New Georgia campaign occurred in the Kula Gulf on the night of July 5, 1943, with Japanese destroyers going against destroyers and cruisers that were supporting the operation under command of Rear Admiral Warden Ainsworth. The light cruiser *Helena* was lost to Japanese destroyer-launched torpedoes, and the Japanese now had a prototype radar in use. The American advantage in radar was no longer absolute. However, new American tactics sank the radar-equipped destroyer cruiser *Niizuki*. A week later Ainsworth's forces were savaged again by the Japanese in battle off Kolombangara, with three cruisers damaged (one severely) by "long-lance" torpedoes in a defeat that mirrored that of Tassafaronga. However, American radar-directed gunfire exacted a toll and sank the Japanese flagship, the light cruiser *Jintsu*.[41] American tactics had still not accounted for the extremely long range of the Japanese long-lance torpedo, even though one had been salvaged early in the year. The Bureau of Ordnance had not forwarded the actual operational ranges of this weapon (over 20,000 yards), because it had not yet received notice of its actual ranges. It seemed that, at sea, the stalemate at night remained, thus favoring attrition—and in the Pacific War, attrition favored the Allies.[42]

The Americans had learned from the bloody Guadalcanal fights that the radar displays should be colocated with the tactical plots in a dedicated space, which became known as the Combat Information Center (CIC). These lessons and others filtered back to Hawaii where they were incorporated into new training for destroyer CIC teams under the veteran destroyer officer J. C. Wylie, who had served in the Guadalcanal battles aboard the destroyer *Fletcher*. They were codified into new doctrine and published as the *CIC Handbook for Destroyers*. This continued the American practice of capturing lessons learned and turning them quickly into standardized doctrine. Wylie was not exceptional in this, as the Navy had done the same thing with its first "ace," Butch O'Hare, after his combat tour, using him to diffuse lessons and train others. The new CIC doctrine and organization were also mirrored in the battleship and cruiser force by innovators such as Rear Admiral Willis Lee. Moreover, the (temporary) loss of the cruisers employed by Ainsworth's covering forces at Kolombangara both pushed the development of tactics serendipitously to the destroyers and provided further lessons for Merrill's cruiser force. Merrill's cruisers and many of the destroyers had the advantage of long operations together, as divisions were under the same commanders.[43]

Significant command changes occurred that brought new names and methods into view. Assuming command of one of Rear Admiral Theodore Wilkinson's destroyer divisions was Commander Arleigh Burke, a pioneer in multigroup destroyer tactics. A key to Burke's approach was to abandon using one group of destroyers and instead use multiple groups. One group would use torpedoes, the other guns, both assisted by radar-CIC plots. In this way they would have a common picture and could be mutually supporting. On the night of August 5, the opportunity to test Burke's tactics came when Commander Frederick Moosbrugger swept Vella Gulf and surprised four Japanese destroyers. Using torpedoes, Moosbrugger's divided formation sank three of the four enemy destroyers, the first such victory of its kind in the South Pacific by Allied naval forces.[44]

The next night battle centered on the Japanese decision to evacuate their ground forces from Kolombangara to Bougainville via an intermediate staging base on Vella Lavella in the Central Solomons. When the Japanese arrived to evacuate the troops from the staging base on October 6, another sea battle occurred: three destroyers under Captain Frank Walker attacked six Japanese destroyers under Rear Admiral Ijiun Matsuji on a clear night. Walker's aggressiveness came in part from his confidence of reinforcement by another division of destroyers. The result was one of the last surface defeats of the Americans at sea during the war: one American destroyer was lost, the other two damaged and out of action. American torpedoes sank one Japanese destroyer. The Japanese transports managed to escape with their troops. The Battle of Vella Lavella proved to be a milestone, though; after it the Americans' improvements finally established their naval dominance in day or night surface actions against the Japanese for the remainder of the war.[45]

A final test of the new doctrine remained. Not long after, in early November 1943, the Allies invaded the large island of Bougainville on their drive northwest toward Rabaul. The Japanese fleet did not stand by idly. Admiral Koga activated Operation Ro, which involved the movement of more carrier aircraft from Truk to Rabaul. American code-breakers picked up this information. What they did not intercept was Rear Admiral Omori Sentaro's sortie with two heavy cruisers, two light cruisers, and six destroyers to try and disrupt the invasion, as well as serving as escorts for a counter-landing force to attack the American lodgment ashore. Rear Admiral A. Stanton Merrill was nonetheless ready for them, and his radars provided him ample warning. Merrill had learned from Ainsworth's defeats and implemented the improved CIC doctrine, and his team was well trained, while Omori's forces were another "scratch" team put together ad hoc at the last moment. Omori remarked prior to leaving Rabaul, "We have never teamed together before, and this can be a dangerous detriment in battle. . . . Admiral Mikawa [of Savo Island fame] managed without a previously trained team, and so can we." His assumptions were soon disproved.[46]

Merrill's forces included four new light cruisers plus two destroyer divisions, both under the command of the intrepid Burke. Merrill's plan was to stand off with his cruisers and use long-range, radar-directed gunfire, but only after releasing Burke's destroyer groups to operate independently using their torpedoes first to achieve maximum surprise. These were Burke's tactics on steroids. The two forces collided on the night of November 2–3. Omori was discovered by an American aircraft during his approach and decided to turn his counter-landing transports around, pressing on to try and attack the American transports reputedly at anchor in the bay. The Americans savaged the Japanese force with well-coordinated tactics underwritten by superior situational awareness in their CICs. One Japanese cruiser and destroyer were sunk, and there was serious damage to one American destroyer. Omori turned for home, believing he had won a tactical victory, and reported sinking heavy cruisers, even though no ships of this type participated on the American side. Omori's superiors disagreed and relieved him from command.[47]

Doctrinal developments did not cease after this point in the war; they continued, but in general they were refinements on a mature way of operations that lasted for the rest of the war in the surface warfare community. By the time the invasion of Okinawa occurred, CIC doctrine had been tested in the hardest school and refined still further. For example, the concept of the picket destroyer emerged and became standard practice in U.S. naval operations throughout the Cold War and beyond as the Positive Radar Identification Advisory Zone (PIRAZ). In effect, Okinawa caused the air and surface doctrines to merge into a more comprehensive overall multidomain doctrine for air and sea.[48]

TENTATIVE THOUGHTS

PAC-10 and CIC doctrine removed the problems for the rapid aggregation and disaggregation of units in the last two years of World War II in the Pacific. No longer did ad hoc or "scratch" teams make it difficult for the Americans to learn lessons, while such problems continued to haunt Japan until the end. When good things happened ad hoc, the Americans routinely tried to institutionalize these instances of serendipity in organization and doctrine. When they did not, the obverse applied.

Standardization of training in the submarine force was even more stringent than the aviation and surface forces. In the submarine force, the same doctrinal dynamic applied and led to a completely unforeseen problem of how to prosecute submarines in an environment where one's own aircraft and destroyers proved as much a threat as enemy submarines, aircraft, and destroyers. The resulting water space management doctrine remains in force inside the U.S. Navy to this day. However, submarines continue to operate almost independently, under loose control of centralized Submarine Operating Authorities.

Did these developments constitute a revolution in warfare? Perhaps. It is rare in the history of warfare to witness the convergence of so many new technologies and their widespread development and adaptation in wars as intense as those of the twentieth century, especially on the global scale of their maritime components. Nonetheless, very few doctrines came about without existing precursors. The sheer scale of World Wars I and II and the Cold War often obscure the evolutionary nature of innovation and adaptation, particularly in doctrine. The scientific metaphor of punctuated equilibrium provides a better comparison and a surprising insight.

The doctrinal stasis that followed World War II is almost as remarkable as these changes. For nearly eighty years (as of this writing) these the doctrines and tactics have served as the bedrock for combat organization in the U.S. Navy. Perhaps one reason for this stasis has precisely been the fact that the Navy has not since had to fight a peer competitor fleet, including the Soviet Red Banner Fleet during the Cold War, in a "blue-water" or littoral environment. War and warfare, especially in a modern combined arms environment of sustained combat, have a way of reordering, and even revolutionizing, tactical development.[49]

NOTES

1. Roy E. Appleman, James M. Burns, Russell A. Gugeler, and John Stevens, *Okinawa: The Last Battle*, United States Army in World War II (Washington, DC: Center of Military History, 1948), 5–30, 101–2.
2. Robin L. Rielly, *Kamikazes, Corsairs, and Picket Ships: Okinawa, 1945* (Philadelphia: Casemate Books, 2008), 141–42; Mark R. Peattie, *Sunburst: The Rise of Japanese Naval Air Power, 1909–1941* (Annapolis: Naval Institute Press, 2001), 300.
3. See especially Trent Hone, *Learning War: The Evolution of Fighting Doctrine in the U.S. Navy, 1989–1945* (Annapolis: Naval Institute Press, 2018).
4. For John F. Kennedy, see Naval History and Heritage Command, "Lieutenant John F. Kennedy, USNR," https://www.history.navy. mil/browse-by-topic/people/presidents/kennedy.html#:~: text=%22Any%20man%20who%20may%20be,Kennedy%20 in%20August%201963 (accessed January 10, 2023).
5. John Byron, "Three Great Apes," U.S. Naval Institute *Proceedings*, May 2005, https://www.usni.org./magazines/proceedings/ 2005/may/three-great-apes.
6. Wayne P. Hughes, *Fleet Tactics: Theory and Practice* (Annapolis: Naval Institute Press, 1986), 88–89.
7. Cited in Russell F. Weigley, *The American Way of War: A History of United States Military Strategy and Policy* (Bloomington: Indiana University Press, 1973), 265.
8. Trent Hone, *Mastering the Art of Command: Admiral Chester W. Nimitz and Victory in the Pacific War* (Annapolis: Naval Institute Press, 2022), 9. See Hal M. Friedman, "Strategy, Language, and the Culture of Defeat: Changing Interpretations of Japan's Pacific War," *International Journal of Naval History*, October 10,

2013, https://www.ijnhonline.org/strategy-language-and-the-culture-of-defeat-changing-interpretations-of-japans-pacific-war-naval-demise/, for a sound corrective about Japanese "failures" in the Pacific War and explanations thereto.

9. The two best sources that describe these activities are Norman Friedman, *Winning a Future War: War Gaming and Victory in the Pacific War* (Washington, DC: Naval History and Heritage Command, 2017), for wargaming. See Albert A. Nofi, *To Train the Fleet for War: The U.S. Navy Fleet Problems, 1923–1940* (Newport, RI: Naval War College Press, 2010), for the annual fleet exercises.

10. John Miller Jr., *Cartwheel: The Reduction of Rabaul*, United States Army in World War II: The War in the Pacific (Washington, DC: Center of Military History 1959), 3–8.

11. Allan Millett, "Assault from the Sea," in Williamson Murray and Allan Millett, eds., *Military Innovation in the Interwar Period* (New York: Cambridge University Press, 1996), 70–93.

12. Edward S. Miller, *War Plan Orange* (Annapolis: Naval Institute Press, 1991), chap. 8, passim; National Archives and Records Administration (NARA), Chief of Naval Operations Correspondence, Record Group (RG) 80 (microfilm), Appendix F WPL-9 Mobile Base Project, December 20, 1923; NARA, RG 38, February 1924 Basic Orange Plan, vol. 2, 89. This section of Orange references "a '*step by step*' *advance* of practically all of U.S. Fleet."

13. AWPD/1, War Department, Washington, DC, Office of the Chief of the Army Air Forces, August 1941; see also Barry D. Watts, *The Foundations of US Air Doctrine* (Maxwell Air Force Base, AL: Air University Press, 1984), 17–22; for advanced bases discussion see John T. Kuehn, *Agents of Innovation: The General Board and the Design of the Fleet That Defeated the Japanese Navy* (Annapolis: Naval Institute Press, 2008), 130–35.

14. Sadao Asada, "Revolt against the Washington Treaty: The Imperial Japanese Navy and Naval Limitation, 1921–1927," *Naval War College Review* 46, no. 3 (1993): 84–84, 90–93.

15. David C. Evans and Mark R. Peattie, *Kaigun: Strategy, Tactics, and Technology in the Imperial Japanese Navy, 1887–1941* (Annapolis: Naval Institute Press, 1997), 282.

16. Sadao Asada, *From Mahan to Pearl Harbor: The Imperial Japanese Navy and the United States* (Annapolis: Naval Institute Press, 2006), 163–77.

17. Hone, *Learning War*, 293.

18. Hughes, *Fleet Tactics*, 89–92.

19. *U.S. Submarine War Patrol Reports and Related Documents, 1941–1945, Reference Documents on Submarine Operations and Submarines* (Washington, DC: U.S. Naval Historical Center, Operational Archives Branch, 1946); Anon., "Submarine Operational History, World War II," 2, Scholarly Resources Inc., Microfilm Edition, Ike Skelton Combined Arms Library, Fort Leavenworth, KS (hereafter USSUBDOCs [microfilm]). These words form the core of Joel Holwitt's *Execute against Japan: The U.S. Decision to Conduct Unrestricted Submarine Warfare* (College Station: Texas A&M University, 2009), which argues that planning for a form of unrestricted warfare did take place prior to America's entry into World War II and it was at odds with senior policymakers in the various interwar administrations, including that of Franklin D. Roosevelt.

20. John T. Kuehn, *America's First General Staff: A Short History of the Rise and Fall of the General Board of the Navy* (Annapolis: Naval Institute Press, 2017), 189–90. The SOC was the General Board's collaborative counterpart inside the Chief of Naval Operations (CNO) staff.

21. David W. Grogan, "Operating below Crush Depth: The Formation, Evolution, and Collapse of the Imperial Japanese Navy Submarine Force in World War II" (unpublished masters thesis, U.S. Army Command and General Staff College, 2011), 23–29; USSUBDOCs (microfilm), 1–2, 16–17.

22. USSUBDOCs (microfilm), 2; Holwitt, *Execute against Japan*, 1–2, 78–81. Holwitt's scholarship emphasizes the stark departure from long-running American foreign policy vis-à-vis merchant shipping and freedom of the seas, and he also describes the interwar training doctrine and exercises.

23. The case for U.S. Navy submarine force adaptation in World War II is also made extensively as a case study in Frank Hoffman's *Mars Adapting: Military Change during War* (Annapolis: Naval Institute Press, 2021), 56–103.

24. Jeffrey K. Juergens, "The Impact of the General Board of the Navy on Interwar Submarine Design" (MA thesis, U.S. Army Command and General Staff College, 2009), 123.

25. See Holger H. Herwig, "Innovation Ignored: The Submarine Problem, Germany, Britain, and the United States, 1919–1939," in Murray and Millett, *Military Innovation in the Interwar Period*, 258–60; email to the author from Trent Hone on the exploder issue, January 30, 2022.

26. Edward Drea, *MacArthur's Ultra: Codebreaking and the War against Japan, 1942–1945* (Lawrence: University Press of Kansas, 1992), 105–9, 130–35; and John Prados, *Combined Fleet Decoded: The Secret History of American Intelligence and the Japanese Navy in World War II* (Annapolis: Naval Institute Press, 1995), 553.

27. Don Keith, *Undersea Warrior: The World War II Story of "Mush" Morton and the USS* Wahoo (New York: Caliber Books, 2011), 5, 9, 45, 96–97. Morton sometimes machine-gunned helpless Japanese sailors and soldiers in the waters around their sinking ships. O'Kane served as "plankholder" and executive officer for Morton on the *Wahoo*.

28. Evans and Peattie, *Kaigun*, 438; the author confirmed the information about the single Japanese staff officer in an email conversation with Sadao Asada.

29. Herwig, "Innovation Ignored," 258–60. For the complacency of the Japanese navy and the destruction of her merchant fleet, see Mark Parillo, *The Japanese Merchant Marine in World War II* (Annapolis: Naval Institute Press, 1993).

30. Parillo, *Japanese Merchant Marine*, 133–38; for the first island chain see Derek Grossman, Nathan Beauchamp-Mustafaga, Logan Ma, and Michael S. Chase, *China's Long-Range Bomber Flights: Drivers and Implications* (Santa Monica, CA: RAND Corporation, 2018), vi.

31. USSUBDOCs (microfilm), 72–75. This term also represented an area of the Pacific Ocean in the Western Pacific on maritime charts used by SUBPAC and submarine captains. Here the term is also used to describe the mindset and process of how anticonvoy tactics and training evolved.

32. USSUBDOCs (microfilm), 69. The most "exclusive" areas, where attacks on submarines were entirely prohibited were classified as Class A areas.

33. National Archives and Records Administration (NARA), Record Group (RG) 80, Proceedings and Hearings of the General Board (Microfilm), May 27, 1930, "Testimony of the Commander-in-Chief U.S. Fleet, in Regard to Needs of the Fleet," 1–2. Admiral Pratt was the commander in chief providing this testimony.

34. John Lundstrom, *Black Shoe Carrier Admiral: Frank Jack Fletcher at Coral Sea, Midway, and Guadalcanal* (Annapolis: Naval Institute Press, 2006), 54–58; Glen Williford, *Racing the Sunrise: Reinforcing America's Pacific Outposts, 1941–1942* (Annapolis: Naval Institute Press, 2010), 324, 341–42.

35. David C. Fuquea, "Task Force One: The Wasted Assets of the United States Pacific Battleship Fleet, 1942," *Journal of Military History* 61, no. 4 (1997): 707–34; John Lundstrom, *The First Team: Pacific Naval Air Combat from Pearl Harbor to Midway* (Annapolis: Naval Institute Press, 1984), 116–17, 137; Jonathan Parshall and Anthony Tully, *Shattered Sword: The Untold Story of the Battle of Midway* (Washington, DC: Potomac Books, 2005), 90. See John T. Kuehn and D. M. Giangreco, *Eyewitness Pacific Theater* (New York: Sterling, 2008), 109–14, for fighter-bomber usage examples prior to PAC-10.

36. Hone, *Learning War*, 256–58.

37. Hone, 256–58; Samuel E. Morison, *Aleutians, Gilberts, and Marshall, June 1942–April 1944, History of the United States Naval Operations in World War II* (Boston: Little, Brown, 1951), 132, 116–18, 337–40.

38. Hone, *Learning War*, 256–59, 295–97; Clark Reynolds, *The Fast Carriers: The Forging of an Air Navy* (Annapolis: Naval Institute Press, 1968), 86; James H. and William M. Belote, *Titans of the Seas* (New York: Harper & Row, 1975), 220–21.

39. Trent Hone, "'Give Them Hell!': The U.S. Navy's Night Combat Doctrine and the Campaign for Guadalcanal," *War in History* 13, no. 1 (2009): 197–98.

40. Craig L. Symonds, *World War II at Sea: A Global History* (Oxford: Oxford University Press, 2018), 397–98. Trent Hone, email to author, January 30, 2022, subject "Torpedoes," based on archival information held by Hone; see also Thomas Wildenberg and Norman Polmar, *Shipkiller: A History of the American Torpedo* (Annapolis: Naval Institute Press, 2010).

41. Hone, *Learning War*, 217–22.

42. Samuel Eliot Morison, *The Two-Ocean War: A Short History of the United States Navy in the Second World War* (Boston: Little, Brown, 1963), 278–79.

43. Hone, *Learning War*, 222–25; John Hattendorf, introduction to J. C. Wiley, *Military Strategy: A General Theory of Power Control* (Annapolis: Naval Institute Press, 1989), xiv–xvii. Rear Admiral Mahlon Tisdale, who was COMDESPAC at the time, was responsible for bringing Wylie back to Pearl to help educate others. Steve Ewing and John B. Lundstrom, *Fateful Rendezvous: The Life of Butch O'Hare* (Annapolis: Naval Institute Press, 1997), 168–73.

44. Hone, *Learning War*, 225–28; Miller, *War Plan Orange*, 126. One must exclude Balikpapan, which did employ a night destroyer strike with torpedoes, but whose main targets were Japanese transports, not warships—and this time the torpedoes were effective.

45. Hone, *Learning War*, 232–35; Miller, *War Plan Orange*, 186. Trent Hone in particular identifies what the U.S. Navy did in these campaigns with doctrine and tactics as a "revolution."

46. Prados, *Combined Fleet Decoded*, 508–9; Samuel Eliot Morison, *Breaking the Bismarcks Barrier, 22 July 1942–1 May 1944*, History of the United States Naval Operations in World War II (Boston: Little, Brown, 1984), 306–8.

47. Hone, *Learning War*, 235–43; Morison, *Breaking the Bismarcks Barrier*, 306–22.

48. For picket destroyer developments and other adaptations to fight the kamikaze threat, see especially Robin L. Rielly, *Kamikazes, Corsairs, and Picket Ships: Okinawa, 1945* (Philadelphia: Casemate Books, 2008). For a discussion of PIRAZ see Garette E. Locker, "PIRAZ," U.S. Naval Institute *Proceedings*, April 1969, 143–46.

49. See John T. Kuehn, "U.S. Navy Cultural Transformations, 1945–2017: The Jury Is Still Out," in Peter R. Mansoor and Williamson Murray, eds., *The Culture of Military Organizations* (New York: Cambridge University Press, 2019), 351, 377. The author's last billet in the U.S. Navy from 1998 to 2000 was as a Combat Direction Center Officer (CDCO) aboard a Navy nuclear-powered aircraft carrier, where the legacies of PAC-10 and CIC doctrine remained in practice and, I have no doubt, where they are still practiced, in a form that aviators and CIC officers in World War II would readily recognize.

CHAPTER ELEVEN

THE MARITIME STRATEGY'S "MISSING MIDDLE"

Ryan Peeks

O n November 4, 1982, Vice Admiral Arthur Moreau briefed the Secretary of the Navy, the Chief of Naval Operations (CNO), and the commandant of the Marine Corps on a strategy for the naval services of "*decisive offensive pressure* on the [Soviet Union] from forward positions" (emphasis in original).[1] This maritime strategy, soon to be known as *the* Maritime Strategy, set the basic outlines of the U.S. Navy's policies through the end of the Cold War. With the Maritime Strategy, the Navy made a positive case for the type of war it wanted to fight (offensive, global) and an implicit case for the type of war and enemy (limited, regional) that it wanted to avoid. Conceptually, the Maritime Strategy focused on the two mission sets that naval leaders were most comfortable with: forward presence and the high-end conventional fight with the USSR. These specific missions bolstered the case for a larger fleet and served to push the Navy away from its role supporting a land war in Vietnam.

Yoked to Secretary of the Navy John Lehman's plans for naval expansion, the Maritime Strategy "successfully marketed the Navy's strategic approach, weapons systems preferences, and . . . revived and reenergized the institution."[2] Accordingly, the historical literature tends to take a positive view of the Maritime Strategy. Likewise, many modern writers on naval policy have held it up as an ideal for contemporary strategists to emulate.[3] Yet we must also consider that it was of limited utility for the fighting the Navy did in the decade after its introduction. As the service conducted successful exercises showing how the fleet would operate against the Soviet Union, it struggled with the real world of "gray zone" operations and a regional war in the Persian Gulf region toward the end of the 1980s.

Limited war with smaller powers hardly appears in the earlier iterations of the Maritime Strategy. Its framers assumed that naval forces sufficient to defeat the Soviet navy were more than sufficient to handle regional powers. The Navy's leadership also deliberately avoided anything that would return the Navy to its Vietnam-era experience as the supporting service in a land campaign. However, as the 1980s and early 1990s showed, fighting against smaller powers required organizational, doctrinal, and structural mindsets that were all but ignored in the Maritime Strategy.

In part, this is because those missions did not help make the case for a larger fleet. The framers of the Maritime Strategy explicitly saw it as a way to advocate for the Navy to receive a larger share of national resources than it had under Presidents Carter and Ford.[4] In 1989, as the Maritime Strategy lost steam, a senior Navy Staff (OPNAV) strategist warned that the Navy need a new strategy to stave off a "budget train wreck."[5] Likewise, it is impossible to untangle one of the Maritime Strategy's main predecessors, Sea Plan 2000, from the budgetary battles of the Carter years.

Following the Vietnam conflict, the U.S. Navy turned to war with the USSR as the strategic and programmatic heart of planning. When married to forward presence—useful as a force-sizing tool—that mission gave the Navy's leaders a successful argument for growth. However, the focus on a Soviet war on one hand, and forward presence on the other, created a "missing middle" in U.S. Navy strategic planning, which ignored combat operations with minor powers. This lack of a "middle" helped create a muddle in Navy planning after the removal of the Soviet threat.

To trace this thread, this chapter will start with a discussion of naval policy and rhetoric in the strategic and budgetary environments of the Ford and Carter administrations. Then it will turn to the birth of the Maritime Strategy in the early 1980s, which built on those efforts. The chapter will end by showing how the process of developing and refining the Maritime Strategy created a force ill prepared for "gray zone" operations in the Persian Gulf in the 1980s and Operation Desert Storm in 1991. This inability, or unwillingness, to devote attention to regional threats left the Navy strategically unmoored at the end of the Cold War.

The road to the Maritime Strategy started with the term of Admiral Elmo Zumwalt (1970–74) as CNO. Zumwalt, who became CNO after commanding naval forces in Vietnam, wanted to shift the service's focus from the ongoing war there to the threat of the growing Soviet navy. Believing that, in a war with the Soviets, "we would lose," Zumwalt tried to de-emphasize projecting power from the sea to land (the primary mission of the Navy in Vietnam) toward the ability to fight and win a war at sea.[6] In line with Zumwalt's pessimism, this would be inherently defensive. Incapable of sweeping the Soviet navy from the seas, the navy would instead pursue "sea control," described by one of Zumwalt's protégés as the ability to "exert air, submarine, and surface control temporarily in an area while moving ships into position to project power ashore or to resupply overseas forces."[7]

It was not lost on Zumwalt, a product of the surface Navy, that sea control was a critical function of the Navy's surface vessels, while power projection was primarily the province of naval aviators flying from expensive aircraft carriers. Power projection was the major mission of the Navy during the Vietnam era, where carriers could launch airstrikes without risking reciprocal attack. Bolstering sea-control forces would improve the relatively weak standing of the surface navy in the fleet of the 1970s and signal a shift away from the frustrations of the Vietnam War toward protecting Atlantic sea-lanes in the event of a Soviet war.[8]

This all came against the background of a precipitous drop in the size of the Navy, as warships built in the World War II era neared the end of their useful service lives.[9] To solve this problem, Zumwalt advocated the construction of a "high-low mix" of ships to replace retiring hulls with some high-end, multimission platforms, and a larger number of "moderate cost, moderate-performance ships that could be turned out in relatively large numbers."[10] Most controversially within the Navy, this included replacing some aircraft carrier construction with smaller, cheaper "sea-control ships" that could provide support for antisubmarine operations.[11]

Zumwalt's successor, Admiral James L. Holloway III (1974–78), believed, like most senior admirals, that Zumwalt's approach was overly defensive and "overall . . . not helpful to the Navy," especially in its seeming deprecation of high-end ships and the power projection mission.[12] Holloway, an aviator, believed that the U.S. Navy was still dramatically superior to its Soviet counterpart and, given that superiority, needed to focus on power projection against the Soviet Union, allowing the Navy to play an *independent*, strategically vital role in wartime.[13] In contrast to Zumwalt's "high-low mix," Holloway wanted to focus construction on expensive combatants, especially aircraft carriers and submarines.[14]

In reality, the approaches of Zumwalt and Holloway had more similarities than the latter was willing to acknowledge. While they disagreed on the importance of power projection versus sea control, both agreed that the focus of the Navy should be preparation for a Soviet war and that almost all other missions were secondary. Despite both admirals' extensive experience in the Vietnam conflict, neither wished to spend much time considering their service's role in a future limited war. As expressed by one veteran of the era, the Navy's goal was to "get back to our natural habitat at sea and stop worrying about 'brown water navies' . . . and that kind of thing; let's talk about fighting the Russians."[15] For better or for worse, Zumwalt, Holloway, and their successors maintained a laser-like focus on the Soviet fleet to the exclusion of all other potential adversaries for the remainder of the Cold War.

Both men also supported, almost unconsciously, a third major conventional mission for the Navy: presence. Though not a specifically combat role, the main peacetime role of the Navy's ships, excluding submarines, was (and remains) rotational deployments to regions of interest to the United States, where American vessels ostensibly deterred conflict, compelled adversary states to cease or avoid undesired behaviors, and reassured allies about American commitment.[16] Starting in the mid-1950s, the U.S. government's general policy was to keep two aircraft carriers on station in the Mediterranean and Western Pacific (from 1973, one carrier has been stationed in Yokosuka, Japan, to facilitate forward presence) at all times.[17]

In the post-Vietnam period, the presence mission became a powerful argument in favor of a larger fleet. Instead of portraying forward presence as simply what one did with the Navy absent a war, some within and outside the Navy began to argue that presence itself justified a certain force level, especially as the Ford and Carter administrations desired a smaller fleet than their admirals. If presence remained based on aircraft carrier battle groups (CVBGs), an argument could be made for retaining more carriers than policymakers desired for a Soviet war, carriers that would still be used against the Soviets in wartime.[18] A widely used (though inaccurate) rule of thumb is that, due to maintenance, training, and transit time requirements, forward presence requires a 3:1 ratio of total ships to deployed ships.[19] In other words, a policy of keeping four aircraft carriers and their escorts forward deployed provided justification for at least twelve aircraft carriers.[20] While naval leaders did not necessarily want carriers *for* forward presence, it was a powerful argument for a large, carrier-based fleet.

Holloway's plans for a larger, more expensive fleet ran into opposition from the Ford administration, which desired the construction of smaller aircraft carriers (CVVs) in lieu of nuclear-powered carriers (CVNs) as a cost-saving measure.[21] The succeeding Carter administration was even more hostile to a projection-focused fleet, viewing it as an expensive distraction from its main defense task of shoring up land and air forces in Europe. Secretary of Defense Harold Brown went so far as to say that the Navy's main wartime job was no longer sea control in a general sense, but merely the defense of the sea-lane running between Norfolk and the English Channel, to facilitate resupply of NATO forces, which did not require the large fleet of expensive combatants desired by Holloway.[22]

Though appointed by Carter, Secretary of the Navy W. Graham Claytor Jr. agreed with the service's uniformed leadership that the administration's policy misused the fleet. To support the Navy's arguments, Claytor chartered a strategy and force structure study, "Sea Plan 2000," which was completed in early 1978.[23] Its conclusions dovetailed neatly with Holloway's critiques of Zumwalt, providing some level of analytical support for a larger fleet oriented around resource-intensive missions. According to Sea Plan 2000's final report, projection was critical to fighting the USSR, where "forward strike operations may prove highly valuable in tying down large Soviet forces. . . . Forward naval operations can have a decisive effect on the outcome of a land war in Europe."[24]

At the same time, Sea Plan 2000 placed a great value on forward presence, the main driver of peacetime operations. In addition to deterring and containing crises "in areas where . . . military force and violence are frequently the primary means of resolving policy disputes," presence also prevented the Soviet Union from expanding its influence in the Third World. Reducing carrier numbers, an obvious outgrowth of the Carter administration's hesitance to continue CVN construction, would risk the loss of one of the fleet's four forward-deployed carriers.[25]

Sea Plan 2000's discussion of offensive naval operations owed a great debt to Admiral Thomas Hayward, the incoming CNO (1978–82). When taking command of Pacific Fleet in 1977, Hayward noticed that the fleet had no war plans for the growing Soviet naval forces in his theater. Instead, it would "swing" most of its carrier strength to European waters, where they would presumably make up the attrition suffered by Atlantic Fleet's carriers in the early stages of the war.[26] Hayward, worried about the effect of this "abandonment" on U.S. allies like Japan and South Korea as well as countering the Soviet Pacific Fleet, set his staff to draw up plans for "prompt offensive action" against the Soviets upon the outbreak of a war.[27] These Navy-led strikes, Hayward hoped, would spur China and Japan to take a pro-American stance in the event of a Soviet war and would prevent the shift of Soviet forces from the Far East to Europe.[28]

Later known as "Sea Strike," this initiative came at the ideal time for the service. First, it demonstrated what offensive power projection against the Soviet Union could look like, a mission that the Navy's bureaucratic opponents had deprecated over the past several years. This argument bolstered the ongoing Sea Plan 2000 study, showing that the uniformed and secretariat wings of the Navy Department were at odds with the Carter administration's defensive, NATO-centric defense strategy and wanted to pursue "forward, offensive operations" against the Soviets.[29]

Sea Strike also suggested how the Navy could use new systems nearing service. Both Hayward's staff and the Sea Plan 2000 team saw that new systems, most notably the F-14 fighter and *Ticonderoga* cruisers, could better protect the fleet from air attack and, if used correctly, could destroy the Soviets' relatively small force of naval bombers before they had a chance to launch their missiles. Other technological advances allowed for the detection and destruction of Soviet submarines at greater ranges.[30]

Alongside new ideas and new technologies, the push for a more aggressive strategy was bolstered by new intelligence that gave high-quality information on the Soviet navy's thought processes and doctrine. By the end of the 1970s, it was obvious, at least to those with the appropriate clearances, that the Soviet navy's focus was resolutely defensive.[31] Not only could the U.S. Navy take on an offensive role in wartime, but it was also increasingly clear that very few Soviet vessels would attempt to cut Atlantic sea-lanes in the event of war.

While the issues above set the stage for the Navy's dramatic shift toward offensive operations under Carter's successor, the last years of the administration also showed the budgetary value of the forward presence mission. From early 1979, the Persian Gulf/Arabian Sea region became a major deployment hub for carrier groups due to unrest in Iran and, at the end of the year, the Soviet invasion of Afghanistan. Lacking basing agreements in the area, Carter deployed two carriers to the region, which placed great strain on ships and crews.[32] These deployments all but forced Carter to resume carrier c onstruction (the future *Theodore Roosevelt*, CVN 71), which he had previously vetoed, in the Fiscal Year (FY) 1980 budget in early October.[33]

The end of the Carter administration presents an interesting conundrum regarding force structure and strategy. Inside the Navy Department, it was clear that the future of the fleet was offensive operations into the teeth of Soviet defenses. This mission required many highly capable warships like CVN 71. Power projection exercised the imagination of naval officers who sought to show policymakers how their service could contribute to the defeat of the USSR in World War III.

However, the funding for CVN 71 only came about because of the Navy's ability to respond to crises in a way that other services could not, with aircraft carriers and their varied escort ships. Middle Eastern deployments, which one senior admiral described as "hell . . . eating us alive," were hardly missions that allowed the service to pressure the Soviet Union.[34] While the coming years would see lurid fantasies of Soviet plans to continue into Iran after their invasion of Afghanistan, the administration agreed to fund CVN 71 months before the Soviet invasion. In other words, the mission the Navy wanted funding for was not necessarily the mission funded, even if the tool—an aircraft carrier—was the same.

Attempting to fix that disconnect would be the job of the new president's first Secretary of the Navy, John Lehman. A reserve naval flight officer, Lehman was an active participant in the carrier battles of the Carter administration, serving as an outside consultant to

Sea Plan 2000 and publishing a short book, *Aircraft Carriers: The Real Choices* (1978), which supported the Holloway-Hayward view of a Navy based on offensive operations around a large carrier fleet. During the 1980 presidential campaign, which he initially started as an adviser to George H. W. Bush, Lehman developed a plank for a "six-hundred-ship Navy" that was inserted into the Republican Party's platform at its convention.[35]

This six-hundred-ship target was the lodestar for Lehman's six-year tenure as secretary, providing a fixed point of reference for planning. The strength of Lehman's advocacy often ruffled feathers within and outside the Navy Department. As one officer who served under Lehman recollected, Lehman often behaved as if his initiatives were "tablets that he's brought down from the mountain. . . . [He has] a pretty healthy ego [but] he has a lot to have a healthy ego about."[36]

At the core of Lehman's six-hundred-ship plan were fifteen carrier battle groups (a target that required more than fifteen hulls, to account for major maintenance periods), as opposed to the eleven available (out of thirteen total hulls) when President Reagan took office in 1981.[37] As Lehman related at the time, "600 ships was a minimum to support the 15 carriers," added to other commitments like nuclear deterrence and amphibious sealift.[38] Initially, the Navy Department defended the plan on the grounds of forward presence: with the new deployments to the Gulf, the international situation warranted the deployment of five carrier battle groups at all times.[39] Using the traditional 3:1 ratio, that called for a force of fifteen deployable aircraft carriers.

Admiral Hayward said much the same thing in front of Congress in February 1981, telling the Senate Armed Services Committee that his service was "trying to meet a three-ocean requirement with a one-and-a-half ocean Navy."[40] New carrier construction would make up this shortfall. A June 1981 draft of the Navy's FY 1983 budget projected funding for new carriers in the FY 1984 and 1986 budgets, which would eventually get the Navy to fifteen deployable carriers.[41] In the meantime, however, no immediate relief was forthcoming.

This mismatch between available and desired forces also affected war plans. While Lehman and Hayward were pushing for a 15-CVBG fleet, the Joint Strategic Planning Document (JSPD) developed by the Joint Staff called for 16 deployable carriers, and another deployable 6 CVVs for a general war scenario, the centerpieces of a 692-ship fleet.[42] As everyone, including its framers, understood, this "fiscally unconstrained" force was nothing more than a wish list cobbled together out of war plans from regional commanders with no sense of what forces Congress and the White House would be willing to fund.[43]

These shortfalls started the Navy down the road toward the Maritime Strategy. In April 1981, Hayward requested a study of "the attainability of the JSPD planning force," which pushed the Navy to develop its own, more realistic strategy rather than relying on the inherently unrealistic JSPD.[44] By mid-1982, Hayward's study merged with criticism from Lehman that financial projections, rather than strategy, were driving force structure development. In order to "set up the [FY 1985 Navy budget] and get the Secretary off OPNAV's back," the OP-603 office in OPNAV was tasked with presenting a "strategic appraisal as the basis for defining the Navy's goals and objectives."[45] That appraisal, briefed to Lehman, the commandant of the Marine Corps, and Admiral James Watkins, the new CNO (1982–86), on November 4 was the first iteration of the Navy's Maritime Strategy.

OP-603's work tied together the two strands of Navy force-sizing rationale, forward presence and global war, almost to the exclusion of everything else. Apart from a single slide on "conflict not involving Soviet forces," the rest of the briefing focused on those two areas, showing how "the U.S. Navy is making a major strategic difference in our peacetime deterrent posture and will make a major strategic impact in the conduct of wartime operations," especially operations conducted as far forward near Soviet territory as possible.[46] Everything else, from sea control to wars with minor powers, was "a lesser included case" that could be handled by the forces needed for these resource-heavy missions.[47]

It is worth pausing to consider what this first iteration of the Maritime Strategy was. It presented neither a new strategy nor a new force structure. In both cases, the Maritime Strategy formalized three main points of the post-Zumwalt conventional wisdom within the service: the Navy needed a large fleet to support forward deployment and facilitate offensive operations against the Soviet Union. These were arguments that Hayward, Holloway, and their supporters in the service had been making for the better part of a decade.

This briefing also conceptualized forward presence according to the desires of Navy, rather than national, leadership. Rather than serving to assert American influence in non-Soviet crises (the rationale behind funding *Theodore Roosevelt*), the briefing perceived forward presence and operations as the first part of a strategy of "global forward deterrence" against the USSR.[48] Explicitly, then, it tied forward presence to the Soviets rather than regional threats. Subsequently, Lehman has made it very clear that regular naval exercises in near-Soviet waters were, for him, the key aspect of putting the Maritime Strategy into action.[49] Indeed, Lehman tried, with limited success, to tie forward operations to these exercises rather than regional security.[50]

These trends carried on into the 1984 iteration of the Maritime Strategy, written from the start to present authoritative Navy Department policy. One of its primary authors, Peter Swartz, later recalled that for the 1984 version "we told a story. . . . Stories are powerful and we told a story. You start off in peace and then all hell breaks loose and there's a crisis and then there's a war."[51] The story told was one in which American sea power leveraged forward deployments to respond to a regional crisis that expanded into a general war with the Soviet Union.[52]

The early pages of the document took pains to note that naval force was applicable "across the entire range of conflict" and pointed out that in 1983 alone, naval forces had been used for crisis response on least six occasions. Still, one of the main reasons noted for peacetime deployments and crisis response was to provide testing, evaluation, and "lessons learned" to be fed back into "strategy for carrying out" global conventional war.[53] The "range of conflict" below general war with the Soviets was not broken out as a separate category of fighting requiring a different approach or force mix.

The Maritime Strategy proved a marvelous success at codifying the navy's offensive turn, providing an intellectual base for operational commanders to sharpen aggressive tactics. In Lehman's hands, it also provided the political rationale for funding the larger fleet needed to fulfill that offensive mindset, backstopping the Navy's success in convincing Congress to fund naval expansion in the early 1980s.[54] Its "story," to borrow Swartz's framing, was one of a campaign against the Soviet Union, where "peace" and "crisis" were rungs on the ladder to World War III. This story matched what naval officers liked to tell themselves: the purpose of the Navy was to fight the Soviets as far forward as possible and "make a major strategic impact" from the sea. This allowed for a rejection of Vietnam-era support of land operations, Zumwalt's sea-control focus, and Carter's SLOC protection strategy.

This is not to say that the Navy did nothing but prepare for a Soviet war during the decade: The service was heavily involved in smaller operations throughout the world from invasions of Grenada and Panama to brief outbreaks of fighting around Libya and Lebanon. As mentioned above, in many ways these contingency operations prevented the Navy from focusing its full attention on preparing for the Soviets. However, preparing a Soviet war, as Zumwalt pressed for in the early 1970s, was virtually the only focus of naval planning and training; other operations did not warrant much in the way of training or serious thought.

The focus on the Soviet Union to the exclusion of other scenarios assumed that forces trained and equipped to strike the Soviet periphery in a prospective World War III could easily handle any other type of operation. The Navy's experience in the Persian Gulf between 1987 and 1991 shows that this assumption was in error. In the "Tanker War" of the late 1980s, the Navy proved itself ill suited to operations against regional powers, in circumstances at the seams of peace, crisis, and war. Later, in Operation Desert Storm, the Navy demonstrated serious capability and organizational shortfalls when operating in concert with other military services in a regional conflict. While this chapter cannot provide a detailed operational history, it can illuminate how the issues discussed above affected the Navy's handling of operations against regional powers, absent the Soviet context.

Focusing on the Gulf region is not accidental. While the Navy was kept busy around the world in the 1980s, the Gulf region was a key forward presence node of the service, regularly visited by carrier battle groups and other combatants as the Iran-Iraq War spilled over into the Gulf, threatening a major part of the world's oil supply. Between its critical sea-lanes and the capabilities of the belligerents, the Gulf also presented specifically maritime challenges that other trouble spots did not. Navy leaders and sailors were familiar with the Gulf and its environs, dramatically outmatched regional powers, yet the Navy's experience there was marked by missteps and errors, even as the service's operations in near-Soviet waters showed the effects of hard-won expertise and tactical excellence.[55]

From the start of the Iran-Iraq War in 1980, American naval vessels kept a wary eye on the belligerents as fighting spread to deliberate attacks on shipping by both sides. Ostensibly neutral, the United States provided aid and support to the Iraqis, which did not stop even after an Iraqi attack on the frigate *Stark*, which killed twenty-seven American sailors in May 1987.[56] Later that year, the country became even more embroiled in the war, when Iranian attacks on Kuwaiti oil tankers led the United States to "reflag" Kuwaiti ships as American and escort them through the Gulf, an operation known as Earnest Will. This decision, made by the Reagan administration, was unwelcome to Navy leaders, who did not view the escort mission as appropriate for their service, especially when those Navy escorts would be placed under the ultimate control of Central Command, then headed by a Marine general.[57]

Seeking to minimize the commitment to the escort mission, Navy leaders declined to make any special provision for Iran's well-documented use of mines to threaten merchant shipping. The very first tanker escorted through the Gulf, the newly renamed *Bridgeton*, hit an Iranian mine, but that did not prevent it from continuing its route. Lacking minesweeping equipment, and much more vulnerable to mine damage, *Bridgeton*'s smaller U.S. Navy escorts were forced to steam in *Bridgeton*'s wake as it sailed out of the Gulf.[58] Following this attack, the Navy flowed minesweepers and minesweeping helicopters to the region.

Between *Bridgeton* and, later, the mining of *Samuel B. Roberts*, mine warfare was the paradigmatic Navy shortfall during the Tanker War, a sign of a force structure *and* a mentality tilted toward major war. As Michael A. Palmer's official Navy history noted, "The United States was…caught woefully unprepared…for the Iranian mining campaign."[59] This unpreparedness was, in a word, inexcusable. As naval leaders were aware, the primary threat to commercial shipping in the Gulf was Iranian mining. Indeed, U.S. Navy divers had found and neutralized several mines in Kuwaiti waters the month before escort operations started, yet these did not prompt calls to move any of the Navy's limited minesweeping assets to the Gulf. Instead, a minesweeping helicopter squadron in Norfolk was put on standby for deployment.[60]

Palmer also hit at the reason for this unpreparedness, albeit couched as an alibi: "The U.S. Navy's priority focus was on the Soviet Union, and justifiably so. The American fleet was designed primarily to fighting within an alliance structure that included a sensible division of labor that assigned most overseas [minesweeping] tasks to European and Asian navies."[61] Minesweeping is barely mentioned in the 1984 and 1985 iterations of the Maritime Strategy: both versions stated, identically, that the Navy "anticipated that the allies would bear the lion's share of the task" as part of the formal division of labor in NATO.[62]

This stance made sense only in the context of a full-scale war with the Soviet Union. Short of that, there was no reason to assume that allies would provide minesweepers on demand for unilateral American operations. In some ways, the minesweeping need was more acute for the service outside of a Soviet war, where much of the fleet would be engaged well offshore in areas unsuitable for mining. In waters near the coast, warships were vulnerable to mining, as Navy leadership well knew from their service's experience during the Korean War. Arguably, mines were the best way a regional power like Iran could inflict serious damage on American naval formations.[63] The strategic focus on the Soviets explains why the U.S. Navy was comparatively underinvested in mine warfare but does not explain why its minimal minesweeping forces were not sent to a theater where mines were the major threat.

It is hard to avoid the conclusion that the Navy did not send its minesweepers to the Gulf before the *Bridgeton* strike because its leaders simply did not want to. As the rush to send minesweepers to the Gulf after *Bridgeton* showed, moving the Navy's aging mine sweepers—often crewed by reservists—from American ports required a major effort, as did providing a large amphibious ship for mine-sweeping helicopters, but these efforts were well within the Navy's capabilities.[64] Prior to *Bridgeton*, naval leaders argued that these efforts were not commensurate with the insignificance of the mission. Secretary of the Navy James Webb viewed the escort mission as an open-ended commitment similar to the Vietnam War, with restricted rules of engagement and no clear mission.[65] Even after *Bridgeton*, senior naval officers, including the CNO, "pressured" Department of Defense (DoD) leadership to "minimize the forces" assigned to operations they saw as inimical to the Navy's primary mission to prepare for war with the Soviet Union.[66]

This disconnect highlights a tension between the vision of forward presence that the Navy pitched to outsiders, and what it told itself. Responding to crises short of war in the Gulf region was the rationale behind Congress funding *Theodore Roosevelt* in 1979 and the Reagan administration's desire to always keep a carrier in the area. From that viewpoint, sending escorts and minesweepers to the region was not a distraction from the Navy's real mission but itself an integral part of the service's peacetime responsibilities.

While the Navy's top leadership tried to wriggle out of Gulf commitments entirely, at least one senior commander, Pacific Fleet's Admiral James "Ace" Lyons, went in the other direction, seeking to apply to Iran operational concepts intended for all-out war with the Soviets. In late 1986, Lyons started developing a plan for "two days of punishing attacks on Iranian military sites" and economic targets to coerce the government into ceasing attacks on neutral shipping.[67] Despite clear lack of interest from policymakers (though with clandestine support from Admiral William Crowe, chairman of the Joint Chiefs of Staff), and the plan's obvious contravention of administration guidance, Lyons proceeded to try to foment a war with Iran until his belligerence forced him into retirement in September 1987.[68]

Tellingly, the most successful naval intervention against Iran came with Operation Praying Mantis in April 1988, which allowed the Navy to conduct large-scale combat operations. After another ship, the frigate *Samuel B. Roberts*, hit a mine in the Gulf, Joint Task Force Middle East was directed to launch a major attack on Iranian naval forces. In Praying Mantis, the mostly naval forces showcased their excellence in kinetic operations, destroying a large portion of the Iranian navy on April 18.[69] As successful as Praying Mantis was, though, it might not have been necessary if the Navy had fulfilled its original escort mission in the Gulf. Operations in the Gulf continued after Praying Mantis; the last major U.S. action of the war was the shooting down of an Iranian airliner by the cruiser *Vincennes*. The factors contributing to that tragedy, including the overly aggressive mindset of its captain, suggest that the U.S. Navy had still not adapted itself to lower-intensity conflict.[70]

By 1988, the Maritime Strategy was losing purchase with policymakers at the highest level, who found it difficult to extricate the Maritime Strategy from Secretary Lehman's six-hundred-ship Navy, the now politically unpalatable budgets of the early Reagan administration, and the declining Soviet threat.[71] In late 1988, the head of the Navy's Office of Legislative Affairs, Rear Admiral T. C. Lynch, told the CNO, Carlisle A. H. Trost (1986–90), that Congress was considering decommissioning older carriers to pay for new escort ships and carrier aircraft. This could perhaps be staved off if Trost was willing to avoid the "old maritime strategy stuff. [Congress wants] a fresh look."[72]

Trost, though, was wedded to the "old maritime strategy stuff," which reflected the preferences of most senior naval officers, telling Lynch that the Navy had a "solid rationale—[we] need to continue to stress the right answers."[73] Trost understood the Maritime Strategy "as a strategy in the general sense of the word: as a means of relating military power to political goals" that remained relevant with or without the Soviet Union or a six-hundred-ship target.[74] To that end, Trost sponsored a new iteration of the Maritime Strategy, released in December 1988, and quickly superseded by a new version in February 1989 that contained more input from the commandant of the Marine Corps.[75]

Essentially, Trost's iteration of the Maritime Strategy tried to reframe its arguments away from a monomaniacal focus on the Soviet threat. Now the Navy also considered "emerging challenges—low and mid-intensity conflict . . . more probable challenges" as a first-order mission for the Navy.[76] However, the document also claimed that "the difference between naval forces designed to fight the Soviets and naval forces designed to fight *anyone else* has narrowed significantly" (emphasis in original), formalizing earlier iterations' implicit assumptions about "lesser included cases."[77] It is unclear *what* changes, if any, the Navy's leadership thought it needed to make to meet this new set of challenges. In fact, as the 1989 Maritime Strategy was nearing completion, Trost's aides were working on an article, later published under his byline, that maintained Lehman's fifteen-carrier target, citing "worldwide commitments" rather than the USSR.[78]

However, after the service's arguments of the previous decade and, indeed its obvious hesitance at performing these sorts of "operations other than war" in the Persian Gulf, few outside observers found Trost's Maritime Strategy and its arguments convincing, especially as the collapse of the Soviet bloc became evident by late 1989. The Navy was also left vulnerable to the "Base Force," an attempt by the chairman of the Joint Chiefs of Staff, General Colin Powell, to manage the inevitable post–Cold War military drawdown using new authorities granted to the chairman in the 1986 Goldwater-Nichols Act.[79] His initial proposal called for cuts of approximately 150 ships and 3 carriers from the Navy's 1989 strength of, respectively, 551 and 15, in line with the cuts proposed for the other services.[80] Believing that Powell's proposed fleet was too small, Trost refused to engage with the Base Force and, joined by Secretary of the Navy H. Lawrence Garrett, pressed for far smaller cuts based around a force of 14 carriers.[81]

In essence, Trost and Secretary Garrett tried to argue that their service should receive a higher percentage of a shrinking budget. Simultaneously, "they maintained that this changed environment called for no shift in the composition of the Navy's own budget," or its force structure. This argument met with markedly little success in front of a skeptical Congress in early 1990, although major cuts were put off to give DoD time to react to the events of late 1989.[82]

As this happened, the Navy faced another conflict in the Persian Gulf, one that again highlighted issues with the Navy's competence to confront regional threats, at an even higher level of intensity. The Navy played an important role in the immediate response to the Iraqi invasion of Kuwait and the buildup of American forces in the region, Operation Desert Shield. Once combat operations started in early 1991, Navy forces in the region faced a litany of problems. Foremost among them was again minesweeping: the cruiser *Princeton* and large amphibious ship *Tripoli* were severely damaged by relatively simple Iraqi mines amid an inadequate mine countermeasures effort.[83] Most problems were caused by the service itself, not Iraqi actions. Naval aviation faced shortages of precision weapons and connectivity issues with other services.[84] These issues were exacerbated by the decision of Central Command's naval commander to remain aboard his flagship rather than joining other senior commanders ashore. This decision largely cut the Navy out of the decision-making process in theater.[85]

In general, Desert Shield/Desert Storm showed that the Navy was underprepared to fight under conditions of "joint" warfare. While its sister services prepared to fight under joint doctrine and command structures, the Navy "got to be part of a doctrinal system it had not practiced . . . or thought about, except to resist . . . and had ignored after it was written."[86] Even after the experience of 1987–88, the Navy continued to prepare for fighting on its desired terms, against its desired enemy. Indeed, the service's leadership had doubled down; recall that Trost's 1989 Maritime Strategy argued that forces designed for the Soviet threat were now *more* appropriate than ever for non-Soviet scenarios.

The Navy's underperformance negatively affected its prospects as the post–Cold War drawdown resumed after the Gulf War. All services faced major cuts after the Cold War, but, as described by Admiral William Owens, who was intimately involved in this process, the Navy faced "deep questions about the efficacy of its operational doctrine" as it tried to defend a force structure optimized for the dead Soviet threat. Desert Storm gave "the Army and Air Force . . . a doctrinal cushion upon entering the new era," while the Navy had none.[87]

Instead, the Navy largely had its future determined for it by Powell's Base Force and the Clinton administration's 1993 Bottom-Up Review. Unable to make a proactive case for independent sea power, the Navy's main mission became rotational forward presence and power projection aimed at regional threats—the exact missions the Navy had eschewed in the previous decade. The dominant Navy strategy document of the period, 1992's ". . . From the Sea," centered on power projection in a joint context, with a focus on fighting in the littorals, which, as recent experience demonstrated, suggested a shift in the Navy's force mix toward smaller surface combatants and minesweepers.[88]

Unlike the Maritime Strategy, though, ". . . From the Sea," and its successor "Forward . . . from the Sea" (1994), "had no direct connection or influence over the Navy's budget and programming process."[89]

On the programming side of the ledger, the Navy strove mightily to maintain the key element of the 1980s force structure: a large number of aircraft carrier battle groups, now twelve instead of fifteen. While the number of carriers did shrink over the 1990s, carriers took a proportionally smaller decrease than other elements of the fleet, preserving the 1980s arrangement of forces for a radically changed strategic context.[90]

Given the fights of the late 1970s and early 1980s, it is easy to see why the Navy ignored intermediate threats in early iterations of the Maritime Strategy. The perceived threat from the Soviet Union overwhelmed all other defense planning. Further, that threat gave Navy leadership license to prepare for the sort of operations they preferred, *and* to advocate for the larger fleet needed for that mission.

Indeed, the fleet built by and for the Maritime Strategy reached a high level of operational proficiency in tasks needed for a global conflict but struggled elsewhere. Twice in four years, naval operations in the Gulf showed that forces built around the Soviet threat faced major shortfalls when confronting the objectively less dangerous threats posed by Iran and Iraq. That may or may not have been a reasonable trade-off, but we must acknowledge that a trade-off existed.

Today the U.S. Navy is focused on another superpower adversary, the People's Republic of China. Again the service is primarily concerned with the systems, doctrines, and training needed to face that adversary. The geography of the Asia-Pacific region mandates that if a conflict were to occur, the American involvement would be spearheaded by the Navy, allowing the service to focus its attention on large-scale maritime operations against a peer competitor. In the 1970s and '80s, a bias toward those operations facilitated the development of the Maritime Strategy, and it is possible a similar dynamic has now taken root.

More than thirty-five years after Goldwater-Nichols, the Navy is certainly better prepared to operate jointly, but it may be setting aside lessons from past "small wars" in favor of the high-end fight. Mine warfare, for example, was the major operational gap adversaries exploited in 1987–91, and today the service only has eight aging, purpose-built mine countermeasures ships, the newest commissioned in 1994.[91] What other capabilities are being allowed to atrophy?

As the Navy's experience in the decade following the first Maritime Strategy shows, focusing on the most dangerous threat to the exclusion of the most likely threat risks strategic and operational tunnel vision. Those risks were compounded because the Soviet threat gave the Navy the license to plan for the sort of operations it wanted to perform and eschew the ones it did not. Turning its attention away from supporting a ground war or fighting in the littorals did not keep the service from having to perform those roles, it just made the Navy less able to succeed in them.

The Navy's overemphasis on the Soviet Union in the 1980s contributed to its strategic dislocation in the 1990s, and the Navy's eventual reliance on forward presence and strike warfare to justify its force structure. That history shows the pitfalls of overemphasizing a single threat or scenario. Today the Navy is applying positive lessons from the 1980s to its preparations for great-power conflict, but hopefully the service can keep the negatives in mind as well.

NOTES

1. OP-603, "Maritime Strategy," presented by Vice Admiral Arthur Moreau, November 4, 1982, reprinted in *U.S. Naval Strategy in the 1980s*, ed. John B. Hattendorf and Peter M. Swartz (Newport, RI: Naval War College Press, 2008), 38.

2. Peter Haynes, *Toward a New Maritime Strategy: American Naval Thinking in the Post–Cold War Era* (Annapolis: Naval Institute Press, 2015), 32.

3. Despite the Maritime Strategy's importance to the U.S. Navy, surprisingly little work has been done on it due, in part, to access restrictions on key primary sources. No one has had access to the full range of material necessary to write a comprehensive history. The best secondary work remains John Hattendorf's *The Evolution of the U.S. Navy's Maritime Strategy, 1977–1986*, Newport Papers 19 (Newport, RI: Naval War College Press, 2004), originally

written for internal Navy use. Hattendorf coedited a collection of the various editions of the Maritime Strategy with Captain Peter Swartz, USN (Ret.), who authored much of the 1984 edition of the strategy. Their commentary alongside the source documents in *U.S. Naval Strategy in the 1980s: Selected Documents* (Newport, RI: Naval War College Press, 2008) is valuable, as are Swartz's *U.S. Navy Capstone Strategies and Concepts* CNA (Arlington, VA, 2011–12) and other material he authored while at CNA. Secretary Lehman has written two books that touch on the creation of the Maritime Strategy, *Command of the Seas* (New York: Scribner, 1988) and the more thoughtful *Oceans Ventured: Winning the Cold War at Sea* (New York: Norton, 2018). Three excellent recent books on U.S. Navy strategy after the Cold War—Peter Haynes' *Toward a New Maritime Strategy: American Naval Thinking in the Post–Cold War Era* (Annapolis: Naval Institute Press, 2015); Sebastian Bruns' *US Naval Strategy and National Security: The Evolution of American Maritime Power* (London: Routledge, 2017); and Steven Wills' *Strategy Shelved: The Collapse of Cold War Naval Strategic Planning* (Annapolis: Naval Institute Press, 2021)—discuss the details of the strategy and how the Navy struggled to replace it in the early 1990s.

4. Hattendorf, *Evolution of the U.S. Navy's Maritime Strategy*, 73; Hattendorf and Swartz, *U.S. Naval Strategy in the 1980s*, 48.

5. Steven Wills, "The Effect of the Goldwater-Nichols Act of 1986 on Naval Strategy, 1987–1994," *Naval War College Review* 69, no. 2 (2016): 35.

6. Edward J. Marolda, *Admirals under Fire: The US Navy and the Vietnam War* (Lubbock: Texas Tech University Press, 2021), 259–62.

7. Vice Admiral Stansfield Turner, "Missions of the U.S. Navy" (1974), reprinted in John B. Hattendorf, ed., *U.S. Naval Strategy in the 1970s: Selected Documents* (Newport, RI: Naval War College Press, 2007), 39.

8. Marolda, *Admirals under Fire*, 263.

9. During Zumwalt's tenure, the size of the Navy shrank from 743 ships to 587. See Naval History and Heritage Command, "US Ship Force Levels," https://www.history.navy.mil/content/history/

nhhc/research/histories/ship-histories/us-ship-force-levels.html (accessed April 30, 2024).

10. Elmo R. Zumwalt Jr., *On Watch: A Memoir* (New York: Quadrangle, 1976), 72.

11. Admiral Elmo R. Zumwalt Jr., "CNO's Project SIXTY Presentation to SECDEF," September 9, 1970, 6–14, folder 8, box 323, Elmo Zumwalt Papers, Operational Archives (OA), NHHC; Rear Admiral W. H. Bagley, "Memorandum: Project SIXTY," September 25, 1970, folder 3, box 23, Zumwalt Papers, NHHC-OA.

12. Marolda, *Admirals under Fire*, 330–31.

13. Marolda, 346.

14. Alva M. Bowen Jr., "U.S. Naval Expansion Program: An Analysis of the Cost of Expanding the Navy from 500 to 600 Ships," Congressional Research Service (CRS), April 7, 1976.

15. Quoted in Marolda, *Admirals under Fire*, 269.

16. Adam B. Siegel, "To Deter, Compel, and Reassure in International Crises: The Role of U.S. Naval Forces," CNA (Alexandria, VA), February 1995.

17. Peter M. Swartz, "Sea Changes: Transforming U.S. Navy Deployment Strategy, 1775–2002," CNA (Arlington, VA), 2021 (originally written in 2002), 52.

18. The concept of a "carrier battle group" was itself invented by Holloway, who introduced the term as part of his reorganization of the Navy's operating forces into battle forces and groups, rather than warship types. James L. Holloway III, *Aircraft Carriers at War: A Personal Retrospective of Korean, Vietnam, and the Soviet Confrontation* (Annapolis: Naval Institute Press, 2007), 386–90.

19. Material prepared by the Navy's Office of Legislative Affairs in 1988 posited a ratio of "4 or 5" carriers to every carrier deployed. Office of Legislative Affairs, "Hard CV Questions," December 5, 1988, enclosure III in Rear Admiral T. C. Lynch to Admiral Carlisle Trost, "Early Retirement of Aircraft Carriers," [early 1989], folder 3, box 14, 1989 Chief of Naval Operations ("00") Files, NHHC.

20. "Back Up for Sen. Stennis Call," OPNAV staff paper, January 24, 1977, 8, folder 1, box 48, 1977 00 Files, Operational Archives, NHHC.

21. Details of the CVN/CVV debate can be found in Ryan A. Peeks, *Aircraft Carrier Requirements and Strategy, 1977–2001* (Washington, DC: Naval History and Heritage Command, 2021), 15–16, 21–23.

22. Alva M. Bowen Jr. and Ray Frank Bessette, "Aircraft Carrier Force Levels," CRS Report, April 28, 1978, 2; Richard P. Cronin, "The FY 1979 Defense Budget," CRS Report, May 10, 1978, 49.

23. Hattendorf, *Evolution of the U.S. Navy's Maritime Strategy*, 13–14.

24. "Sea Plan 2000 Naval Force Planning Study: Unclassified Executive Summary," March 28, 1978, 7.

25. "Sea Plan 2000," 7–10.

26. James M. Patton, "Dawn of the Maritime Strategy," U.S. Naval Institute *Proceedings*, May 2009, 57–58.

27. Hattendorf, *Evolution of the U.S. Navy's Maritime Strategy*, 17–18; Frederick H. Hartmann, *Naval Renaissance: The U.S. Navy in the 1980s* (Annapolis: Naval Institute Press, 1990), 27–28; Patton, "Dawn of the Maritime Strategy," 58–59.

28. Hattendorf, *Evolution of the U.S. Navy's Maritime Strategy*, 19.

29. Hattendorf, 20–21.

30. Norman Friedman, *Fighters over the Fleet: Naval Air Defence from Biplanes to the Cold War* (Annapolis: Naval Institute Press, 2016), 383.

31. Lehman, *Oceans Ventured*, 41–43. For more on the shift in intelligence assessments of Soviet strategy see Lieutenant Commander Christopher A. Ford, USNR, with Captain David A. Rosenberg, USNR, *The Admiral's Advantage: U.S. Navy Operational Intelligence in World War II and the Cold War* (Annapolis: Naval Institute Press, 2005), 77–108.

32. Harry D. Train II, *The Reminiscences of Admiral Harry D. Train II, U.S. Navy (Retired)*, interviewed by Paul Stillwell (Annapolis: Naval Institute Press, 1997), 454–56.

33. Jimmy Carter, "The State of the Union Address Delivered before a Joint Session of the Congress," January 23, 1980, in Gerhard Peters and John T. Woolley, *The American Presidency Project*, https://www.presidency.ucsb.edu/documents/the-state-the-union-address-delivered-before-joint-session-the-congress (accessed April 30, 2024); George C. Wilson, "Carter Gives Up on Blocking New Navy Nuclear Carrier," *Washington Post*, October 2, 1979.

34. Train, *Reminiscences*, 454–56.

35. Lehman, *Command of the Seas*, 101–2; Republican National Committee, "Republican Platform: Family, Neighborhood, Work, Peace, Freedom," July 14, 1980, quoted in Joseph B. Gorman, "A Survey of Policy Positions Supported by the 1980 Republican National Convention That Would Require Congressional Action for Implementation," Congressional Research Service, January 6, 1981, 22.

36. Captain Peter M. Swartz, USN (Ret.), interviewed by Drs. Justin Blanton and Ryan Peeks, July 2019, Naval History and Heritage Command. An edited version of this interview is available at https://www.history.navy.mil/research/library/oral-histories/navy-strategy/swartz-oral-history.html; however, quotations used in this paper are taken from the raw transcripts in the author's personal files.

37. On January 20, 1981, the U.S. Navy possessed thirteen carriers, but two, *Enterprise* and *Saratoga*, were undergoing major refits that left them unable to deploy. A fourteenth carrier, *Carl Vinson*, commissioned in early 1982 and made its maiden deployment in early 1983. Peeks, *Aircraft Carrier Requirements*, 52.

38. Hattendorf, *Evolution of the U.S. Navy's Maritime Strategy*, 50.

39. OP-090 (OPNAV Navy Program Planning), "Aircraft Carrier Force Planning," April 1981, folder 6, box 9, John F. Lehman Jr. Papers, NHHC-OA.

40. Admiral Thomas B. Hayward, "Department of Defense Authorization Appropriations for Fiscal Year 1982, Hearings before the Committee on Armed Services, United States Senate," 9th Cong., 1st sess., part 2, February 5, 1981 (Washington, DC: GPO, 1981), 849.

41. Vice Admiral M. Staser Holcomb, "Navy Program Objectives Memorandum (POM-83) Overview," Briefing for the JCS (Joint Chiefs of Staff), June 10, 1981, folder 35, box 891, OP-004 Records, NHHC-OA.

42. Commander J. W. Bailey and Captain J. Daigenault, OP-605, "JCS 2143/557-2—Joint Strategic Planning Document for FY 1983–90 (JSPD FY 83–90, Part II)," and attachments, February 9, 1981, folder 35, box 915, OP-004 Records, NHHC-OA.

43. Lieutenant Colonel John M. Vann, "The Forgotten Forces," *Military Review* 67 (August 1987): 4–9, quoted in Richard K. Betts, *Military Readiness: Concepts, Choices, Consequences* (Washington, DC: Brookings Institution Press, 1995), 123–24.

44. Colonel F. J. McConville, "Terms of Reference for a JCS Planning Force Attainability Study," July 21, 1981, folder 7, box 808, OP-004 Records, NHHC-OA.

45. Swartz, interviewed by Blanton and Peeks, July 2019, NHHC; Hattendorf, *Evolution of the U.S. Navy's Maritime Strategy*, 65–72.

46. OP-603, "Maritime Strategy," 21–43.

47. Swartz, interviewed by Blanton and Peeks, July 2019, NHHC.

48. OP-603, "Maritime Strategy," 35–36.

49. Lehman, *Oceans Ventured*, xxviii.

50. House Armed Services Committee, *Defense Department Authorization and Oversight: Hearings on H.R. 2287, Department of Defense Authorization of Appropriations for Fiscal Year 1984 and Oversight of Previously Authorized Programs* (Statement of John Lehman, Admiral James Watkins, and General Robert Barrow, February 17, 1983), 98th Cong., 1st sess., HASC No. 98-6, 888–89.

51. Swartz, interviewed by Blanton and Peeks, NHHC.

52. OP-603, "The Maritime Strategy," May 4, 1984, reprinted in Hattendorf and Swartz, *U.S. Naval Strategy in the 1980s*, 48–104.

53. OP-603, "Maritime Strategy," May 4, 1984, 48–52.

54. The particulars of the Maritime Strategy remained secret until the release of an unclassified version in 1986, but Navy leadership aired the basic concept in a variety of unclassified forums beforehand.

55. Lehman, *Oceans Ventured*, 273–74.

56. David Crist, *Twilight War: The Secret History of America's Thirty-Year Conflict with Iran* (New York: Penguin, 2012), 84–106. Of course, for the period of the "Iran-Contra Affair," the United States also supplied arms to the Iranians.

57. Crist, 249.

58. Michael A. Palmer, *On Course to Desert Storm: The United States Navy and the Persian Gulf* (Washington, DC: Naval Historical Center, 1992), 116–23; Crist, *Twilight War*, 240–47.

59. Palmer, 129.

60. Crist, *Twilight War*, 239–41.

61. Palmer, *On Course*, 129–30.

62. OP-603, "Maritime Strategy"; *The Maritime Strategy: Global Maritime Elements for U.S. National Strategy*, 1985, reprinted in Hattendorf and Swartz, *U.S. Naval Strategy in the 1980s*, 90, 179.

63. Iran possessed several relatively unsophisticated coastal defense cruise missiles that were a threat to merchant shipping, but likely not to an alert USN warship.

64. Crist, *Twilight War*, 249–55.

65. Robert Timberg, *The Nightingale's Song* (New York: Simon & Schuster, 1995), 402–4; Palmer, *On Course*, 119.

66. Crist, *Twilight War*, 240–41.

67. Crist, 257.

68. Crist, 269–72.

69. Palmer, *On Course*, 133.

70. Crist, *Twilight War*, 363–70.

71. Haynes, *Toward a New Maritime Strategy*, 41–42.

72. [Navy] Office of Legislative Affairs, "Hard CV Questions," December 5, 1988, enclosure III, Rear Admiral T. C. Lynch to CNO Trost, "Early Retirement of Aircraft Carriers," January 6, 1989, folder 3, box 14, 1989 00 Files, NHHC-OA.

73. Trost, "CNO Comment Sheet: Early Retirement of Aircraft Carriers," January 17, 1989, folder 3, box 14, 1989 00 Files, NHHC-OA.

74. Haynes, *Toward a New Maritime Strategy*, 43.

75. Hattendorf and Swartz, *U.S. Naval Strategy in the 1980s*, 270–71.

76. Admiral Carlisle A. H. Trost, *The Maritime Strategy*, revision IV, OPNAV 60 P-1-89, reprinted in Hattendorf and Swartz, *U.S. Naval Strategy in the 1980s*, 277–78.

77. Trost, *Maritime Strategy*, revision IV, 283.

78. OP-00K, "Navy Force Level Requirements," February 10, 1989, folder 3, box 10, 1989 00 Files, NHHC-OA, 1–7. For more on this article, see Peeks, *Aircraft Carrier Requirements*, 81–82.

79. Lorna S. Jaffe, *The Development of the Base Force, 1989–1992* (Washington, DC: Joint History Office, 1993), 9–13.

80. Jaffe, 15.

81. Department of the Navy Secretariat, "Draft POM-92 DNCPPG: Planning and Programming Guidance," January 10, 1990, 1–2, box 47, 1990 00 Files, NHHC-OA, 1–2.

82. Ronald O'Rourke, "Congressional Watch," U.S. Naval Institute *Proceedings*, May 1991, 168–72.

83. For a full assessment of the Navy in Desert Shield/Desert Storm, see Edward J. Marolda and Robert J. Schneller Jr., *Shield and Sword: The United States Navy and the Persian Gulf War* (Washington, DC: Naval Historical Center, 1998), 355–85.

84. Government Accountability Office, "Naval Air Operations: Interservice Cooperation Needs Direction from the Top," GAO Report NSIAD-93-141, May 1993, 16–22.

85. Marolda and Schneller, *Shield and Sword*, 366–67.

86. Swartz, interviewed by Blanton and Peeks, August 2019, NHHC.

87. Admiral William Owens, *High Seas: The Naval Passage to an Uncharted World* (Annapolis: Naval Institute Press, 1995), 121–22.

88. Haynes, *Toward a New Maritime Strategy*, 80–81.

89. Wills, *Strategy Shelved*, 198.

90. Peeks, *Aircraft Carrier Requirements*, 155–58.

91. Naval Vessel Register, "Ship Class: MCM 1," https://www.nvr.navy.mil/NVRSHIPS/HULL_SHIP_MCM_1_5_1.HTML, accessed October 10, 2023. The Navy intends to replace these ships with Littoral Combat Ships outfitted with mine countermeasures modules, though these modules have faced significant developmental issues.

CHAPTER TWELVE

DETERRENCE OR ESCALATION?

A REAPPRAISAL OF THE 1980s MARITIME STRATEGY

Sebastian Bruns

O n June 8, 1982, the Rolling Stones played a concert for a sold-out crowd at the West Berlin Waldbühne.[1] Carlo Karges, guitarist for the up-and-coming German band Nena, and Uwe Fahrenkroog-Petersen, keyboarder and songwriter, attended the gig that day. At the end of the event, a few hundred helium balloons were released into the summer night. As the bunches of colorful orbs slowly floated away, both men wondered whether the balloons might drift across the Berlin Wall and be mistaken for enemy aircraft, only to be shot down by overeager East German and Soviet air defenses. This would, their reasoning went, unintentionally spiral into a nuclear war. At the height of the late Cold War, the risk of inadvertent escalation between the West and the East appeared very real.[2] Karges and Fahrenkroog-Petersen went home and wrote "99 Luftballons," the world hit later rereleased as "Ninety-Nine Red Balloons" in the English-speaking world, which captured the spirit of the time.[3]

At the same time, in Washington, DC, work was already in progress on the Maritime Strategy, a novel strategic document—or, rather, a series of documents that cumulated in an unclassified, public version that was released in 1986.[4] As opposed to the fear of superpower conflict exhibited by two concertgoers in West Berlin, in America the appetite for a more aggressive stance against the Soviet Union was noticeable. Buoyed by the presidency of the staunchly anticommunist Ronald Reagan since 1981, the Maritime Strategy was a cumulation of ideas that stretched far back into the previous decade.

This essay discusses how the U.S. Navy thought about possible enemies in the context of this capstone document. This is particularly noteworthy because, unlike other major naval strategies that were tested in classical maritime confrontation, the Maritime Strategy never was. Critics of the strategy, both at the time and since, have been quick to make this point.[5] On the other hand, the Maritime Strategy has emerged as a gold standard for many considerations of what a successful capstone document should look like.[6]

Designed as a critical reappraisal, this essay will address the contemporary thinking in the U.S. Navy that informed the Maritime Strategy. In line with an overarching objective in this collection of essays, it will speak to a potential "Plan B" in the face of strategic failure. It will also apply lessons for today as it addresses learnings for the great-power competition, or perhaps even "New Cold War," in this twenty-first century.

FROM NAVAL *BAISSE* TO STRATEGIC RENAISSANCE

In the 1970s, the Vietnam War and its legacy had left the U.S. Navy with an aging fleet and, worse still, with tremendous retention and morale problems.[7] In addition, the political trade winds were positioned against the Navy. Domestic political turmoil around Richard Nixon's Watergate affair and two presidents who were relatively weak or constrained on defense issues—Gerald Ford and Jimmy Carter—spelled significant challenges for the seagoing services. Nevertheless, the Navy undertook a significant amount of modernization, including introducing the first of ultimately fifty-one new guided-missile frigates of the *Oliver Hazard Perry* class in 1977. The same period saw the Navy commission the first of the sixty-two *Los Angeles*–class attack submarines, two more *Nimitz*-class aircraft carriers, and six nuclear-power cruisers of the *California* and *Virginia* classes. Rather unplanned were the four *Kidd*-class guided-missile destroyers originally slated for Iran, based on the *Spruance*-class destroyer hull (a total of thirty-one were procured in the 1970s). The innovative *Ticonderoga*-type guided-missile cruisers with their game-changing Aegis combat systems were in development but would not join the fleet until the 1980s.[8]

Despite all these additions, in 1979, a consolidated U.S. Navy operated almost a third fewer warships than it did in 1970.[9] While the issue of ship-counting and derivation of naval strength is a futile exercise, the fleet size and composition remain a key metric, certainly in the political sphere. Quantity has a quality of its own. In any case, this shrinking U.S. Navy was remarkable given the geopolitical events of the decade. After a period of détente among the superpowers, the Soviet Union appeared to be on the upswing once more. The dispatch of modern SS-20 "Saber" nuclear-tipped intermediate ballistic missiles in Eastern Europe from 1976 challenged the strategic balance on the continent. Western allies reacted with the NATO double-track decision, which would, in turn, modernize the missile arsenal after Moscow declined to enter disarmament talks.

The buildup of the Soviet navy under the leadership of Sergej Gorshkov included the development of numerous cruise-missile-carrying surface ships, a vast investment in more capable submarines, a modernization in naval aviation, and the deployment of the Fifth Eskadra task force to the Mediterranean Sea. This was a key driver in the American naval buildup.[10] In addition, the revolution in Iran in 1979 cumulated in the U.S. Embassy hostage crisis, which lasted 444 days and included a failed release attempt undertaken by American military forces. Meanwhile, the Second Oil Shock created unfavorable economic conditions throughout the West. The Soviet invasion of Afghanistan on December 26, 1979, created difficult political conditions going into the 1980s. In response to the Southwest

Asian turmoil and what was seen as an attempt of the Soviet Union to establish hegemony in the region, on January 23, 1980, President Carter established his "Carter Doctrine," which declared security and stability in the Persian Gulf a core U.S. national interest.[11] This was to no avail; that same year, the Iran-Iraq War broke out and contributed to the election of Reagan, who was seen as more hawkish on U.S. national security and America's global role.

Because the United States remained preoccupied with Vietnam and its domestic issues, the Soviet Union's aspirations to field a large, modern, and capable navy reversed the Soviet postwar trend of naval consolidation.[12] Two massive naval exercises in 1970 and 1975 were the most visible sign that American and by extension Western-allied sea control, long since seen as a given, were under siege. Moscow's naval exercises considerably rattled naval planners and analysts alike. In the spring of 1970, the rapidly growing Soviet navy conducted history's largest peacetime fleet exercise. Labeled "Okean" (Ocean), the event included eighty-four surface combatants, more than eighty submarines (fifteen of which were nuclear powered), and forty-five naval auxiliary and intelligence-collection ships, plus several hundred aircraft.[13]

Quietly, U.S. Navy leaders had already begun to work developing strategic narratives for their service. Project Sixty (1970) and Sea Plan 2000 (1978) had laid some important conceptual groundwork for larger and more modern fleets centered around nuclear-powered aircraft carriers in anticipation of a conflict that would pit the navy against a sea-control challenger, a peer competitor.[14] Proposals for a larger U.S Navy had also found its ways into the Republican Party's presidential campaigns as early as 1976.[15]

Such a significant naval force appeared to underline the argument that in wartime, a Soviet fleet would attempt to wrestle choke point control from the West and attack the North Atlantic sea lines of communication. Unlike the Navy's role in the Vietnam War, where it exercised a significant degree of sea control absent a peer competitor, and unlike the Carter administration's early views of the service as a kind of maritime railroad service that would bring supplies to the Central European front, a new role for the Navy emerged: to fend off a sea-control challenger with capable blue-water assets. The idea of this "Third Battle of the Atlantic" was much closer in imagination to its predecessors,[16] fought in the same waters during World War I and II, respectively.[17] Soviet advances in submarine technology and the advent of nuclear-tipped missiles were not quite factored in, which, coupled with an incorrect American reading of Moscow's naval intentions at the time, skewed this particular mirror-imaging assessment.

THINKING ABOUT THE ENEMY

Through careful analysis of Soviet naval doctrine, and later confirmed by intelligence, the Center for Naval Analyses (CNA), based in the DC metro area and affiliated with the U.S. Navy, over the course of fifteen years argued that

> the Soviets planned to withhold their SLBM force during the conventional phases of a war with the North Atlantic Treaty Organization (NATO) and during initial nuclear strikes "in order to provide either a second-strike capability or to retain a bargaining chip during [war-termination] negotiations." To this end, CNA believed that Moscow would operate its SSBNs [submarine, ballistic missile, nuclear] within special "bastions" protected by naval forces dedicated to sea control missions as a means of strategic defense. . . . This analysis led CNA analysts to suggest the need for the U.S. Navy to attack or threaten Soviet strategy by developing antisubmarine warfare capabilities in Soviet home waters and thereby enhance the deterrent effect of U.S. naval power.[18]

This thinking encapsulated a lot of the ideas that found their way into the Maritime Strategy of the 1980s. It codified some significant changes in the American naval mindset. In parallel, Western allies had begun to gather and properly analyze intelligence that corresponded with American findings.[19]

As a new mindset, it gave the U.S. Navy a reinvigorated mission outlined above that was based on offensive, forward-deployed, and forward-stationed forces—a far cry from the more diffuse naval roles and missions in Vietnam and the limited sea-control imagination of the Carter administration.[20] A voracious force posture would come at certain costs, but the Maritime Strategy rightfully assumed that a rising tide in military spending and a more forceful rhetoric under Reagan would lift all boats.

Geographically, the U.S. Navy would focus on the attack at the source, namely the Soviet SSBN bastions. This meant operating in harsher conditions in the Norwegian Sea, the North Atlantic, and the Arctic Circle. A similar strategy was developed against the Soviet Pacific Fleet and its bastions there.[21] To get to station, forces would have to be properly designed, equipped, manned, and trained to exercise their role. That required extended endurance, and given the nature of NATO as a transatlantic multilateral alliance, a mix of rotationally and permanently forward-deployed capabilities that interacted in and around the European peninsula.

Operationally, that meant naval presence north of the GIUK Gap (the Greenland/Iceland/United Kingdom area that served as a passageway for Soviet naval assets and was heavily monitored by U.S. and NATO allies) and bringing aircraft carriers far forward into the contested spaces. Consequently, and under the command of the U.S. Second Fleet, whose jurisdiction stretched all across the Atlantic Ocean from the North Pole to the South Pole, and from the eastern continental United States to the central northern tip of the USSR, American warships would operate forward and in novel areas such as deep inside Norwegian fjords.[22] The objective was to practically hide the big deck capital ships from Soviet radar and defense perimeters. At the same time, the U.S. Navy's Sixth Fleet—fielding a significant posture in the Mediterranean Sea since the early Cold War to provide stability in the region and to blunt Soviet naval activities on the southeastern European flank—routinely "comprised two supercarriers, multiple escorting destroyers, cruisers, frigates, submarines, and an amphibious ready group with helicopters and several thousand embarked Marines."[23] It operated from the Strait of Gibraltar into the Eastern Mediterranean, and into the Black Sea within the boundaries of the Montreux Convention, which governs nonlittoral states' access to and activity in that region. Exercises had a major function, certainly more so when they featured U.S. Navy capital ships, as seen in this Norwegian analyst's perspective: "High points were the deployments of U.S. Navy aircraft carriers, elements of Supreme Allied Commander, Atlantic's (SACLANT's) Striking Fleet Atlantic, into northern Norwegian coastal waters in Vestfjorden, outside Bodø: in 1985, USS *America* (CV 66) and, in 1987, USS *Forrestal* (CV 59) in Exercise OCEAN SAFARI; in 1988, USS *Theodore Roosevelt* (CVN 71) and *Forrestal* in TEAMWORK; and in 1989, *America* in NORTH STAR."[24]

Tactically, much of the innovation of the Maritime Strategy rested on the shoulders of then–Vice Admiral James "Ace" Lyons, commander Second Fleet. Significantly, Lyons changed the way exercises were handled, transforming them from mere training events to real-world simulations and fleet practices.[25] Lyons tore up the old operations order and established new orders. His fleet's dispersed disposition was decidedly more difficult to decipher for the Soviets—even though they had successfully planted the Walker spy ring in the Navy, which fed large swaths of classified information to Moscow until it was discovered in 1985. Lyons' gung-ho style and appetite for going on the offensive, paired with tactical innovation, led to such feats as the interception of long-range Soviet naval bombers from some one thousand miles away, coupled with simulated attacks on them before they even got close to missile launch position. Lyons also brought in attack submarines to provide direct support of battle groups, and he introduced NATO airborne warning and control system (AWACS) aircraft into naval operations during exercises—an exercise in jointness even before the term became popular in the mid-1980s.[26]

Multilaterally, while the Maritime Strategy was a national document designed for the U.S. Navy and the Marine Corps, it implicitly and explicitly drew on allied and partner navies: "As early in the drafting process as 1982, Chief of Naval Operations Admiral James D. Watkins insisted that the Navy's strategy should be 'focused on cooperation with allies.'"[27] Meanwhile, Western European navies had modernized, standardized, and often increased their warships and naval aviation assets by the early 1980s.[28] For instance, the Royal Netherlands Navy and the West German Bundesmarine procured modern frigates of a similar design, the ten *Kortenaer*-class and eight *Bremen*-class ships, respectively. Germany also shed its post–World War II, Western European Union–imposed tonnage and geographical reach limits. On the other side of the North Sea, the declining Royal Navy, the long-standing and arguably closest ally of the U.S. Navy, found itself battle-tested after the Falklands War in 1982. In the era of the Maritime Strategy, it brought to bear three light aircraft carriers of the *Invincible*-class. These ships, along with modern nuclear-powered submarines, defined the Royal Navy at the time.[29] Admiral Richard G. Colbert, U.S. Navy, proposed maritime partnerships with allies to contain and deter the Soviet Union at and from the sea.[30] Under the Supreme Allied Command Atlantic, this contingency force was approved by NATO in December 1967 and activated a month later as Standing Naval Force Atlantic, known today as Standing NATO Maritime Group 1. Conceptually, northwestern European allies also adapted to the Maritime Strategy and the idea of forward defense with their own capstone document: the "Concept of Maritime Operations," which embodied the culmination of the development of Atlantic naval, strategic, and operational thought and was mainly driven by West Germany and Canada. The original document was published in 1985, and an updated version appeared in 1988, though both versions remain classified.[31]

Buoyed by a much larger, ultimately six-hundred-ship navy, the U.S. Navy would also hold Soviet Pacific naval ambitions in check, such as by operating deep in the Sea of Okhotsk and near the

Vladivostok naval base. This would do away with the "Swing Strategy" of the Carter administration, which imagined swinging Pacific naval assets to the Atlantic theater—or vice versa—in case of open conflict and crisis, thus exposing the rear. The Japanese Maritime Self-Defense Force (JMSDF) was a crucial ally in the Pacific that lacked the number and quality of partner navies that American planners found in Europe. There was also no equivalent to NATO. Absent a system of collective defense like that, bilateral partnerships gained even more leverage and significance.

Building on the century-long experiences and strategic culture of a two-ocean navy (one stationed on the U.S. West Coast and in the Pacific, the other one stationed on the U.S. East Coast and forward in Europe), the U.S. Navy that the Maritime Strategy envisioned would not merely be a tool in the president's kit for when a major crisis or theater war erupted; rather, it would be used as a two-ocean multitool on the peacetime-to-conflict spectrum that would deter the Soviet Union and the Warsaw Pact, hold Moscow's second-strike capability at risk, and assure allies through a rotational and offensive forward presence.[32] This was more reminiscent of naval diplomacy—understanding gray-painted ships and white-capped sailors as ambassadors of American national interest and resolve—than of a narrow military understanding and use of naval power. The diplomatic use of navies had gained some attention in the late 1970s just when navies seemed to be looking for a wider spectrum of use to demonstrate to political leaders the futility of concentrating on a single fault line and potential military battleground.[33]

Domestically, the effects of the procurement programs begun in the 1970s were felt to full effect in the United States as shipyards and factories around the country churned out what the six-hundred-ship Navy required. This was a welcome by-product to obtain congressional support for the Maritime Strategy, even in districts far from oceans and naval installations. A strategic basing initiative designed at spreading the wealth around but masked as a measure of resilience against a prospective Soviet decapitation strike enabled the Navy to gather more congressional and public support. Secretary of the Navy John Lehman appeared frequently in front of congressional leaders and committees on Capitol Hill to explain, defend, and ultimately sell his strategy, fully aware of the political bargaining chips this required.

CHALLENGING THE STRATEGY

Throughout the evolution and implementation of the Maritime Strategy, it goes without saying that the world continued to turn. International developments along with domestic politics and policies factored in highly, as should be expected. A relatively sharp contrast is that of the two Ronald Reagan administrations. Whereas in his first term (1981–85) the president was very vocal about a strong and powerful America in the Cold War (in no small part to carry on his campaign themes), his second term (1985–89) was marked by a significantly toned-down approach that also affected defense and naval policy.[34]

During the first half of the 1980s, a rapid succession of frail USSR leaders and the onset of the "Second Cold War" after Soviet SS-20 missiles were stationed in Europe led to growing fears of superpower confrontation. In response, Reagan's "Peace through Strength" sought to rebuild American military, strategic, and diplomatic clout. NATO implemented a double-track decision in Europe to pair diplomacy with deterrence and missile modernization. In parallel, smaller but hardly less important crises challenged U.S. resolve. Managing the military and diplomatic fallout of the Tehran hostage crisis and supporting America's closest ally, the United Kingdom, in its retaking of the Falkland Islands (1982) were a mere run-up to the ultimately disastrous intervention in Lebanon, where a suicide attack on the U.S. Marines in Beirut claimed the lives of 241 service members on October 23, 1983. A U.S. intervention on the island of Grenada just a few days later was less costly, though with more direct American-Soviet confrontation. Earlier in 1983, President Reagan's public characterization of the USSR as an "evil empire," and the proposed Strategic Defense Initiative (SDI), rattled the Soviet Union. The shooting down of Korean Airlines Flight 007 on September 1, mistakenly thought to be an American military aircraft that had unlawfully penetrated Soviet air space in the Far East, claimed the lives of 269 people on board, including Representative Larry Donald (D-GA) and 61 other Americans. Finally, the Soviet misreading of the NATO exercise Able Archer in November 1983 brought the world as close to the brink of a nuclear exchange as during the Cuban Missile Crisis some twenty-one years prior.[35]

In the second half of the 1980s, American-Soviet relations appeared markedly different. In March 1985, Mikhail Gorbachev assumed the leadership of the USSR and introduced such policies as "Glasnost" (openness) and "Perestroika" (reconstruction). He engaged in bilateral Strategic Arms Reduction Talks (START) with Reagan, who seized the momentum to call on the General Secretary of the Communist Party to "tear down that [Berlin] wall" to end the Cold War for good.[36] American defense spending continued unabated, and the U.S. Navy was underway to achieve its stated six-hundred-ship navy goal. Inter alia, two aircraft carriers USS *Carl Vinson* (CVN 70) and USS *Roosevelt* (CVN 71) were commissioned, and all four *Iowa*-class battleships returned to the Navy (among them USS *Missouri* [BB 63] and USS *Wisconsin* [BB-64] during Reagan's second term). In the meantime, domestic challenges mounted for the fortieth president. The Iran-Contra Affair about unlawful weapon shipments to Iran and discrete funding to Nicaraguan rebels created significant turmoil. Although a congressional investigation did not implicate the president directly, some of his closest—and arguably most colorful—advisers were deeply involved in this scheme.[37] The administration's handling of the emerging AIDS crisis and the wide-ranging effects of its economic policies ("Reaganomics") complicated policymaking and took some of the president's attention off defense and naval issues. The Black Monday stock market crash on October 19, 1987—the first of its kind since World War II—shocked the American public even further. With Reagan's focus elsewhere, the Maritime Strategy was released in an unclassified version in January 1986. Critics of the administration immediately gravitated to the document and, against the background of thawing East-West relations, challenged it.

With Reagan's top cover receding, Lehman sought to fend off some of that criticism himself, although his retirement in 1987 (after six intense years in office and at least in part over having been implicated in rowdy behavior at an earlier "Tailhook" naval aviation conference) preempted a more public conversation.[38] One of the most vocal critics, both of the substance of the Maritime Strategy and of the Secretary of the Navy, was Harold Brown. As secretary of defense under President Jimmy Carter, Brown had argued for a more army- and air-force-centric defense effort in support of the European central front. When the Maritime Strategy successfully argued for investment in a larger and more powerful navy and using the maritime flanks to charge at the Soviet Union, Brown sought to conserve the legacy of the Carter policies through television appearances and interviews.

An unlikely challenge emerged from academia in 1986, just as the Maritime Strategy was publicized. John Mearsheimer, a Chicago-based political scientist who by 2023 rose to be one of the preeminent if hotly contested academics of this trade, and Linton Brooks, a career naval officer with an undergraduate degree in physics who in the 1990s became vice president at the CNA, used the unlikely forum of academic journals to argue on the issue of inadvertent nuclear escalation, which hinged on the offensive mindset lurking in the Navy's strategy. The debate was substantive and conducted at a high level of sophistication, though parts of it were reminiscent of the thoughts of the two Rolling Stones concertgoers in Berlin described in the opening paragraph of this essay. Mearsheimer's criticism and Brooks' emphatic affirmation were printed back-to-back in an issue of *International Security*.[39] It provided a much more nuanced discussion than some of the 1980s popular culture products on the Cold War—from "99 Red Balloons" to the mid-1980s hit movie *Top Gun*—ever could.

The Maritime Strategy continued to be tested at sea. Exercises to refine the ideas of the capstone document continued to be held and professionalized, but the operating pace slowed down in the second half of the 1980s.[40] A notable exception was the deployment of the reinstated battleship USS *Iowa* (BB 60) to the Baltic Sea in 1985 and again in 1989. Firing a full broadside in a cordoned-off area east of Bornholm (Denmark), the venerable battleship's shots were meant to be seen and heard around the Baltic perimeter and certainly as far away as Moscow. But the real cause of concern for Red Navy planners was the *Ticonderoga*-class guided missile cruisers with the new Aegis system.[41] Meanwhile, the Soviet navy halted many of its forward deployments, not least as a cost-cutting measure, including that of submarines patrolling off the U.S. coasts.[42]

Two major naval operations tested the U.S. Navy relatively far from the Soviet bastions, though the strategic signaling was important: operations against Libya (Operation El Dorado Canyon) and in the Persian Gulf as part of the protection of merchant shipping in the Iran-Iraq "Tanker War."[43] These operations gave the Navy exposure to a wide range of conventional threats to their ships and aircraft. It afforded them hard lessons in antiship missile defense, mine countermeasures, and damage control. It also provided the ability to forward operate Aegis cruisers with some success in the Gulf of Sirte, but with a disastrous operation in the Persian Gulf that mistakenly downed an Iran Air flight in 1988.

LEGACY OF THE MARITIME STRATEGY

A few months later, the Soviet Union and the Warsaw Pact dissolved. Germany, long at the frontline of a superpower clash, was reunited peacefully. For the Maritime Strategy, this meant that its business model had essentially been nullified. In fact, whereas many resources had poured into the document, its application, and the corresponding six-hundred-ship navy throughout the decade, that tempo slowed down considerably after the 1986 legislation that mandated a joint approach to military planning (Goldwater-Nichols Act) and John Lehman's 1987 departure.

If the deterrence that was vested in the Maritime Strategy had failed, the Navy would have been well placed to fight a war with the Soviet Union.[44] If deterrence had continued in the expected way, the U.S. Navy's force-level goal of 600 warships might have been achieved in the 1990s (it leveled off at 594). By 1991, with the implosion of the Soviet Union, the Cold War ended. The Maritime Strategy was successful. Or was it? Naval leaders postulated that the document was to be kept on the shelf in case of a resurgence of superpower tensions but were unable or unwilling to produce a convincing "Plan B" for much of the 1990s.[45] As Swartz summarized,

> The Maritime Strategy remained the template for the U.S. Navy strategy until its replacement in 1992 by . . . From the Sea (updated in 1996 [sic] as Forward . . . From the Sea). The Maritime Strategy described U.S. Navy thinking on the prosecution of naval operations in peacetime, crises, and war. Its focus, however, was on war with the Soviets. The U.S. Navy viewed such a war as being inevitably (and optimally) conducted globally—especially in the North Atlantic, the Mediterranean and the North Pacific.[46]

Amid force reductions, challenges to planning and organization thanks to Goldwater-Nichols, strategic disorientation, and a row of scandals,[47] the Navy went on a long and often painful path toward a new strategic mindset in the 1990s, one that eventually led to "A Cooperative Strategy for 21st Century Seapower" in 2007.[48] Meanwhile, the generation of navalists who conceptualized, drafted, and refined the Maritime Strategy in the 1980s began to share their best practices in private and public. The more the Navy and America's post-9/11 reputation appeared to be challenged, the more warmly the Maritime Strategy was regarded. Absent a sea-control challenger like the Soviets, naval planning appeared to be less from the same mold.

Whereas the Maritime Strategy allowed all relevant players to be singing from the same sheet of music, strategic ambiguity (notwithstanding the fundamental changes in technology, military legislation, and global security throughout the 1990s and 2000s) reigned. That, and the orchestrated and focused mentoring of the Maritime Strategy makers, has influenced a generation of naval leaders and academics.[49] It turned the old document into something of a gold standard for naval strategists of the twenty-first century who would often aspire to bring back the effects of the Maritime Strategy, even at the risk of mirror-imaging the Cold War of the 1980s and, in a failure of imagination, apply it the Indo-Pacific of the 2020s.[50]

Four decades after its development and implementation, it is apparent that the Navy did not have a proper "Plan B." One can assume that a considerable degree of enthusiasm for the Maritime Strategy existed at the time, certainly within Navy circles. Enjoying the political backing of the executive and legislative branch, having found a new sense of purpose for the 1980s, and the palpable successes and breakthroughs large and small (in military technology, modern naval operations, strategic thinking inside the organization, etc.) led the Navy to abandon broadening the Maritime Strategy beyond the Soviet-U.S.-centric struggle. Smaller contingencies off Libya and in the Persian Gulf, costly as they might have looked, provided a distraction to countering the Soviet Union, rather than being understood as both an integral part of maritime deterrence from the sea and foreshadowing naval operations in a unipolar or multipolar world. The Navy also appears to have failed in reimagining its role in a world without powerful allies in the Pentagon, in the White House, and on Capitol Hill. It did not properly account for a range of systemic shocks to the strategy's business model, such as the accession of Mikhail Gorbachev to the top of the Soviet leadership in 1985, or the 1986 Goldwater-Nichols legislation, which established joint planning and conduct of military business. A proper "Plan B" would also have included a force structure that proposed alternatives to the seemingly arbitrary number of six hundred ships. The Navy appears to have spent little effort and time to avoid criticisms of its document, and simply assumed that increasing defense spending would supply what it needed. While Secretary Lehman made a point of the strategic homeporting initiative and giving naval bases and shipyards around the country a slice of the pie, one wonders why the same effort was not in-vested in such less glamourous subjects as active and reserve personnel or logistics in the case of a prolonged conventional war.

The Navy also assumed that its allies and many partners would follow suit in maritime strategic planning, exercising, and operational synchronization. Some did, but others did not. Furthermore, domestic policy challenges from the mid-1980s onward consumed much of the Navy's attention and the service failed to prepare for contingencies in a post–Cold War world. The use of the Navy in the Gulf War offers an excellent case study for how the service tried to apply its forces to a novel contingency in the Goldwater-Nichols world, to modest successes. A review of the demise of naval strategy planning since then only emphasizes a downward trend.[51]

The narratives of the successes of the Maritime Strategy, in no small part led by the fathers of the documents and their mentees, eclipsed the documents' shortcomings. Whereas the verdict for con-temporary U.S. maritime and naval strategy is still out, the Maritime Strategy lives on in a wealth of publications and in the imagination and experience of a generation of navalists, and more. That is rather remarkable for a document that, unlike its interwar period predeces-sors, was never fully battle-tested.

I am indebted to Dr. John D. Sherwood and Captain Peter M. Swartz (USN, Ret.) for reviewing earlier versions of this chapter. All mistakes remain mine, of course.

NOTES

1. The Waldbühne is an open-air stage in the Charlottenburg-Wilmersdorf section of (West) Berlin.
2. See also Taylor Downing, *The World at the Brink: 1983* (Boston: Little, Brown, 2018).
3. "99 Luftballons und das Chaos der Gefühle," *Der Spiegel*, March 25, 1984. For a contextualization, see Lutz Fahrenkrog-Petersen, "Soziokulturelle Bedeutung," in *Die unglaubliche Geschichte von "'99 Luftballons,"* at https://uwefahrenkrogpetersen.com/99luftballons/ (accessed January 24, 2023).

4. Sebastian Bruns, *US Naval Strategy and National Security: The Evolution of American Sea Power* (London: Routledge, 2018), 75.

5. John B. Hattendorf and Peter Swartz, eds., *The Evolution of the U.S. Navy's Maritime Strategy*, Newport Papers 19 (Newport, RI: Naval War College Press, 2004).

6. See, for example, Steve Wills, *Strategy Shelved: The Collapse of Cold War Naval Strategic Planning* (Annapolis: Naval Institute Press, 2021); and Sebastian Bruns, "The U.S. Navy's Role in National Strategy, Especially between 1980 and Today," in Michael Crawford, ed., *Need and Opportunities in the Modern History of the U.S. Navy* (Washington, DC: Naval History and Heritage Command, 2018), 281.

7. For the U.S. Navy in the Vietnam War, see, for example, Carsten Fries, "A Chronology of the U.S. Navy in Vietnam and Southeast Asia, 1950–75" (Washington, DC: Naval History and Heritage Command, 2018), https://www.history.navy.mil/browse-by-topic/wars-conflicts-and-operations/vietnam-war0/chronology.html (accessed January 24, 2023).

8. "My list of what entered the fleet in the 1970s shows LCC, P-3C, KA-6D, A-6E, EA-6B and upgrades, Mk 48 torpedo, E-2C, RH-53D minesweeping helicopter, Paveway guided bombs, F-14A Tomcat, S-3A, AIM-54 Phoenix air-to-air missiles, upgraded AIM-9L Sidewinder air-to-air missiles, *Nimitz*-class CVN, quiet *Spruance*-class ASW gas turbine DD, *Los Angeles*–class SSN, *Perry*-class FFG, *Pegasus*-class PHM, *Mystic*-class Deep Submergence Rescue Vehicle (DSRV), *Pigeon*-class catamaran submarine rescue ships (ASR), LHA, LVTP-7, Harpoon Block 1, Sea Sparrow RIM-7H, 5-inch/62 caliber Mk 45 gun, FLTSATCOM, NAVSTAR GPS, CAPTOR mines, Mk 62 Quick strike aircraft-laid bottom mine (bomb-to-mine conversion), Mk 67 Submarine-launched mobile mine (SLMM), NTPF, FLTSATCOM, next generation ELINT satellite system, Trident I C4 missile, W76 SLBM nuclear warhead, Navy TENCAP, AN/SQS-53 surface combatant hull-mounted sonar, AN/BQQ-5 submarine bow sonar, AN/SLQ-32 jammer shipboard electronic warfare system, Prairie-Masker radiated noise reduction systems, AN/SSQ-50 Command Activated Sonobuoy System (CASS), AN/SSQ-62 Directional Command Activated

Sonobuoy System (DICASS), A-6E Target Recognition Attack Multi sensor (TRAM), Standard Tension Replenishment Alongside Method (STREAM) underway replenishment system, FRAM upgraded torpedo, missile, sensor and other military capabilities on Hamilton-class USCG cutters, etc. *But the numbers of each system entering the fleet were too small*" (emphasis in the original). Peter Swartz, email to author, February 6, 2023.

9. In 1970, there were 743 active ships; by 1979, that total had dropped to 533, a decline of 28 percent. See Naval History and Heritage Command, "U.S. Navy Active Ship Force Levels, 1970–1979," https://www.history.navy.mil/research/histories/ship-histories/us-ship-force-levels.html (accessed March 3, 2023).

10. John D. Sherwood, email to author, February 14, 2023.

11. Jimmy Carter, "The State of the Union Address Delivered before a Joint Session of the Congress," January 23, 1980, in Gerhard Peters and John T. Woolley, *The American Presidency Project*, https://www.presidency.ucsb.edu/documents/the-state-the-union-address-delivered-before-joint-session-the-congress (accessed January 20, 2023).

12. Norman Polmar, Thomas Brooks, and George Fedoroff, *Admiral Gorshkov: The Man Who Challenged the U.S. Navy* (Annapolis: Naval Institute Press, 2019), 152–71.

13. Norman Polmar, "OKEAN: A Massive Soviet Exercise, 50 Years Later," U.S. Naval Institute *Proceedings*, April 2020, 406. The Soviet Union held comparable exercises in 1975 and again in 1980.

14. For a rich discussion see Hattendorf and Swartz, *Evolution of the U.S. Navy's Maritime Strategy*; and Bruns, *US Naval Strategy*, 54–76. See also Peter Haynes, "Elmo Zumwalt's Project SIXTY: Driving Institutional Change in an Era of Great Power Competition at Sea," in Sebastian Bruns and Sarandis Papadopoulos, eds., *Conceptualizing Maritime and Naval Strategy: Festschrift for Captain Peter M. Swartz, United States Navy (Ret.)* (Baden-Baden: Nomos, 2020), 91–112.

15. "Republican Party Platform of 1976. Adopted by the Republican National Convention, August 18, 1976, at Kansas City, Mo.," in Gerhard Peters and John T. Woolley, *The American Presidency*

Project, https://www.presidency.ucsb.edu/documents/republican-party-platform-1976 (accessed January 20, 2023).

16. Magnus Nordenman, *The New Battle for the Atlantic: Emerging Naval Competition with Russia in the Far North* (Annapolis: Naval Institute Press, 2019), 42–43.

17. For an overview, see Nordenman, 21–41. In recent years, the argument was made that the twenty-first-century naval confrontation between the United States and Russia was akin to a new conflict, the "Fourth Battle of the Atlantic." See James Foggo and Alarik Fritz, "The Fourth Battle of the Atlantic," U.S. Naval Institute *Proceedings,* June 2016, 1360; Commander, 2nd Fleet, "Trans-Atlantic Leaders Gather for Fourth Battle of the Atlantic Tabletop Exercise," Defense Visual Information Distribution Service, January 7, 2020; James Foggo, "The Fourth Battle of the Atlantic Is Underway," Center for European Policy Analysis, January 17, 2023. The Navy appears to have adopted this concept, for there is already an acronym: 4BOA.

18. Christopher Ford and David Rosenberg, *The Admirals' Advantage: U.S. Navy Operational Intelligence in World War II and the Cold War* (Annapolis: Naval Institute Press, 2005), 79. For the fifteen-year project mentioned above, see Peter Swartz, with Michael Connell, "Understanding an Adversary's Strategic and Operational Calculus: A Late Cold War Case Study with 21st Century Applicability to U.S. Views on Soviet Navy Strategy and Operations," Center for Naval Analyses, 2013, 9–36.

19. See, for example, Bundesministerium der Verteidigung, *Sowjetische Seekriegskunst—der Arktische Ozean als Schauplatz von Kriegshandlungen* [Soviet art of naval warfare—the Arctic Ocean as a theater for actions of war] (Bonn: Bundesministerium der Verteidigung, 1987).

20. Dov Zakheim, "The U.S. Sea Control Mission: Forces, Capabilities, and Requirements," Background Paper (Washington, DC: Congressional Budget Office, 1977).

21. Narushige Michishita, "The U.S. Maritime Strategy in the Pacific during the Cold War," in Bruns and Papadopoulos, *Conceptualizing Maritime and Naval Strategy,* 223–39.

22. Eric Grove with Graham Thompson, *Battle for the Fiords: NATO's Forward Maritime Strategy in Action* (Annapolis: Naval Institute Press, 1991).

23. Seth Cropsey, "Restore the U.S. Sixth Fleet," *National Review*, November 2, 2015.

24. Jacob Børresen, "Alliance Naval Strategies and Norway in the Final Years of the Cold War," *Naval War College Review* 64, no. 2 (2011): 1.

25. David Winkler, "Maritime Strategist Ace Lyons Remembered," Naval Historical Foundation (NHF) blog, December 17, 2018, https://navyhistory.org/2018/12/maritime-strategist-admiral-ace-lyons-remembered/.

26. Lyons in conversation with the author, Washington Navy Yard, September 21, 2012. The author and Naval History and Heritage Command hold copies of the recording and a transcript.

27. Jon-Wyatt Matlack, "Allies through Thick and Thin: U.S. Navy Strategic Communication, 1986–1994, in Transatlantic Context," *Journal of Advanced Military Studies* 13, no. 2 (2022): 33–55.

28. See Eric J. Grove, *NATO Major Warships—Europe: A Tri-Service Pocket Book* (London: Tri-Service, 1990); and, correspondingly, Eric J. Grove, *NATO Major Warships—USA and Canada: A Tri-Service Pocket Book* (London: Tri-Service, 1990). The narrow focus on ship types and numbers somewhat cloaks allied-advances in the introduction of naval aircraft such as the F/A-18 Hornet and the diversity of the fleets that spanned from carrier-based F-14 Tomcats to P3 Orion Maritime Patrol Aircraft, to the rotary-wing workhorses such as the SH-2 Seasprites. See Adrian Symons, *US Naval Aviation in the 1980s: Atlantic and Pacific Fleet Air Stations* (Strout, U.K.: Amberley, 2023). For allied navies, recall the SeaLynx helicopter operated by a number of navies, the carrier-variant Harrier jump jet, or the navalized Tornado naval strike bomber.

29. Nick Childs, *The Age of Invincible: The Ship That Defined the Modern Royal Navy* (Barnsley, U.K.: Pen & Sword, 2009).

30. John B. Hattendorf, "Admiral Richard G. Colbert," *Naval War College Review* 61, no. 3 (2008): 11–13.

31. Peter Swartz, "Preventing the Bear's Last Swim: The NATO Concept of Maritime Operations (ConMarOps) of the Last Cold War Decade," in I. Loucas and G. Maroyanni, eds., *NATO's Maritime Power, 1949–1990* (Piraeus, Greece: European Institute of Maritime Studies and Research, Inmer Publications, 2003). See also Udo Sonnenberger, "Die 'Forward Maritime Strategy' der NATO in den 1980er-Jahren als Reaktion auf eine sich wandelnde Bedrohungsperzeption? Eine Studie zur militärischen Strategieentwicklung und deren Umsetzung" [NATO's "Forward Maritime Strategy" of the 1980s as a reaction to a changing threat perception? A study on military strategy development and implementation] (PhD diss., University of Halle-Wittenberg, forthcoming).

32. John Lehman, *Oceans Ventured: Winning the Cold War at Sea* (New York: W. W. Norton, 2018), 101.

33. See Ken Booth's remarkable book *Navies and Foreign Policy* (London: Routledge, 1977). His contemporary James Cable (1994) described the slightly derogatory term "gunboat diplomacy" as "the use or threat of limited naval force, otherwise than as an act of war, in order to secure advantage or to avert loss, either in furtherance of an international dispute or else against foreign nationals within the territory or the jurisdiction of their own state." Cited in P. K. Gosh, "Revisiting Gunboat Diplomacy: An Instrument of Threat or Use of Limited Naval Force," *Strategic Analysis: A Monthly Journal of the IDSA* 26, no. 11 (2001): 2005–17.

34. For an overview, see Bruns, *US Naval Strategy*, 73–93.

35. Simon Miles, "The War Scare That Wasn't: Able Archer 83 and the Myths of the Second Cold War," *Journal of Cold War Studies* 22, no. 3 (2020): 86–118.

36. Ronald Reagan, "Remarks on East-West Relations at the Brandenburg Gate in West Berlin," June 12, 1987, in Gerhard Peters and John T. Woolley, *The American Presidency Project*, https://www.presidency.ucsb.edu/documents/remarks-east-west-relations-the-brandenburg-gate-west-berlin (accessed February 2, 2023).

37. Three of them were graduates of the U.S. Naval Academy: Oliver North, Robert McFarlane, and John Poindexter. See Robert Timberg, *The Nightingale's Song* (Annapolis: Naval Institute Press, 1995).

38. William H. McMichael, *The Mother of All Hooks: The Story of the U.S. Navy's Tailhook Scandal* (New Brunswick, NJ: Transaction, 1997).

39. John Mearsheimer, "A Strategic Misstep: The Maritime Strategy and the Deterrence in Europe," *International Security* 11, no. 2 (1986): 3–57; Linton Brooks, "Naval Power and National Security: The Case for the Maritime Strategy," *International Security* 11, no. 2 (1986): 58–88.

40. Including the remarkable Ocean Safari '85 and '87 exercises, the latter of which featured significantly fewer American warships than two years prior and also incorporated more allies; "NATO Exercise Begins in the Atlantic," Associated Press, August 31, 1987, https://apnews.com/article/e6c7a05075396466b8bf81d cfeb1fc5d.

41. Sebastian Bruns, "From Show of Force to Naval Presence, and Back Again: The U.S. Navy in the Baltic, 1982–2017," *Defense and Security Analysis* 35, no. 2 (2019): 117–32.

42. Lehman, *Oceans Ventured*, 221.

43. Bruns, *US Naval Strategy*, 88–91.

44. For a scenario, see Tom Clancy, *Red Storm Rising* (New York: G. P. Putnam's Sons, 1986).

45. Secretary of the Navy H. Lawrence Garrett III, Chief of Naval Operations Admiral Frank B. Kelso II, and Commandant, and U.S. Marine Corps General A. M. Gray, "The Way Ahead," U.S. Naval Institute *Proceedings*, April 1991, 36–47. The first formal and public attempt by the U.S. Navy's leadership to replace the Maritime Strategy with a concept more in keeping with the times, noting, "The Maritime Strategy . . . remains on the shelf." Cited in Hattendorf and Swartz, *Evolution of the U.S. Navy's Maritime Strategy*, 275.

46. Swartz, "Preventing the Bear's Last Swim," 53–54. The capstone document "Forward ... From the Sea" was actually published in December 1994.

47. These ranged from repeated instances of sexual assault at various "Tailhook" symposia, to the *Iowa* turret explosion in 1989, which claimed the lives of forty-seven, to the suicide of Chief of Naval Operations Admiral Jeremy Boorda in 1996.

48. Pete Haynes, *Toward a New Maritime Strategy: American Naval Thinking in the Post–Cold War Era* (Annapolis: Naval Institute Press, 2015).

49. Sarandis Papadopoulos, "Peter Swartz's Republic of Letters: Recent World on the U.S. Navy and Strategy," in Bruns and Papadopoulos, *Conceptualizing Maritime and Naval Strategy*, 155–78. See also the contributors to that volume whose geographic range spans from Austria and Switzerland to Japan, Germany, Poland, and obviously the United States.

50. One of the often-overlooked aspects is the Strategic Studies Group that was a backbone in the strategic thinking that went into the creation of the Maritime Strategy. It would be worthwhile re-creating. See John T. Hanley Jr., "Creating the 1980s Maritime Strategy and Implications for Today," *Naval War College Review* 67, no. 2 (2014): 11–30.

51. Bruns, *US Naval Strategy*, 111–68.

CHAPTER THIRTEEN

BACK TO ITS COMFORT ZONE

THE RUSSIAN NAVY'S VIEWS OF ITS PRINCIPAL ADVERSARIES, STRATEGY AND FORCE APPLICATION, AND CAPABILITY DEVELOPMENT

Alexey D. Muraviev

In early 2023, the Russian Ministry of Defense (MoD) reported that approximately one hundred Russian warships and auxiliaries were on deployments across major maritime theaters of operations.[1] This figure was reflective of the tempo of Russian naval activities over the past five to six years. Despite operational commitments to the war in Ukraine, the Russian Federation Navy (RFN) was clearly demonstrating its regrown potential after two decades of decline and decay.

The evolution of Russian naval power since the end of the Cold War until the war in Ukraine has been a complex and dramatic process. Once the pride of the Soviet Union and the world's largest standing naval force, the navy went through painful processes of reductions, disintegration, and repositioning. Its political weight and influence, which had peaked under the architect of the Soviet oceangoing navy, Admiral of the Fleet Sergei Gorshkov, faded away, and its funding was cut.

The struggle for survival and a search of a purpose in the 1990s gradually gave way to a steadier period of its development in 2000s. Under the presidency of Vladimir Putin, the RFN regained some of its lost ground regarding its role and place in the system of national security and defense, as well as its strategic weight within the Russian defense establishment. It also developed a more coherent narrative concerning future force design.

This chapter will critically review the circumstances that affected the transformation of post-Soviet Russian naval power. It will examine the evolution of Russia's views and assessments of its principal adversarial maritime force, the U.S. Navy (USN), and it will identify patterns in the ongoing force modernization and development as well as its operational experience in the 1990s and 2000s.

FRIENDLIES OR HOSTILES? PERCEPTIONS OF THE USN AND ALLIED NAVIES

Historically, Russia has struggled to balance the urgency of addressing threats to its land frontiers with an ongoing strategic imperative of protecting its vast landmass from the sea-based threats. The country's strategic geography makes it susceptible to political-military pressures, which could be applied by superior adversarial naval forces. Approximately half of the entire Russian population lives either along, or in the vicinity of, the country's seacoast, and around 60 percent of the nation's industrial potential is concentrated in coastal and nearby areas, thus making them dependent on littoral shipping, and consequently vulnerable to maritime threats. As a result, the overall need to invest in national naval power has never gone off the table for the Russian ruling elite. But in times of political and economic upheavals it was questioned, thus forcing Russia's naval planners to adopt a degree of flexibility in their thinking and planning, and also to accommodate political agendas of the day.

Dramatic turns in the progression of Russian naval power in the 1990s and early 2000s reflected the evolution of Moscow's appreciation of its principal potential adversaries in the maritime domain. Two competing influence groups—loosely, if at all, organized—shaped how the Russian naval planners and operators perceived the USN, the North Atlantic Treaty Organization (NATO), and other allied navies.

Senior naval commanders knew that their best chance to develop national naval power was to convince Russia's ruling elites of their cause. By winning the minds of the Politburo elite, for example, Gorshkov had been able to build his dream navy. His successors under Mikhail Gorbachev and Russia's first president, Boris Yeltsin, had less luck in receiving such support. We can identify two broad approaches to influencing political opinions since 1991: what we might call *positivists*, on the one hand, and *neo-Gorshkovtsy*, on the other.

In the 1990s, the Kremlin's strategic agenda prioritized a positive relationship between Russia and the West.[2] Positivists' views effectively mirrored the official political sentiment of the Kremlin and the MoD with respect to geopolitical agenda of the day. The naval positivists argued against keeping the vast and expensive oceangoing navy and advocated instead for a close cooperation with Western navies. For example, in 2010, then–Chief of the RFN (CN-RFN) Admiral Vladimir Vysotskiy argued for the importance of maintaining good links with NATO counterparts, particularly in the fields of counter-piracy, narcotraffic, and search-and-rescue.[3] The maintenance of good order at sea encouraged the RFN to cooperate with foreign navies. As Vysotskiy's argument suggests, the positivists retained significant influence over naval affairs well into the twenty-first century as part of a broader development of robust and pragmatic links between the Russian and U.S. defense establishments. Positivist influence was strong enough to affect formulations of the official views, which were reflected in principal doctrinal documents. It was only after Russian relations with the West declined dramatically from 2012 to 2014 that positivists started losing influence.

By contrast, the traditionalists, or neo-Gorshkovtsy, consisted of a large pool of naval experts, many of whom were retired senior naval personnel, alongside some active-duty senior officers.[4] The principal position of the neo-Gorshkovtsy was that despite the warming of Russia's relations with the West, the West retained hostile intent toward Moscow and continued to perceive Russia as a potential military adversary. The traditionalists continued to develop threat assessments based on high-end warfighting scenarios, in which the RFN would have to counter the combined might of the USN and allied navies across several maritime theaters of operations. For example, the threat estimates for the Atlantic and European maritime theaters factored in the combined might of all operational units drawn from the USN and NATO navies present at sea at any given time (table 13.1).

TABLE 13.1 Russian assessments of U.S. and NATO naval forces on deployment, 1999

Task groups/fleets; core capability	Navy	Composition, platforms, systems (Russian estimates)	Composition, personnel (Russian estimates)
SSBNs	USN, U.K., French	10 to 13 (288 SLBMs)	—
SSGNs/SSNs	USN	10 to 12 (up to 160 SLCMs)	—
Fleets (Third, Sixth, Seventh)	USN	Approx. 60 units, over 200 aircraft	7,000 marines on board
Three permanent task groups	NATO's combined naval force	Up to 30 units	—

Source: *Morskoi Sbornik*, no. 12 (1999)

Elaborated threat assessments dealt specifically with the capacity of the USN and allied forces to mount sea-based aerial and cruise missile strikes from those areas of operations against strategically sensitive areas in Russia.[5] In making these assessments, the neo-Gorshkovtsy used the Soviet-era formula, which was based on estimating the overall combat value of the deployable capability of the USN in any given theater in addition to combat value estimates of the most significant regional naval forces (table 13.2).[6] For example, in 2008, Russia's leading naval journal, *Morskoi Sbornik*, published a detailed three-part analysis of major strategic risks to Russia and the European maritime theaters (the Baltic, Black Sea, and Mediterranean), which was largely driven by this approach.[7]

TABLE 13.2. General frameworks of threat assessment and combat potential estimates of Russian naval fleets vis-à-vis potential adversarial naval forces, 1990s and 2000s

Maritime theater	USN	NATO	Specific regional navies (bench markers)
Arctic Ocean	Yes	Yes	Norway
Atlantic Ocean	Yes	Yes	—
Baltic Sea	Yes	Yes	German, Polish, Swedish
Black Sea	Yes	Yes	Turkish
Caspian Sea	—	—	Iranian
Mediterranean Sea	Yes	Yes	—
Pacific (Northwestern) Ocean	Yes	—	Canadian, JMSDF, RoK

Sources: *Morskoi Sbornik* (2000–23); *Krasnaya Zvezda* (2000–23); *Voenno-Promyshlenny Kurier* (2013–22); data collected by the author

Consequently, the future RFN had to be developed on the basis of maintaining balanced fleets in all maritime theaters sufficient to counter the combined might of the adversarial forces without relying on the ability to move forces between the theaters.[8] Many views expressed by representatives of the neo-Gorshkovtsy resonated positively in the Kremlin and with Putin. Eventually, Russia's MoD adopted a dedicated concept for the development of Russian future naval power until 2050 that was partially based on the expert input of the neo-Gorshkovtsy.

Despite the absence of united views on Russia's potential naval adversaries until the mid-2010s, Russia's MoD, including the Main Operational Directorate of the General Staff, the Naval Staff, its associated bodies, and leading naval experts, continued closely assessing the transformation of Western naval power. Regular published analysis in open-source defense and other publications suggest that the Russian professional and expert community focused on (1) up-to-date assessments of the current thinking and changes to doctrines by potential adversaries (for example, ". . . From the Sea," "Sea Power 21," "A Cooperative Strategy for 21st Century

Seapower," and others); and (2) assessments of new capabilities and their combat performance in campaigns involving the USN and allied navies. With respect to the latter, the Russians tended to focus on the U.S.-led campaigns against Iraq (1991 and 2003), NATO-led campaigns against former Yugoslavia (1999) and Libya (2011), and the initial phase of Operation Enduring Freedom (2001), which saw extensive employment of USN's strike assets against targets in land-locked Afghanistan.

Russian experts identified several major trends in the evolution of U.S. naval strategy and force application. In their view, the focus of the USN in the unipolar world was on stabilization activities in forward areas as part of the continuous expansion of U.S. influence. With the gradual emergence of a multipolar system, the USN and allied navies shifted their focus toward global naval presence by means of "deterrence by intimidation based on the possibility of an immediate proactive response in a particular area of the world."[9] Russian observers noted that the USN was less concerned with fleet-versus-fleet confrontations and more focused on "from the sea" operations against land powers.[10] They also perceived a shift in U.S. deterrence posture from one based on sea-launched nuclear weapons to one based on a new generation of kinetic and nonkinetic systems. Another area of interest for the Russians was how the USN conducted multidomain operations with other elements of the U.S. military and with its allies, through the Global Maritime Partnership.

Critical evaluation of published analysis reveals several areas of sustained professional interest for the Russian navy. Operationally, Russian observers were interested in the effectiveness of U.S. multi-domain/multisphere operations, particularly as a counter to Russia's A2/AD (antiaccess/area-denial) operational concept.[11] They noted with interest the introduction of a network-centric approach to warfighting across the aerospace and maritime domains. How well the USN integrated the space-based, airborne, sea-based, and ground-based intelligence-gathering elements into one coordinated system, and how that was then integrated with the airborne and sea-based strike systems for the conduct of coordinated offensive strikes in a real-time environment, was a frequent topic of discussion. Some noted that in this system, data about the enemy is immediately processed and transmitted to the strike elements that carry out immediate responses, which was something that the Soviet military trialed back in the 1980s under Marshal Nikolai Ogarkov but never institutionalized.[12]

Russian naval strategists and planners classified this new form of war as strategic aerospace-and-sea operation (*vozdushno-kosmicheskaya morskaya operatsiya*, or C^3O), and they saw it as particularly useful during limited local conflicts or regional wars. Military strikes against enemy targets are carried out by combined combat reconnaissance-strike systems, primarily comprising space-based reconnaissance and data-processing systems (satellites) and sea-based and airborne combat platforms (warships and multirole aircraft), with delivery systems of long-range, high-precision weapons (cruise missiles, smart bombs, and others). Thus, in their view, C^3O carried out within one theater was becoming the primary form of warfighting in the twenty-first century.[13]

The Russians were equally interested in examining U.S. experiences in mobilizing forces during the escalation phase of naval confrontation.[14] In their estimates the USN could mobilize up to one thousand merchant vessels and other ships to support its transoceanic operations. The overall capacity to commence large-scale, sustained operations with the support of allied navies following partial mobilization was estimated to be twenty to thirty days.[15]

There was also significant discussion within Russian professional naval circles about the impact of the U.S. littoral strategy on Russia's national security and defense. One of the publications emphasized that the U.S. littoral strategy represented a "qualitative jump" in the execution of U.S. operations "against the shore," particularly against large geopolitical entities such as Russia.[16]

Another important vector was assessments of various variables concerning the effectiveness of combat employment of Russian existing and incoming combat strike systems against the USN and

NATO navies. One of the major emphases of these studies was an analysis of these systems' combat performance in the so-called distant maritime zone (dal'nyaya morskaya zona, or DMZ).[17] One of the studies, which was published in Russia's open defense source raised concerns about the effectiveness of the Russian navy's ability to inflict substantial damage on adversarial naval forces (for example, carrier battle groups) during a hypothetical engagement in a DMZ. In particular, the authors highlighted the "guaranteed detection of aerial and surface targets" by the U.S. and NATO forces by means of multilayered concentration of all types of electronic intelligence and tracking, including the AWACS aircraft. The study argued that a network-centric approach of warfighting at sea adopted by the USN and NATO fleets effectively neutralizes the ability of Russian joint forces to jam adversarial communications and electronic systems by means of electronic countermeasures (ECMs) and electromagnetic spectrum warfare (ESW). It also valued highly the USN and NATO battlegroups' ability to deploy multilayered air defense (AD) and ballistic missile defense systems (BMDS) via ship-based missiles, artillery systems, and shipborne aircraft, as well as incoming guided laser interceptors.[18]

Finally, Russian observers analyzed the significance of the USN fielding new-generation combat and other systems, including lasers and underwater unmanned reconnaissance and attack vehicles.[19] The realization of the transformed potential of U.S. naval power combined with an urgent need to modernize its own declining power compelled the Russian political-military leadership to act. Moscow revised its naval strategy and established new parameters for its future force design.

RUSSIA'S VIEWS ON THE APPLICATION OF NATIONAL NAVAL POWER IN THE 1990s AND 2000s

These new circumstances, as well as the lessons of the Cold War naval confrontation, called for the reassessment of Russian naval strategy. In the 1990s Russian naval staff developed a new set of tasks for the navy to accomplish in peace and wartime based on the new political and military-strategic realities, the current state of Russian naval capabilities, and the ability of the state to support fleet activities. In peacetime, the main objectives of the RFN would be

- Strategic nuclear deterrence
- Conventional deterrent operations, including combined-arms deterrent operations against potentially hostile naval forces, combat service (*boyevaya sluzhba*), and combat duty (*boyevoe dezhurstvo*)
- Joint containment and peace-enforcement activities, as well as combined-arms operations to prevent or localize border conflicts threatening Russia's security
- Forward presence and naval diplomacy
- Humanitarian and disaster relief operations and supporting United Nations–led peacekeeping operations
- Special operations, such as surveillance, intelligence gathering, oceanography, hydrography, meteorology, and search-and-rescue)

In wartime, the main missions of the navy would include

- *Strategic missions*—nuclear deterrence and strategic strike; limited strategic antisubmarine warfare (ASW) operations against enemy nuclear-powered ballistic missile submarines (SSBNs); attacks against enemy land-based infrastructure and its military-industrial potential
- *Operational-tactical missions*—anticarrier warfare and specialized ASW operations against enemy nuclear power attack submarines (SSNs) or nuclear-powered submarines armed with guided cruise missiles (SSGNs); other combat operations and maritime defense of the littoral
- *Tactical missions*—anti-SLOC warfare and conventional ASW; mine warfare; amphibious operations and coastal defense; protection of friendly shipping
- Generally, combined-arms operations against adversarial forces[20]

Regarding the navy's role in the system of national strategic nuclear deterrence, the current provisions of Russia's application of the nuclear triad in times of war leaves the sea-based strategic nuclear component with the strategic retaliatory strike responsibility, which will become an essential element in the planned strategic deterrent forces operation (*operatsiya strategicheskikh sil sderzhivaniya*).[21]

In the first decade of the twenty-first century, senior Russian naval commanders argued that the RFN should focus on preemptive operations aimed at containing adversarial hostile intent toward Russia and its allies. Containment was supposed to be achieved by means of positioning naval task groups in conflict zones with an aim to contain of restrain fighting or supporting Russia's interests through indirect or direct cohesion falling short of direct combat. The Russians classified these activities as strategic-level noncontact operations (StratNocOps). In the opinion of Admiral Mikhail Mot-sak (then chief of staff of the Russian Northern Fleet), StratNocOps would become the definitive form of the use of Russian naval forces in the new millennium.[22] These types of operations were considered to be best force commitment options in in response to low-intensity conflicts or limited-scale local and regional wars.

Two strategic-level operations where naval forces can effectively participate during wartime were identified. In the event of a possible C^3O against Russia, or the limited C^3O in one of Russia's strategic theaters, forces of the entire navy or individual fleets (flotillas) responsible for the defense of that specific geographic zone would repel the attacks. Meanwhile, the SSBN force would take part in the strategic nuclear operation of the Russian strategic deterrent forces. It is expected that the Russian nuclear-powered submarines armed with submarine-launched cruise missiles (SLCMs) would also participate in such operation.[23]

Several combat commitments in this period shaped changes to the strategic application of Russian naval power in peacetime and wartime. In October 2022, the then CN-RFN, Admiral Nikolai Evmenov, referred to three such operations since 1992: the war in Georgia, the war in Syria, and the war in Ukraine.[24] Yet the analysis of the entire operational activity of the navy between 1992 and late 2022 identifies no fewer than seven contingencies (table 13.3), which can be divided into three main categories. In nonstrategic, noncontact operations (NosNocOps) in zones of armed conflict, elements of the RFN were committed to combat support roles (reconnaissance; shadow operations; fleet-in-being, etc.). In contact operations in zones of armed conflict, elements of the RFN were operationally assigned and performed combat and combat support roles combined with other operational activities. Finally, the RFN also conducted special operations, mainly counter-piracy operations (CPOs) or counterterrorism patrols (CTPs).

The RFN's involvement in limited NosNocOps, such as the former Yugoslavia and Iraq, was a case of reluctant ad hoc operational commitments largely driven by the Kremlin's political agenda, rather than a carefully planned operation with an expectation that force deployments to conflict zones would produce any favorable outcomes. For example, in 1999, the RFN's delayed response to NATO's Operation Allied Force was limited to intelligence-gathering deployments to the Adriatic by two *Oscar II*–class SSGNs.[25] Similarly, in 2003, after publicly promising a powerful response to the invasion of Iraq, Moscow ended up committing a task force to limited-term operations in the Arabian Sea sufficiently distant to avoid direct confrontation with the USN.[26]

In contrast, the navy's involvement in combat operations in Syria (from 2015) and Ukraine (from 2022) was a result of advance contingency planning based on capability assessments, studies of the theater of war, threat assessments of adversarial intent, and studies of logistics. Both campaigns highlighted the growing fighting potential of Russian naval power, particularly in its matured capacity to execute large-scale cruise missile strikes against land as well as the ability to engage in StratNocOps. At the same time, these campaigns revealed ongoing shortfalls in combat performance and the capacity to partake in high-end operations against a technologically developed adversary.

TABLE 13.3. RFN's combat operational activity, 1992–early 2023

Type of activity	Year(s)	Maritime theater(s)	Reason	Mission(s)
NosNocOps	1992–93	Black Sea	Civil war in Georgia	Maritime evacuation from Abkhazia; onshore marine ops; containment naval ops against the Georgian forces
	1999	Adriatic/ Mediterranean	NATO operation against Serbia	Reconnaissance and shadow ops; limited deterrent ops against the USN and NATO navies
	2003	Northern Indian Ocean	Operation Iraqi Freedom	Naval and aerial ops in the Arabian Sea
Special operations	2007	Mediterranean	Maritime terrorism risks	CTPs
	From 2009	Northwestern Indian Ocean	Piracy attacks off the Horn of Africa	CPOs; convoy ops
Contact ops in zones of armed conflict	2008	Black Sea	Five-Day War with Georgia	Sea lift, naval blockade, naval surface warfare, aerial defense, special forces ops
	From 2015	Mediterranean	Russia's intervention in the Syrian conflict	Amphibious lift and sealift; naval strike; aerial defense; onshore marine and special forces ops; enforcing favorable maritime regime and deterrent ops (against the USN and NATO)
	From 2022	Black Sea and Mediterranean	Russia's invasion of Ukraine	Amphibious lift and sealift; naval strike; aerial defense; onshore marine and special forces ops; maritime defense, deterrent ops (against the USN and NATO)

Sources: *Morskoi Sbornik* (1992–23); *Krasnaya Zvezda* (1998–23); *Voenno-Promyshlenny Kurier* (2013–22); *Nezavisimoe Voennoe Obozrenie* (1999–23); *TASS* (2000–2023); data collected by the author

From the vantage point of early 2023, the Russian navy has lost its capacity to engage in stand-alone strategic-level naval operations, meaning sustained high-tempo, large-scale operations within one maritime theater. There are several overlapping reasons for this failure. The RFN lacks sufficient oceangoing forces, a robust auxiliary element, and overseas shore infrastructure. Its naval airpower has been depleted and relies too heavily on shore-based aircraft. The RFN has abandoned the Soviet commitment to forward sea-control operations in favor of a more realistic littoral sea-control and limited "blue-water" sea-denial missions. Russian naval forces prioritize operations within the 300 km inner defensive zone, complemented by limited operations within the 2,000–2,500 km outer-defensive perimeter. Their future ability either to retain these limited capabilities or to increase their strategic reach is linked to the ongoing naval modernization and capability enhancement program.

PRIORITIES IN FORCE DEVELOPMENT AND NAVAL CONSTRUCTION

The post–Cold War modernization of the RFN underwent several dramatic turns, suffering from the effects of the USSR's disintegration, the poor state of the national economy, and resultant absence of funding, as well as conflicting views on the future force composition advocated by the two competing influence groups.

The collapse of a once-united and integrated naval shipbuilding industry was the first major challenge for Moscow after 1992. Most Soviet naval shipbuilding infrastructure was located west of the Ural Mountains, on the shores of the Baltic and Black Seas. When the USSR disintegrated, Russia inherited 113 out of the 170 facilities of the former Soviet shipbuilding industry.[27] But Moscow lost access to a powerful network of shipyards in Ukraine, which specialized in the construction of many types of surface combatants, submarines, auxiliaries, and ship turbines. Also, production of some ASW weapons systems and navigational equipment was left in Kazakhstan, Kyrgyzstan, and Azerbaijan, respectively.[28]

As a result, Moscow had to rebuild the collapsed supply chain while simultaneously developing designer competence and manufacturing expertise in areas once provided by the former Soviet republics.

Severe lack of funding became another major disruptor. Until the middle of the first decade of the twenty-first century, the navy suffered from inadequate funding even to sustain ongoing operational units, let alone plan for new warship construction. The last large-scale naval construction program ended in 1990, after which state procurement orders for the navy dropped by 2,000 percent.[29] High inflation seriously complicated this situation. Between 1992 and 2000, Russian naval shipyards were capable of only finishing building some Soviet-era projects, though they did attempt to commence the construction of new-generation platforms.[30]

Finally, Russia's military leadership under Yeltsin effectively neglected the naval sphere. Russia's first Military Doctrine, which was released in 1993, did not mention the role of the navy in the new national security concept. In the national white paper titled *What Should the Russian Defence Doctrine Be?*, Andrei Kokoshin, who served as the First Deputy Minister of Defense between 1992 and 1997, argued in favor of a smaller non-oceangoing force: "A totally new concept is needed also for Russia's and CIS's [Commonwealth of Intendent States] navy. Moderate and non-aggressive goals of Russia . . . do not require such a large high seas navy which began to be built after N. S. Khrushchev's overthrow and which for many years had been connected to the name of Admiral Gorshkov."[31] The situation began gradually changing in the 2000s, particularly with the adoption of the State Armaments program until the Year 2020, in which about 25 percent of total funding was assigned toward naval construction. The naval modernization of the early 2000s largely reflected future force design provisions, which had been formulated in late 1990s on the basis of the following major strategic considerations:

- The navy was supposed to partake in strategic deterrent operations in peacetime while being ready to launch counter or counter-value strategic nuclear strikes;
- The navy should have the combat potential sufficient to defeat adversarial forces during a low-intensity conflict or a local war by means of peacetime strength force supported by elements of partial mobilization; and
- The navy should have sufficient capacity to defeat adversarial forces in one regional war (within one maritime theater) while actively deterring and containing hostile forces at other theaters after full mobilization of personnel and assigning of additional assets (transition to a wartime strength, including reinforced order of battle).[32]

Naval construction can be sorted into three tiers, in descending order of importance (chart 13.1).

CHART 13.1. The three-tier priority approach in Russia's naval construction, 2000s

Sea-based strategic nuclear deterrent (SSBNs)	
Subsurface submarine sea-denial component (SSGNs, SSNs, SSKs)	Surface-action component (SBCM carriers)
Amphibious element / Auxiliary element	Naval aviation

In terms of future force development, it was suggested that priority should be given to the qualitative replenishment of the sea-based strategic nuclear deterrent in order to prevent a "considerable qualitative and quantitative gap of these systems from the level of the U.S., even for a limited time."[33] The future SSBN force and its associated support components (the sea-based missile-nuclear system, *morskaya raketno-yadernaya sistema*) was envisaged to comprise ten to fifteen fourth-generation boats of the *Borey* and *Borey-A* classes.[34] As a result of these findings, *Tier One* has been focusing on the qualitative upgrade of the existing SSBN force by replacing the remaining *Delta-III* and *Typhoon* classes, and eventually *Delta-IV*-class, with *Borey/Borey-A*-class *submarines*. The current state defense order has a provision for ten units with a possibility of ordering additional boats in the near future. This tier gets an absolute priority in terms of funding and state support, at times at the expense of other naval procurement programs.

Tier Two is the second most important force development program for the RFN. It covers multirole nuclear and conventional submarine construction as well as a series of littoral and ocean-going surface strike combatants: sea-based cruise missile (SBCM)/submarine-launched cruise missile (SLCM) carriers such as 3M24 *Uran* (SS-N-25 Switchblade), 3M55 *Oniks* (SS-N-26 Strobile), 3M14 *Kalibr-NK/PL* (SS-N-30A), and now 3M22 *Tsirkon* (SS-N-33). One of the main reasons behind the prioritization of the large-scale construction of platforms capable of carrying different types of long-range SBCM/SLCMs was modeling which suggested that multiecheloned ECMs and AD/BMD could neutralize some of these weapons systems.[35]

As part of the multirole submarine force upgrade, Russia pursues the simultaneous construction of three types of submarines: nuclear-powered (Project 855 for the Northern and Pacific fleets and conventional projects 636.3 and 677 for all four fleets). By 2023, Russia's MoD placed an order for 26 boats (14 of which have already been commissioned) with an additional 12 under construction or expected to be laid down in due course (table 13.4). In addition, the RFN ordered a major overhaul and refit of a select number of *Oscar II*–class as well as all *Akula*-class SSNs to equip them with enhanced detection and SLCM strike capabilities, including increased payload.

TABLE 13.4. Russian submarine warfare construction programs (SLCM launchers), early 2023

		Conventional		Nuclear-powered
Project		636.3 Improved Varshavyanka	677 Lada	855 Yasen' / Yasen'-M
Construction program launched		2010	1997	1993
Displacement, full (tons)		3,950 (dived)	2,650 (dived)	13,800 (dived)
Main missile armament		Kalibr-PL	Kalibr-PL	8 × 5 Kalibr-PL OR 8 × 4 Oniks, Tsirkon
Numbers ordered		12	5	9
Fleet	Northern	(3)	1 (4)	2 (3)
	Pacific	4 (2)	—	1 (3)
	Baltic	(1)	—	—
	Black Sea	6	—	—
Further planned		+4	—	—

Sources: *Military Balance* (1993–2023); *Morskoi Sbornik* (1992–23); *Krasnaya Zvezda* (1998–23); *Voenno-Promyshlenny Kurier* (2013–22); *Nezavisimoe Voennoe Obozrenie* (1999–23); *TASS* (2000–2023); data collected by the author

The capability upgrade of the conventional surface element was more controversial. Partially inspired by similar programs in the United States, the Russian senior naval command lobbied for the launch of expensive series of littoral warfare ships (Project 22160) as well as multimission modular design platforms (Project 20386).[36] Eventually, it was agreed to prioritize the construction of surface SBCM carriers designed for both littoral and open-ocean operations.

A growing disparity between U.S. and Russian SCBMs and their carrier platforms had long been a source of concern for Russian senior naval commanders. According to the Russian estimates, in 1997 the USN operated 136 surface and subsurface platforms armed with 4,784 SBCM launchers.[37] The RFN projected that by 2000 the USN would be operating various combat platforms armed with 7,500 SBCM launchers (over 4,000 SBCMs).[38] By contrast, the RFN's public data in 1997 said it had some 20 strike platforms capable of launching SBCMs (about 100 launchers). Fearing the continuous decline of state support for the navy, the Russian Naval Staff estimated that by 2000 the number of SBCM carriers (and launchers) would be cut eightfold,[39] thus making the RFN's future capacity to carry out long-range high-precision missile strikes almost nominal. The authors particularly noted the urgent need to increase the arsenal of antiship missiles and their shipborne and airborne carriers in order to achieve relative force parity with the USN and NATO combined forces.[40] Consequently, they proposed a construction program of launchers and missiles sufficient to "meet the navy's needs for guaranteed repulsion of aggression from maritime directions, among them delivery of strikes against enemy forces at a considerable distance from Russia's shores."[41]

The SCBM factor in Russia's post–Cold War and current thinking and planning could possibly be explained by lessons drawn from the Soviet Cold War naval playbook. Between the 1950s and early 1980s, when the USSR was trying to achieve strategic parity at sea with the United States and its allies, sea denial and limited sea control over coastal waters was at the heart of Soviet thinking and operational planning. The large-scale introduction of various types of shipborne missiles and surface, underwater, and aerial delivery systems in the order of battle of the Soviet Navy made the SCBM factor one of key determinants of then Soviet and now Russia's force calculations.

In 2001, Russia commenced an ambitious surface warfare upgrade program designed to compensate for the shortfall of SBCM surface carriers as well as to replace partially the aging littoral warfare and oceangoing platforms. Five series of surface combatants (sixty-two units) began construction, effectively making it the largest surface warfare upgrade program in Europe (table 13.5). Although most of the platforms built were smaller-hulled warships, the Russians gradually turned their focus to an oceangoing element.[42] In early February 2023, it was revealed that Russia's MoD was planning to order six additional Project 22350 hulls and the first 22350M guided-missile frigates (FFGs), all to be built at the Amur shipyard in Komsomol'sk-na-Amure.[43] If this contract comes through, it will be another indicator that, despite the ongoing commitment to ground operations in Ukraine, the Russian political-military leadership remains committed to the continuous modernization of its navy.

TABLE 13.5. Russian surface warfare construction programs (SBCM launchers), early 2023

		Littoral			Oceangoing	
Project		21631 Byan-M	22800 Karakurt	20380/20385 Steregush-chiy/ Gremyashchiy[a]	11356R Admiral Grigoro-vich[b]	22350 Admiral Gorshkov
Program launched		2010	2015	2001	2010	2006
Displacement, full (tons)		949	870	2,250 (20380) 2,430 (20385)	4,035	5,400
Main missile armament		1 × 8 3C14 Kalibr-NK, Oniks	1 × 8 3C14 Kalibr-NK, Oniks	2 × 4 Uran (20380) 1 × 8 3C14 Kalibr-NK, Oniks (20385)	1 × 8 3C14 Kalibr-NK, Oniks	2 × 8 3C14 Kalibr-NK, Oniks 4 × 8 3C14 (from fifth unit)
Numbers ordered		12	16	18	6	10
Fleet	Northern	—	—	—	—	2 (2)
	Pacific	—	(4)	4 (8)	—	(4) + (6)
	Baltic	3 (1)	3 (4)	4	—	—
	Black Sea	4	1 (4)	(2)	3	(2)
	Caspian	3 (1)	—	—	—	—
Further planned		—	+2	—	—	+6

Sources: *Military Balance* (1993–2023); *Morskoi Sbornik* (1992–23); *Krasnaya Zvezda* (1998–23); *Voenno-Promyshlenny Kurier* (2013–22); *Nezavisimoe Voennoe Obozrenie* (1999–23); TASS (2000–2023); data collected by the author

[a] Although Projects 20380 and 20385 were originally designed as littoral warfare combatants, commissioned units were extensively drawn in support of open-ocean long-range deployments.

[b] The initial order was for six units. However, problems with receiving ship turbines from Ukraine after 2014 forced the Russian naval command to limit the series to three commissioned units.

Tier Three illustrates Russia's efforts to modernize the amphibious, auxiliary, and naval aviation arm of the RFN. Although this tier does not receive same degree of priority as the first two, it nonetheless shows the extent and comprehensiveness of Russia's modernization efforts. According to the Russian estimates, the RFN's amphibious and auxiliary arms' capability gap is as high as 70 percent.[44] The immediate focus is on the construction of a new line of support platforms equipped with indigenous technologies.[45] The amphibious element should receive fewer but more potent platforms, including landing ship, tank (LSTs), and landing helicopter docks (LHDs) designed for prolonged operations and overseas contingencies (table 13.6).

TABLE 13.6. Russian amphibious warfare construction programs, early 2023

Project type, class	Commissioned, ordered	Fleet	Displacement, full (tons)	Maximum range, n.m.	Capacity
LST					
Project 11711	2	Northern	6,600	4,000	Up to 13 MBTs OR 36 APCs, up to 300 marines; 2 Ka-29
Vladimir Andreev	(2)	Pacific	Up to 8,000	5,000	Up to 40 heavy equipment; up to 400 marines; 3 to 5 helicopters
LHD					
Project 23900	(2)	Pacific Black Sea	Up to 40,000	6,000	Up to 75 heavy equipment, approx. 900 marines; 16 to 20 helicopters, 4 UAVs

Sources: *Morskoi Sbornik* (1992–23); *Krasnaya Zvezda* (1998–23); *Voenno-Promyshlenny Kurier* (2013–22); *Nezavisimoe Voennoe Obozrenie* (1999–23); *TASS* (2000–2023); data collected by the author

Moscow's decision to move toward a mature expeditionary capability is driven by both the conceptualization of the StratNocOps, which called for the creation of a potent expeditionary component, as well as operational experience gained from staging contact operations NosNocOps. The extensive and successful operational experience of the USN and NATO navies was also taken into account. Finally, Russia's MoD's decision to expand its naval infantry/marine capability by converting five existing brigades into full-strength divisions (with at least two being assigned to the Pacific Fleet) correlates with the continuous construction of LSTs and LHDs.[46]

This analysis of the ongoing Russian naval construction programs suggests that Moscow's current approach toward the development of its naval power resembles the Soviet experience, where the emphasis was on the development of a powerful sea-based strategic nuclear deterrent as well as potent submarine attack force. The latter, combined with a consistent effort to acquire a fleet of surface strike platforms, indicates a defensive rather than offensive force posture with clear sea-denial and substrategic strike capabilities, but a limited ability to contest sea control in distant areas. Nevertheless, the gradual expansion of larger hull construction would still make the future Russian navy a force with a considerable reliance on smaller assets. Even in the 1980s, only 15 percent of the Soviet naval force were oceangoing surface combatants, while some 64 percent were littoral warfare ships (out of which 30 percent were light combatants).[47] This force structure is likely to prevail for the foreseeable future.

CONCLUSION

Since the end of the Cold War the Russian navy has endured a turbulence that any naval force would be desperate to avoid. Between 1991 and 2000, the RFN lost almost one thousand naval platforms, which was roughly comparable to a total defeat in a high-intensity conflict. It struggled to win budget battles, and the budget itself shrank dramatically. Not only did Russia's political leadership fail to appreciate the navy's role, but also it was internally divided on fundamental questions including force design and its relationship with Western navies. The 1990s RFN was unable to come up with useful plans for future conflicts both because it did not know whom it would be fighting and because every year the budgetary situation seemed worse than the one before.

However, the past fifteen years have seen an impressive turn-around, and the RFN has a much better sense of its role in national strategy and how it envisions confronting Western navies. The resumption of out-of-area deployments, the intensification of the overall operational activity, and the launch of several ambitious naval construction programs signaled of a renaissance of Russian naval power. Putin's desire to rebuild Russia's naval power sparked this transformation. Nevertheless, despite possessing a blue-water component, Russian naval posture remains largely oriented toward home littoral waters. The ongoing prioritization of the multirole submarine force combined with the construction of a large number of littoral warfare strike surface combatants (echoing Soviet approaches to addressing problems of threat containment in distant and littoral areas) serves as additional illustration of this current thinking and planning.[48]

By prioritizing operations in the vicinity of home waters, Russian naval leadership not only acknowledges the force's existing limitations but also has a realistic understanding of how to maximize the use of its available naval potential. The Russians assume that the difference between defense and offense in naval warfare is almost irrelevant. It is possible to imagine a Russian battle group fighting a defensive engagement somewhere in the Sea of Japan or Okhotsk under the umbrella of friendly shore-based aviation and succeeding in destroying an adversarial strike force, all without ever needing a significant high seas component. Finally, it is worth remembering the old but time proven Soviet naval concept of *total deployed forces*. The Russian way of assessing the level and efficiency of operational commitment at sea includes both out of area and in-area deployments. In fact, staging operations in the latter are viewed to be as important as operational commitments to forward areas.

The RFN's combat performance in Syria and Ukraine offered opportunities both to appreciate the growing combat value of the force as well as analyze its ongoing problems. Russia's invasion of Ukraine exposed several strategic shortfalls in the country's preparations and conduct of the initial phases of the campaign. Furthermore, sustained losses and the need to replenish stocks of munitions forced Moscow to rethink and reassess its commitments to national security and defense. Given the dominant nature of ground operations over the 2022 campaign and early 2023, questions were raised whether the navy would remain among the priority areas for the Russian MoD.[49] However, on December 29, 2022, while taking part in the official commissioning of several new warships, Putin emphasized that his government will "increase the pace and volume of construction of ships of various designs, equip them with the most modern weaponry, conduct operational and combat training of sailors [also by] taking into account the experience gained, including during the special military operation."[50] This indicates the ongoing resolve by Putin's administration to continue the progression of the national naval power reconstruction no matter the current military situation or the cost.

The rationale is clear. The strategists in Moscow understand too well that Russia's deepening strategic collision with the United States and its allies will not be limited to land or cyberspace. As noted earlier, Russia's strategic geography makes it susceptible to military-strategic threats coming from the maritime domain. The enhanced strike capabilities of the USN and allied navies reduce the advantage of Russia's strategic depth by making highly populated areas (including strategic centers of gravity such as Moscow) and major industrial centers potentially accessible targets. For Moscow, the navy will always remain an unavoidable element of its national security and defense posture. Unless Russia goes through a democratic regime change or experiences a catastrophic collapse of its national economy, its ambitions to rebuild the oceangoing navy are likely to remain unchanged.

NOTES

1. Yulia Kozak, "Vernykh i bezopastnykh kursov!'" [(Wishing) accurate and safe (navigational) courses!], *Krasnaya Zvezda*, January 25, 2023, 5.
2. Names given to this quasi-group and its ideological counterpart are indicative, as they reflect views and operational philosophies of respective informal bodies.
3. Andrei Gavrilenko, "Perspektivy flota" [The navy's perspectives], *Krasnaya Zvezda*, August 4–10, 2010, 3.
4. Supporters of Gorshkov's school of naval thought, strategy, and planning. Another way to refer to this quasi-group and its followers are traditionalists, e.g., supporters of the organic development of national naval power based on the principle of a design and development of a balanced force.
5. Effectively, these potential strikes could hit targets across 80 percent of the entire country, which houses 60 to 65 percent of its total military-industrial potential as well as critical coordination, command and control centers, and largest population centers. Sergei Kozlov, "Voenno-Morskoi flot i obespechenie natsional'nykh interesov Rossii v mirovom okeane" [The navy and the provision of Russia's national interests in the world ocean], *Upravlencheskoe Konsul'tirovanie* 2 (2006): 60, 72.
6. Rear Admiral (Ret.) Georgiy Kostev, *Voenno-Morskoi Flot Strany 1945–1995* [The country's navy, 1945–1995] (Saint Petersburg: Nauka, 1999), 597–98. NB: In some cases, threat assessments included regional naval forces of countries with nonalignment status but a history of strategic confrontation with Russia, or if these doctrines considered Russia as a potential threat (e.g., the Swedish navy in the Baltic).
7. Captain 1st Rank A. Smolovskiy, "Istoki nestabil'nosti v operatsionnykh zonakh VMF RF" [Sources of instability within the operational zones of the Russian navy], *Morskoi Sbornik*, no. 8 (August 2008): 72–81; no. 9 (September 2008): 56–65; and no. 10 (October 2008): 54–60.
8. For example, the *neo-Gorshkovtsy* proposed that the future RFN's order of battle should have no less than 14–15 SSBNs;

90 nuclear-powered and conventional attack submarines; about 45 oceangoing surface combatants, some 130–140 smaller combatants; up to 60 mine warfare ships; and 600 fixed-wing and 300 rotary aircraft. Kostev, *Voenno-Morskoi Flot Strany 1945–1995*, 576.

9. For example, M. Boitsov, "Ob evoliutsii strategiy i strategicheskikh kontseptsiy VMS SShA" [On the evolution of strategies and strategic concepts of the U.S. Navy], *Morskoi Sbornik*, no. 4 (April 2011): 50.

10. Captain 2nd Rank A. Repin, "Perspektivy razvitiya teorii porazheniya nazemnykh o'bektov stranami NATO" [Perspectives of the development of a theory of striking land-based targets by NATO countries], *Morskoi Sbornik*, no. 10 (October 2016): 63–71.

11. Col. A. V. Khomutov, "O protivodeistvii protivniku v usloviyakh vedeniya im 'mnogosfernykh operatsiy'" [On countering an adversary in times when it stages "multisphere" operations], *Voennaya Mysl'* 5 (May 2021): 27–41.

12. The Russians openly acknowledge that the United States displays superior capacity in situational awareness, the speed of making and executing decisions in battlefield situations. Khomutov, 55.

13. Admiral (Ret.) I. Kapitanets, "Voenno-Morskaya nauka i perspektivy ee razvitiya" [Naval art and perspectives of its development], *Morskoi Sbornik*, no. 5 (May 2002): 37.

14. Captain 2nd Rank V. Evseev, "Morskie perevozki VS SShA v voennoi operatsii 'Svoboda Iraka'" [Maritime transport operations of the U.S. military during the operation Iraqi Freedom], *Morskoi Sbornik*, no. 10 (October 2008): 61–66.

15. Captain 1st Rank (Ret.) A. I. Ismailov, Captain 1st Rank (Ret.) V. V. Puchnin, and Rear Admiral A. Iy. Sysuyev, "Problemy mobilizatsionnogo obespecheniya Rossiiskogo voenno-morskogo flota i vozmozhnye puti ikh razreshenya" [Problems of the mobilizational support of the Russian navy and possible ways to resolve them], *Voennaya Mysl'*, no. 12 (December 2022): 69, 71.

16. A. Mozgovoi, "Litoral'ny boyevoi korabl': Kakim on dolzhen byt'?" [A littoral warfare ship: How should it look?], *Morskoi Sbornik*, no. 7 (July 2009): 44–52; A. Mozgovoi, "Natsional'naya Sistema PVO i 'Litoral'naya' Strategiya SShA" [The national ballistic missile defense system and the U.S. "littoral" strategy], *Morskoi Sbornik*, no. 2 (February 2021): 58.

17. The DMZ is understood to be an area of operations that stretches beyond two hundred nautical miles from a friendly coastline.

18. Lieutenant Colonel S. Golubchikov, "Perspektivy razvitiya sistemy PRO morskogo bazirovaniya AEGIS" [Perspectives of the development of the sea-based ballistic missile defence system AEGIS], *Morskoi Sbornik*, no. 2 (February 2015): 67–76; I. Spirin and Colonel V. Alferov, "Osobennosti porazheniya o'bektov v dal'nei morskoi zone" [The peculiarities of striking objects in a distant maritime zone], *Morskoi Sbornik*, no. 12 (December 2015): 43–44.

19. Captain 1st Rank (Ret.) D. V. Zerniukov, "Rol' i mesto sverkh-bol'shikh avtonomnykh neobitayemykh podvodnykh apparatov v morskoi strategii Soedinennykh Shtatov Ameriki" [The role and place of extra-large autonomous uninhabited underwater vehicles in the maritime strategy of the United States of America], *Voennaya Mys'l* 1 (January 2023): 149–57.

20. Vice Admiral V. Ilin, "Sootvetstvovat' zadacham svoego vremeni" [To comply with tasks of its time], *Morskoi Sbornik*, no. 1 (January 1998): 7; see also Vladimir Kuroyedov, "O morskoi strategii Rossii" [On Russia's naval strategy], *Voenny Parad* 2, no. 26 (1998): 8–9; Vladimir Kuroyedov, "Kompleksny podkhod k razvitiu morskoi sily gosudarstva" [A comprehensive approach toward the development of the sea power of a state], *Morskoi Sbornik*, no. 8 (August 1999): 5.

21. Lieutenant-General I. R. Fazletdinov and Colonel (Ret.) V. I. Lumpov, "Rol' raketnykh voisk strategicheskogo naznacheniya v protivodeistvii strategicheskoi mnogosfernoi operatsii NATO" [The role of the strategic missile forces in countering NATO's strategic multidomain operation], *Voennaya Mysl'* 3 (March 2023): 59–60.

22. Mikhail Motsak, "S pritselom na nepryamye strategicheskie deistviya" [With an aim on the nonstrategic activities], *Nezavisimoe Voennoe Obozrenie* 3 (2000): 4.

23. See the report by Kuroyedov, "The Navy's Role in the Defence of the State: Forms and Ways of Employment," in "Kompleksny podkhod k razvitiu morskoi sily gosudarstva," 5–6.

24. N. Evmenov, "Rol' i mesto voenno-morskogo flota v voihakh i vooruzhennykh konfliktakh" [The navy's role and place in wars and armed conflicts], *Morskoi Sbornik*, no. 11 (October 2022): 5.

25. In particular, RFS *Kursk* staged covert operations in the Mediterranean and RFS *Omsk* in the Pacific with a likely mission to track
carrier and other battle groups operating in respective theaters.
· "Itogi i perspektivy" [Results and perspectives], *Morskoi Sbornik*,
no. 12 (December 1999): 3–4.

26. Alexey D. Muraviev, "Russia," in Howard M. Hensel, ed., *Security Dynamics in the Gulf and the Arabian Peninsula* (London: Routledge: 2023), 300, 306.

27. G. Voronin, "O kraine tyazhelom polozhenii VMF" [On the navy's
extremely difficult situation], *Morskoi Sbornik*, no. 2 (February
1996): 13.

28. Rear Admiral L. Belyshev, "Ostanetsia li Rossiya velikoi morskoi
derzhavoi" [Will Russia remain a great maritime power], *Morskoi
Sbornik*, no. 7 (July 1992): 8. See also interview with Belyshev in
"Korablestroenie i remont: Gruz problem na vesakh biudzheta"
[Shipbuilding and maintenance: Burden of problems on a budget's
balance], *Morskoi Sbornik*, nos. 8–9 (August–September 1992): 8.

29. Captain 1st Rank Boris Makeev, "Ugrozy iz okeana: Vek XXI"
[Ocean-based threats: The twenty-first century], *Krasnaya Zvezda*
5 (August 2000): 2.

30. For example, in 1993, the Sevmash shipyard launched the Project
855 *Severodvinsk* class SSGN and in 1996 the Project 955 Borey
class RFS *Yuri Dolgorukiy* SSBN. The construction of both lead
units turned into a lengthy saga.

31. Kokoshin's remarks were quoted from Duk-Ki Kim, *Naval Strategy in Northeast Asia: Geo-Strategic Goals, Policies and Prospects*
(London: Frank Cass, 2000), 110.

32. Captain 1st Rank V. Apanasenko, "Sokhranyat' sposobnost' protivostoyat' ugrozam s morya" [To be able to retain a capacity to
repel sea-based threats], *Morskoi Sbornik* 11 (November 1997): 5.

33. Apanasenko.

34. Captain 1st Rank B. Makeev, "Morskie strategicheskie yadersnye
sily i podderzhanie strategicheskoi stabil'nosti" [Sea-based strategic nuclear forces and the maintenance of strategic stability],
Morskoi Sbornik, no. 9 (September 2001): 24.

35. In particular, the study mentioned earlier proposed to plan and
execute missiles strikes comprising launches of different types of

missiles against designated targets or the "use of means [operating] in different environments." To increase the cost-effectiveness of missile strikes, friendly strike aircraft and naval platforms should avoid entering the so-called hit zones, where they could be targeted by adversarial forces. Spirin and Alferov, "Osobennosti porazheniya o'bektov v dal'nei morskoi zone," 45.

36. In particular, the decision to build a series of 1,800-ton Project 22160 corvettes was a result of growing commitment to support CTPs and CPOs. Russian naval studies acknowledged that some elements of the so-called peacekeeping operational activities fell outside the traditional spectrum of operations. They also required more specialized platforms, which the navy had no initial plans to acquire. Captain 3rd Rank I. Garmatenko, "Vzaimodeistvie VMF Rossii c inostrannymi VMS i bezopastnost' na more" [The interaction of the Russian navy with foreign navies and security at sea], *Morskoi Sbornik*, no. 7 (July 2013): 46.

37. The Russians estimated the USN's SBCM arsenal at 2,537 missiles, including 382 nuclear-armed.

38. Apanasenko, "Sokhranyat' sposobnost' protivostoyat' ugrozam s morya," 4.

39. Apanasenko.

40. Spirin and Alferov, "Osobennosti porazheniya o'bektov v dal'nei morskoi zone," 45.

41. Apanasenko, "Sokhranyat' sposobnost' protivostoyat' ugrozam s morya," 5.

42. Just like with the submarine arm, the Russian navy has commenced modernization of a select number of its oceangoing Soviet-era units (three Udaloy class guided-missile destroyers (DDGs) and one Ushakov class RFS *Admiral Nakhimov* nuclear-powered guided-missile battle cruiser (CGN). The modernized warships will receive larger complements of SBCMs and enhanced AD, communications, and tracking systems.

43. "Istochnik: Na forume 'Armiya 2023' podpishut kontrakt na stroitel'stvo shesti fregatov" [Source: A contract for the construction of six frigates will be signed at the Army 2023 forum], *TASS*, February 2, 2023, Источник: на форуме "Армия-2023" подпишут

контракт на строительство шести фрегатов (tass.ru) (accessed February 3, 2023).

44. Ismailov, Puchnin, and Sysuyev, "Problemy mobilizatsionnogo obespecheniya rossiiskogo voenno-morskogo flota i vozmozhnye puti ikh razreshenya," 69.

45. Roman Kretsul and Aleksei Ramm, "Suda i delo: VMF obnovit 'voenno-buksirny' flot" [Ships and business: The navy would replenish the "military-tug" fleet], *Izvestia*, March 6, 2023, 3. Prior to the imposition of Western sanctions, the Russian shipbuilders used to order a considerable portion of onboard equipment for the navy's auxiliaries abroad. The current state of hostility in Russia-West relations forces Russian design and production bureaus to compensate the emerged capability shortfalls by developing indigenous analogues.

46. "Vse tseli, kotorye my pered soboi stavim, budut, bezuslovno, dostignuty" [All tasks, which we appoint to ourselves, without a doubt will be met], *Krasnaya Zvezda*, December 23, 2022, 4.

47. V. Aleksin and E. Shevelev, "O reformirovanii nashego VMF" [On the reform of our navy], *Morskoi Sbornik*, no. 3 (March 1995): 13; Aleksin and Shevelev, "Su'dby Rossii i flota nerazdelimy" [The fates of Russia and the navy are inseparable], *Morskoi Sbornik*, no. 6 (June 1996): 10.

48. Adding to that, is the operational requirement to shield friendly SSBNs, which will continue to operate within the protected SSBN bastions close to Russian shores.

49. There was a growing belief that the naval share of Russia's future defense spending would be the first to go in favor of more funding being allocated toward the ground force and air force elements.

50. Yulia Kozak, Andrei Gavrilenko, and Timur Gainutdinov, "'My budem povyshat' tempy i ob'emy stroitel'stva korablei raznykh proektov . . .'" [We will increase the pace and volume of construction of ships of various designs . . . , *Krasnaya Zvezda*, December 30, 2022, 1.

CHAPTER FOURTEEN

ADVERSARIES AND PLANNING ASSUMPTIONS

CHINA'S NAVY AND THE POST–COLD WAR WORLD

Andrew S. Erickson

T his chapter explains how and why the People's Republic of China (PRC)'s People's Liberation Army Navy (PLAN) has responded to changing circumstances—mainly its perception of foreign threats and technology—in the post–Cold War era.[1] It probes the assumptions about the nature of the adversary and the required tasks that have shaped PLAN fleet design and development. China studies the U.S. military assiduously for both lessons for its own development and insights into how to counter in furtherance of key strategic goals, with unification over Taiwan long the ultimate objective.[2] Here paramount leader Xi Jinping's determination to both develop a world-class navy and to make historic achievements across the Taiwan Strait, his preoccupation with the United States as his most formidable enemy in the latter regard, and his perception of a limited window of opportunity are raising the risks of conflict.

CHANGING CIRCUMSTANCES AND STRATEGY

Specifics of Beijing's maritime strategy and development can be challenging to glean. As a Peking University scholar explains,

317

China's national government has never set forth a comprehensive list of its maritime interests, especially its core maritime interests. One reason for this is that China is developing
too rapidly, so it is quite difficult to be certain of its interests,
which are changing. Being intentionally vague will allow policy leeway in dealing with future uncertainties. Furthermore,
vagueness also has some benefits of its own. Maintaining a
vague position on the major issues of the East China Sea and
the South China Sea is not only advantageous for flexibly
handling maritime disputes with other countries, but helps
to ease potential pressure from domestic public opinion and
reduces unnecessary policy risk.[3]

Nevertheless, carefully examining pedigreed sources reveals the
broader outlines of China's maritime trajectory.

PLAN thought is rooted in mid-twentieth-century history,[4] but it
has evolved considerably over the ensuing decades. Sino-American
rapprochement in the 1970s ended the most difficult and threatening
period of the Cold War for Beijing by removing American threats,
affording support in deterring Soviet threats, and allowing for Beijing's
first naval efforts beyond its coastal waters. The People's Republic's
unprecedented seaward turn was springboarded by the relatively intact
and significant potential of its shipbuilding industry, which had been
saved from the worst of Maoist malpractice by its physical unsuitability
for relocation into China's remote interior during the disastrous Third
Front movement. As part of his modernization drive in the early 1980s,
Deng prioritized shipbuilding industrial development to facilitate the
export of manufactures around the world. In 1985, he assigned the
PLAN its first-ever independent strategy: "Near Seas Active Defense,"
focused on the Yellow, East, and South China Seas. There Beijing has
the world's most numerous and extensive disputed island and feature
claims, with the largest number of other parties; none looms larger than
Taiwan. The 1995–96 Taiwan Strait Crisis and 1999 Belgrade Embassy
Bombing catalyzed a concerted People's Liberation Army (PLA) and
PLAN buildup that has already yielded dramatic results.[5]

Xi, the PRC's first navalist leader, now seeks to transform China into a "maritime great power." Two years after assuming office, in 2015, he added "Far Seas Protection"—a more modest version of U.S. and Western allied-style sea-lane security—to the PLAN's strategy. Subsequently, as two researchers explain, "on April 12, 2018, Xi Jinping attended the naval parade in the South China Sea, during which he called for [the service to] 'strive to comprehensively build the People's Navy into a world-class navy.'" They elaborate, "The only way to consider oneself a world-class navy is to have the power to match, contend with, and square off against any opponent; deter and win possible maritime conflicts; and forcefully support the country's status as a world-class great power."[6]

Circa 2018, as part of this effort, Xi extended the PLAN's strategic and operational writ to all the world's oceans, adding a third layer of PLAN strategy to include "near seas defense, far seas protection, [global] oceanic presence, and expansion into the two poles."[7] This latest, largest layer of PRC naval strategy and its operationalization remains a work in progress. A China Central Television Reporter's interview of Yin Zhongqing, deputy chairman of the Finance and Economy Committee at the Thirteenth National People's Congress, reveals similar language: "China must . . . do a better job protecting our territorial sea and controlling the near seas, enter the deep ocean, and move toward distant oceans until we reach Antarctica and the Arctic."[8]

Thus prioritized, funded, and tasked, the PLAN is charged with leading the maritime component of Xi's timeline for the "Great Rejuvenation of the Chinese Nation." By 2027, the timeline calls for achieving the "Centennial Military Building Goal" of capabilities to realize the PLA's "founding mission" of vanquishing the Kuomintang (KMT), now on Taiwan. By 2035, it calls for completing military modernization. By 2049, it calls for becoming a strong country with world-class armed forces. There is a strong maritime component to national strategy throughout. As two researchers contend, "Threats to China's national security primarily come from the sea, the focus of military struggle is at sea, and the center of gravity of China's expanding national interests is also at sea."[9]

Even approaching Xi's ambitious goals would require eroding, and in some cases overturning, formidable Western advantages. The PLAN's efforts to do so include (1) working increasingly jointly with other forces, including China's land-based, missile-heavy "anti-Navy" forces; (2) attempting to impose risk by maximizing the numbers of PLAN vessels and the numbers of antiship missiles deployed on them, while accepting risk in battle damage survivability to reduce costs; and (3) pursuing new technologies and ways of war, such as unmanned systems and autonomous operations enhanced through artificial intelligence, that may disproportionately advantage China or target adversary vulnerabilities.

STRONG SHIPBUILDING SURGE

Beijing has gone to sea with scale, sophistication, and superlatives that no continental power previously sustained in the modern era.[10] By around 2020, China had built and deployed the world's largest navy, coast guard, and maritime militia by number of ships—the ultimate manifestation of strategy at sea.[11] The development of China's three major sea forces, with the navy by far the most sophisticated and demanding to produce and operate, has been fueled by strong, consistent national political and military prioritization, and formidable funding. Propelled by the world's largest shipbuilding industry, it has been guided by a succession of naval strategies that are radiating increasingly further outward globally, connected to military capabilities and operations in every domain, while increasingly intense in their focus on addressing "core" security interests along China's maritime periphery—foremost among them, resolving Taiwan's status on Beijing's terms.

Several factors in particular have enabled China's historically impressive warship modernization and production rate: the largest, fastest shipbuilding capacity expansion since World War II, and part of the largest postwar military buildup. Supported by the world's second-largest economy and defense budget, and what until very recently was indisputably the world's largest population and fastest-growing multi-trillion-dollar economy, coherent, stable national political, military, and maritime strategies maintain high prioritization. Formidable, consistent funding is provided through all-encompassing Five-Year Plans. China's shipbuilding facilities, the world's largest in aggregate, are prioritized as national assets and accordingly receive great investment. Additionally, Beijing employs the world's largest human-organizational technology acquisition and application infrastructure to ingest foreign technology and ship-building practices, which allows China to skip much research and focus on development. Specifically, through a process of imitative innovation, China seeks, obtains, evaluates, and adapts technologies, systems, and processes on a scale approached by no other nation. The results are design and production processes, systems, and platforms firmly entrenched in the spiral development concept: an iterative process for developing a weapon system's capabilities in which the developer, tester, and user interact with one another so as to refine and improve the system's performance.[12]

PRC civilian and military ship production is highly integrated. China boasts many yards, of large capacity, with newbuild layout efficiency. Most shipyard production has been of merchant ships for foreign customers; China's commercial shipbuilding industry, the world's largest with over 40 percent of oceangoing vessel construction,[13] subsidizes overhead costs for construction of all three sea forces' vessels; an impossibility for America's military-focused shipbuilding industry. China likely uses a hybrid civilian-military production standard that enables it to shift shipbuilding personnel between civilian and military production, resulting in a cost-effective, "good-enough-quality" solution.

China thus enjoys some key advantages over the United States in warship production, and it has made the most of them to maximize its comparative advantages and resulting output.[14] The result is that the PLAN already has substantially more battle force ships than the U.S. Navy, although its heretofore meteoric building rates may finally be slowing down, and it faces mounting maintenance/

overhaul needs.[15] Nevertheless, the PLAN continues to dramatically expand its fleets, in part by adding modern surface combatants.[16]

The China Coast Guard (CCG) has benefited from the transfer of twenty-two "early flight" variant Type 056 *Jiangdao*-class corvettes from the PLAN in 2021. These corvettes lacked the towed-array sonar and hence substantial antisubmarine warfare (ASW) capabilities of their successors, which made them an easily sustained loss for the PLAN but a big boost for the CCG.[17] It speaks to particularly deep, increasing integration between these two PRC sea forces. Despite the resulting dip to a current PLAN battle force of around 340 platforms, China's navy is expected to have 400 ships by 2025 and 440 by 2030.[18]

Superior ship numbers are a comparative advantage that Beijing pursues relentlessly in peacetime competition and preparation for conflict contingencies. When it comes to deployment, even the most advanced vessel simply cannot be in more than one place at once; particularly regarding the growing Sino-American strategic competition where Washington plays a distant away game. U.S. Coast Guard cutters are primarily focused near American waters, far from any international disputes, while the U.S. Navy is dispersed around the world, with many forces separated from maritime East Asia by responsibilities, geography, and time. Meanwhile, all three PRC sea forces remain focused first and foremost on the contested Near Seas and their immediate approaches, close to China's homeland bases, land-based air and missile "anti-navy," and supply lines. There China regularly deploys sea forces far greater numerically than the size of the entire U.S. Navy.

OPERATIONALIZING STRATEGY, NEAR AND FAR

Beijing's threat to Taiwan is mounting toward Xi's key PLA capabilities preparation target year of 2027 and the PLA's growing panoply of weapons and increasingly focused training toward that prioritized goal.[19] PRC military operational options vis-à-vis Taiwan, which might be employed individually or in combination, may be divided primarily into three categories: bombardment, blockade, and invasion. China's sea forces would have role(s) to play in all three operations.

Accordingly, it is hardly surprising that in 2022, the PLA conducted frequent amphibious training, with more than 120 instances in a three-month period.[20] The Pentagon rightly emphasizes China's organization and integration through training of civilian maritime vessels (roll on–roll off, or RO-RO, ships in particular) to help fill remaining gaps in amphibious sealift.[21] The year 2021 also witnessed growing frequency and realism in PLA island-seizure drills; the more than twenty exercises conducted that year representing a large increase over the thirteen witnessed in 2020.[22] For all these efforts, however, Taiwan remains substantially protected against amphibious invasion by complex weather, tides, mudflats, coastal barriers, and a growing array of asymmetric weapons designed to capitalize on this natural moat and its ramparts.

Beyond Taiwan and its other disputed sovereignty claims in the Near Seas, Beijing's maritime interests and efforts to secure them are increasingly global in nature. With its long land borders, difficult neighbors, and hemming in by "island chains" fortified with American and allied military bases,[23] China has undeniable challenges to overcome. One group of researchers goes so far as to argue that "China should go eastward first, recover Taiwan's deep-water ports, and open a gap in America's oceanic blockade. First, China's aircraft carriers and nuclear submarine forces can use this to approach Guam, Hawaii, and even the West Coast of the U.S. The U.S. military will lose the vast depth of the Western Pacific Ocean, and the situation of offense and defense in the Western Pacific will change."[24]

For combat scenarios vis-à-vis the Near Seas, the PLAN remains the first responder and first line of defense; but the CCG is an increasingly capable second line that can backfill lower intensity missions in the Near Seas and additionally offer some capacity beyond. Sea-lane and energy/resource import security has long been a driver of the expansion of the PLAN's force structure and capabilities. Xi's signature Belt and Road Initiative, a catch-all framework for much of his ambitious foreign policy, requires growing overseas protection efforts, led by the PLAN. Increasing PRC polar resource pursuits and related activities likewise call for PLAN participation first and foremost.[25]

Here as elsewhere, submarine forces have a special role to play. As three researchers at the PLAN Submarine Academy in Qingdao envision, "Our submarine forces must not only advance to the Pacific Ocean. They must also advance towards the Indian Ocean. Indeed, in the future they must also advance towards the Atlantic Ocean and the Arctic Ocean. This will effectively ameliorate the difficulties of our submarine force operating in waters facing China; it can also provide vast maritime strategic space for China's rise as a great power."[26]

Characteristically, China proceeds in layers. Beyond a global network of more than ninety-five PRC-invested ports,[27] and a more constrained pursuit of "strategic support points,"[28] widespread efforts to develop overseas access and basing appear underway. China's first overseas military support base, in Djibouti, has now received PLAN ships at a new 450-meter pier large enough to accommodate PLAN carriers. Beyond that, Beijing has apparently established its first Indo-Pacific overseas base in Ream, Cambodia;[29] and has courted the Solomon Islands and Vanuatu, in addition to Namibia (where China's PLA Strategic Support Force, or SSF, already operates one of its eight or more tracking, telemetry, and control (TT & C), ground stations to support space missions).

The Pentagon specifies: China's "military facility at Ream Naval Base in Cambodia will be the first PRC overseas base in the Indo-Pacific.... If the PRC is able to leverage such assistance into a presence at Ream Naval Base, it suggests that the PRC's overseas basing strategy has diversified to include military capacity-building efforts." More broadly, the PLA "has likely considered Cambodia, Myanmar, Thailand, Singapore, Indonesia, Pakistan, Sri Lanka, United Arab Emirates, Kenya, Seychelles, Equatorial Guinea, Tanzania, Angola, and Tajikistan among other places as locations for PLA military logistics facilities. *The PRC has probably already made overtures to Namibia, Vanuatu, and the Solomon Islands. The PLA is most interested in military access along SLOCs from China to the Strait of Hormuz, Africa, and the Pacific Islands*" (emphasis added).[30]

POTENTIAL FOR INTERSERVICE RIVALRY

The increasingly global, all-domain orientation and operations of China's armed forces brings new challenges that will convulse the PLAN. Increasing emphasis on the roles, missions, and capabilities of the PLAN (as well as the PLA Air Force [PLAAF] and PLA Rocket Force [PLARF], in particular), enhances potential for another challenge long-plaguing advanced militaries: interservice rivalry. Growing PRC external interests have eroded the ground forces' formerly dominant power. As the ground forces continually diminish in relative clout, competition among the PLAN and its fellow services will likely intensify. If defense spending increases slow down or reverse, this will be accentuated. Each pursues development frontiers; each boasts cutting-edge capabilities. With the most external geopolitical orientation and operations, the PLAN may claim a growing budgetary portion. Moving from its current Near Seas–centered three-fleet structure, as some PRC analysts have suggested, toward a bifurcated Pacific and Indian Ocean navy, and beyond, would demand more, better vessels. It may generate further PLAN-PLAAF competition as both services maintain land-based air forces with overlapping Near Seas missions, even as PLAN carriers bring more aircraft to distant seas. The PLARF, similarly, seeks space responsibilities: China's burgeoning orbital assets are a circum-global capability vital to supporting, and disrupting, information-age warfare. Growth of China's nuclear ballistic-missile submarine (SSBN) force—already patrolling and fielding a PLAN-based element of China's nuclear triad—and ongoing PLAAF development of its own leg may both generate further friction.

THE MOUNTING COST OF CHINESE SEA POWER

One of the greatest challenges facing Xi and his ambitions ashore and at sea is that even as comprehensive implementation remains challenging over the next few years, larger structural factors are already beginning to slow China's economic growth overall. PRC national power growth faces dissipation and disruption.

The economic model that propelled China through three-plus decades of meteoric growth is taking on water. China already suffers from acute domestic problems, including resource constraints, environmental degradation, corruption, urban-rural division, and ethnic and religious unrest. All these, combined with looming demographic and gender imbalances, may strain both China's economic development and internal stability. An additional risk factor is the global economy's potential to change (e.g., restructuring supply chains) faster than China can adjust. These problems could combine with rising nationalism to motivate Xi to adopt more confrontational military approaches, particularly concerning unresolved claims in the Near Seas. Rather than portending an impending "collapse," however, these factors may herald China's version of the same slowdown in national trajectory that has afflicted great powers throughout history. This has direct implications for PLA/PLAN development.

History suggests that great powers tend to follow an "S-curved" trajectory in which the very process of growth and development sows the seeds for its eventual plateauing. In fact, the unleashing of PRC society in 1978 followed a century of foreign predation and internal turmoil, and three subsequent decades of abnormally constricted individual and economic possibilities. This terrible past may have disguised China's post-1978 economic boom—facilitated though it was by pragmatic policies and globalization—as a "new normal." In fact, it is more likely an exceptionally well-managed but unsustainable catch-up period. Beijing's one-time opportunity to funnel this pent-up national potential has produced the seeds of peaking: urbanization of unprecedented scale and rapidity, tragically exacerbated by history's greatest artificial demographic restriction. These factors are slowing China faster than any other major power previously. Recent relaxation of the "one-child policy" comes too little, too late: demographic decline is already unstoppable. Already a labor-shortage economy, China may be further along the "S-curve" than many realize.

Moreover, even if implemented with the greatest success conceivable, some of the key reforms Xi proposes—and many of those most likely to garner popular support sufficient for their successful implementation—can themselves strengthen potent "S-curve" headwinds, and will even accelerate and deepen their impact. Some challenges stem from societal patterns that the United States and other Western nations are already suffering from, and which even China cannot escape—and may well narrow the gap quickly, before China is well prepared. A rapidly aging society with rising expectations, burdened with rates of chronic diseases exacerbated by sedentary lifestyles, will probably divert spending from both military development and the economic growth that sustains it. Expanding China's welfare state, in particular, will crowd out other forms of spending, yet the floodgates appear already to be opening.

One of China's greatest strengths in recent years has been its ability to allocate tremendous resources rapidly to programs for security, infrastructure, and technology development. Many of these programs are seen as extremely inefficient. As competition for resources intensifies, the leadership's ability to allocate increasingly scarce funds effectively will face unprecedented tests.

Domestic challenges may place increasing demands on, and funding claims by, China's internal security forces, whose official budget already exceeds the PLA's if funding for the paramilitary People's Armed Police is counted as internal (in keeping with China's own budget structure). Potential drivers include unrest in ethno-religiously restive borderlands (e.g., Xinjiang, Tibet) as well as disaster relief, exacerbated by environmental degradation and climate change. Rising living costs and societal expectations may greatly increase the expense of current security approaches, which rely in part on large numbers of relatively low-paid individuals to provide physical security, surveillance, and monitoring of data from security cameras and other sources.

This has a special significance for China's ability to continue developing external military capabilities, particularly its massive, maintenance-hungry naval buildup. For two-plus decades, Beijing has funded multiple overlapping megaprojects simultaneously. China's shipbuilding industry—which, aside from its missile, space, and electronics industries, produces China's most advanced indigenous defense products—has long proven able to do this through simultaneous construction of multiple modern submarine and warship classes, together with a profusion of prototypes. China's military aviation industry, traditionally laggard, is catching up. In many key areas, China's number of multiple simultaneous programs is now unrivaled. But how long such dynamic investment can be sustained is unclear.

Within this larger context, manifold factors will likely increase costs and technological requirements and hence reduce the purchasing power of each yuan allocated to defense spending and restrain further budget growth and focus. These include

- Weapons systems and associated infrastructure, which are more expensive to build, operate, and maintain than their less advanced predecessors
- Investments in structural and organizational reform and associated demobilization costs
- Rising salaries and benefits to attract, educate, train, and retain technologically capable professionals
- Growing entitlements, particularly as more retirees draw benefits over longer lifespans

The closer the PLA/PLAN approaches leading-edge capabilities, the more expensive and difficult it will be for it to advance further, or even to pace the general increase in global capabilities. China's cost advantages decrease as military equipment becomes less labor-intensive and more technology- and materials-intensive. The more sophisticated PLA/PLAN systems become, the less relative benefit China can derive from acquiring and indigenizing foreign technologies, and the less cost advantage it will have in producing and maintaining them.

Here China, its navy, and Commander in Chief Xi are on a demanding treadmill that has long bedeviled advanced militaries. Maintaining a leading navy or air force, for instance, is increasingly expensive. Military shipbuilding cost escalation approximates that of other weapons systems, such as military aircraft, making this a revealing example.[31] Cost control is complicated by relatively small production numbers (in the *best* of cases) and rising standards—today's ships and the conditions under which they are produced and operated are far more complex than their predecessors. In his classic treatise, Philip Pugh marshals considerable historical data to suggest that while countries tend to spend a constant percentage of their economy on defense over time, the cost of ships and weapons increases faster than inflation—typically at 9 percent. At 2 percent inflation, this would compound to costs doubling each decade. Pugh finds that even 2 percent per annum naval budget growth—excessively optimistic for most developed Western nations—would tend to require an annual average 3.5 percent reduction in fleet numbers. In practice, navies find ways to save costs and innovate (e.g., by shifting given missions to smaller platforms).[32] In an example of its emphasis on civil-military integration, China is accomplishing just such a mission shift by strengthening its coast guard (and, to a lesser extent, its maritime militia) and assigning them missions PLAN forces previously fulfilled. Eventually, however, the cost-growth challenge proves overwhelming, forcing relentless numbers reductions.

A RAND study similarly concludes that the cost-growth rate for U.S. Navy vessels over the past half century is 7–11 percent, with economy-related factors approximating inflation and customer-driven demands accounting for the remaining majority. Of these, ship weight, power density, and sophistication are the largest cost drivers.[33] In Pugh's analysis, such dynamics make it essential to avoid the "Everest syndrome"—constant selection of the most advanced ship possible over a more conservative approach based on competition with actual adversary capabilities.[34] Mass production of the Type 056 *Jiangdao*-class corvette and Type 022 *Houbei*-class fast-attack craft suggests PRC avoidance of the "Everest syndrome" in pursuing proximate priorities thus far. China's ongoing buildup of destroyers, cruisers, aircraft carriers, and other large vessels, by contrast, risks changing that dynamic to Beijing's detriment.

A combination of rapid GDP growth and shipbuilding prowess puts a country in an enviable sweet spot. Between the world wars, for instance, Japan's rapid economic growth enabled it to bear ever-increasing ship development costs at a constant defense burden.[35] World naval powers, including Holland, the United Kingdom, and the United States, have likewise enjoyed such conditions in their rapid-growth years. Today China enjoys a similar confluence but may finally be nearing the end of one of history's great runs.

By developing and deploying advanced technologies, Beijing is raising the bar for regional capabilities competition. An action-reaction cycle forces it to spend ever more on more-advanced systems to narrow the gap with the United States and key allies like Japan and Australia, while staying ahead of other regional rivals. Political scientist Minxin Pei warns that by pursuing incomplete reforms Beijing risks a "trapped transition" instead of transformation into a full market economy. An analogous "trap" may also emerge for the PLA/PLAN as it strives to transition from a homeland and periphery-focused, people-intensive, mechanized force into a broader-ranging, technology-intensive, information-enabled force. A slowdown in the PLA/PLAN's recently rapid progress looms as fewer easy improvements remain available and the costs of advancement rise even as objectives grow more ambitious than ever.

Here, China may partially fall back on its continentalist approach of "using the land to control the sea" with an "anti-Navy" of long-range, land-based missiles, delivery systems, and related "counter-intervention" weapons.[36] However, by wielding asymmetric weapons, China suggests their efficacy and writes potential adversaries a potent playbook. This portends a new era in counter-intervention systems, which PRC forces themselves may face increasingly. The United States, Japan, Taiwan, and Vietnam in particular may attempt to deploy missiles, naval mines, and torpedoes to complicate potential PRC predations. While China can already exploit its geographical proximity to nearby conflict zones by deploying many overlapping forces to attempt to overwhelm and defeat such approaches, it is far from being able to defend its forces effectively if they face such challenges from a capable power farther afield (e.g., India in the Indian Ocean, and the United States there and beyond). The likelihood that the PLA will get "trapped" in its region with respect to high-end warfighting capabilities will increase still further if China's growing military power and assertiveness leads its neighbors to accelerate countermeasures against it.

Certainly, there are important caveats to this larger analysis. First, there is a lag effect. Ships purchased on favorable terms today can benefit Beijing for years to come. China currently lacks the unstable business and vendor base of its Western shipbuilding counterparts, factors that increase costs. No other major shipbuilder appears poised to overtake China as the world's foremost civil shipbuilder by volume, and it is working up the value chain in both military and civil domains.

Second, slowdown could stimulate innovation. Today's massive R&D coupled with tomorrow's slowdown could generate revolutionary PRC military capabilities that both surprise and challenge U.S. and allied forces.[37] China is presently investing in military R&D supported by an economy that grows fast enough to afford the faster-than-inflation growth of military technology. "S-curve" factors are likely to render this unsustainable, however, eventually leaving China with an increased sense of its own capabilities, perhaps some form of overseas commitments (protecting citizens, property, and critical resource access), and all of the problems maintaining forward military progress that presently plague the U.S. and allied militaries. At that point, China, seeking relief from the cost-compounding treadmill, may strive to field radical, disruptive new capabilities to achieve its goals more efficiently. Such an approach already emerged at a lower level of PRC capacity, when the 1999 Belgrade Embassy Bombing persuaded Beijing's leaders to fund "assassin's mace" megaprojects to develop weapons of disproportionate effect like the land-based, antiship ballistic missile (ASBM). More than two decades later, the Type 055 cruiser is projected to take ASBMs of its own to sea.[38]

In conclusion, history suggests that Beijing will face difficult choices in the future, particularly as China's overall national growth slows. Lower economic growth rates tend to tighten shipbuilding and operational budgets. The PLAN's trajectory will ultimately depend on China's trajectory.

XI'S TIME AND TIDES

However these structural dynamics play out in China, a particularly concerning prospect involves thinking about adversaries, particularly the most powerful. Xi may well perceive China's strategic window of opportunity to be closing during the 2020s, a dynamic further accentuated by traversing his own eighth decade and facing undeniable human limits on his otherwise domestically unrivaled power. Meanwhile, Xi may well perceive the primary enemy and obstacle to his making historical achievements regarding Taiwan and other sovereignty claims—the United States—to be presently in disarray and slow to rally, yet nevertheless favored by longer-term trends.

While accidental great power wars are arguably unlikely, particularly since the advent of nuclear weapons, miscalculation may well remain the significant risk factor that it has proven in the past. Consider Stephen Van Evera's research on "windows of opportunity and vulnerability," which he judges "a potent cause of war. They create incentives for war and for war-risking belligerence by declining states. . . . Windows impose haste. Cooperation is undercut by expectations of war, which windows create."[39] Among many historical examples of this phenomenon, Van Evera highlights Germany's policies from 1933–45 and Japan's in 1940–41. Geographical, military, and maritime analogues to today's worst scenarios make imperial Japan's case loom particularly large. "In 1941 Japan perceived a window of enormous size," Van Evera explains. "The caprice of world politics had raised Japan momentarily to a historic pinnacle of power. Ahead, Japan's leaders believed, lay a rapid descent to helpless weakness unless Japan acted."[40] Obfuscation widened the window: "Japan cloaked its 1937–41 naval buildup in dark secrecy to avoid provoking a U.S.

reaction. As a result the U.S. response lagged until 1940, giving Japan a window of opportunity in 1941–42 that helped move it to war."

Such a temporary window, at least in his own perception thereof, might heighten Xi's determination to push for progress vis-à-vis Taiwan and his resolve not to be deterred by any means. For their part, a U.S. president thus confronted might well see America's credibility and values; regional security and alliances; and vital strategic technological interests threatened fundamentally. This, in turn, could set the stage for tremendous tensions and crises, if not a far more frightening prospect: the first-ever kinetic conflict between two nuclear-armed great powers. Time and tides waiteth not for Xi, and now the United States is more determined than ever to convince him that the time and tides will *never* be right for him to move militarily against Taiwan.

The rising PLAN has set its sights on becoming at least a leading fleet, and perhaps even ultimately the preeminent sea service in the world. The strong and consistent support of PRC leaders over the past two-plus decades; and particularly Xi, China's first navalist leader; explains why the PLAN has continued to receive such a high level of investment, over time making the funding leap gradually at first, then seemingly all at once. That growth's real nature is cloaked in social and political opacity, however, and for a variety of reasons cited in this chapter may not continue at anywhere near its present pace. Whatever contingencies ultimately come to pass, however, the PLAN will play an important role.[41] Facing naval history's latest version of age-old problems, China under Xi will attempt its own solutions. The results will shape the future of the world, for good or for ill, both at sea and on land.

NOTES

1. The views expressed here are mine alone. I thank many anonymous reviewers for helpful inputs.
2. See, for example, 师小芹, 刘晓博 [Shi Xiaoqin and Liu Xiaobo], 中美全方位海上竞争的序幕即将拉开—美最新海上战略评析 [The prelude to all-encompassing maritime competition between China and the U.S. is about to begin—an appraisal of America's newest maritime strategy], 中国南海研究院 [website of the

National Institute for South China Sea Studies], December 29, 2020, http://www.nanhai.org.cn/review_c/506.html (CMSI translation). Shi is a researcher in the National Institute for South China Sea Studies' World Naval Research Institute. A retired PLA Senior Colonel, Shi has worked at the PLA Academy of Military Science, Central Military Commission Department of Strategic Planning, and the Office of the National Security Council. She researches sea power, maritime security, and naval strategy; see https://rwsk.zju.edu.cn/rwskdj/2018/0522/c30587a1260995/page.htm. Liu is director of the World Naval Research Institute. A former naval officer, Liu worked at the PLAN Naval Research Institute from 2007 to 2017. From 1993 to 2007 he was assigned to the first destroyer detachment of the PLAN's North Sea Fleet; see http://www.nanhai.org.cn/team_c/193.html.

3. 胡波 [Hu Bo], 论中国的重要海洋利益 [On China's important maritime interests], 亚太安全与海洋研究 [*Asia-Pacific Security and Maritime Affairs*], no. 3 (2015) (CMSI translation). Dr. Hu is director of the Center for Maritime Strategy Studies and Research Professor at the Institute of Ocean Research, Peking University, and director of the South China Sea Strategic Situation Probing Initiative. His books include *China's Sea Power in the Post-Mahan Era* (Beijing, Ocean Press, 2018) and *Chinese Maritime Power in the 21st Century* (London: Routledge, 2019).

4. Toshi Yoshihara, *Mao's Army Goes to Sea* (Washington, DC: Georgetown University Press, 2022).

5. Andrew S. Erickson, *Chinese Anti-Ship Ballistic Missile Development: Drivers, Trajectories, and Strategic Implications* (Washington, DC: Jamestown Foundation/Brookings Institution Press, 2013).

6. 刘丽娇, 陈文华 [Liu Lijiao and Chen Wenhua], 改革开放以来海军战略理论的发展及经验启示 [Theoretical development of naval strategy since reform and opening up and implications for today], 中国军事科学 [*China Military Science*], no. 6 (2018): 59–65 (CMSI translation). Senior Captain Liu is a researcher at the Naval Research Institute. Lieutenant Chen is a master's student at the PLA Navy Command Academy, studying military strategy.

7. Yu Wenbing, 乘势而上建设一流军事指挥学院 [Take advantage of the situation to build a world-class military command college]

人民海军 [*People's Navy*] July 13, 2018, 3; Ryan D. Martinson, "The Role of the Arctic in Chinese Naval Strategy," *Jamestown China Brief* 19, no. 22 (2019), https://jamestown.org/program/ the-role-of-the-arctic-in-chinese-naval-strategy/. See also Andrew S. Erickson, "The Ryan Martinson Bookshelf: Illuminating Xi/ China's Maritime Policies, Forces and Ops, Including Latest re Whitsun Reef/Spratlys," *China Analysis from Original Sources*, June 14, 2021, https://www.andrewerickson.com/2021/06/the-ryan-martinson-bookshelf-illuminating-xi-chinas-maritime-policies-forces-ops-including-latest-re-whitsun-reef-spratlys/.

8. 尹中卿:目前发展海洋经济面临四个突出的问题 [Yin Zhongqing: Development of the marine economy currently faces four major problems], 新华 [*Xinhua*], March 10, 2019, www.xinhuanet.com/ politics/2019lh/2019-03/10/c_137883595.htm.

9. 史常勇, 陈炎 [Shi Changyong and Chen Yan], 试论新时代海军战略定位 [On the Navy's strategic positioning in the new era], 国防 [*National Defense*], no. 5 (2018): 34–36 (CMSI translation). Senior Captain Shi is the director of the teaching and research section of the Strategy and Campaign Department at the Naval Command Academy in Nanjing. Senior Captain Chen is an associate professor in the same department.

10. Andrew S. Erickson, Lyle J. Goldstein, and Carnes Lord, eds., *China Goes to Sea: Maritime Transformation in Comparative Historical Perspective* (2009; repr., Annapolis: Naval Institute Press, 2021).

11. For additional PRC maritime superlatives, see Andrew S. Erickson, foreword to Manfred Meyer, *Modern Chinese Maritime Forces*, ed. Larry Bond and Chris Carlson, 2nd ed. (Admiralty Trilogy Group April 1, 2024), 3.

12. Ronald O'Rourke, *Evolutionary Acquisition and Spiral Development in DOD Programs: Policy Issues for Congress* (Washington, DC: Congressional Research Service, 2006), https://www.everycrsreport.com/files/20061211_RS21195_5cd6d2d08c1c17db74e4b-b7e3c035f774504ce4f.pdf; Andrew S. Erickson, ed., *Chinese Naval Shipbuilding: An Ambitious and Uncertain Course* (2016; repr., Annapolis: Naval Institute Press, 2023).

13. Secretary of the Navy Carlos Del Toro, "SECNAV Delivers Remarks at Harvard KennedySchool," September 26, 2023, https://www.navy.milPress-Office/Speeches/display-speeches/Article/3538420/secnav-delivers-remarks-at-harvard-kennedy-school/.

14. China does not appear to build naval vessels *faster* than the United States—it is simply building many more ships simultaneously. Building time is carefully managed and minimized, but PLAN vessels spend more time at the fitting-out pier than their American counterparts do; a sample of Type 052C and 052D destroyers and 055 cruisers suggests that production time of PLAN vessels is in fact approximately 25 percent longer.

15. Captain Christopher P. Carlson, USNR (Ret.), *PLAN Force Structure Projection Concept: A Methodology for Looking Down Range*, China Maritime Report 10 (Newport, RI: Naval War College China Maritime Studies Institute, November 2020), https://digital-commons.usnwc.edu/cmsi-maritime-reports/10/.

16. Sam LaGrone, "Pentagon: Chinese Navy to Expand to 400 Ships by 2025, Growth Focused on Surface Combatants," *USNI News*, November 29, 2022, https://news.usni.org/2022/11/29/pentagon-chinese-navy-to-expand-to-400-ships-by-2025-growth-focused-on-surface-combatants.

17. Office of the Secretary of Defense, *Military and Security Developments Involving the People's Republic of China 2022* (Washington, DC: Department of Defense, November 29, 2022) (hereafter CMPR 2022), 53, https://media.defense.gov/2022/Nov/29/2003122279/-1/-1/1/2022-MILITARY-AND-SECURITY-DEVELOPMENTS-INVOLVING-THE-PEOPLES-REPUBLIC-OF-CHINA.PDF.

18. CMPR 2022, 52.

19. Andrew S. Erickson, "PRC Pursuit of 2027 'Centennial Military Building Goal' (建军一百年奋斗目标): Sources and Analysis," *China Analysis from Original Sources*, December 19, 2021, https://www.andrewerickson.com/2021/12/prc-pursuit-of-2027-centennial-military-building-goal-sources-analysis/.

20. CMPR 2022, 129.

21. CMPR 2022, 129.

22. CMPR 2022, 107.

23. Andrew S. Erickson and Joel Wuthnow, "Barriers, Springboards and Benchmarks: China Conceptualizes the Pacific 'Island Chains,'" *China Quarterly*, no. 225 (March 2016): 1–22.

24. 孙亮, 张军, 张木, 张典, 卜晓东, 许啸 [Sun Liang, Zhang Jun, Zhang Mu, Zhang Dian, Bu Xiaodong, and Xu Xiao], 我国未来作战方向拓展分析研究 [Analysis and research regarding the future expansion of China's operational direction], 舰船电子工程 [*Ship Electronic Engineering*], no. 5 (May 2020): 4–8 (CMSI translation). Sun, a senior engineer working in the China Academy of Launch Vehicle Technology (Beijing)'s Tactical Weapons Division, primarily researches systems warfare. Zhang Jun, a researcher in the Nanjing University of Aeronautics and Astronautics' School of Aeronautics and Astronautics, primarily researches experimental aerodynamics, computational fluid dynamics, computational heat transfer, and systems warfare. Zhang Mu is a colleague of Sun Liang. Zhang Dian is a colleague of Zhang Jun. Xu works at Jiangsu University of Science and Technology's School of Mechanical and Electrical Engineering.

25. See, for example, 黄加强 [Huang Jiaqiang], 北极航行对潜艇航行性能影响研究 [Research on submarine navigation in the Arctic], 舰船电子工程 [*Ship Electronic Engineering*] 40, no. 9 (September 2020), 62–66 (CMSI translation). The author, a senior engineer at the PLAN's Naval Equipment Department military representative office in Wuhan, Hubei, primarily researches overall ship design. Research for this article was supported by a grant from a PLA key research project titled "XXX Polar Operational Use Design Requirement Study" (serial no. HJ20172A01016).

26. 胡冬英, 黄锐, 蔡广友 [Hu Dongying, Huang Rui, and Cai Guangyou], 推进潜艇兵力走向远洋的几点思考 [Several thoughts on advancing the submarine force to distant oceans], 舰船电子工程 [*Ship Electronic Engineering*], no. 1 (2017), 1–3 (CMSI translation). All three authors are based at the PLA Navy Submarine Academy (Qingdao). Hu, a graduate student and engineer, primarily researches submarine operational command theory and methods. Huang, a staff officer, primarily researches weapon and equipment management and technical support. Cai, an associate

professor, primarily researches submarine operational command theory and methods.

27. Isaac B. Kardon and Wendy Leutert, "Pier Competitor: China's Power Position in Global Ports," *International Security* 46, no. 4 (2022): 9–47, https://direct.mit.edu/isec/article-abstract/46/4/9/111175/Pier-Competitor-China-s-Power-Position-in-Global?redirectedFrom=fulltext.

28. 胡中建 [Hu Zhongjian] and 胡欣 [Hu Xin], "布局与破局: 中国的海外战略支撑点" [Making and breaking the status quo: China's overseas strategic support points], 现代军事 [*Contemporary Military*], no. 12 (2015): 34–41 (CMSI translation).

29. Ellen Nakashima and Cate Cadell, "China Secretly Building PLA Naval Facility in Cambodia, Western Officials Say," *Washington Post*, June 6, 2022, https://www.washingtonpost.com/national-security/2022/06/06/cambodia-china-navy-base-ream/.

30. CMPR 2022, 145.

31. Mark V. Arena, Irv Blickstein, Obaid Younossi, and Clifford A. Grammich, *Why Has the Cost of Navy Ships Risen? A Macroscopic Examination of the Trends in U.S. Naval Ship Costs over the Past Several Decades* (Santa Monica, CA: RAND, 2006), 20, http://www.rand.org/content/dam/rand/pubs/monographs/2006/RAND_MG484.pdf.

32. Philip Pugh, *The Cost of Seapower: The Influence of Money on Naval Affairs from 1815 to the Present Day* (London: Conway Maritime, 1986), 143–51, 272–77.

33. Arena et al., *Why Has the Cost of Navy Ships Risen?*, xiv–xv, 22–49.

34. Pugh, *The Cost of Seapower*, 316.

35. Pugh, 294.

36. Andrew S. Erickson and David D. Yang, "Using the Land to Control the Sea? Chinese Analysts Consider the Anti-ship Ballistic Missile," *Naval War College Review* 62, no. 4 (2009): 53–86, https://digital-commons.usnwc.edu/nwc-review/vol62/iss4/6/.

37. Andrew S. Erickson, "China's Approach to Conventional Deterrence," in Roy D. Kamphausen, ed., *Modernizing Deterrence: How China Coerces, Compels, and Deters* (Seattle: National Bureau

of Asian Research, 2023), 12–27, https://www.nbr.org/publication/chinas-approach-to-conventional-deterrence/.

38. Daniel Caldwell, Joseph Freda, and Lyle Goldstein, *China's Dreadnought? The PLA Navy's Type 055 Cruiser and Its Implications for the Future Maritime Security Environment*, China Maritime Report 5 (Newport, RI: Naval War College China Maritime Studies Institute, February 2020), https://digital-commons.usnwc.edu/cmsi-maritime-reports/5/.

39. Stephen Van Evera, *Causes of War: Power and the Roots of Conflict* (Ithaca, NY: Cornell University Press, 1999), 73–74.

40. Van Evera, 89.

41. 孙盛智, 裴春宝, 侯妍 [Sun Shengzhi, Pei Chunbao, and Hou Yan], 太空信息在海军远洋精确打击作战中的应用 [The application of space information in distant-ocean precision strike naval operations], 火力与指挥控制 [*Fire Control and Command Control*] 44, no. 12 (2019): 12–15 (CMSI translation). Hou is a professor in the PLA Strategic Support Force Space Engineering University's Aerospace Command College. Sun is a PhD candidate there, and a lecturer in the China Coast Guard Academy's Department of Electronic Technology. Pei is a lecturer at the University of Tibet's School of Information Science and Technology.

CHAPTER FIFTEEN

NAVIES AND STRATEGIC SURPRISES

THE POST–COLD WAR U.S. NAVY

Norman Friedman

B etween 1989 and 1991 the Cold War ended. With it ended the threats that had defined the U.S. Navy for more than forty years. How well was the U.S. Navy prepared for the post–Cold War world? The historian must reckon with the lack of released official records. The two major defense reviews completed after the end of the Cold War (the Bush administration's Base Force analysis and the Clinton administration's Bottom-Up Review) are well known, but not the Navy's interaction with them.[1] The main evidence must be physical: what the Navy did and did not do after the end of the Cold War, with some indications of what it was forced to do by the big defense reviews.

The key events with naval resonance in this period were the first Gulf War (1991), the wars in the former Yugoslavia, the Bottom-Up Review, and the War on Terrorism that began in 2001. The major public factors were the election of Bill Clinton, with his interest in reaping a post–Cold War dividend, and the election of George W. Bush, who brought in Donald Rumsfeld as secretary of defense.

It was one of Clinton's secretaries of defense, former congressman Les Aspin, who demanded particularly deep cuts in defense, including naval forces. Rumsfeld was determined to save more money by pressing the "Revolution in Military Affairs," which meant far greater automation.[2]

Navy funding was and is controlled by key actors in Washington: the Office of the Secretary of Defense and various congressional committees. They tend to have a land-oriented point of view, which is well adapted to the regionally oriented U.S. command system. Late in the Cold War the U.S. defense organization was reorganized by the Goldwater-Nichols Act, nominally intended to improve interservice coordination. The U.S. naval leadership fought it on the ground that the navy was fundamentally different from the other services, and that the country benefited greatly from a pluralistic approach to defense. The fundamental difference is that the Navy is not geographically oriented. For example, the late Cold War Maritime Strategy concentrated on the effect of naval pressure exerted on the flanks of the Soviet Union, but the unified European command concentrated on the threat Soviet ground and tactical air forces posed to the NATO defense of the Central Front in Germany. The Maritime Strategy succeeded because naval pressure on the flanks, particularly on sanctuaries for Soviet strategic submarines, offered impacts the Soviet leadership had to take very seriously. The naval view was, and remains, that tying naval forces to particular regional commands robs the country of the flexibility inherent in them.[3]

In addition, the classic naval view of the nature of a war differs radically from that of land and associated air forces. The Pacific War is a case in point. The Army view, as expressed in the first volume of its official history, is that the war was about the Philippines, in 1941 a U.S. possession seized by the Japanese. The Navy view was that the war was about Japan. A defeated Japan would disgorge what it had seized, and would be unable to repeat its aggression. The Navy opposed the decision to invade the Philippines in 1944 on the ground that the gain to be expected was disproportionate to the

effort involved. Its preferred alternative was to seize a base on Formosa (Taiwan) from which Japan could be more effectively blockaded,
the idea being that the point of the war was to defeat Japan, and the
obvious method was strangulation by blockade. This strategy had
been espoused by the Navy for at least the past thirty years.[4]

These ideas were revived with the Maritime Strategy of the 1980s.
The question then was whether a war, if it broke out, would be about
the future of Germany or about the wider question of defeating the
Soviet Union. The U.S. Army certainly took the former viewpoint,
as of course did European NATO governments. However, given the
sheer strength of the Soviet and Warsaw Pact armies and their tactical air arms, it was widely believed that NATO could not win a
European land war. Declared NATO policy was to escalate to using
a few tactical nuclear weapons to convince the Soviets to stop their
advance. If that did not stop the Soviets, NATO would keep escalating,
ultimately to using strategic weapons.

As it developed the Maritime Strategy, the Navy asked what
would happen if the Soviets reached the Channel. Would that end
the war? Should it? Was there some deterrent, the use of which would
not amount to mutual suicide? Around 1981 the Navy began to argue
that maritime strike forces offered a deterrent, in that they could
rescue U.S. forces caught by a Soviet advance and keep up the fight
by striking at the maritime flanks of the Soviet Union. That the
United States would keep fighting might encourage Europeans to
keep fighting. The ultimate war aim, if the Soviets started a war, would
be their defeat, not merely to limit a Soviet advance into Western
Europe.[5] Not surprisingly, this strategy was not popular with the U.S.
Army and the U.S. Air Force, who had devoted most of their tactical
strength to the direct defense of West Germany. The naval view was
that strategy without an envisaged endgame was self-defeating.

In a broader sense, the Navy argued later that the United States
benefited from the reality that the naval view differed from that of
the two ground-oriented services. Plurality served the United States
much better than forced unanimity.

THE COLD WAR FLEET

Through most of the Cold War, the Soviet Union operated by far the world's most numerous submarine fleet. In the West, it was generally assumed that in wartime this fleet would reenact the Battle of the Atlantic, threatening shipping routes across the North Atlantic. As during World War II, much of what would keep a NATO army fighting would come from North America. It seemed to follow that the main naval task in NATO was to defeat the Soviet submarine force. As Soviet submarines improved, the cost of antisubmarine forces rose rapidly.

Beginning in 1955, the U.S. Navy conducted formal studies of its long-term future. An early conclusion, both by the Navy and by others, was that war in Europe was very unlikely, since it would carry a strong threat of nuclear escalation. President Eisenhower cut his army, which he considered too small to make much difference in Europe. He and the naval analysts saw no reason for East-West tension to vanish; they assumed that its armed expression would move to the Eurasian periphery, to places like Malaya and Taiwan, where there would be little or no danger of nuclear escalation. Eisenhower saw the U.S. Navy's carrier force as a means of dealing with such outbreaks.

The U.S. Army protested that Eisenhower was ensuring that any outbreak in Europe would escalate uncontrollably; the army should be built up sufficiently that a U.S. government (and NATO) would have a nonnuclear alternative. Once it was accepted that NATO should be able to fight a protracted nonnuclear war in Europe, it followed that the shipping route across the Atlantic had to be protected, because much of what would enable a NATO army to keep fighting would come, as in World War II, from North America. The NATO European scenario was studied intensely in the 1970s and 1980s, not only by the Army and the Air Force but also by the Office of the Secretary of Defense (OSD), whose power had increased enormously under Secretary of Defense Robert S. McNamara. He favored numerical studies of defense issues, and this emphasis survived his departure in 1967.[6]

Many naval strategists distinguished two main roles: sea control and power projection. The peripheral strike role was power projection. Cold War antisubmarine warfare was sea control. Typically, sea control involved large numbers of specialized surface ships (mainly frigates), submarines, and maritime patrol aircraft. Power projection involved limited numbers of capital ships (carriers) and their escorts, as well as amphibious formations. The Cold War U.S. Navy considered strike warfare its most important role, although it accepted the need for a substantial sea-control force. As the Cold War continued, other navies found power projection less and less affordable, the Royal Navy being a particular case in point. However, from the 1960s on sea control came to include defending shipping against long-range Soviet naval bombers armed with antiship missiles. If they were taken seriously, carrier fighters were required to help maintain sea control.

The election of Jimmy Carter created a crisis for the Navy.[7] Carter rejected the idea that the United States would probably have to fight on the Eurasian periphery; he expected "soft power" to settle problems there.[8] That left the possibility of war in Europe. Determined to balance the budget, Carter saw the Navy's power projection force as a target. The Navy felt compelled to show how its power projection capability offered unique advantages not only on the periphery but also in the NATO war that Carter imagined. For example, it argued that by applying naval pressure in the Far East, the power projection fleet could prevent the Soviets from moving their large Far Eastern ground and air forces to Europe; this was called "virtual attrition." Naval strategists also argued that, given emerging technology, the fleet could gain sufficient supremacy in the West that it could threaten the flanks of any Soviet advance. The new naval strategy based on power projection became the explicit U.S. Maritime Strategy.

The Maritime Strategy in turn justified the composition and character of the six-hundred-ship fleet built up during the 1980s. It emphasized carrier strike groups and, to some extent, amphibious forces. By this time U.S. and British submariners had demonstrated that they could trail Soviet strategic submarines in the open ocean;

the Soviet response was to move those submarines into "bastions" protected by most of their fleet: the White Sea and the Sea of Okhotsk.[9] The new strategy emphasized the use of U.S. and British submarines to hunt Soviet strategic submarine in the bastions. There was no attempt to cut back existing sea-control assets (frigates and maritime patrol aircraft), but no new frigates were ordered, and annual programs cut back new maritime patrol aircraft production.

For some years the Soviets had been building up their naval ballistic missile force. Some strategists had argued that the main wartime role of the Soviet fleet was to tip the strategic balance in the Soviets' favor by hunting down Western ballistic missile submarines while protecting their own. With the balance obviously favoring them, the Soviets imagined, they could force a Western surrender. Sometime in the early 1980s, sensitive intelligence confirmed this view. Suddenly the power projection navy had the potential to win a war by tippingthe strategic nuclear balance against the Soviets. The fleet could destroy the Soviet naval force intended to protect the bastions. U.S. and British attack submarines could hunt the Soviet ballistic missile submarines in the bastions, while it was unlikely that Soviet attack submarines could sink Western strategic submarines. The big force of Soviet attack submarines would be occupied defending the bastions and trying to deal with the attacking U.S. strike fleet. The U.S. Navy pressured the Soviets by running massive exercises, which showed that it could execute the new strategy. After the Cold War ended, Soviet naval officers confirmed that the U.S. strategy had succeeded; sufficient protection of the bastions, particularly that in the White Sea, had become unaffordable.[10]

Other NATO navies did not share the new U.S. orientation, as indeed they had not shared interest in peripheral warfare (the French were the major exception). The British and the Dutch, for example, built widely admired antisubmarine frigates. The British did retain just enough power-projection capacity to win the war in the Falklands—just as their defense minister had been about to eliminate it.[11]

THE SURPRISE

Navies require considerable long-term investment in ships and aircraft, which of course reflect particular guesses as to future requirements. The abrupt end of the Cold War forced all Western navies to confront the question of how well their choices were adapted to drastic changes in circumstances and in government perceptions.

The U.S. government announced the beginning of a new world order in which all involved would try to live in, and benefit from, peace. A State Department official, Francis Fukuyama, published *The End of History and the Last Man*. He argued that Western victory in the Cold War had demonstrated the superiority of democracy and free-market economics. The main driver of history had been the attempt by all governments to organize their societies for the greatest economic good. Clearly free markets had demonstrated their superiority. Surely the collapse of the Soviet Union proved that; the post-Soviet Russian government favored free enterprise and greater participation in the globalized economy. China had already opted to move in this direction, and it was already benefiting hugely. Governments primarily interested in keeping their populations prosperous would not risk war or even the threat of war. Fukuyama accepted that other forces might cause wars, but surely they would be localized.[12]

U.S. naval leaders knew how important the explicit Cold War Maritime Strategy had been in convincing Congress and others in Washington to support the naval programs of the Reagan era.[13] An explicit strategy was a vital means of achieving coherence within the service and of gaining necessary support outside. Any stated naval strategy had to be consistent with the largely unexpressed national strategy.

The new situation was somewhat analogous to that immediately after 1945, before it was clear that the Soviets were so hostile. In March 1946, Chief of Naval Operations Fleet Admiral Chester Nimitz published an article in *National Geographic*, at that time very widely read: "Your Navy as Peace Insurance." It is not clear how many within the Navy remembered it in 1990, but they ended up making much the same argument: the navy was badly needed in a disorderly postwar world. It should not be subject to the same degree of run-down as the land-oriented services.

The first Gulf War of 1991 might be seen either as the last gasp of the Cold War outside Europe or as the first conflict of a new world *dis*order. Its naval end was fought by the power projection forces built during the Cold War. The Navy was the only force immediately available after the Iraqi invasion of Kuwait, its carriers the only immediately available insurance against a continued Iraqi thrust into that country. On a subtler level, because they enabled the United States to defend Saudi airspace without Saudi permission, Iraqi pressure to deny Saudi airfields to U.S. and other Western aircraft fell flat. Since the war to liberate Kuwait was staged largely outside Saudi Arabia, and since the Iraqis had hoped to prevent that staging, it seems that the U.S. naval presence was decisive. The Navy failed to make that clear.[14]

The Navy pointed out that something like 70 percent of the world population lived in (and depended on) littoral strips.[15] They were defined as the strip of sea and shore which interacted. The first versions of post–Cold War, explicit U.S. naval strategy described how the Navy and the Marines could keep the peace by dominating the littoral strips and, if necessary, by fighting in them. Concentration on the littorals had real consequences. The capacity to mount deep airstrikes was no longer particularly vital, since nearly all potential targets were not far from the sea. Surely the new Tomahawk land-attack missile would suffice against deeper targets, and the air force could take care of any others.[16] This was an important way to save money; it justified retiring the Navy's older longer-range strike bombers (A-6 and A-7) and relying on the short-range F/A-18.

Operation in the littorals also changed the threat facing the fleet. During the Cold War, the main air threat was saturation by large numbers of bomber-launched missiles. Responses included antisaturation modernization of many ships (New Threat Upgrades). The new AEGIS system was also an antisaturation measure, but it had the added virtue of being capable of very quick reaction to sudden (pop-up) threats. The most prominent pop-up threats were relatively short-range, land-based missiles, such as the Silkworm fired at the battleship *Missouri* during the first Gulf War.[17] The New Threat Upgrade ships represented a huge investment, and they could have been kept in service for decades to come. They were discarded instead. In addition to their obsolescence from a combat system point of view, almost all of them were steam-powered, meaning that they required much more manpower than their gas turbine successors. The Office of the Secretary of Defense was willing to pay for them to go into reserve.

The other change was in the character of the submarine threat: from deepwater nuclear submarines to diesel submarines often operating inshore. Western navies, including the U.S. Navy, quickly retired the bulk of their Cold War antisubmarine forces, most visibly large numbers of sophisticated frigates. Some frigates and antisubmarine patrol aircraft survived.[18]

The Navy's littoral strategy was directed at the Washington policymakers who decided the fates of the services' programs. They shared Fukuyama's vision: governments would share the goal of maintaining prosperity. Prosperity in turn would cause countries to become friendlier. For example, trade with the West would convince the Chinese government to abjure hostile intentions. China would develop a prosperous middle class, which would force the future Chinese government to concentrate on maintaining its prosperity by strengthening its trade ties. If China was to become permanently friendly, the United States would not face any future peer competitor. The Navy could and should concentrate on local problems. This was not really very different from the pre-Carter, Cold War view of the U.S. naval function.

The difference was that budgets were now being cut. Since the U.S. Navy already wanted to abandon its previous sea-control force, it suffered less than other Western navies: it retained most of its power projection strength. It and the U.S. government understated the extent of post–Cold War disorder. It seems that no one in government wanted to face the dark possibility that resentment against the secular, prosperous West might be a driving force in much of the world. This was not jealousy; it was fear that by its existence the West might undermine the very different societies in much of the world. For example, many Islamic fundamentalists contrasted the values of the West with their own religious values. Such a societal conflict seemed to have been illustrated by the 1993 attack on the World Trade Center. At the time the U.S. Navy was developing its first post–Cold War strategy. Raising the possibility that its main role might be to defend against hatred of the West was distinctly unpopular, and it was never used to justify the global navy.

The force of nationalism was also underestimated. It was evident during the breakup of Yugoslavia, resulting in a problem so serious that the United States led a NATO coalition to crush the Serbians. The war against Serbia certainly demonstrated the value of the power projection navy the United States retained. For example, although the NATO force had access to many airfields in Italy, which lay across the Adriatic from the former Yugoslavia, carriers made a disproportionate contribution to the NATO air effort. They could maneuver out from under weather that often closed down bases ashore. Even a very small British carrier often launched more sorties than the NATO land bases. This experience convinced the British government to include carriers in its future defense plan.[19]

The fleet also demonstrated the capability of its long-range Tomahawk precision missile. Its use demonstrated the wisdom of a decision made during the Cold War, to equip the fleet's destroyers and cruisers with vertical launchers suitable for both air defense missiles and Tomahawks. During the Cold War, the point of Tomahawk capability was that the destroyers were potential nuclear threats to the Soviet Union; as such they had to be tracked so that they could be hit early in a war. That in turn helped dissipate Soviet naval efforts. After the Cold War, the nuclear Tomahawks were retired in favor of conventional ones with precision navigation. The vertical launch cells made it possible for fleet air defense ships to become precision attack ships.

SECOND SURPRISE

The second shock was much worse than the collapse of the Soviet Union. Given the belief that economics was the primary driver of international events, those in Washington seem to have discounted terrorism (a kind of nationalism). During the Cold War, most terrorism was state-sponsored, either by the Soviet Union or by Arab governments backed by the Soviets. The end of the Cold War eliminated direct Soviet support (and cover). Too, without the Soviets to back and protect them, Arab governments previously inclined to attack the West were far less willing to do so. In the 1990s, the only state supporting terrorists was North Korea, and it was interested only in attacking South Korea.

The possibility that groups without any national support might be able to mount effective attacks against the West was discounted, even after Al-Qaeda managed to carry out massacres in Africa. Thus, the 9/11 attacks were a terrible surprise. A small group of highly motivated individuals, led by a man in distant Afghanistan, managed to kill more than three thousand Americans and to endanger the U.S. government. It was not at all clear, then or later, what to do about such terrorists. Were they primarily a police problem? An intelligence problem? A hidden enemy state problem?

Afghanistan was asked to hand over the man behind 9/11, Osama bin Laden. When it refused, the U.S. government joined with local leaders already opposed to the Afghan government to attack those who had backed bin Laden. Afghanistan is landlocked, hence might seem not to have any naval aspect. Before U.S. forces became involved, a former Soviet general wrote that without bases close to Afghanistan, the United States would surely have to use nuclear weapons there. Given the horrors of the Soviet war in Afghanistan, for him this prospect was presumably a happy one.

Reality was rather different. The United States did have bases, but they were floating ones: aircraft carriers. U.S. and allied forces operating in Afghanistan needed aircraft on call rather than aircraft rushing in to drop bombs on preselected targets. The Navy's decision to abandon deep strike proved unfortunate; its shorter-range strike aircraft had to depend heavily on aerial refueling to enable them to loiter over Afghanistan. They depended on tankers based around Afghanistan, including some in Pakistan.

An important naval contribution went unsung. As U.S. and allied forces surged into Afghanistan, members of Al-Qaeda had to run. Their best bet was to cross the Arabian Sea to refuges, mainly in Africa. The only reliable way to get there was over water. The U.S. and allied navies operated a blocking force in the Bay of Bengal. It is not clear how many terrorists it caught, but at the least it seems to have made it difficult for Al-Qaeda to regroup quickly. This was a classic naval mission, connected intimately to the most basic fact of naval warfare: that the sea is the world's primary highway.

A NEW FLEET?

The important feature of 9/11, as the Navy came to see it, was that it was now possible for a few individuals to mount an attack the United States had to answer with major forces. During the Cold War, it had been assumed that the Soviets would be reluctant to present the United States with multiple more or less simultaneous crises, for fear of U.S. overreaction and consequent escalation. For that matter, the Soviets themselves were ill adapted to run multiple crises at the same time. This calculation in turn justified the U.S. policy of being able to handle two crises at a time—say, one due to the Soviets plus one other. If, however, the crises were initiated by a few individuals at a time, the United States might have to deal with many at about the same time.

The sort of strategy espoused after 1991 implied a need for a Navy to be present all over the world—a numerous Navy, not just one with extremely capable power projection ships. This need was not clearly articulated, and after 1991 the fleet was run down to about half its strength at the end of the Cold War.

Now it seemed that multiple crises might be the rule. The Navy would have to be in more places at the same time, in each case with significant combat power. In 2002 it circulated a briefing, one slide of which was labeled "a bad day in 2003." Illustrative crises included the collapse of the Egyptian government and a new Iraqi attack against Kuwait, neither of which happened. At this time the U.S. Navy had twelve operational carriers, which were associated with twelve amphibious ready groups. If a lot more naval formations were needed, the obvious way to create them was to make the twelve major amphibious ships the cores of new formations, which were called Expeditionary Strike Groups (ESGs). There had been proposals to use the big amphibious ships as low-capability carriers, but this time the idea was that the Marines on board those ships would be the offensive punch of the ESGs. In addition, Surface Action Groups (SAGs) could be created, their survivability ensured by the inclusion of existing ships with high-capability Aegis air defense systems. The new formations had to be filled out with additional surface combatants.

The briefing argued that the existing fleet was about seventy surface warships short. For so many to be affordable, the new ships had to be defined by their unit cost: a quarter as much as a missile destroyer. The briefing said nothing about either how this cost was to be achieved or about desired capabilities. However, it was apparent that the number could be reached only if the new ships replaced multiple old ones. Important replacement candidates were mine countermeasures ships and coastal patrol ships. It seems to have been accepted at the outset that the new ships would have to be modular, combining a standard hull with alternative mission packages. The Royal Danish Navy was already using modular warships whose mission packages could, in theory, quickly be changed out.[20]

The new ships were called littoral combat ships (LCS), probably because something (undefined) called LCS was the only surface combatant other than a missile destroyer (DDG) under discussion around 2001. The littoral designation reflected the U.S. Navy's expectation that it would fight mainly in littoral areas. The designation has not been particularly meaningful.

Within about a year the U.S. conclusion was that the mission packages would be built around unmanned systems, such as drones. At some point, another requirement was added, that the new ships should be capable of very high speed, about 45 knots. No public justification was ever offered. It may have been argued that modular operation demanded speed. Ships operating at any distance from their base would have to run back to base to pick up alternative modules.[21]

The demand for a specific (high) speed trumped the more fundamental decision to gain flexibility by developing a range of modules and unmanned vehicles. Very high speed in ships has always been very expensive, not only in terms of money but also with regard to other qualities. The high monetary cost badly retarded development of the modules.[22] High speed required that hulls with seakeeping problems be chosen. One of them (*Freedom*-class) required extraordinarily high power and consequently very high fuel consumption. The other (*Independence*-class) needed much less power but had to be built with a rather flimsy structure, so that it was impossible, for example, for a heavy helicopter to use its large flight deck. It was understood at the outset that modules had to include specialized personnel, so that an LCS would have a basic crew plus the specialists to operate the particular module embarked. That turned out to be impractical. Twenty years after conception, the LCS program, the main, concrete naval consequence of 9/11, is largely being abandoned. A few LCS are being fitted to support mine countermeasures using unmanned systems.

The range of new naval formations envisaged in 2002 has not materialized, although some ESGs did operate using existing ships. On the other hand, neither has the vision of a world exploding in uncoordinated warfare, which would have stretched the Navy, perhaps beyond its capacity. Even so, the current U.S. Navy is badly stretched, and it certainly could have used the numbers it had in, say, January 1991. The difference from the vision offered in 2002 is that the stretch is against a single potential adversary, China, which demands a much more coordinated fleet than the dispersed one envisaged two decades ago.

A THIRD SHOCK

Through the late 2010s it became clear that the central post–Cold War idea was wrong: the Chinese were not being drawn into amity based on participation in the global economy. Neither were the Russians. The governments of both countries appeared concerned mainly with maintaining and expanding national power, at whatever cost to their populations. Both seemed confident that they could ignore any internal problems connected with the cost of expanding power. Neither accepted the idea, central to the West, of a rules-based international order.

The rise of a hostile China was particularly painful for the U.S. government. The measures to open U.S. markets to China had destroyed many U.S. jobs and consequently had created considerable enmity in parts of the United States. Now it seemed that the Chinese were determined to seize control of the Far East, ejecting the United States. This was back to something much like the Cold War, but it had new features. Unlike the Soviets, the Chinese had built a prosperous economy with the potential to build a powerful military without accepting poverty. The strategy of containment, which had won the Cold War, did not seem applicable to China, and no alternative was being suggested.

It seemed clear that allies in the Far East had to be backed against possible Chinese attack or economic pressure. In contrast to the situation during the Cold War, there was no land frontier between China and major U.S. allies. One possible equivalent was the Taiwan Strait, which separated the PRC from Taiwan, which it claimed. Another might be the land frontiers between the PRC and its enemies, such as Vietnam and India. The United States had to demonstrate resolve in supporting local allies. The principal means of doing so was to continue naval operations in waters near China, including waters the Chinese claimed in the face of adverse legal decisions. It is not yet clear whether the Chinese have an inbuilt maritime vulnerability like the Soviet strategic submarine bastions.

U.S. naval strike capacity is still embodied mainly in aircraft car-riers. They are the only warships to which weapons can be trans-ferred at sea, hence the only ones capable of fighting on a sustained basis. Their great combat power justifies building surface warships nearly limited to supporting them. The Chinese navy is currently considerably stronger than the U.S. Navy numerically, but it lacks numbers of carriers. On the other hand, the Chinese claim that their land-based missiles are effective carrier-killers.

It is not clear what would be needed in a war against China. Are there crucial targets that can or should be struck from the sea? The Chinese navy has justified the enormous investment it embodies largely on the basis of Chinese dependence on seaborne trade. Is that trade the most valid maritime target in a war? Or do we contemplate a limited war over Taiwan in which the maritime target is the Chi-nese invasion force? To what extent is attack against land targets in China unlikely due to Chinese nuclear deterrence?

Whatever the answers to these questions, U.S. numbers are insufficient. There is uneasiness about depending on a relatively small carrier fleet. It is possible that the eleven carriers currently in service will be supplemented by adapted amphibious ships operating F-35B STOVLs (short take-off and vertical landing aircraft), despite their limited endurance and payload. It seems less likely that the solu-tion will be more surface missile ships, simply because surface ship payloads are so limited. Other solutions currently being advocated include construction of numerous unmanned ships (including unmanned missile ships) and incorporation of offensive missile launchers onboard many ships currently without them ("if it floats, it fights" is the relevant slogan).

U.S. ships are increasingly expensive to build, but it can be argued that this is due largely to very limited production rates. For example, the United States now builds two submarines per year, but during the Cold War it built ten, using the same two yards. The country keeps the yards active to maintain the ability to ramp back up (and to hold prices down through competition). What happens to unit prices if the United States does ramp up, and if the yards can hire more workers? Can production automation change matters?

There is also the more basic question of how naval warfare has changed in the last three decades. In 1991 the U.S. Navy relied heavily on satellites, but a few years earlier a carrier battle force commander warned that in war the satellites would soon be gone, and his force would have to rely heavily on its own resources. And now? The Chinese threat to U.S. forces offshore relies heavily on means of detecting and tracking that force, using space-based and other sensors. Can we deny those sensors to the Chinese as they try to deny ours to us? Will decoying and deception change naval warfare? Will they make capital ships more or less survivable in combat?

Post–Cold War shocks badly stressed all of the Western navies. The U.S. Navy seems to have fared much better than the others, thanks to its insistence on power projection—which remained vital after the Cold War—as the single most important naval task. In 1991 it was already moving toward discarding much of its sea-control element—the element that was basic to most other NATO navies. The power projection fleet turned out to be well equipped for the post–Cold War world. The question now is whether it forms the appropriate core for what is needed to face China.

NOTES

1. Ryan A. Peeks, *Aircraft Requirements and Strategy 1977–2001* (Washington, DC: Naval History and Heritage Command, 2020), 87–102, 125–29.

2. The "Revolution in Military Affairs," or RMA, was an important theme for Andrew Marshall, the founder and chief of the Office of Net Assessment. An account of RMA as he saw it is in Andrew Krepinovich and Barry Watts, *The Last Warrior: Andrew Marshall and the Shaping of Modern Defense Strategy* (New York: Basic Books, 2015), 194–214. The name came from the Soviet announcement of a "Revolution in Military Affairs" due to the emergence of nuclear weapons and missiles. RMA was typically used by the Army and the Air Force; the Navy used the term

"network-centric warfare" for much the same development. In each case, the idea was that the new precision weapons, supported by precision reconnaissance, could destroy key targets using far less firepower than in the past. For example, see David S. Alberts, John J. Garstka, Richard E. Hayes, and David A. Signori, *Understanding Information-Age Warfare* (Washington, DC: Department of Defense Command and Control Research Program, 2001). Readers may also find my own book *Network-Centric Warfare: How Navies Learned to Fight Smarter through Three World Wars* (Annapolis: Naval Institute Press, 2009) useful. There is also considerable literature debunking the RMA of about 2000 as a false revolution. See, for example, Michael O'Hanlon, "A Retrospective on the So-Called Revolution in Military Affairs, 2000–2020," *Brookings*, September 2018.

3. For more on the Maritime Strategy, see chaps. 11 and 12.

4. I have described U.S. Navy strategy for a Pacific War in my analysis of interwar wargaming at the U.S. Naval War College, *Winning a Future War* (Washington, DC: Naval History and Heritage Command, 2019), available on the NHHC website. The connection between wargaming and war planning was that the War College acted as the planners' laboratory. The endgame of the war was always the same: strangulation of Japan by blockade. What varied was the way that would be approached. As early as 1929, joint war planners offered an alternative. If the blockade failed to convince the Japanese to abandon a war, they could be bombed from the same islands needed to support the blockade, the idea being that Japanese cities were unusually vulnerable because they were so flammable.

5. My account of the U.S. Maritime Strategy is based on my experience working as a personal consultant to Secretary of the Navy John Lehman. I joined his Office of Program Appraisal (in effect his personal office) in 1984, assigned to write the history of his administration (it was never released). After Dr. Lehman left, I remained as a consultant doing quick studies for that office. I published my own account of the Maritime Strategy as *The U.S. Maritime Strategy* (London: Jane's Information Group, 1988). I was influenced by my experience at the Hudson Institute in 1973–84, when the conventional wisdom among analysts, at least

before the 1980s, was that if NATO escalated to using tactical nuclear weapons it would still be defeated by the Soviets, only in a more devastating manner. At that time the war analysts generally considered a Soviet attack in Central Europe.

6. I worked in a think tank, Herman Kahn's Hudson Institute, from 1973 through 1984. Our defense business was largely financed by OSD, and the great bulk of it was focused on the problem of defending against a Soviet land attack in Central Europe. One of our staff members, Frank Armbruster, showed that such an attack was extremely unlikely because both sides would be acutely aware of the possibility of nuclear escalation, but that seems to have had no impact on the general feeling that the European war scenario was the one that counted. Only later did I meet naval officers who pointed out that, if it was difficult to ignite a European land war, perhaps that was the wrong scenario on which to concentrate. Until President Jimmy Carter took office, the Navy concentrated on the much likelier scenario of a limited war on the Eurasian periphery, as in Vietnam. It did have contingency plans for a European war, but they were secondary. This point was made by a slide in the standard Maritime Strategy briefing plotting the possible severity of a crisis against the probability that it would erupt, with the big European war high on the scale of potential severity and very low in probability. See my book *The Fifty-Year War: Conflict and Strategy in the Cold War* (Annapolis: Naval Institute Press, 2000). The relationship between U.S. and NATO strategy is a very tangled and complex subject.

7. The crisis is suggested by Peeks, *Aircraft Requirements*, 20–23. See also John B. Hattendorf, *The Evolution of the U.S. Navy's Maritime Strategy, 1977–1986*, Newport Paper 19 (Newport, RI: U.S. Naval War College Press, 2004), chap. 1. Reading the official Department of Defense account of President Carter's secretary of defense, Dr. Harold Brown, it seems significant that he was credited with the application of microcomputers to U.S. ground forces in Europe, without any reference to their impact on naval operations. The Navy's *Sea Plan 2000* devoted considerable space to the proposition that the new technology would reverse the naval balance in places near the Soviet Union, "maritime air superiority" being mentioned

(thanks to the combination of the Aegis system on ships and the F-14/Phoenix on fighters). This potential in turn helped justify the forward strategy adopted under President Reagan, and demonstrated in major fleet exercises. I have discussed the impact of the Carter administration in detail in the revised edition of my *U.S. Aircraft Carriers: An Illustrated Design History* (Annapolis: Naval Institute, 2019), which draws on declassified Carter administration documents and also on the reminiscences of retired Rear Admiral Jim Stark, who was involved in the Navy reaction to the administration's demands for analyses to support its planned cuts.

8. During the 1976 campaign, a fellow staff member, Dr. William H. Overholt, who had been close to Zbigniew Brzezinski, worked on the Carter campaign. He personally explained to me that Carter distinguished the East-West problem (the conflict with the Soviets) from the North-South problem. He was determined to avoid military solutions to North-South problems; the only military issue for him was the fate of the Central Front in Europe. Carter's subsequent policy decisions seemed to follow this predicted pattern.

9. Christopher A. Ford and David A. Rosenberg, "The Naval Intelligence Underpinnings of Reagan's Maritime Strategy," *Journal of Strategic Studies* 28, no. 2 (2005): 379–409.

10. John Lehman, *Oceans Ventured: Winning the Cold War at Sea* (New York: Norton, 2018), 199–200.

11. When the Falklands were invaded, HMS *Invincible*, the first of the three British VSTOL carriers, had been sold to Australia as part of the fleet reduction ordered by Defence Secretary John Nott as a result of the 1981 Defence Review. In his memoir, *Here Today, Gone Tomorrow* (London: Politico's, 2002), 203–44, Nott wrote that he concentrated on deterring war in Europe. He doubted that the Royal Navy could have any impact before the Soviets overran Germany, which he thought could be done within a week. On that basis Nott wanted to concentrate his limited resources on the British land force in Germany and on the RAF supporting it. The *Invincible* sale (intended as part of a reduction from three to two small carriers) was canceled, and HMS *Invincible* went to the Falklands together with HMS *Hermes*, the other operational British carrier. The other two *Invincibles* were still under

construction. Initially the Australians were told that they could have one of the carriers under construction to replace *Invincible*, but then the sale was abandoned altogether (*Hermes* was sold to India). See David Hobbs, *The British Carrier Strike Fleet since 1945* (Annapolis: Naval Institute Press, 2015), 522, for the post-Falklands decision to retain the three small British carriers.

12. Francis Fukuyama, *The End of History and the Last Man* (New York: Free Press, 1992).

13. This is from my own experience working in the Secretariat when the first post–Cold War expression of naval strategy was being written. It also reflects my experience with the Maritime Strategy as a source of coherence under Dr. Lehman and various senior naval officers.

14. The Saudis had long considered their country sacred Muslim soil; the Iraqis threatened to show Saudis that their government had lost its legitimacy by allowing infidels to defend it. Carriers in the Gulf and the Red Sea could provide air defense without any presence ashore. Knowing that Saudi Arabia would be defended whether or not they made their arguments, the Iraqis gave up the effort; it was pointless to expend their public relations capital that way. Ultimately land-based aircraft based in Saudi Arabia had a much larger footprint, but it was several months before they and, as importantly, their supporting equipment and spares, were in place. Well after the Saudis had welcomed them, spares and support for land-based fighters were not yet available. The fact that carrier-based aircraft could provide essential support whether or not local countries accepted U.S. aircraft was again vitally important in the Afghan War, particularly in convincing the Pakistanis to allow U.S. tankers to operate from their airfields. This comment is based on my own experience immediately after the Gulf War, when I was working in the Navy Secretariat and there was considerable discussion of how difficult it had been to secure base rights. I have not seen any open discussion, but I mentioned the issue in my book on the war, *Desert Victory* (Annapolis: Naval Institute Press, 1992).

15. The first post–Cold War expression of U.S. naval strategy was a paper, ". . . From the Sea: Preparing the Naval Service for the 21st Century," signed by the Chief of Naval Operations, the

commandant of the Marine Corps, and the Secretary of the Navy, and released in September 1992. Buried in this document is the idea that the Navy would operate forward in the littorals of the world. A follow-on paper, "Forward . . . From the Sea," was issued in 1994. It emphasized the ability of naval forces to prevent conflicts and control crises.

16. The older aircraft were much more expensive to maintain than the F/A-18. At this time the A-6 Intruder and the A-7 Corsair II were being retired, and the question was whether the A-6 should be retained in reserve or scrapped. They were scrapped. There were obviously skeptics, who justified development of the longer-range Super Hornet (F/A-18E and -18F). In the late 1990s the Navy also converted some surviving F-14 Tomcat fighters into "Bombcats." Neither it or the Super Hornet approached the combined bomb capacity and range of the A-6. See my book *U.S. Naval Attack Aircraft, 1920–2020* (Annapolis: Naval Institute Press, 2021). It is based largely on official papers.

17. That the missile was destroyed by a previous-generation system aboard a British missile destroyer suggests that the contrast between Aegis and its predecessors in a littoral situation may have been overestimated at the time.

18. For the changes in force structure, see standard handbooks of the world's fleets. For the United States, Stephen Chumbley, ed., *Conway's All the World's Fighting Ships, 1947–1995* (Annapolis: Naval Institute Press, 1996), documents the rise and fall (by scrapping) of the U.S. surface fleet, with additional discards documented in A. D. Baker III, ed., *The Naval Institute Guide to Combat Fleets of the World, 2002–2003* (Annapolis: Naval Institute Press, 2002). The decline of the British and Dutch escort fleets is evident in later editions of *Jane's Fighting Ships* (some of the ships were sold to Chile). By the 2010 edition, the Royal Netherlands Navy had discarded all of its pure ASW frigates, retaining only some antiaircraft ships with missiles. The Royal Navy was down to seventeen frigates (ASW ships), four of which were soon discarded. Not all of the remaining thirteen have been modernized as planned. *Jane's* and *Combat Fleets* also show aircraft strengths, though the reader has to compare different editions to see the decline in maritime patrol aircraft strength.

19. The effectiveness of the small British carriers in the Adriatic apparently explains the 1998 decision, as explained in the British Strategic Defence Review released that year, to build two new larger carriers. See Hobbs, *British Carrier Strike Fleet*, 541, for an analysis of the politics involved. These ships eventually materialized as HMS *Queen Elizabeth* and HMS *Prince of Wales*.

20. *Burke*-class missile destroyers have 96 vertical launch cells; *Ticonderoga*-class cruisers have 122. Note that their offensive capability is dwarfed by that of a carrier, which may accommodate more than 2,000 tons of ammunition, the airplanes serving as reusable boosters. The retired (and discarded) missile ships could not be refitted with vertical launch cells. However, it did prove possible to install such cells on board many *Spruance*-class destroyers, giving them an important new role. No such option was available for the much smaller surface warships in other NATO navies.

21. I have not seen a good connected account of the naval side of the Afghan War. The U.S. Naval History and Heritage Command has published a chronology of the naval side of the Afghan War, 2001–2, which concentrates heavily on the air and land campaigns, and barely mentions the Maritime Interdiction Force in the Arabian Sea. A paper written at the Naval War College by Lieutenant Commander Alexander E. Carr, titled "Maritime Interdiction Operations in Support of the Counterterrorism War" (ADA 438554, dated February 4, 2002) does address the role of maritime interdiction; it mentions the coalition force in the Indian Ocean (the Arabian Sea). There is also a Naval War College paper by Lieutenant Colonel Damian I. Spooner, USMC, "Decision Points: A Case Study of Naval Expeditionary Task Force 58," submitted May 5, 2016, but it mentions maritime interdiction only in passing. I became aware of the role and scope of maritime interdiction in the Arabian Sea through long discussions with the late Rear Admiral James Goldrick RAN, who commanded the international interdiction force for a time.

22. This paper has not been released, but in his account of the LCS story, *Why LCS? How We Got Here and Why* (2014, released by the Undersecretary of the Navy, ADA 594372), Robert O. Work

(who was undersecretary) refers to its place in a new battle force architecture and, fleetingly, to the new 1-4-2-1 strategy embodied in the 2001 Quadrennial Defense Review (QDR), published on September 30, 2001. The latter replaced the earlier requirement that U.S. forces be able to deal with two major conflicts. Instead, U.S. forces had to be able to deal with multiple simultaneous regional conflicts, their numbers increasing as their intensity decreased (hence the 4-2 part). According to the QDR, for planning purposes U.S. forces would be structured to defeat quickly attacks against U.S. allies and friends in two overlapping time frames. At the president's direction, however, they would be capable of decisively defeating an enemy in one of the two theaters. The unclassified QDR does not appear to specify the number or the character of lower-level contingencies, the 1-4-2-1 part. My own experience was that the 2002 Navy paper, which seems to have been the basis for OSD approval of a large number of smaller combatant ships, did not mention the QDR conclusion at all. It argued that the existing naval structure did not support simultaneous crisis reactions. Nothing could be done about the major combatant ships, which took so long to build. In the past, Amphibious Ready Groups (ARGs) had operated with Carrier Strike Groups, which provided support, for example against submarines. There were far too few major surface combatant ships to support the number of independent striking forces, which the 2002 Navy paper required. The 2002 Navy paper proposed forming independent Expeditionary Strike Forces (ESGs) and Surface Action Groups. A large number of new surface warships were needed to fill out these formations. Hence the LCS, which was unspecified except for its cost. I remember meeting someone from the OpNav group framing LCS requirements, who said just that; the only other requirement at the time was that the ship have a "lily pad," a helicopter pad, suitable for refueling but not necessarily a hangar. Everything else came later, in my view. Work emphasizes the Navy mission to defeat antiaccess/area-denial threats, which was inherent in the strategy made explicit in the 1990s. He recalls that OSD demanded that the Navy include a small combatant in its plans to complement the big DD-21

(*Zumwalt* class) it wanted. To that extent, the Navy's 2002 paper may have been designed to fit OSD demands. Initially, the Chief of Naval Operations proposed a family of ships that would include a land-attack destroyer, a cruiser optimized for tactical missile defense, and a small "focused" combatant.

23. The Danes containerized their weapons, exploiting computer power, which made it possible for a ship's combat system computer to carry simultaneously the software for all the alternative weapons, making it possible to change them out quickly (at least in theory). In the course of a war, the Danish fleet could execute a sequence of roles without needing an unaffordable number of craft. For example, it might start by laying defensive mines, then shift to missiles to defend against incoming invaders, and eventually sweep the mines it (and perhaps the invaders) laid, among other functions. It turned out, incidentally, that it was a lot more difficult to train a crew to carry out multiple functions. In some cases, too, merely dropping a container into place was not enough; weapons had to be aligned, sometimes laboriously. The Danish StanFlex concept was widely publicized by the Royal Danish Navy in the 1980s; I attended commercial meetings sponsored by the British arm of the U.S. Technology Training Corp. in London in the 1980s (at which I was a speaker) at which a Royal Danish Navy spokesman, Captain Hans Harboe-Hansen, repeatedly explained the logic of StanFlex. A substantial official Danish brochure describing the initial StanFlex ship, *Standard Flex 300: The True Multi-Role Ship*, is available on marinehist.dk. It was published by Danyard, which built the initial StanFlex corvettes, by NobelTech, which was responsible for the containers, and by Terma Elektronik, which was responsible for the adaptable command/control system. It is dated March 1992 (the first of the StanFlex corvettes was completed in 1989). Baker, *Combat Fleets, 2002–2003*, 154, describes the StanFlex corvettes in detail, including their modular combat systems. Later versions of StanFlex equip more recent Danish warships.

24. Work reports that the Chief of Naval Operations, Admiral Vern Clark, and a group he assembled for an LCS offsite in February 2003 concluded that high sprint speed would offer "responsive mobility" (to concentrate rapidly in forward theaters from a

globally dispersed posture), increased search volume, and threat evasion (particularly against torpedoes). High sprint speed comes with a loss of endurance; a self-deployment range of 3,500 nautical miles at 18 knots was specified (later reduced to 3,500 nautical miles at 14 knots, with a goal of 3,500 nautical miles at 16 knots), planners accepting that long-range deployment would require development of a fuel bladder mission module. The idea seems to have been that divisions of LCS would be forward-based, so that the limited endurance would not be a problem. It was considered acceptable that LCS would require replenishment every three to five days, which had not been unusual during carrier operations in the 1980s. The February 2003 arguments for high speed are not entirely convincing. The ability to deploy rapidly from dispersed forward positions can be read as a rationalization for desired very high speed. Whether high speed would equate to high search volume is questionable, particularly in the case of ASW. For other kinds of search, organic helicopters would provide most of the desired search area. As for torpedoes, the LCS as actually built carries no torpedo detection sensors, and it therefore seems very unlikely that any were ever specified. Without such sensors, high speed would be a meaningless form of self-defense against underwater weapons. The arguments for high speed thus seem to have been intended to support an unspoken earlier demand for it. It may be relevant that as a junior officer, Admiral Clark served on fast *Asheville*-class fast gunboats assigned to the Sixth Fleet to trail Soviet "tattletales," fast warships assigned to trail carriers and other high-value U.S. targets.

25. There was also a subtler cost. It is not difficult to specify a particular characteristic, such as a desired speed (or, for that matter, range). It is impossible to require flexibility, although a ship can be designed to be flexible. Contractors offering candidate LCS designs had to show that they could perform to desired levels of speed and endurance, but flexibility was a different proposition. Important LCS modules depend on unmanned vehicles, and in some cases it seems difficult to provide for them. It is also arguable that by relying on unmanned vehicles LCS is a kind of carrier for them—and that experience with aircraft carriers suggest the importance of being able to mix and match the vehicles.

CONCLUSION

Paul Kennedy and Evan Wilson

There is always a reason to think that we will not make the mistakes of our predecessors. Historical study provides us with details of those mistakes, and it is easy to convince ourselves that it should be enough to allow us to avoid them. More subtly, though, we combine knowledge of the past with access to new and emerging technologies, approaches, and knowledge. Our superior capabilities, we think, will insulate us from past mistakes. Exciting new ways of engaging with the world around us—big data, artificial intelligence, whatever comes next—make a splash precisely because they promise to destroy existing barriers to understanding the present and the future. We would not be human if we did not think that we will not be so foolish as our ancestors.

Of course, every navy under study in this volume thought that, too. Whether it was simply avoiding the mistakes of the last war or, more ambitiously, deploying a cutting-edge, disruptive technology like submarines or aircraft to fight the next war in a new way, navies are apt to convince themselves that they have the right plan in place. Sometimes they did—it is important not to lose sight of times when a navy's plans actually came to fruition, more or less like they had hoped. But the times when they did not are also instructive. Navies cannot be so arrogant as to think that they have achieved a break-through in human affairs, that they are insulated from the perils of prediction. They must try to understand the mistakes of their predecessors, to see why their plans went awry, and to understand that,

366

while their plans are unlikely to go awry in precisely the same way, there will be fog and there will be friction.

It is not too much to suggest here, then, that both naval planners and operational leaders alike, in any one of the world's contemporary large navies, had they the time to peruse this volume and then reflect a bit on their own "best-laid plans," might wish to order a scrutiny of their armed service's present strategic beliefs; current force structure; existing naval and marine infantry deployments; technological deployments; and supporting economic, high-tech, and shipbuilding capacities. Do any of today's navies, for example, have the nerve and intellectual capacity to create an in-house (or closely situated) office whose task it is to keep challenging all current assumptions, an office that would be a sort of mix of the Pentagon's Office of Net Assessment and the papacy's former devil's advocate function? That is, to keep pushing both their naval and national leaders on their tendency toward best-case scenarios, and to keep asking how their possible opponents might be looking at the world or planning for conflict differently?

It is not difficult to imagine that the most serious current students of future naval operations, including best-laid plans that might go awry, could be the operational planners and logistics officers of the People's Republic of China's People's Liberation Army Navy (PLAN). In the first place, this navy is undertaking the largest fleet expansion of modern times. Grappling with the implications of its changing capabilities will surely prove to be an immense challenge. It does appear, however, that the PLAN has clearly defined goals: to develop a world-class navy and unify Taiwan. Most other navies must be reactive; the PLAN will likely be able to choose the time and method of its attack, if it receives such an order. On the other hand, all the Chinese open discussion about securing the "first island chain" and then, later, more distant lines of island groups and archipelagos, not to mention those well-known strategic choke points that would allow both Chinese surface warships and commercial vessels greater access to the Indo-Pacific, suggest ambitions beyond Taiwan. What, exactly, does China hope to do with its large navy? And does the PLAN have a good understanding of its role in Chinese grand strategy? Do their plans for operations around Taiwan and further afield take into consideration their own heavy losses in surface craft and submarines, and a scheme for constant reinforcements to the battle fronts? From the outside, these appear to be important and unresolved questions, though the discussion inside the PLAN undoubtedly looks very different.

Any consideration of where and how the U.S. Navy, still the world's most powerful by most measurements of naval force projection, might find its plans and preparations for future war going badly awry should begin with a succinct description of America's place in the world and the grand strategy, which flows from that. Such a description, done along hard, classical lines, would recognize the incredibly fortunate geostrategic position the United States possesses as compared to that of any of the leading great powers of the past and as compared, even more so, to the constrained positions of the competing great powers—Russia, India, and even China—in today's world. America's first military task is to prevent its own homeland and people from severe damage, defeat, and destruction. There is no higher strategic aim than that, but the United States could not be better placed to accomplish that task. A huge continent-wide nation of nearly 340 million, possessing a giant economy that was galvanized first by industrial and then by high-tech economic expansion, comfortably protected by Canada to its north and Mexico and the rest of a basically nonhostile hemisphere to its south, and sheltered by three thousand miles of Atlantic Ocean on one side and seven thousand miles of the Pacific on the other, is free from having China and Russia's geographic fate of having uncertain land and littoral problems all around.

America's second most important strategic task, and one pursued unwaveringly since around 1942, has been and is the protection of its own assets and closest allies in Western Europe, in the West and Southwest Pacific, and in the Mediterranean and Middle East. It flows from this that the third most vital (and intricately connected) aim must lie in assuring the integrity and safety of the sea lines of communication (SLOCs) to and from those overseas places. There may exist other significant American diplomatic purposes to be pursued in the world (e.g., giving support to the United Nations or providing assistance to African nations), but none are as basic as the three strategic objectives listed above.

It is relatively easy, therefore, to see where the U.S. Navy's roles can be fitted into its larger strategic posture, and therefore to consider whether its weaponry and its planning might be vulnerable to the possibility of going awry against a well-prepared opponent. America's strategic task remains, as it was historically, a two-fronted one. Across the Pacific, the sea-air posture necessary to deter a Chinese attack on Taiwan requires close integration with and support from vital allies like Japan, South Korea, and the Philippines. Across the Atlantic, the U.S. Navy plays an essential role in the sea-air-land posture necessary to bolster NATO and still, despite increasing domestic production, protect the supply of oil out of the Persian Gulf.

Where are these plans likely to go awry? To borrow Donald Rumsfeld's framing, technological disruption is a known unknown. Artificial intelligence may be announcing its arrival on the battlefield soon—or not, depending on whom you ask. But getting it wrong, either by falling behind its development or misunderstanding its strengths and weaknesses, is surely a source of concern. Some of the enclosed waters in which the U.S. Navy expects to operate present known challenges: from the Persian Gulf to the South China Sea, surface ships will face threats from land-based and air-launched missile systems that demand advance preparation. Other areas, once a source of great concern, seem to present a diminished challenge. The SLOCs to Europe, long the site of some of the most consequential naval warfare in modern history, may not require the same resources in the next war.

As with all predictions about the future, however, the historian is no more likely to get it right than the naval planner. There are too many unknown unknowns. Neither the English nor the Dutch understood when the war began that the particular contours of their conflict would launch a revolution in naval tactics that would last a century and a half. Historians are still untangling the causes and effects of the French Revolution—imagine how hard it was to respond to it in real time. Who saw the collapse of France in 1940 coming, or the fall of the Berlin Wall in 1989? We can say with some certainty only that the United States faces more challenges now than it has since 1991, and that it can no longer afford to ignore its sealift and shipbuilding capabilities. Nor does it have the luxury of spending billions of dollars on unproven experimental ship designs. It is academic whether the relative decline in U.S. naval strength is yet another major turn in the centuries-long Mackinder-versus-Mahan oscillation between land power and sea power. The fact is that the best-laid plans of the U.S. Navy, both in its transpacific and in its European-Mediterranean-Gulf objectives, could be seriously disrupted if not completely upset by a substantive foe possessing disruptive technologies.

It is not too difficult to suggest that the political and naval leaders who might best be advised to ponder over the historical lessons of best-laid plans could be those in recent U.K. Tory governments who have suggested that the Royal Navy return to a regular and significant east-of-Suez posture, perhaps even with its largest warships—the new *Queen Elizabeth*–class carriers—being part of that presence. If that strategic posture was a difficult enough one to maintain in the 1930s, as Geoffrey Till's essay explored, it is hard to see how it might work today. The surface fleet of the Royal Navy is a dramatically shrunken one, given that so much of its budget has been allocated to the carriers and the submarine forces, and any glance at the geographic distance between Portsmouth and Hong Kong suggests that the Royal Navy's operational areas should more sensibly focus on the North Sea/Baltic, the Eastern Atlantic, and (within a NATO context) the Western Mediterranean. Within those more realistic boundaries, then, its further task will be to keep up with—or to *keep keeping up with*—the demanding challenges of ever more sophisticated technologies and ever-rising budgets. It is difficult to envision how a Brexit-damaged British economy might provide the foundations for such an effort. Partnerships seem likely to produce better results, and it will be fascinating to follow how the Australia-U.K.-U.S. (AUKUS) submarine deal will shape the strategic situation east of Suez.

Today's even further reduced French navy, the once-vaunted "Royale," may have mainly resisted any temptation to significant east-of-Suez deployments and therefore be more sensibly situated in Mediterranean and Eastern Atlantic waters. If that is so, then its challenges in future strategic environments are the same as those facing all other medium-sized/medium-budget navies: how to keep up with, and how to pay for, the spiraling newer air-sea technologies and the costs they bring.

What can one say about the Russian Navy? As Alexey Muraviev explored, the vacillations in Russian naval policy since 1991 have produced mixed results. But saying much more than that, as the Russo-Ukrainian War still rages, draws a line of emphasis under the challenges of thinking about the future. The Russian invasion of Ukraine in February 2022 was not on anyone's horizon when the conference from which these essays are drawn was conceived. By the time we met, the invasion was underway, but its outcome was still uncertain. It remains so today, as this volume goes to press.

It has been well said that "historians are deeply unreliable, and never more so than when they are foolish enough to predict the future."[1] But perhaps we can say two things in favor of the case studies presented here. Historians cannot hope to predict the future with any confidence, any more than the navies whose plans went awry did. Unlike historians, however, navies must try. In this effort, historians can and should play a role. The study of the past forms the greatest part of any serious planning effort, because as N. A. M.

Rodger has said, "the alternative is not other people with better information but other people with no information, for it is the past that makes the present and the future."[2] When we study the past, moreover, we need to look not for lessons directly applicable to the present and the future but, rather, for questions to ask. By accessing the full range of naval experiences, navies can gain new perspectives that, if all goes well, will equip them for whatever the future brings.

NOTES

1   N. A. M. Rodger, "The Hattendorf Prize Lecture: The Perils of History," *Naval War College Review* 66, no. 1 (2013): 7–15.
2   Rodger, 7.

ABOUT THE EDITORS

PAUL KENNEDY is J. Richardson Dilworth Professor of History and Distinguished Fellow of the Brady-Johnson Program in Grand Strategy at Yale University. He is internationally known for his writings and commentaries on global political, economic, and strategic issues. He holds many honorary degrees and is a fellow of the Royal Historical Society, the American Philosophical Society, and the American Academy of Arts and Sciences. He was made Commander of the Order of the British Empire (CBE) in 2000 for services to history and elected a fellow of the British Academy in 2003. Kennedy is author or editor of twenty books. His best-known work is *The Rise and Fall of the Great Powers*, which provoked an intense debate on its publication in 1988 and has been translated into more than twenty languages. His newest book is *Victory at Sea: Naval Power and the Transformation of the Global Order in World War II*.

EVAN WILSON is an associate professor in the Hattendorf Historical Center at the U.S. Naval War College in Newport, Rhode Island. A recipient of the Sir Julian Corbett Prize in Modern Naval History, he is the author or editor of six books, most recently *The Horrible Peace: British Veterans and the End of the Napoleonic Wars*. His work has appeared in the *English Historical Review*, the *Journal of Military History*, the *Mariner's Mirror*, and other journals. Before coming to Newport, he was the Caird Senior Research Fellow at the National Maritime Museum (U.K.) and the Associate Director of International Security Studies at Yale University. He holds degrees from Yale, Cambridge, and Oxford.

ABOUT THE CONTRIBUTORS

MARTIN S. ALEXANDER is Professor Emeritus of International Relations and Strategy at Aberystwyth University in Wales. He held a Franco-British Council Research Fellowship in 1980–82 and a John M. Olin Visiting Fellowship at Yale in 1988–89 and was associate professor of strategy and policy at the Naval War College in 1991–92. He focuses on French planning and performance in twentieth-century conflicts. His books include *The Republic in Danger: General Maurice Gamelin and the Politics of French Defence, 1933–39* (1992), *Knowing Your Friends: Intelligence in Alliances and Coalitions* (1998), and, coedited with J. F. V. Keiger, *France and the Algerian War, 1954–62: Strategy, Operations and Diplomacy* (2002). In 2023 he contributed to Jonathan Krause and William J. Philpott, eds., *French Generals of the Great War: Leading the Way*, and he is now writing a new operational history of the fight for France in 1940.

SEBASTIAN BRUNS is a naval strategist and sea power expert based in Germany, where he works as Senior Researcher at the Institute for Security Policy Kiel University (ISPK). He is also a Senior Associate at the Center for Strategic and International Studies (CSIS), Washington, DC. Previously, Sebastian taught political science and naval strategy at the U.S. Naval Academy as the inaugural McCain-Fulbright Distinguished Visiting Professor. From 2010 to 2011, he worked as a defense and military staffer in the U.S. House of Representatives. He is the founder of the Kiel International Seapower Symposium, Europe's dedicated annual maritime strategy conference. He is the author or editor of seven books, including *US Naval Strategy and American National Security* (2018) and *Conceptualizing Maritime and Naval Strategy: Festschrift for Captain Peter M.*

Swartz, United States Navy, retired (2020). Dr. Bruns holds a PhD in political science (Kiel, 2014) and an MA in North American studies (Bonn, 2007).

ANDREW S. ERICKSON is a professor of strategy in the Naval War College's (NWC) China Maritime Studies Institute (CMSI) and a Visiting Scholar in Residence in Harvard's Department of Government. A core founding member, he helped establish CMSI and stand it up officially in 2006, and has played an integral role in its development; from 2021 to 2023 he served as Research Director. CMSI inspired the creation of other research centers, which he has advised and supported; he is a China Aerospace Studies Institute Associate. Erickson received NWC's inaugural Civilian Faculty Research Excellence Award and the National Bureau of Asian Research's inaugural Ellis Joffe Prize for PLA Studies. He serves on the editorial boards of *Naval War College Review* and *Asia Policy*. Erickson blogs at www.andrewerickson.com.

NORMAN FRIEDMAN is a strategist and historian interested in the intersection between defense technology and national policy. He spent more than a decade at a prominent U.S. think tank and then another decade with the Office of the Secretary of the Navy. For two years he was futurologist to the Headquarters, U.S. Marine Corps. He has been a contractor to defense organizations, including the U.S. Navy and some of its major contractors. Dr. Friedman has lectured widely on naval topics for the U.S. Navy and for private organizations. His books include *Winning a Future War*, a study of the impact of wargaming at the U.S. Naval War College between wars; *The Fifty-Year War*, a history of the Cold War; *Seapower as Strategy*; and *Network-Centric Warfare: How Navies Learned to Fight Smarter in Three World Wars*, as well as histories of U.S. and British warships, naval systems, and naval aircraft. He was awarded a lifetime achievement medal by the British Nautical Research Society and the Commodore Dudley H. Knox medal by the U.S. Naval Historical Foundation. He received his PhD in physics from Columbia University.

JOHN B. HATTENDORF is the Ernest J. King Professor Emeritus of Maritime History, a chair he occupied at the U.S. Naval War College from 1984 to 2016. He served as chairman of the College's Advanced Research Department from 1986 to 2003 and chairman of the Maritime History Department and director of the Naval War College Museum from 2003 to 2016. A former surface warfare officer, he earned his degrees in history from Kenyon College (AB, 1964), Brown University (AM, 1971) and the University of Oxford (DPhil, 1979; DLitt, 2016). His most recent books are *Recovering Naval Power: Henry Maydman and the Revival of the Royal Navy* (with Geoffrey Till, 2024) and *Reflections on Naval History: Collected Essays* (2023).

JOHN T. KUEHN is the past General William Stofft Professor of Military History and has taught military history at U.S. Army Command and General Staff College since 2003, retiring from the naval service in 2004. He earned a PhD in history from Kansas State University in 2007. He is the author of *Agents of Innovation* (2008), *Eyewitness Pacific Theater* (2008, with D. M. Giangreco), *A Military History of Japan* (2014), *Napoleonic Warfare* (2015), *America's First General Staff* (2017), and *100 Military Disasters* (2020), as well as numerous articles and editorials. He was awarded a Moncado Prize in 2011 and a Vandervort Prize in 2023, both from the Society for Military History. His most recent book is *Strategy in Crisis: The Pacific War, 1937–1945.*

PETER MAUCH teaches modern Japanese history at Western Sydney University (Australia). He has authored *Tojo* and *Sailor Diplomat: Nomura Kichisaburō and the Japanese-American War* (2011). He has contributed essays to the *Cambridge History of the Second World War* (2015) and *The Road to Pearl Harbor: Great Power War in Asia and the Pacific* (Naval Institute Press, 2022), and he has published with such journals as *Diplomatic History, Pacific Historical Review, Diplomacy and Statecraft, War in History,* and the *Journal of American-East Asian Relations.* He is currently engaged in a critical reassessment of Emperor Hirohito's role in Japan's delayed decision to surrender.

JOHN H. MAURER serves as the Alfred Thayer Mahan Distinguished Professor of Sea Power and Grand Strategy at the Naval War College. He is the author or editor of books examining the outbreak of World War I, military interventions in the developing world, naval competitions between the two world wars, a study on Winston Churchill and British grand strategy, and the great-power contest in Asia and the Pacific that led to Pearl Harbor. At the Naval War College, he served as chair of the Strategy and Policy Department. In recognition of his contribution to professional military education, he has received the U.S. Navy's Meritorious Civilian Service Award and Superior Civilian Service Award.

KEVIN D. McCRANIE is the Philip A. Crowl Professor of Comparative Strategy at the U.S. Naval War College, where he is a member of the Strategy and Policy Department. He is the author of *Admiral Lord Keith and the Naval War against Napoleon* as well as *Utmost Gallantry: The U.S. and Royal Navies at Sea in the War of 1812*. His recent writing compares the sea power and maritime strategic theories of Alfred Thayer Mahan and Sir Julian Corbett in a Naval Institute Press book titled *Mahan, Corbett, and the Foundations of Naval Strategic Thought*. His articles have appeared in *Naval History*, the *Journal of Military History*, the *Naval War College Review*, and the *Northern Mariner*.

ABIGAIL MULLEN is an assistant professor in the History Department at the United States Naval Academy. Her book *To Fix a National Character: The United States in the First Barbary War, 1800–1805* was published in 2024. She teaches naval, maritime, and digital history at the Naval Academy. In her previous role as a history professor and head of R2 Studios at George Mason University, she created historical podcasts such as *Consolation Prize*, a podcast about the history of U.S. consuls.

ALEXEY D. MURAVIEV is an associate professor of national security and strategic studies at Curtin University, Perth, Western Australia. He is the founder and director of the Strategic Flashlight forum on national security and strategy at Curtin. Alexey is the former head of Curtin's Department of Social Sciences and Security Studies. Between 2016 and 2021, he was academic lead of Curtin's strategic defense initiative. He has published widely in the field of national security, strategic studies, and defense studies. His research interests include problems of modern maritime power; contemporary defense and strategic policy; Russia as a Pacific power; Russia's naval power; and other topics. Among his latest publications is Alexey D. Muraviev, *Battle Reading the Russian Pacific Fleet, 2023–2030* (2023).

RYAN PEEKS is a historian in the Joint Staff's History and Research Office. He previously worked at the Naval History and Heritage Command and the Historical Office of the Office of the Secretary of Defense. His publicly available works include *Aircraft Carrier Requirements and Strategy, 1977–2001*, and articles in *Naval War College Review*, the U.S. Naval Institute's *Proceedings*, and *War on the Rocks*. He holds graduate degrees from the University of North Carolina and a BA from Amherst College.

GEOFFREY TILL is Emeritus Professor of Maritime Studies at King's College London. Once Dean of Academic Studies at the U.K. Joint Services Command and Staff College, he is author of over three hundred books, chapters, and articles. Since 2009 he has been a visiting professor, Senior Research Fellow, and adviser at the Rajaratnam School of International Studies, Singapore. He held the Dudley W. Knox Chair for Naval History and Strategy at the U.S. Naval War College and is now a Non-resident Research Fellow at its Hattendorf Historical Center. His *Understanding Victory: Naval Operations from Trafalgar to the Falklands* was in 2014, and his *How to Grow a Navy: The Development of Maritime Power* was published in 2022. With John Hattendorf, he edited *Recovering Naval Power: Henry Maydman and the Revival of the Royal Navy* (2023). He is now working on a fifth edition of his *Seapower: A Guide for the 21st Century Seapower*, first published in 2005.

RYAN WADLE is an associate professor of naval and maritime history in the John B. Hattendorf Center for Maritime Historical Research at the U.S. Naval War College. He is the author of several publications, including the book *Selling Sea Power: Public Relations and the U.S. Navy, 1917–1941*. His work has been recognized by the Society for Military History and the North American Society for Oceanic History. Prior to joining the Hattendorf Center, he served on the faculty at Air University's eSchool of Graduate Professional Military Education and also as part of the Afghanistan Study Team at the U.S. Army's Combat Studies Institute.

INDEX